Hêliand

Medieval European Studies II

Hêliand

Text and Commentary

Edited by
James E. Cathey

West Virginia University Press
Morgantown 2002

West Virginia University Press, Morgantown 26506
© 2002 by West Virginia University Press

All rights reserved

First edition published 2002 by West Virginia University Press
Printed in the United States of America

10 09 08 07 06 05 04 03 02   9 8 7 6 5 4 3 2

ISBN 0-937058-64-5 (alk. paper)

Library of Congress Cataloguing-in-Publication Data

Hêliand. Text and Commentary / edited by James E. Cathey.
    p.   cm. -- (Medieval European Studies ; 2)
  1. Heliand (Old Saxon Poem). 2. Old Saxon language--texts. 3. Old Saxon language--grammar. I. Title. II. Cathey, James E. III. Series.
IN PROCESS

Library of Congress Control Number: 2002104486

Cover design by Alcorn Publication Design
Cover motif adapted from image of St John in Vienna, Weltliche
    Schatzkammer, Coronation Gospels (saec. viii *ex.*)
Typeset by P. W. Conner
Printed in USA by Lightning Source, Inc.

Table of Contents

Preface ix
Introduction 1
The Historical Setting of the *Hêliand* 3
    The Saxons 3
    The Early Missions 4
    The Arian and Moslem Threats 6
    The English Mission.. 7
    Charlemagne and Europe 8
    Charlemagne and the Saxons 9
    Consolidation of Power 11
    Semantic Hurdles to the Task of Conversion 12
The Work 16
    Hêliand Verse 18
    The Dating of the *Hêliand* and the *Prefatio* 20
    The Manuscripts 22
    The *Fitten*... 24
A Comparison of the 'M' vs. 'C' Manuscripts 26
Excerpts from the text of the *Hêliand* 29
    Introduction 29
    Elizabeth's Child 32
    The Birth of John.. 35
    Mary's Child... 36
    The Birth of Jesus 39
    Signs of Jesus' Birth... 40
    Jesus in the Temple 42
    The Three Wise Men.. 43
    Herod's Threat 45
    The Flight to Egypt 46
    John the Baptist 49
    The Baptism of Christ 51
    The Tempting of Christ... 52
    Jesus Returns to Galilee 54
    The Sermon on the Mount 57
    Admonitions 58
    Hearing the Sermon... 62

Table of Contents

Swearing Oaths 64
The Lord's Prayer 65
Lilies of the Field 66
Pearls before Swine 67
Bad Tree - Bad Fruit 67
The Narrow Gate 68
A House upon Sand 69
Lambs among Wolves 70
Entering Heaven 71
Water to Wine 72
Reward and Punishment 74
Raising the Dead 75
Calming the Storm 76
The Sower and the Seed 78
Interpretation 80
The Wheat in the Field 81
Herodias' Daughter Dances 83
The Death of John 84
Jesus Walks on Water 85
Saint Peter's Keys 86
The Transfiguration 87
Fishing for Coins 88
The Rich Man and Lazarus 89
Workers in the Vineyard 92
Going to Jerusalem 93
The Blind Men 94
Entering Jerusalem 96
A Thane's Duty 97
Judgment Day 97
Raising Lazarus 98
Jesus as Threat 100
Apocalypse 101
Washing Feet 104
Jesus Identifies the Betrayer 105
Jesus in Gethsemane 107
The Capture of Christ 108
Peter Denies His Lord 112
The Fate of a Bad Thane 114
Pilate 115

Table of Contents

    The Death of Judas 116
    Christ before Pilate 117
    Christ before Herod 118
    The Second Hearing before Pilate 119
    Pilate's Offer 120
    Satan's Attempt and Pilate's Wife 121
    Pilate's Soldiers Take Jesus 123
    The Crucifixion 124
    The Death of Jesus 126
    The Burial 129
    The Resurrection 131
Commentary to the Readings 133
References 253
A Brief Outline of Old Saxon Grammar 263
    The Sound Systems of Primitive Germanic and Old Saxon . 263
    Old Saxon Reflexes of Germanic Vowels 266
    Strong Noun Declension 269
    Weak Noun Declension 275
    Pronouns 276
    Adjective Declensions 279
    Comparison of Adjectives 281
    Adverbs 282
    Numerals 282
    Verbal Types 284
    Verb Conjugations 289
Glossary 293

Preface

The present work was written partly in order to present the *Hêliand* to English speakers who may lack knowledge of German, a language in which the overwhelming body of scholarship on Old Saxon is written, and partly to provide a version of the *Hêliand* in the original language with apparatus in English. The standard edition by Otto Behaghel, now periodically reprinted in the series *Altdeutsche Textbibliothek,* dates from 1882. Although it has passed through the capable hands of further editors such as Walther Mitzka and Burkhard Taeger, a more accessible treatment is due. The Old Saxon to German glossary in the *ATB* version has its faults, for example, and there is little further apparatus that the student can turn to.

The anonymously-composed *Hêliand* with its preserved 5983 lines of alliterative poetry tells the story of Christ in a form presentable to a still largely pre-Christian audience of the early 800s. It is thus contemporaneous with some of the oldest preserved literary documents of Old English and Old High German. For this reason alone it seems appropriate to make this splendid telling of the story available to students of Old English, who – if they lack knowledge of German – would be denied access to it, for there are points of comparison with the closely-related Old English that may profitably be studied.

The audience of the *Hêliand* remains speculative. It may have been written for the purpose of being read aloud during mealtimes in refectories at monasteries where young Saxon novitiates were being trained in biblical knowledge; it may have been written to be read episodically in missionary churches; or it may have been written for some other purpose. For whatever reason, it was written in a style calculated to appeal to a native Germanic audience. The poetic form is that of Germanic epic tales; the analogy of Christ's role is to that of a presumably familiar kind of military leader (*drohtin*); there are notes in the text itself that explain Jewish law and custom; and there

Preface

are emendations and insertions that are nowhere found in the bible. As Ronald Murphy (1992) puts it,

> The audience of the *Hêliand* was probably to be found in mead-hall and monastery. The epic poem seems not to have been designed for use in the church as part of official worship, but is intended to bring the gospel home to the Saxons in a poetic environment in order to help the Saxons cease their vacillation between their warrior-loyalty to the old gods and to the 'mighty Christ.' Internal evidence, as well as liturgical tradition, would indicate that the epic was designed for after-dinner singing in the mead-hall and the cloister. It is clearly addressed to the Saxon warrior-nobility, and the mead-hall scenes in the *Hêliand* (the wedding-feast at Cana) show a familiar touch, one that might deliberately reproduce the very situation in which a singer of the *Hêliand* might find himself. One occasionally hears as well an exhortation that sounds much more like an oblique address to the monks who are in charge of the conversion of the Saxons, rather than to the Saxon nobility themselves (p. xvi).

The overarching tasks of the unknown author(s) of the *Hêliand* were to tell the story of Christ in a theologically sound manner, while contriving somehow to use native vocabulary to describe concepts unknown to the culture of the Saxons during this period, and to keep the attention of the audience. The first of these goals was accomplished through adherence to Christian theology as represented by scholars at the monasteries at Fulda, Corvey, Hersfeld, and elsewhere. When new concepts had to be introduced, Christian terminology was inserted in explicatory juxtaposition with native words as, for instance, where the pre-Christian concepts 'fates' *uurdigiscapu* and 'marked by a/the divine measurer' *metod gimarcod* are explained as *maht godes* 'the power of God' in lines 127-128. The audience's attention was presumably held by the innovative vocabulary and dramatic presentation, as when the apostle Peter draws his sword to defend Christ or when the death of Judas is drastically portrayed, although similar examples abound.

The present work seeks to provide an entry point to study of the *Hêliand*. To that purpose this volume contains a short description of time and place (THE HISTORICAL SETTING), a description of the poetic form and of manuscripts (THE WORK), approximately one half of the almost six thousand lines of the *Hêliand* set into sections (that, however, differ from the manuscript's division into *Fitten*), commentaries on each of the sections selected, a brief grammar, an Old Saxon to English glossary, and a list of references.

The author would like to express his great thanks for corrections suggested by users of previous drafts of this book in courses at Indiana University and Harvard University. Many thanks to Susanne Hoeller Wagner, Kristen Jones, and Betheny Moore, whose diligent work with the first version of this draft in 1996 already led to a considerable number of corrections and improvements. My special thanks also go to many both graduate and undergraduate students in subsequent years at the University of Massachusetts Amherst, including particularly Antonio Ornelas who during the most recent trial use of the book in Spring 2000 assiduously rooted out more typos and made excellent suggestions for improvement of the layout and presentation. Special thanks go also to Prof. G. Ronald Murphy, S.J. at Georgetown University and to Patrick W. Conner, Director of the West Virginia University Press. Remaining infelicities are, of course, attributable to the author.

JAMES E. CATHEY
Amherst, Massachusetts
May 2001

Introduction

The Old Saxon life of Christ, which was composed in about the year 830 and given its name by the scholar Johann Andreas Schmeller in the first edition titled *Hêliand oder die altsächsische Evangelien-Harmonie* (1830), belongs to the 'best' literature written in an ancient Germanic language. The adjective 'best' can be used here because the work while being theologically correct is written in a lively, engaging manner to appeal to its audience in terms that the Saxons of the time could presumably identify with. The style of the telling is also one to appeal to the contemporary audience with its Germanic alliterative form of poetry (see THE WORK).

In addition to its intrinsic interest, this volume will, it is to be hoped, serve the purpose of introducing the *Hêliand* to students of Old English who do not read German (or do so only with difficulty) and to all others interested in becoming acquainted with this version of the Life of Christ. The affinity between Old Saxon and Old English is clear and should make the study of both an obvious desideratum, but the standard scholarly editions have been published with German as the language of the glossaries and other apparatus, and most of the secondary literature has appeared in German.

This book is also an attempt to be all-inclusive in that the necessary apparatus (historical background, readings, commentaries, grammar, and glossary) strives for completeness. It is *not* all-inclusive to the extent that only about one half of the *Hêliand* is presented here. The grammar is intended to be reasonably comprehensive and offer some comparison with that of Old English. The glossary is keyed to the grammar, so that the student can quickly classify words as to their type and see their paradigmatic alternations. The glossary furthermore improves on its precursors in that definitions are more accurate and for the first time given in English. The commentaries to the reading selections include quotes from secondary literature, and some of them are thus in German. May this be viewed as an encouragement to learn to read German, as that skill will be indispensable to anyone seriously interested in studies in Germanic philology. Translations are provided in footnotes.

The sections chosen from the *Hêliand* do not correspond to the 'fits' (*Fitten*) into which the work is divided but rather were selected on the basis of biblical or cultural interest. The *Hêliand* retells the story of Christ partly in ways that do not correspond with the versions we are normally familiar with. There are large and small additions or embellishments to the biblical story, and some Old Saxon cultural traits can be discerned from the manner in which story is told. The commentaries to the readings are meant to address some of these points.

The Historical Setting

of the

Hêliand

The Old Saxon telling of the gospel, titled *Hêliand* (Savior) by J. A. Schmeller in his edition of 1830, was not written in a vacuum but was, as is everything, a product of its place and time. The *Hêliand* was composed in what is now part of northern Germany in the first half of the 9th century. The time was approximately in the middle of the period extending from the first Christian missions to the north of Europe in the 500's to the end of the 1100's, by which time most Europeans excepting the Balts and Prussians had at least superficially been converted. It is the political and religious background of that period which provides a context in which to understand the missionizing intent of the *Hêliand* and the political as well.

THE SAXONS

The Roman historian Tacitus placed the precursors of the Saxons in southern Denmark, north of the Eider river, in the first century A.D. According to the Greek explorer Ptolemaus, they lived in what is now Holstein (between Eider and Elbe rivers) during the second century A.D. As Herbert describes them from the point of view of the Angles, ancestors of the English:

> South of [the Angles], in the lands around the lower Elbe and Weser, were the Suebic tribes. The first Roman writer to mention the English makes no reference to the Saxons. Like Franks, it is the name of a later confederation of tribes from this area. The Saxons were of Suebic stock; their earlier English neighbors called them *Swæfe*; later they were known as Old Saxons, to distinguish them from the folk who had crossed to Britain (p. 9).

3

The Saxons did not expand their territory beyond the Elbe until the third century but were fighting with the Franks to their south by 350 in the area between the lower Rhine and upper Weser rivers. By the 400s they were plundering the coasts of southern England and of France and together with the Angles some of them settled in England beginning in about 450.

Toward the end of the 600s the continental Saxons were as far south as the Lippe river and in Thuringia, but by the 700s the Franks were able to exert sufficient pressure to contain them in Westphalia and parts north.

THE EARLY MISSIONS

Germanic groups were up to the time shortly preceding the composition of the *Hêliand* still in the process of settling their territories and frontiers. Their world view was by definition pre-Christian. Although the Frankish king Clovis had been converted to Roman Catholicism through baptism in 496, the general population had been left largely undisturbed by missionizing efforts. Only later did the mission come, but not, as we might expect, directly northward from Rome but rather it took a long sweep through time and geography.

The effort to missionize the Saxons had its historical roots with the Celts of Roman Britain, where Christian churches had been established during the third century. From post-Roman Britain the effort of conversion proceeded to Ireland in the fourth century. The increasing settlement of England by Anglo-Saxons from the continent during the fifth century interrupted communications between Rome and Britain, and the center of the Celtic Church shifted to Ireland, a land little touched by Roman influence. The Irish, in turn, brought the Church back to Britain by establishing northern monasteries at Iona and Lindisfarne. From these outposts Irish monks preached the gospel in Scotland and northern England, while the English south remained a mixture of pagan and Anglo-Roman Christian.

The missionizing effort conducted by the Irish did not stop at attempts to convert the Scottish Celts and Anglo-Saxons. The first great missionary to the continent was also Irish. St. Columban (born about 545) left Bangor in northern Ireland reportedly along with the apostolic number of twelve fellow monks in the decade before 600.

The Historical Setting

He (and they) established monasteries adhering to the Celtic Church in what is now eastern France and, later, at Bobbio in northern Italy, where Columban died in 615 on his mission to the Langobards. One companion of Columban, Gall (born in Ireland about 550, died around 630), remained in what is now Switzerland when his patron continued on to Italy. The great monastery at St. Gallen carries his name.

The Franks had long been on the periphery of Roman influence, particularly after they entered northern Gaul, which retained a continuation of Roman administration in the form of the Gallo-Roman church. The key turning point in the history of this Church in the West came with the conversion of the Frankish king Clovis to Roman Catholicism when, according to the story in the *History of the Franks* by Gregory of Tours, Clovis' god of battle (i.e. Wodan) failed him but his calling upon Christ routed the enemy. (Hillgarth, p. 82) From that time the Franks were at least nominally Catholic.

At about the same time that the Celtic Catholic Columban was establishing his Burgundian monastery at Luxeuil in the French Vosges, the Roman Catholic Pope Gregory I in 596 sent a mission in the opposite direction, from Rome to Britain, led by Gregory's appointee as Bishop of London, but who was later to be known as St. Augustine of Canterbury (died in 605). Augustine began the work of converting the southern Anglo-Saxons, concentrating first on their ruler Ethelbert, king of Kent. His efforts resulted in the nominal baptism of allegedly 10,000 of Ethelbert's followers in the Roman Church. The ground rules for conversion were set down by Gregory in a letter sent from Rome in 601 to give guidance to Augustine. These rules stated, in part, that idols were to be removed from heathen temples, but the temples themselves should be purified by removal of altars on which sacrifice had been performed and Christian altars should be set up in their place. In other words, the tactic was to replace the content of the old forms, including the content (semantics) of certain vocabulary (cf. Hempel, p. 57). Since kings were understood in their native, pre-Christian context as intermediaries with the gods, their conversion was always paramount. (As we will see, the ancient poetic form likewise received new content in the *Hêliand*, which retains abundant allusions to older conditions.)

The Arian and Moslem Threats

The great competition within Christian religiosity in Western Europe was between Roman Catholicism and Arianism, which did not hold with the unity of Father, Son, and Holy Spirit (the Trinity). The Burgundians and the Visigoths at the borders of Clovis's territory were Arian in belief, and converting them to Roman Catholicism was virtually equivalent in importance to converting pagan groups like the Alamanni and Saxons. Already in a letter from Bishop Avitus of Vienne to Clovis in about 496 we read the exhortation to go out and subdue pagans (i.e. Arians) for the sake of the Christian mission:

> The followers of [Arian] error have in vain, by a cloud of contradictory and untrue opinions, sought to conceal from your extreme subtlety the glory of the Christian name. [...] Since God, thanks to you, will make of your people His own possession, offer a part of the treasure of Faith which fills your heart to the peoples living beyond you, who, still living in natural ignorance, have not been corrupted by the seeds of perverse doctrines [that is, Arianism]. Do not fear to send them envoys and to plead with them the cause of God, who has done so much for your cause. So that the other pagan peoples, at first being subject to your empire for the sake of religion, while they still seem to have another ruler, may be distinguished rather by their race than by their prince. (Hillgarth, pp.76-78)

Russell notes (p. 154), however, that "[f]rom the death of Clovis in 511 until the arrival of the Irish missionary monk Columban in Gaul about 590, the progress of Christianization among the Germanic peoples, aside from the Merovingian court, was negligible," but he asserts further (p. 156) that "the heroic self-discipline and asceticism of Irish monasticism may have appealed to the Germanic warrior spirit" and that "[w]hatever the sources of attraction were, Columban and his followers succeeded in establishing a network of monasteries, free from local episcopal control, on the property of the northern Frankish aristocrats." Whether this attraction represents the continuation of pre-Christian religious control by the nobility or new ways of thinking or even so mundane a matter as the teaching of innovative methods of agriculture by the monasteries, the church had effectively found a method of influencing the Franks and eventually recruiting them to its teachings — or perhaps it was rather that the Frankish aristocracy used the church for the sanctioning of its domination.

While England was being missionized, a competing monotheistic religion born on the Arabian Peninsula swiftly rose to power and began to threaten Europe. In 622 Mohammed moved from Mecca to Medina, proclaiming that 'there is no God but God, and Mohammed is the prophet of God.' By the time of his death in 632 Mohammed had kindled a religious fervor that let Islam conquer most of North Africa and Spain within the next eighty years. The Arabs were halted in 732 by Charles Martel, who defeated the Mohammedan forces at Poitiers in the middle of France. It was not obvious during these centuries that Europe as a whole would become and remain Christian. The effort to convert the Saxons approximately one hundred years after the victory at Poitiers was still part of an attempt to consolidate Europe for Christianity.

Power politics and the Church in Rome were inextricably linked during the period under consideration. Rome was under pressure from Byzantium to the east, and Europe as a whole was pressed by the Arabs coming from the south through Spain. Rome had reached a nadir of power. Syria, Palestine, North Africa, and Spain had all converted to Islam. Greece and Southern Italy (Sicily and Calabria) came under the influence of the Eastern Rite in Byzantium after 731. The Germanic Langobards, who adhered to Arianism, threatened Rome from the north, and only central Italy and France remained under the Roman Church. Arianism as a rival theology ceased to be a threat to the Roman Church by the middle of the 7th century, but the disposition of the Franks seemed uncertain indeed. The position of the Pope threatened to be reduced to that solely of the Bishop of Rome.

THE ENGLISH MISSION

From southern England the next great Christian missionary journeyed south. Wynfrith, known as Boniface, (born about 675, died in 754) was educated in the abbey of Nursling near Winchester. Upon being elevated to the rank of bishop in 722 he was charged by Pope Gregory II to work in Germany. At Geismar near Fritzlar in

Hessia Boniface toppled the pillar that supported the heathen world view, a great oak dedicated to the god Thor. In not being punished by the gods for his heresies, Boniface and his fellow missionaries demonstrated the primacy of the Christian God among the heathen. The foundation by Boniface of the monastery at Fulda in 743 was less dramatic than the cutting down of the oak at Geismar but key to the ongoing effort to missionize the entire north of the continent. Thus were the first blows struck for Christianity on Saxon territory about one hundred years prior to the composition of the *Hêliand* at a time when Islam was firmly established in Spain and posed a considerable threat to the Roman Church (then restricted to part of what is now Italy).

It was Boniface who began to change the situation by calling a synod in 747 at which all Thuringian, Bavarian, and Frankish bishops swore allegiance to Rome. Four years later, following the deposition of the last in the line of Merovingian kings, Pippin III (714-768) was anointed in 751 as king of the Franks in the presence of Boniface. Pippin subsequently pledged by oath in 754 to Pope Stephen II to protect the Roman Church against the Langobards, thereby effecting the rescue of Rome, which otherwise would probably have sunk to the status of a minor power. The consolidation of Frankish allegiance to and protection of Rome continued under the reign of Pippin's son Karl (768-814), known as Charlemagne, the greatest of Frankish kings.

CHARLEMAGNE AND EUROPE

Charlemagne was not the only son of Pippin III. Charlemagne and his younger brother, Karlmann, were both anointed by Pope Stephan II in 754 and along with their father, Pippin, were granted the honorific title Patricius Romanorum, which almost guaranteed later conflict. In 770 Charlemagne defied the wishes of the Pope and married the daughter of the Langobardian king Desiderius in an attempt to isolate Karlmann politically. Karlmann, however, died suddenly the following year, and Charlemagne (ignoring the rights of inheritance of Karlmann's sons) seized all of the Frankish kingdoms. He sent his wife back to her father in 771, and, now following the wishes of the Pope, he turned against Desiderius in 773. The sons of Karlmann had fled to the Langobardian court, and Desiderius urged the Pope to anoint them as kings. Charlemagne prevailed, however, and took the title Rex Langobardorum.

Meanwhile, Charlemagne was also concerned about his southern flank and eventually secured the borders against the Arabs, although not before the first Frankish campaign across the Pyrenees ended with the defeat of Roland in 778. Within the following ten years, however, he extended his realm to southern France and far enough to the east to include the Bavarians.

CHARLEMAGNE AND THE SAXONS

The Saxons were the only large unconverted grouping left in the west of the continent, and Charlemagne led numerous campaigns against them in the period 772-804. Even before then Charlemagne's father Pepin had led expeditions against the Saxons in 743, 744, 747 and according to the *Royal Frankish Annals* in 758 "went into Saxony and took the strongholds of the Saxons at Sythen by storm. And he inflicted bloody defeats on the Saxon people. They then promised to obey all his orders ..." (Scholz 13, 42). The Saxons were not a single people but rather a confederation of different groups which occupied the northern German areas of Westphalia, Eastphalia, Engern, and North Albingia with their various political or juridical districts. There was no single king, and Charlemagne had to fight grueling wars against separate entities. The only unifying instance was an annual assembly at Marklo on the Weser River. Present at the assembly were about 3700 representatives: the heads of the hundred political districts (*Gaue*) with thirty-six elected representatives from each district, twelve each for the three estates of the nobles, freemen, and tenant farmers. Only the thralls were excluded. During the reign of Charlemagne a strong champion emerged on the side of the Saxons in the person of the Westphalian duke Widukind, who had a strong following among all the people.

The Saxons gained strength under Widukind and took some Frankish territory to the south of Westphalia. Charlemagne recognized the danger and swore in 775 either to Christianize the Saxons completely or to liquidate them. He penetrated their territory to the east of the Weser for the first time in that year and met the Eastphalians near Goslar and the Engern at Bückeberg, but the Saxons did not resist. Instead Charlemagne showered the leaders of Eastphalia and Engern with gifts, and they delegated hostages to him. The Eastphalians were faced with Slavs on their eastern frontier and could scarcely afford a two-front war. The Westphalians, however, resisted, and Charlemagne was forced to fight them at Lübbecke, after which they offered hostages and swore allegiance to Charlemagne.

Unfortunately for Charlemagne, this brief foray into Saxon territory and the co-opting of some leaders of the Eastphalians, Westphalians, and Engern did not result in pacification of the whole area. In 777 Charlemagne moved with a large army to Paderborn and convened the Frankish assembly there on Saxon territory, at which location he also ordered the Saxons to convene their assembly. Charlemagne required those whose representatives attended to pledge to him and to the Christian faith their fealty or risk losing their freedom and property. Those Saxons then promised loyalty to Charlemagne and accepted Christianity, which meant in effect that the southern part of Saxon territory became part of Charlemagne's Frankish lands. A mass baptism took place, and Abbot Sturm from the newly-founded monastery at Fulda with its approximately 400 monks took charge of further religious instruction. However, because of the procedure followed by the monks from Fulda in setting baptism as the first goal of their mission and in mercilessly carrying it out by destroying all heathen cult sites, they triggered a reaction on the part of the Saxons.

Widukind had not challenged Charlemagne up to this point but had instead withdrawn to the protection of the Danish court. After the aggressive behavior of the monks from Fulda, however, the general populace was prepared to resist this strange and seemingly destructive new religion and united in great numbers behind Widukind, who in 778 led a campaign that destroyed churches and cloisters in the west of the territory all the way to Deutz by Cologne and south to the mouth of the river Lahn. Only a defense by the Alemans and East Franconians saved the monastery at Fulda. Charlemagne countered in 779 by moving back into Saxon territory, and all went as before. The Eastphalians and Engern gave hostages and cooperated. Charlemagne reshuffled the structure of the mission, and the situation quieted. He made his next move in 780, when he called together an assembly at the source of the river Lippe at which he partitioned Saxony into missionary dioceses and appointed bishops, priests, and abbots from other parts of his territories to run them: the Bishop of Würzburg went to Paderborn, the Abbot of the cloister at Amorbach went to Verden, etc. Charlemagne was back in Italy in 781, and all was quiet in Saxony.

In 782 Charlemagne held another assembly at Lippspringe, this time to dissolve the old Saxon political structure. Instead of bringing in Frankish nobility, he installed Saxons from notable families as dukes on the Frankish model in an effort to co-opt at least part of the previously loosely-organized political system.

Widukind and his followers reacted strongly to the confiscation of property, the introduction of mandatory tithing, and the overthrow of the old way of government by annual assembly. This time he and his troops attacked missionaries and the newly-installed dukes and nobles. Charlemagne ordered loyal Eastphalians, Palatinates, and allied Saxons together with Frankish forces to meet Widukind. Charlemagne's forces were wiped out almost completely. Charlemagne hurried north and conferred with the leader of his loyal Saxon troops, after which the survivors of the battle against Widukind were marched up, and he had them all executed. Even though Widukind won the battle, he must, however, also have suffered great losses, as he returned to the Danes after this victory.

Charlemagne persevered and in 783 led a campaign to Detmold, where the Saxons had prepared to do battle. Charlemagne won a bloody victory and withdrew to Paderborn to await reinforcements. His next move was to the river Hase where he won a bitter battle against Saxon forces. In spite of these successes, a new campaign was necessary in 784, but nothing decisive came of it. Charlemagne convened the assembly again in Paderborn in 785, but no record survives of what transpired there. In any case, following the assembly of 785 there were no more hostilities in the middle and southern territories. Charlemagne began negotiations with Widukind, and they exchanged hostages. The result was that Widukind along with his hostages from Charlemagne traveled to Attiguy and was baptized there in 785. Charlemagne himself was Widukind's sponsor.

THE CONSOLIDATION OF POWER

The law known as *Capitulatio de partibus Saxoniae* came into force on October 28, 797, in which was stipulated that only the king,

Hêliand

Charlemagne in this case, could convene a Saxon assembly. The position of the church was strengthened in that the death penalty was imposed for heathen belief and practices. Attendance at mass and the hearing of sermons as well as tithing was made obligatory. The Saxons had to build new churches, each with a house of worship and two manses. For every group of 120 men a servant and a servant girl had to be assigned for work in the church. In other words, the draconian measures that had led to rebellion in 778 were codified and legally reinforced, but the struggle continued for the northern territories, and Charlemagne was involved until 804 with subduing Saxon groups there.

As in the advice given by Pope Gregory I in his letter of 601, the leader was here again the key figure in the process of conversion. After Widukind submitted to baptism, the missionaries had at least an easier time of converting the populace. The *Hêliand* was likely still a part of the effort of persuasion and pacification when it was composed some forty years after Widukind's baptism.

SEMANTIC HURDLES TO THE TASK OF CONVERSION

One overriding concern is the meaning (semantics) of the Old Saxon words in the work of conversion to Christianity. Deep cultural divides had to be crossed on the way to conversion, not the least of which was the gap between a world-accepting native religiosity and a world-rejecting,[1] extra-mundane religion, Christianity. Putting missionaries in the field among uncomprehending or even hostile Saxons was hazardous enough, but perhaps the most difficult practical problem was the translation of Christian concepts, as the pre-Christian Saxon conception of the world and of behavior in it were at considerable odds with the message of Christianity.

The Saxons practiced some form or another of religious practice common to Germanic groups. There was no uniform ritual but various forms were tolerated, i.e., there was no one specific way to worship but rather many ways to (attempt to) gain the favor of the gods. Sacred springs and trees were worshiped, and there were cult sites. The monk Ruodolf of Fulda (died in 865) reported that the Saxons also worshiped in open air a wooden idol of considerable

---

[1] See Russell (1994)

size that was placed vertically. They called it the *Irmensûl*, a world pillar (as has been worshiped by various groups in various parts of the world). There was a store of treasure at the temple, where gods called Saxnot (perhaps another name for Wodan), Thor, and others were honored.[2] To the Saxon mind the world was ruled by forces in it, not apart from it. When the world perished at the end of our time, everything including the gods would go down with it. Thus one of the primary messages to be imparted was of a God Who stands eternally beyond the visible.

Perhaps more troublesome were socio-cultural standards that had to be overthrown in order that Christianity might prosper. The very vocabulary with which this new religion had to be described contained meanings at odds with the Christian message, most particularly as regards the place of the individual among other members of society and the attitude of the individual to God. The missionaries had to persuade converts that the proper attitude was one of humility before God and good will towards their fellow humans, but Old Saxon had no native word to render the Latin term *humilitas*. The pre-Christian mind set was rather the opposite, and the words with which the new message had to be conveyed were in themselves frequently opposite to what was meant. It was thus necessary for the mission to persevere and subvert old words to convey new meanings, as imported words from Latin would necessarily have remained in a foreign realm apart from daily life.

The Germanic ethic required behavior that with Christian sensibility was understood as *superbia*. To the traditional Germanic, and thus Saxon, mind set the egocentric goal of achieving fame in this world as an individual (and proper status for one's family) was all that would live on after one's death. Tales told of dead heroes constituted the only transcendent realm in a world defined merely by what is here and now.

Fame was attained not through good works but rather through glorious and brave deeds on one's own behalf and/or against one's opponents. Positive words of praise, including adjectives like *bald* 'brave, bold', *frôkni* 'bold', *gêl* 'boisterous', and *ôbarmôdig* 'proud'

---

[2] A brief description is to be found in Leube, Vol. 2, p. 468. The literature on this topic is expansive and can be referred to in bibliographical entries cited below.

or nouns like *êra* 'honor,' *gelp* 'terrifying battle cry' or *hrôm* 'fame', were not matched by words in the Saxon vocabulary like 'reticent,' 'modest,' 'gentle,' or 'humble.' Belief in one's own might was paramount.

The egocentric native concepts of 'honor,' 'fame,' and etc. were not directly confronted by the Church, as this would have been counterproductive. Russell writes,

> The notion of Christian honor, with its goal of individual salvation, directly opposed the supremacy of the Germanic concept of ... the bond of kinship which could be extended to others through an oath of loyalty... This bond included the duty to avenge a kinsman or lord's death, as well as the obligation to follow one's lord into a battle, even if death was imminent. To survive one's lord in battle was cause for disgrace, exceeded in shamefulness only by acts of cowardice and outright betrayal. (p. 121)

Although the societal context was not chaotic, not 'every man for himself,' homicide was a common means of achieving individual goals, be it for maintenance of property rights or in order to gain renown as a member of a fighting troop. Great leaders attained their position through eloquence, bravery, and strength, and their followers gained fame in turn for the same qualities along with their faithfulness to the leader. There was a strong bond to kinship and prestige group, but these bonds were maintained through individual strength instead of humanitarian sympathy. Ethical values were posited on individual qualities instead of considerations for the good of the group. Hempel writes, "Daher ist die Kirche genötigt, in Morallehre wie Gesetz immer wieder den Totschlag ..., die Rache ..., den Raub ... als Todsünden zu brandmarken und ihnen breite Aufmerksamkeit zu widmen" (p.. 53).[3] The Church in its preaching focused on the deadly sins of homicide, revenge, and pillage.

To convey the message of Christian charity and ego-denying *humilitas* the native words that were negative and pejorative in the context of Christian sensibilities were employed with the (indeed eventually realized) hope that the Christian content would also convert their meanings (cf. Hempel, p. 57). Subversion of the vocabu-

---

[3] "The Church is thus required repeatedly to condemn manslaughter, ... vengeance, ... abduction, ... as mortal sins and to pay great attention to them in moral teachings as well as law."

lary was the only possible method available to spread the gospel. As Russell puts it,

> Instead of directly confronting this opposing value system and attempting to radically transform it—an approach which almost certainly would have resulted in an immediate rejection of Christianity—the missionaries apparently sought to redefine the Germanic virtues of strength, courage, and loyalty in such a manner that would reduce their incompatibility with Christian values, while at the same time 'inculturating' Christian values as far as possible to accommodate the Germanic ethos and world-view. (p. 121)

To Saxons presented with the story of Christ in the form of the *Hêliand*, a work necessarily written in way that would appeal to a pre-Christian or newly converted audience, the choice of vocabulary that rang with old associations and carried old meanings must have at least somewhat clashed with the religious world of the story.

In some cases, however, the old meanings and cultural values may have actually helped to illustrate the Gospel story which the poet was recasting for his Saxon audience. Murphy (1997) in his analysis of the use of light and bright imagery argues interestingly that the author of the *Hêliand* relied on the use of bright images and light in John's Gospel to portray a path from birth into this 'light' and death into the 'other light' in analogy with images from Germanic mythology, as for example *bifrǫst*, a bridge of light (rainbow) from this world to the abode beyond earthly existence. Some of these possible cruxes are pointed out in the COMMENTARIES TO THE READINGS.

The Work

The Old Saxon *Hêliand* is preserved in 5,983 lines of verse edited from the M and C manuscripts (cf. THE MANUSCRIPTS below). The work was composed during the long period of decline of Germanic culture and slow encroachment of European culture during which Christianity had begun to replace ancient forms of worship, while the poetic forms, although not given up, were abandoning their strict alliterative and metrical constraints everywhere on the continent. The *Hêliand* shows a mixture of the more strictly controlled old poetic form and a discursive, prose-like overlay. (See HÊLIAND VERSE below.)

Although the new culture was slowly and against considerable odds being introduced to northern Germany from the monasteries at Fulda or Werden (as Drögereit argued) or Corvey (Gantert, pp. 91 ff.), the old culture had very deep roots indeed. We will observe throughout the corpus of the *Hêliand* words and phrases whose semantic content at least historically referred to conditions of earlier belief and behavior, although it seems clear that by the time of the composition of the work many of the meanings had changed. Nevertheless, we can wonder what reactions certain words and phrases would have triggered in a contemporary audience still cognizant of (or even still practicing) pre-Christian habits of thought.

The assumption here is that because of its traditional, alliterative form the *Hêliand* was written to be read aloud. Taeger (1978) discusses the musical notation found over lines 310-313 in manuscript M and tentatively concludes "...daß auch der 'Heliand' vor dem Horizont halbliturgischen Gebrauchs zu sehen sein dürfte."[4] The question of which audience it addressed cannot be settled with finality. Perhaps it was intended as an exercise for monks or even as meal time devotionals read aloud to them. Perhaps it was written in order to be read (or 'sung') in episodes before groups of potential converts who had already suffered baptism by coercion and who now

---

[4] "...that the *Hêliand* can also be viewed as intended for a 'half-liturgical' use."

needed to be persuaded of the validity of the new faith. Drögereit (1970) hypothesizes that "der unbekannte Dichter, wohl ein Friese, [verfaßte] sein Predigt-Epos nicht einmal für Mönche, sondern für adlige Damen in einem der zahlreichen Kanonissenstifte, nämlich Essen"[5] (p. 465).

The question of the site of composition has been debated for a century and a half. The general body of opinion tends to favor Fulda, for among other reasons because the *Hêliand* reflects the commentary on Matthew written by the Abbot of Fulda, Hrabanus Maurus, and because there was a copy of the work known as *Tatian* there. A version of *Tatian* was used as a basis for the structure of the *Hêliand*. There are, however, arguments in favor of other monasteries. Drögereit (1978) favors Werden on paleographic evidence, namely the fact that only at Werden was the letter <b> used, which is characteristic of the M and P manuscripts, and on evidence of the presence of Frisian monks there. The *Hêliand* evinces so-called Frisianisms in the spellings <kiasan> and <niate> in lines 223 and 224. These views are, however, challenged by Bischoff (1952) who claims that many manuscripts that Drögereit attributes to Werden were instead brought there from the monasteries at Corbie in France or its Saxon offshoot Corvey or from elsewhere or never were there at all. Another scholar, Krogmann, believes that Fulda must be excluded as the site of composition on the basis of the word *pâscha* instead of *ôstar / ôstarun* for 'Easter.' The latter word was used only in the Archdiocese of Mainz, and Fulda was in its territory. Werden was under the Archdiocese of Cologne, where *pâscha* was the term for 'Easter,' and Krogmann also adduces the paleographic evidence of <b> in favor of Werden (cf. Krogmann [1973], pp. 25-26). Gantert (1993) points out that the sons of Saxon nobility had been schooled in Corbie in the Picardy and were then instrumental in founding the monastery at Corvey in 815 on Saxon territory, which at least would provide a fertile ground for the reception of the *Hêliand*.[6]

---

[5] "The unknown poet, probably a Frisian, [composed] his sermon-epic not for monks but for noble ladies in one of the many religious communities of canonesses, namely in Essen."

[6] Markey (1976: 259 ff.) provides a summary of paleographic and other evidence (or lack of same) regarding the provenance of the *Hêliand*.

Hêliand

In any case, whether composed at Fulda or Werden or Essen, the *Hêliand* adheres faithfully to the Christian gospel while the work is couched in terms acceptable to a northern audience familiar with stories of Germanic mythology and historical culture presented in alliterative verse.

HÊLIAND VERSE

Pre-literate societies preserve their literary monuments in memorized, oral form. Essential to long recitations is a mnemonic code to cue speakers when memory lags. The Germanic code had as a constant over the span of centuries alliteration and a fixed number of dynamic stresses per line. In the simplest, and perhaps original, form the 'long line' consisted of eight syllables containing four stresses, two in each 'half line' on either side of a pause (Latin *caesura*; German *Zäsur*). Schematically, we can represent a basic line as:

$$/\smile/\smile \quad /\smile/\smile$$

where the / indicates a stressed syllable and $\smile$ an unstressed syllable.

Alliteration was superimposed on the pattern of stresses. (A certain leeway in filling the syllables, which is called *Füllungsfreiheit* in German, was allowed.) The term alliteration (German *Stabreim*) indicates an initial "rhyme" of consonants or vowels with each other in such a manner that certain specified stressed syllables each begin with either the same single consonant, with identical clusters of initial *s*- plus a consonant, or with initial vowels of any quality. (End rhyme, which affected unstressed syllables, did not play a role here and – in any case – was a later borrowing, perhaps from Latin hymns.) The key position was the first stress in the second 'half-line' (the third stressed syllable from the beginning of the 'long line'), which should contain a 'heavy' syllable defining the alliteration on the whole line. (A 'heavy' syllable is one that has a stressed vowel followed by a consonant cluster or one that has a diphthong.) That is, if the third stressed syllable started with /h/, then the first stressed syllable had to, and commonly the second stressed syllable then also started with /h/. The fourth stress (second stress in the second 'half-line') could not alliterate. An ancient example in North Germanic is found on the Gallehus horn from about 400 A.D.:

ek hlewagastiR holtijar   horna tawidō

'I Hlewagast, son of Holt, made this horn.'

In the Gallehus inscription we hear alliteration on the /h/ in /horn-/ in the first and second stressed syllable, and we also find various unstressed syllables including one before the first stress in /hlewa-/. The presence of an initial unstressed syllable (Greek *anacrusis*, German *Auftakt*), here /ek/, is thus also an ancient feature of the poetic form, which we will see much used and expanded on in the *Hêliand* — also before other than the first stressed syllable.

The *Hêliand* does not, on the whole, represent an ideal of alliterative verse. Dynamic stress played less of a role in Old Saxon than in earlier stages of Germanic dialects, and the author was constrained to proselytize with a theologically sound message as well as to entertain. We are thus confronted with a great mixture of lines varying from what might be termed "pure" alliterative to almost prose-like poetry. Within close proximity of each other one finds a variety of lines, as in the sequence 978-981. An example of a rather well-formed line in the historical alliterative tradition is

978: dôpte allan dag   druhtfolc mikil.

In this line we see that the third (and 'heavy') syllable /druXt/ in *druhtfolc* (a noun: 'retainers; people') sets the alliteration, which is carried through in the verb *dôpte* ('baptized') and *dag* in the phrase *allan dag* ('all day') in the first and second stresses. The fourth stressed syllable, /mi-/ in *mikil* (an adjective: 'great') properly lacks alliteration. Line 979 is also fairly well-formed, although it contains a few extra unstressed syllables. This line alliterates on /w/, here again on a noun phrase (*uualdand Krist* 'ruling Christ') in the key third position.

979 uuerod an uuatere   endi ôk uualdand Krist.

The next line, 980, is also a good example, this time alliterating in /h/ on the third stress in the phrase *handun sînun* 'with his hands':

980 hêran heƀencuning   handun sînun.

An example of a more typical line in the *Hêliand* is 981, which properly alliterates in /b/ but shows many more unstressed syllables:

981 an allaro baðo them bezton   endi im thar te bedu gihnêg.

In this last example we find a fairly long anacrusis before the first alliterating syllable in *baðo* and a very long unstressed anacrusis before the key alliteration in the third stressed syllable in *bedu* ('and bowed [*gihnêg*] there to him in prayer [*te bedu*]'). Although line 981 alliterates, it is so filled out with unaccented syllables that it is more discursive while yet still true to the poetic convention. McLintock (1985) has this to say about the form of the *Hêliand*:

> The biblical epic in alliterative verse flourished in England, and the *Hêliand* may have been composed in imitation of such works as a consequence of Anglo-Saxon participation in the conversion of the Saxons. A literary link with England is attested not only by the Cotton manuscript but also by the existence of an Old English translation of the *Genesis* (the so-called *Genesis B*). Differences in verse technique may be explained partly by the differing grammars of the two languages. Notable features of Old Saxon verse are density of alliteration and the proliferation of unstressed syllables, especially before the first ictus of the *b* [second half-line] verse. (p. 150)

Many words have been written about alliterative verse and about the language of the *Hêliand*. A good overview is given by Lehmann (1973). See also Doane (1991:89-92).

THE DATING OF THE *HÊLIAND* AND THE PRAEFATIO

The direct evidence which, according to Drögereit (1978), links the letter <ƀ> to Werden also frames the date of composition. Drögereit adduces paleographic features he claims were used only at Werden and only between about 850 and 900, stating that

> "[ƀ] begegnet während einer kurzen periode n u r in Quellen der um 800 gegründeten Abtei Werden, und zwar in einem lateinisch-altsächsischen Glossar von ca. 850 und vor allem in den Werdener Heberegistern von ca. 900. Wir können dieses [ƀ] ferner noch für die etwa 864 dort abgefaßte Originalhandschrift der dritten Vita Liudgers, des friesischen Gründers Werdens, erschließen" (p. 53).[7]

---

[7] "[ƀ] is found during a short period *only* in manuscripts from the abbey in Werden, which was founded around the year 800, namely in a Latin-Old Saxon glossary from about 850 and particularly in the tax lists from about 900. We can also re-

A certain form of large <N> also appearing in the M and P manuscripts of the *Hêliand* was written that way only in Werden up to the period in question (Drögereit, *op. cit.*, p. 54). This dating, which Drögereit (1951) first established, contradicts the previous accepted dating made on the basis of the Latin *Praefatio*.

The Latin *Praefatio et Versus* is customarily divided into *Praefatio A*, *Praefatio B*, and *Versus*. Although the preface has not been seen physically attached to any manuscript of the *Hêliand* — at least since its publication by Flacius Illyricus in 1562 — there is internal and external evidence that the two at one time were connected.

The *Praefatio A* describes the commissioning of a translation of the New Testament with the words: *Præcepit namq[ue] cuidam uiro de gente Saxonum, qui apud suos non ignobilis Vates habebatur, ut [uetus ac] nouum Testamentum in Germanicam linguam poetice transferre studeret, quatenus non solum literatis, uerum etiam inliteratis sacra diuinorum præceptorum lectio panderetur.*[8] This passage has been thoroughly dissected by Krogmann (*op cit.*), among others, and revealed to have its faults, including words and phrases added at a date later than its original composition. The phrase *vetus ac* is perhaps among them, although it could be taken to refer to the Old Saxon *Genesis* if the *Praefatio* was introductory to both works. The grammatical subject of *præcepit* is *Ludouuicus pijssimus Augustus*, identified by most scholars as Louis the Pious (Ludwig der Fromme), who ruled from 813 to 840. The *Praefatio* thus seems to establish a *terminus ante quem* of Louis' death date, if the perfect form *præcepit* is understood to mean that the *Hêliand* was commissioned during his lifetime — and if *Ludouuicus pijssimus Augustus* indeed refers to Louis the Pious. Drögereit (1951a) points out, however, that a son of Louis the Pious, Louis the German, was called *augustus* in the year of his birth in 805, which — if this is the correct *Ludouuicus* — would push the possible dating of composition to his death in 876. Against this argument stands the dating of the manuscript and fragments, of which three can be restricted to about 850.

construct this [ƀ] from the original manuscript of the third Vita Liudgers, the Frisian founder of Werden, which was written there in about 864."

[8] "For [he] ordered a certain man of the Saxon people who was deemed among them to be no inglorious bard to devote himself to a poetic translation into the German language of the Old and New Testaments so that the holy reading of the divine commandments might be diffused not only to the literate but also to the illiterate."

Hêliand

The prose *Praefatio B* is a rendering of Bede's story of Caedmon's dream, in which the poet, a simple herdsman, while asleep receives divine impulse to compose in verse. The *Versus* relates basically the same poetically, establishing the modest credentials of the divinely inspired, humble man of the countryside (cf. Andersson [1974]).

The *terminus post quem* for the composition is generally linked to the composition of Hrabanus's commentary on Matthew, which was finished in 822.

The allusion to Caedmon and his dream-inspired talent as a poet serves to set the *Hêliand* in a tradition of Germanic divinely-inspired eloquence. North (1991) in discussing the 'unflawed gift' of poetry cites Cynewulf's *Elene* and claims that "Cynewulf's poetic predecessors ... before the Conversion ... believed in the divinely invested integrity of poetic skill" (p. 26). The *Hêliand* makes many allusions to the prestige and importance associated with speaking eloquently, which we can with some certainty view as an attribute of leadership as practiced in earlier times. Cathey (1996) expands on this topos. Of course, the *Hêliand* itself was written in alliterative verse for reasons of prestige and as an aid to its reception among the Saxons.

THE MANUSCRIPTS

The surviving manuscripts are the M in Munich, the C in the British Museum, the P in Prague, the S found at Straubing, and the V at the Vatican. M and C descend from a common prior manuscript *CM, while P and V seem to stand apart from that and from each other. According to Taeger (1979) there are indications for a connection SM as against C but also for CS as against M, a finding which demands further clarification. Taeger (1984) admits the possibility that identical mistakes in C and M could have been made independently by different scribes. In his introduction to the ninth edition of *Hêliand und Genesis* Taeger also postulates a common line of descent connecting C and P, evidently posterior to *CM. In any case, he correctly states (1979) "Ein vollständiger Stammbaum ist natürlich nicht voll erweisbar, wenn er außer aus zwei Handschriften nur aus Fragmenten konstruiert wird, die sich an keiner Stelle überlagern"⁹ (p. 187). From these manuscripts, chiefly C and M, 5,983 lines can be edited to make up our reading of the *Hêliand*. There is evidence also for a lost manuscript *L from the library in Leipzig, about which very little is known.

The Monacensis (M) manuscript in Munich dates from the 9th century and still contains 75 leafs. The original was larger by at least six, although it is not clear by exactly how many, as the first is missing along with gaps after leafs 33, 37, 50, 57, 67, and a larger one after leaf 75. The M is considered the best manuscript in spite of its missing beginning and ending in that its language is relatively consistent and is written in just one hand. Drögereit (1951b) claims it for the scriptorium at Werden, while Bischoff (1979) states flatly "die Handschrift M ist in Corvey geschrieben" (p. 161).[10]

Cotton Caligula A. VII, the C manuscript, is younger than M and is likely to be from the 10th century. C contains more corrections than M and shows less consistency in its forms. Franconian features are more prominent, especially in the diphthongization of Saxon /e:/, spelled <ê>, to /ie/, spelled <ie>, and of /o:/, <ô>, to /uo/, <uo>, and in the third plural present indicative ending *-ent*. Priebsch (1925) placed the site of composition of C in England at Winchester, perhaps by a Saxon scribe. C contains the beginning of the *Hêliand*, but it also lacks the ending.

The manuscript in Prague (P) consists of a single leaf from around the year 850 containing lines 958-1006. As noted above, it is allied to manuscript C and descended along with it from a postulated *CP.

The Vatican manuscript (V) contains excerpts from the Old Saxon *Genesis* along with lines 1279-1358 of the *Hêliand* and is from the third quarter of the 9th century. Since only V maintains the original reading of line 1308 as against the shortened version in M and the altered one in C, it is revealed as independent of and anterior to *CM (Taeger [1984], p. xvii).

Manuscript S, which was discovered only in December of 1977 during a search for fragments of Carolingian manuscripts in the libraries of Straubing, is the furthest removed from *CM, descending along with M from a postulated *MS. (A key to the relationship of S

---

[9] "A complete stemma is of course not completely demonstrable when, beyond the two manuscripts, it is constructed only from fragments that do not overlap."

[10] "Manuscript M was written at Corvey."

with M is line 508, where S has *antheti* [with an accent mark over the <n>, M has *anthehti*, but C has *an ehti*.) The fragment is badly mangled, as it was used in the binding of a *Weltchronik* from 1493, but contains 25 lines grouped in bunches between lines 351 and 722. S can be dated to around the year 850.

THE FITTEN

The entire *Hêliand* was composed in what perhaps were 75 episodes or divisions, called *Fitten* in German (English 'fitt'). The Latin *Praefatio* describes way in which the *poeta* divided the episodic composition into *Fitten*, using the word in the accusative plural form *vitteas* as a direct loan from Old Saxon, but only the C manuscript indicates the division of the narrative into *Fitten*, which was the Anglo-Saxon practice of the time. Rathofer (1962) in his interesting but controversial book describes a symmetry around the center that involves the thirteen central *Fitten* (symbolizing Christ and the Twelve) with the account of the Transfiguration (*Fitte* 38) in the middle. The whole work is, according to Rathofer, divided into thirds by *Fitten* in the proportion 31-13-31. He furthermore sees a second pattern in the form of a cross (a *figura crucis*) that involves the number four (p. 561). The first and final 22 *Fitten* thus constitute the horizontal bars of such a cross, while the central 31 form vertical bars of 15 each, with *Fitte* 38 again in the center. The first *Fitte* itself is, according to Rathofer, symbolically structured with the numbers three (The Trinity) and four (the Four Evangelists). He adduces much material to support his hypotheses and, taken on their own terms, his arguments seem persuasive. Almost needless to say, Rathofer's views have drawn considerable fire. Wolf (1975) concludes that "der Helianddichter ... [hat] dieser Fitte zahlhafte Struktur verliehen.... Das ... 'geistliche Zählen' epischer Variationen bestätigte sich aber nicht"[11] (p. 20). Cordes (1967) in a lengthy review comes to the blunt conclusion: "Wenn man die obigen Ausführungen noch einmal durchsieht, hat doch eigentlich – bei allem Fleiß und aller Vorsicht – kein einziges Argument Stich gehalten. Der 'Bauplan' ist

---

[11] "The author of the *Hêliand* gave a numerical structure to this fitt.... The 'sacred counting' of epic variations can, however, not be confirmed."

auch für den *Hêliand* nicht zu beweisen..."[12] (p. 78). Liberman (1995) points out that "the poem is too long to be read straight through from beginning to end, so its attractiveness must have been based on something other than number symbolism and the like" (p. 194). Murphy (1992) sees the Transfiguration as being at the center of the narrative but that "due to the formal unwieldiness of the gospel story itself, the poet could not order the entirety of the gospel's incidents into parallel episodes in his composition, but rather selected a number of them based on his spiritual insight into their appropriateness" (p. 222). Murphy states in reference to the Transfiguration on the mountaintop that it,

> "suggests two other mountain scenes in the epic in which the author brings the gospel story to a striking climax in Germanic imagery: the epic 'battle scene' on Mr. Olivet, in which Peter defends his Chieftain with the sword, and the brilliant recasting of Christ's teachings in Germanic terms in the Sermon on the Mount. The scene on Mt. Olivet is in song 58, exactly twenty songs away from the Transfiguration's song [division or *Fitte*] 38, and the Sermon on the Mount reaches the conclusion of its first part in Song 18 – also twenty songs away from song 38. I do not thing this placement is accidental" (p. 224).

Murphy (1992) then proposes his own scheme of parallel episodes (p. 229), advocating a structure based on a symmetrical arrangement around the scenes brilliantly illuminated on the three mountains with images of light.

---

[12] "If you once again look through the arguments given above, not a single one holds up in spite of all the energy and care invested. The 'plan of construction' cannot be proven for the *Hêliand*."

A Comparison of the 'M' vs. 'C' Manuscripts

See THE WORK for a description of the two principal manuscripts of the *Hêliand*. Here we present a side-by-side comparison of the same excerpt — lines 2906b to 2919a — in order to illustrate particularly the kinds of orthographic distinctions that obtain between them. This sample is taken from Sievers (1878), who provides facing pages that, where possible, show matching lines in manuscripts M and C; also compare these lines below with those from the present text in the normalization provided by Taeger (1984) which follows on the next page.

Manuscript M	*Manuscript* C
Tho letun sie *an* suidean strom	Thuo lietun sia an suithean strom
hohhurnid skip hluttron udeon	hohhurnid scip hluttron uthion
skedan skir uuater. Skred lioht dages,	scedan scirana uuatar. Scred lioht dages,
sunne uuard an sedle; the seolidandean	sunno uuarth an sedle; thia seolithandiun
naht nebulo biuuarp; nathidun erlos	naht neflu biuuarp; nathidun erlos
forduuardes an flod: uuard thiu fiorthe tid	forthuuardes an fluod: uuarth thiu fiorða tid
thera nahtes cuman — neriendo Crist	thero nahtes kuman — neriendi Crist
uuarode thea uuaglidand—: tho uuard	uuaroda thiu uuaglithand—: thuo uuarth
uuind mikil,	uuind mikil
hoh uueder afhaben: hlamodun udeon	ho uueder ahaban: hlamodun uthion,
storm an strome; stridiun feridun	strom an stamne; stridion feridun
thea uueros uuider uuinde: uuas im	thia uueros uuidar uuinde: uuas im
uured hugi,	uureth hugi,
sebo sorgono ful: selbon ni uuandun	sebo sorogono full: selbon ni uuandun
lagulidandea an land cumen	lagolithanda an land cumin
thurh thes uuederes geuuin.	thuru thes uuedares giuuin.

A Comparison of the 'M' vs. 'C' Manuscripts

The first difference to strike one is in the spelling. Not only do these two versions differ from each other, but they are also different from that contained in this book:

    Thô lêtun sie suîðean strôm,

   hôh hurnidskip hluttron ûðeon,

   skêðan skîr uuater. Skrêd lioht dages,

   sunne uuarð an sedle; the sêolîđandean

2910 naht neƀulo biuuarp; nâðidun erlos

   forðuuardes an flôd; uuarð thiu fiorðe tid

   thera nahtes cuman — neriendo Crist

   uuarode thea uuâglîðand —: thô uuarð uuind mikil

   hôh uueder afhaƀen: hlamodun ûðeon,

2915 strôm an stamne; strîdiun feridun

   thea uueros uuiðer uuinde, uuas im uurêð hugi,

   seƀo sorgono ful: selƀon ni uuândun

   lagulîðandea an land cumen

   thurh thes uuederes geuuin.

A careful comparison will give an inkling into choices made in the normalized text last edited by Taeger. Note, for example, the spelling <th> in *uuarth* in C (line 2911) as against <d> as in *uuard* in M, which is generally resolved in <ð>; or in <b> as against <f> in *nebulo* / *neflu* in line 2910 that represents the phoneme /ƀ/.

The long vowel phoneme spelled as <ô> in our text appears either unmarked as <o> or as the Franconian diphthong <uo>, for example *Thuo* in line 2906b. The same holds for <e> vs. <ie> in *lietun* (2609b), which is resolved as long <ê> in the normalized text. It is the presence of the contrasting spelling of <uo> and <ie> that really shows that unmarked <o> and <e> in parallel positions are long. Other factors played a role in normalization, including etymological knowledge from related languages.

As we see from the strange blunder *scirana uuatar* in line 2908 of the C-manuscript with a masculine accusative ending on an adjective referring to a neuter singular noun, editors also had to correct some syntactical problems. The choice between 'storm' and 'stream' (*storm* and *strom*) and between 'on the stream' and 'on the stem' (*an strome* vs. *an stamne*) in line 2915 offered a different sort of editorial conundrum.

Mitzka states in the eighth edition of *Heliand und Genesis* (Altdeutsche Textbibliothek Nr. 4):

> Die Ausgabe von Sievers, die genaue Abdrücke von *M* und *C* liefert, hat für alle sprachlichen Untersuchungen den Ausgangspunkt zu bilden. Die beiden Haupthandschriften stimmen in ihren Lauten und Formen nicht überein; welche von ihnen der Sprache des Originals näher steht, wissen wir nicht (p. XIV).[13]

It is, perhaps ironically, the version published by Otto Behaghel in Altdeutsche Textbibliothek Nr. 4 that itself has since become the standard to which one appeals.

---

[13] The edition by Sievers, that provides exact reproductions of *M* and *C*, must be the point of departure for all linguistic examinations. The two main manuscripts do not agree in their sounds and forms; we do not know which of them is closer to the language of the original.

Excerpts† from the
Hêliand

§1. Introduction

M anega uuâron,   the sia iro môd gespôn,
....   that sia bigunnun uuord godes,
reckean that girûni,   that thie rîceo Crist
undar mancunnea   mâriða gifrumida
5   mid uuordun endi mid uuercun.   That uuolda thô uuîsare filo
liudo barno loƀon,   lêra Cristes,
hêlag uuord godas,   endi mid iro handon scrîƀan
berehtlîco an buok,   huô sia is gibodscip scoldin
frummian, firiho barn.   Than uuârun thoh sia fiori te thiu
10 under thera menigo,   thia habdon maht godes,
helpa fan himila,   hêlagna gêst,
craft fan Criste, —   sia uurðun gicorana te thio,
that sie than êuangelium   ênan scoldun
an buok scrîƀan   endi sô manag gibod godes,
15 hêlag himilisc uuord: sia ne muosta heliðo than mêr,
firiho barno frummian,   neuan that sia fiori te thio
thuru craft godas   gecorana uurðun,

---

† The sixty-seven excerpts included here are divided into sections chosen for their general interest as cultural cues to Old Saxon life and thought and/or accommodation to Christian theology. The *Commentary*, pages 133-254, is keyed to the sections and their line numbers. These sections, however, do not necessarily correspond to the traditional division of the Hêliand into so-called *Fitten*. Consult *Hêliand und Genesis*, hrsg. von Otto Behaghel, 9. Auflage bearbeitet von Burkhard Taeger 1984, (Altdeutsche Textbibliothek Nr. 4) for the full text.

Hêliand

    Matheus endi Marcus, — sô uuârun thia man hêtana —
    Lucas endi Iohannes;   sia uuârun gode lieƀa,
20 uuirðiga ti them giuuirkie.   Habda im uualdand god,
    them heliðon an iro hertan   hêlagna gêst
    fasto bifolhan   endi ferahtan hugi,
    sô manag uuîslik uuord   endi giuuit mikil,
    that sea scoldin ahebbean   hêlagaro stemnun
25 godspell that guoda,   that ni haƀit ênigan gigadon huergin,
    thiu uuord an thesaro uueroldi,   that io uualdand mêr,
    drohtin diurie   eftho derƀi thing,
    firinuuerc fellie   eftho fîundo nîð,
    strîd uuiđerstande —,   huand hie habda starkan hugi,
30 mildean endi guodan,   thie thes mêster uuas,
    aðalordfrumo   alomahtig.
    That scoldun sea fiori thuo   fingron scrîƀan,
    settian endi singan   endi seggian forð,
    that sea fan Cristes   crafte them mikilon
35 gisâhun endi gihôrdun,   thes hie selƀo gisprac,
    giuuîsda endi giuuarahta,   uundarlîcas filo,
    sô manag mid mannon   mahtig drohtin,
    all so hie it fan them anginne   thuru is ênes craht,
    uualdand gisprak,   thuo hie êrist thesa uuorold giscuop
40 endi thuo all bifieng   mid ênu uuordo,
    himil endi erða   endi al that sea bihlidan êgun
    giuuarahtes endi giuuahsanes: that uuarð thuo all mid
        uuordon godas
    fasto bifangan,   endi gifrumid after thiu,
    huilic than liudscepi   landes scoldi
45 uuîdost giuualdan,   eftho huar thiu uueroldaldar
    endon scoldin. Ên uuas iro thuo noh than

§1. Introduction

    firio barnun biforan,   endi thiu fîƀi uuârun agangan:
    scolda thuo that sehsta   sâliglîco
    cuman thuru craft godes   endi Cristas giburd,
50 hêlandero bestan,   hêlagas gêstes,
    an thesan middilgard managon te helpun,
    firio barnon ti frumon   uuið fîundo nîð,
    uuið dernero duualm.   Than habda thuo drohtin god
    Rômanoliudeon farliuuan   rîkeo mêsta,
55 habda them heriscipie   herta gisterkid,
    than sia habdon bithuungana   thiedo gihuilica,
    habdun fan Rûmuburg   rîki giuunnan
    helmgitrôsteon,   sâton iro heritogon
    an lando gihuem,   habdun liudeo giuuald,
60 allon elitheodon.   Erodes uuas
    an Hierusalem   oƀer that Iudeono folc
    gicoran te kuninge,   sô ina thie kêser tharod,
    fon Rûmuburg   rîki thiodan
    satta undar that gisîði.   Hie ni uuas thoh mid sibbeon bilang
65 aƀaron Israheles,   eð iligiburdi,
    cuman fon iro cnuosle,   neuan that hie thuru thes kêsures
        thanc
    fan Rûmuburg   rîki habda,
    that im uuârun sô gihôriga   hildiscalcos,
    aƀaron Israheles   elleanruoƀa:
70 suîðo unuuanda uuini,   than lang hie giuuald êhta,
    Erodes thes rîkeas   endi râdburdeon held
    Iudeo liudi.   Thana uuas thar ên gigamalod mann,
    that uuas fruod gomo,   habda ferehtan hugi,
    uuas fan them liudeon   Levias cunnes,
75 Iacobas suneas,   guodero thiedo:
    Zacharias uuas hie hêtan.   That uuas sô sâlig man,

Hêliand

    huand hie simblon gerno   gode theonoda,
    uuarahta after is uuilleon;   deda is uuîf sô self
    — uuas iru gialdrod idis: ni muosta im erƀ iuuard
80   an iro iuguðhêdi   giƀ ið ig uuerðan —
    libdun im farûter laster,   uuaruhtun lof goda,
    uuârun sô gihôriga   heƀ ancuninge,
    diuridon ûsan drohtin: ni uueldun derƀ eas uuiht
    under mancunnie,   mênes gifrummean,
85   ni saca ne sundea.

§2. Elizabeth's Child

Ik is engil bium,
120   Gabriel bium ic hêtan,   the gio for goda standu,
    anduuard for them alouualdon,   ne sî that he me an is ârundi huarod
    sendean uuillea.   Nu hiet he me an thesan sîð faran,
    hiet that ic thi thoh gicûð di,   that thi kind giboran,
    fon thînera alderu idis   ôdan scoldi
125   uuerðan an thesero uueroldi,   uuordun spâhi.
    That ni scal an is lîƀ a gio   lîðes anbîtan,
    uuînes an is uueroldi: sô haƀed im uurdgiscapu,
    metod gimarcod   endi maht godes.
    Hêt that ic thi thoh sagdi,   that it scoldi gisîð uuesan
130   heƀ ancuninges,   hêt that git it heldin uuel,
    tuhin thurh treuua,   quað that he im tîras sô filu
    an godes rîkea   forgeƀ an uueldi.
    He quað that the gôdo gumo   Iohannes te namon
    hebbean scoldi,   gibôd that git it hêtin sô,
135   that kind, than it quâmi,   quað that it Kristes gisîð

§2. Elizabeth's Child

an thesaro uuîdun uuerold   uuerðan scoldi,
is selbes sunies,   endi quað that sie sliumo herod
an is bodskepi   bêðe quâmin.
Zacharias thô gimahalda   endi uuið selban sprac
140   drohtines engil,   endi im thero dâdeo bigan,
uundron thero uuordo: 'huuô mag that giuuerðan sô,' quað he,
'aftar an aldre?   It is unc al te lat
sô te giuuinnanne,   sô thu mid thînun uuordun gisprikis.
Huuanda uuit habdun aldres êr   efno tuêntig
145   uuintro an uncro uueroldi,   êr than quâmi thit uuîf te mi;
than uuârun uuit nu atsamna   antsibunta uuintro
gibenkeon endi gibeddeon,   siðor ic sie mi te brûdi gecôs.
Sô uuit thes an uncro iuguði   gigirnan ni mohtun,
that uuit erbiuuard   êgan môstin,
150   fôdean an uncun flettea,   — nu uuit sus gifrôdod sint,
habad unc eldi binoman   elleandâdi,
that uuit sint an uncro siuni gislekit   endi an uncum sîdun lat;
flêsk is unc antfallan,   fel unscôni,
is unca lud giliðen,   lîk gidrusnod,
155   sind unca andbâri   ôðarlîcaron,
môd endi megincraft,   — sô uuit giu sô managan dag
uuârun an thesero uueroldi,   sô mi thes uundar thunkit,
huuô it sô giuuerðan mugi,   sô thu mid thînun uuordun gisprikis.'

§3. The Birth of John

  Thô uuarð sân aftar thiu maht godes
gicûðid is craft mikil;   uuarð thiu quân ôcan,
idis an ira eldiu: scolda im erƀiuuard,
195 suîðo godcund gumo   giƀiðig uuerðen,
barn an burgun.   Bêd aftar thiu
that uuîf uurdigiscapu.   Skrêd the uuintar forð,
geng thes gêres gital.   Iohannes quam
an liudeo lioht: lîk uuas im scôni,
200 uuas im fel fagar,   fahs endi naglos,
uuangun uuârun im uulitige.   Thô fôrun thar uuîse man,
snelle tesamne,   thea suâsostun mêst,
uundrodun thes uuerkes,   bihuî it gio mahti giuuerðan sô,
that undar sô aldun tuêm ôdan uurði
205 barn an giburdeon,   ni uuâri that it gibod godes
selƀes uuâri: afsuoƀun sie garo,
that it elcor sô uuânlîc   uuerðan ni mahti.
Thô sprak thar ên gifrôdot man,   the sô filo consta
uuîsaro uuordo,   habde giuuit mikil,
210 frâgode niudlîco,   huuat is namo scoldi
uuesan an thesaro uueroldi: 'mi thunkid an is uuîsu gilîc
iac an is gibârea,   that he sî betara than uui,
sô ic uuâniu, that ina ûs gegnungo   god fon himila
selƀo sendi.'   Thô sprac sân aftar
215 thiu môdar thes kindes,   thiu thana magu habda,
that barn an ire barme: 'hêr quam gibod godes,' quað siu,
'fernun gêre,   formon uuordu
gibôd, that he Iohannes   bi godes lêrun
hêtan scoldi.   That ic an mînumu hugi ni gidar

§3. *The Birth of John*

220 uuendean mid uuihti,   of ic is giuualdan môt.'
Thô sprac ên gêlhert man,   the ira gaduling uuas:
'ne hêt êr giouuiht sô,' quað he,   'aðalboranes
ûses cunnies eftho cnôsles.   Uuita kiasan im ôðrana
niudsamna namon: he niate of he môti.'
225 Thô sprac eft the frôdo man,   the thar consta filo mahlian:
'ni gibu ic that te râde,' quað he,   'rinco negênun,
that he uuord godes   uuendean biginna;
ac uuita is thana fader frâgon,   the thar sô gifrôdod sitit,
uuîs an is uuînseli: thoh he ni mugi ênig uuord sprecan
230 thoh mag he bi bôcstabon   brêf geuuirkean,
namon giscrîban.'   Thô he nâhor geng,
legda im êna bôc an barm   endi bad gerno
uurîtan uuîslîco   uuordgimerkiun,
huat sie that hêlaga barn   hêtan scoldin.
235 Thô nam he thia bôk an hand   endi an is hugi thâhte
suîðo gerno te gode: Iohannes namon
uuîslîco giuurêt   endi ôc aftar mid is uuordu gisprac
suîðo spâhlîco: habda im eft is sprâca giuuald,
giuuitteas endi uuîsun.   That uuîti uuas thô agangan,
240 hard harmscare,   the im hêlag god
mahtig macode,   that he an is môdsebon
godes ni forgâti,   than he im eft sendi is iungron tô.

§4. Mary's Child

Thô ni uuas lang aftar thiu,   ne it al sô gilêstid uuarð,
sô he mancunnea   managa huîla,
245 god alomahtig   forgeben habda,
that he is himilisc barn   herod te uueroldi,
is selbes sunu   sendean uueldi,
te thiu that he hêr alôsdi   al liudstamna,
uuerod fon uuîtea.   Thô uuarð is uuisbodo
250 an Galilealand,   Gabriel cuman,
engil des alouualdon,   thar he êne idis uuisse,
munilîca magað: Maria uuas siu hêten,
uuas iru thiorna githigan.   Sea ên thegan habda,
Ioseph gemahlit,   gôdes cunnies man,
255 thea Dauides dohter: that uuas sô diurlîc uuîf,
idis anthêti.   Thar sie the engil godes
an Nazarethburg   bi namon selbo
grôtte geginuuarde   endi sie fon gode quedda:
'Hêl uuis thu, Maria,' quað he,   'thu bist thînun hêrron liof,
260 uualdande uuirðig,   huuand thu giuuit habes,
idis enstio fol. Thu scalt for allun uuesan
uuîbun giuuîhit. Ne habe thu uuêcan hugi,
ne forhti thu thînun ferhe: ne quam ic thi te ênigun frêson herod,
ne dragu ic ênig drugithing.   Thu scalt ûses drohtines uuesan
265 môdar mid mannun   endi scalt thana magu fôdean,
thes hôhon hebancuninges suno.   The scal Hêliand te namon
êgan mid eldiun.   Neo endi ni kumid,
thes uuîdon rîkeas giuuand,   the he giuualdan scal,

§4. Mary's Child

    mâri theodan.'   Thô sprac im eft thiu magað angegin,
270 uuið thana engil godes   idiso scôniost,
    allaro uuîbo uulitigost: 'huô mag that giuuerðen sô,' quað siu,
    'that ic magu fôdie?   Ne ic gio mannes ni uuarð
    uuîs an mînera uueroldi.'   Thô habde eft is uuord garu
    engil thes alouualdon   thero idisiu tegegnes:
275 'an thi scal hêlag gêst   fon heƀanuuange
    cuman thurh craft godes.   Thanan scal thi kind ôdan
    uuerðan an thesaro uueroldi.   Uualdandes craft
    scal thi fon them hôhoston   heƀancuninge
    scadouuan mid skimon.   Ni uuarð scôniera giburd,
280 ne sô mâri mid mannun,   huand siu kumid thurh maht
        godes
    an these uuîdon uuerold.'   Thô uuarð eft thes uuîbes hugi
    aftar them ârundie   al gihuorƀen
    an godes uuilleon.   'Than ic hêr garu standu,' quað siu,
    'te sulicun ambahtskepi,   sô he mi êgan uuili.
285 Thiu bium ic theotgodes.   Nu ik theses thinges gitrûon;
    uuerðe mi aftar thînun uuordun,   al sô is uuilleo sî,
    hêrron mînes;   nis mi hugi tuîfli,
    ne uuord ne uuîsa.'   Sô gifragn ik, that that uuîf antfeng
    that godes ârundi   gerno suîðo
290 mid leohtu hugi   endi mid gilôƀon gôdun
    endi mid hluttrun treuun.   Uuarđ the hêlago gêst,
    that barn an ira bôsma;   endi siu ira breostun forstôd
    iac an ire seƀon selƀo,   sagda them siu uuelda,
    that sie habde giôcana   thes alouualdon craft
295 hêlag fon himile.   Thô uuarð hugi Iosepes,
    is môd giuuorrid,   the im êr thea magað habda,

Hêliand

    thea idis anthêttea,   aðalcnôsles uuîf
    giboht im te brûdiu.   He afsôf that siu habda barn undar iru:
    ni uuânda thes mid uuihti,   that iru that uuîf habdi
300 giuuardod sô uuarolîco: ni uuisse uualdandes thô noh
    blîði gibodskepi.   Ni uuelda sia imo te brûði thô,
    halon imo te hîuuon,   ac bigan im thô an hugi thenkean,
    huô he sie sô forlêti,   sô iru thar ni uurði lêðes uuiht,
    ôdan arbides.   Ni uuelda sie aftar thiu
305 meldon for menigi: antdrêd that sie manno barn
    libu binâmin.   Sô uuas than thero liudeo thau
    thurh then aldon êu,   Ebreo folkes,
    sô huilik sô thar an unreht   idis gihîuuida,
    that siu simbla thana bedskepi   buggean scolda,
310 frî mid ira ferhu: ni uuas gio thiu fêmea sô gôd,
    that siu mid them liudiun leng   libbien môsti,
    uuesan undar them uueroda.   Bigan im the uuîso mann,
    suîðo gôd gumo,   Ioseph an is môda
    thenkean thero thingo,   huô he thea thiornun thô
315 listiun forlêti.   Thô ni uuas lang te thiu,
    that im thar an drôma quam   drohtines engil,
    hebancuninges bodo,   endi hêt sie ina haldan uuel,
    minnion sie an is môde: 'Ni uuis thu', quað he, 'Mariun
        uurêð,
    thiornun thînaro;   siu is githungan uuîf;
320 ne forhugi thu sie te hardo;   thu scalt sie haldan uuel,
    uuardon ira an thesaro uueroldi.   Lêsti thu inca uuinitreuua
    forð sô thu dâdi,   endi hald incan friundskepi uuel!
    Ne lât thu sie thi thiu lêðaron,   thoh siu undar ira liðon êgi,
    barn an ira bôsma.   It cumid thurh gibod godes,
325 hêlages gêstes   fon hebanuuanga:
    that is Iêsu Krist,   godes êgan barn,

§4. Mary's Child

uualdandes sunu.   Thu scalt sie uuel haldan,
hêlaglîco.   Ne lât thu thi thînan hugi tuîflien,
merrean thîna môdgithâht.'

§5. THE BIRTH OF JESUS

　　Thô uuarð fon Rûmuburg　　rîkes mannes
340　oƀar alla thesa irminthiod　　Octauiânas
　　ban endi bodskepi　　oƀar thea is brêdon giuuald
　　cuman fon them kêsure　　cuningo gihuilicun,
　　hêmsitteandiun,　　sô uuîdo sô is heritogon
　　oƀar al that landskepi　　liudio giuueldun.
345　Hiet man that alla thea elilendiun man　　iro ôðil sôhtin,
　　heliðos iro handmahal　　angegen iro hêrron bodon,
　　quâmi te them cnôsla gihue,　　thanan he cunneas uuas,
　　giboran fon them burgiun.　　That gibod uuarð gilêstid
　　oƀar thesa uuîdon uuerold.　　Uuerod samnoda
350　te allaro burgeo gihuuem.　　Forun thea bodon oƀar all,
　　thea fon them kêsura cumana uuârun,
　　bôkspâha uueros,　　endi an brêf scriƀun
　　suîðo niudlîco　　namono gihuilican,
　　ia land ia liudi,　　that im ni mahti alettean mann
355　gumono sulica gambra,　　sô im scolda geldan gihue
　　heliðo fon is hôƀda.　　Thô giuuêt im ôc mid is hîuuisca
　　Ioseph the gôdo,　　sô it god mahtig,
　　uualdand uuelda:　　sôhta im thiu uuânamon hêm,
　　thea burg an Bethleem,　　thar iro beiðero uuas,
360　thes heliðes handmahal　　endi ôc thera hêlagun thiornun,
　　Mariun thera gôdun.　　Thar uuas thes mâreon stôl
　　an êrdagun,　　aðalcuninges,

Dauides thes gôdon,   than langa the he thana druhtskepi
    thar,
erl undar Ebreon   êgan môsta,
365 haldan hôhgisetu.   Sie uuârun is hîuuiscas,
cuman fon is cnôsla,   cunneas gôdes,
beðiu bi giburdiun.   Thar gifragn ic, that sie thiu berhtun
    giscapu,
Mariun gimanodun   endi maht godes,
that iru an them sîða   sunu ôdan uuarð,
370 giboran an Bethleem   barno strangost,
allaro cuningo craftigost: cuman uuarð the mâreo,
mahtig an manno lioht,   sô is êr managan dag
biliði uuârun   endi bôcno filu
giuuorðen an thesero uueroldi.

§6. Signs of Jesus' Birth

Thô uuarð that managun cûð
oƀar these uuîdon uuerold,   uuardos antfundun,
thea thar ehuscalcos   ûta uuârun,
uueros an uuahtu,   uuiggeo gômean,
390 fehas aftar felda: gisâhun finistri an tuuê
telâtan an lufte,   endi quam lioht godes
uuânum thurh thiu uuolcan   endi thea uuardos thar
bifeng an them felda.   Sie uurðun an forhtun thô,
thea man an ira môda: gisâhun thar mahtigna
395 godes engil cuman,   the im tegegnes sprac,
hêt that im thea uuardos   uuiht ne antdrêdin
leðes fon them liohta: 'ic scal eu', quað he, 'lioƀora thing
suîðo uuârlico   uuilleon seggean,
cûðean craft mikil: nu is Krist geboran

§6. Signs of Jesus' Birth

400 an thesero selƀun naht,   sâlig barn godes,
     an thera Dauides burg,   drohtin the gôdo.
     That is mendislo   manno cunneas,
     allaro firiho fruma.   Thar gi ina fîðan mugun,
     an Bethlemaburg   barno rîkiost:
405 hebbiad that te têcna,   that ic eu gitellean mag
     uuârun uuordun,   that he thar biuundan ligid,
     that kind an ênera cribbiun,   thoh he sî cuning oƀar al
     erðun endi himiles   endi oƀar eldeo barn,
     uueroldes uualdand'.   Reht sô he thô that uuord gisprac,
410 sô uuarð thar engilo te them ênun   unrîm cuman,
     hêlag heriskepi   fon heƀanuuanga,
     fagar folc godes,   endi filu sprâkun,
     lofuuord manag   liudeo hêrron.
     Afhôƀun thô hêlagna sang,   thô sie eft te heƀanuuanga
415 uundun thurh thiu uuolcan.   Thea uuardos hôrdun,
     huô thiu engilo craft   alomahtigna god
     suîðo uuerðlîco   uuordun loƀodun:
     'diuriða sî nu', quâðun sie,   'drohtine selƀun
     an them hôhoston   himilo rîkea
420 endi friðu an erðu   firiho barnun,
     gôduuilligun gumun,   them the god antkennead
     thurh hluttran hugi.'   Thea hirdios forstôdun,
     that sie mahtig thing   gimanod habda,
     blîðlîc bodskepi: giuuitun im te Bethleem thanan
425 nahtes sîðon;   uuas im niud mikil,
     that sie selƀon Krist   gisehan môstin.

§7. Jesus in the Temple

Thô quam thar ôc ên uuîf gangan
ald innan them alaha: Anna uuas siu hêtan,
505 dohtar Fanueles;   siu habde ira drohtine uuel
githionod te thanca,   uuas iru githungan uuîf.
Siu môsta aftar ira magaðhêdi,   sîðor siu mannes uuarð,
erles an êhti   eðili thiorne,
sô môsta siu mid ira brûdigumon   bôdlo giuualdan
510 sibun uuintar saman. Thô gifragn ic that iru thar sorga gistôd
that sie thiu mikila maht   metodes tedêlda,
uurêð uurdigiscapu.   Thô uuas siu uuidouua aftar thiu
at them friðuuîha   fior endi antahtoda
uuintro an iro uueroldi,   sô siu nia thana uuîh ni forlêt,
515 ac siu thar ira drohtine uuel   dages endi nahtes,
gode thionode. Siu quam thar ôc gangan tô
an thea selbun tîd: sân antkende
that hêlage barn godes   endi them heliðon cûðde,
them uueroda aftar them uuîha   uuilspel mikil,
520 quað that im neriandas ginist   ginâhid uuâri,
helpa hebencuniges: 'nu is the hêlago Krist,
uualdand selbo   an thesan uuîh cuman
te alôsienne thea liudi,   the hêr nu lango bidun
an thesara middilgard,   managa huuîla
525 thurftig thioda, sô nu thes thinges mugun
mendian mancunni.'   Manag fagonoda
uuerod aftar them uuîha: gihôrdun uuilspel mikil
fon gode seggean.   That geld habde thô gilêstid
thiu idis an them alaha,   al sô it im an ira êuua gibôd
530 endi an thera berhtun burg   bôk giuuîsdun,
hêlagaro handgiuuerk.

§8. The Three Wise Men

Thoh thar than gihuilic hêlag man
Krist antkendi, thoh ni uuarð it gio te thes kuninges hoƀe
them mannun gimârid, thea im an iro môdseƀon
540 holde ni uuârun, ac uuas im sô bihalden forð
mid uuordun endi mid uuerkun, antthat thar uueros ôstan
suîðo glauua gumon gangan quâmun
threa te thero thiodu, thegnos snelle,
an langan uueg oƀar that land tharod:
545 folgodun ênun berhtun bôkne endi sôhtun that barn godes
mid hluttru hugi: uueldun im hnîgan tô
gehan im te iungrun: driƀun im godes giscapu.
Thô sie Erodesan thar rîkean fundun
an is seli sittien, slîðuurdean kuning,
550 môdagna mid is mannun: — simbla uuas he morðes
    gern —
thô quaddun sie ina cûsco an cuninguuîsun,
fagaro an is flettie, endi he frâgoda sân,
huilic sie ârundi ûta gibrâhti,
uueros an thana uuracsîð: 'huueðer lêdiad gi uundan gold
555 te geƀu huilicun gumono? te huî gi thus an ganga kumad,
gifaran an fôðiu? Huat, gi nêthuuanan ferran sind
erlos fon ôðrun thiodun. Ic gisihu that gi sind eðiligiburdiun
cunnies fon cnôsle gôdun: nio hêr êr sulica cumana ni
    uurðun
êri fon ôðrun thiodun, sîðor ik môsta thesas erlo folkes,
560 giuualdan thesas uuîdon rîkeas. Gi sculun me te uuârun
    seggean
for thesun liudio folke, bihuuî gi sîn te thesun lande
    cumana'.

Hêliand

Thô sprâcun im eft tegegnes   gumon ôstronea,
uuordspâhe uueros: 'uui thi te uuârun mugun', quâðun sie,
'ûse ârundi   ôðo gitellien,
565 giseggean sôðlîco,   bihuuî uui quâmun an thesan sîð herod
fon ôstan te thesaro erðu.   Giu uuârun thar aðalies man,
gôdsprâkea gumon,   thea ûs gôdes sô filu,
helpa gihêtun   fon hebencuninge
uuârun uuordun.   Than uuas thar ên giuuittig man,
570 frôd endi filuuuîs   — forn uuas that giu —,
ûse aldiro ôstar hinan,   — thar ni uuarð sîðor ênig man
sprâkono sô spâhi—; he mahte rekkien spel godes,
huuand im habde forliuuan   liudio hêrro,
that he mahte fon erðu   up gihôrean
575 uualdandes uuord: bithiu uuas is giuuit mikil,
thes thegnes githâhti.   Thô he thanan scolda,
ageben gardos,   gadulingo gimang,
forlâten liudio drôm,   sôkien lioht ôðar
thô he is iungron hêt   gangan nâhor,
580 erbiuuardos,   endi is erlun thô
sagde sôðlîco: — that al sîðor quam,
giuuard an thesaro uueroldi —:   thô sagda he that hêr scoldi
   cuman ên uuîscuning
mâri endi mahtig   an thesan middilgard
thes bezton giburdies;   quað that it scoldi uuesan barn godes
585 quað that he thesero uueroldes   uualdan scoldi
gio te êuuandaga,   erðun endi himiles.
He quað that an them selbon daga,   the ina sâligna
an thesan middilgard   môdar gidrôgi,
sô quað he that ôstana   ên scoldi skînan
590 himiltungal huît,   sulic sô uui hêr ne habdin êr

§8. The Three Wise Men

    undartuisc erða endi himil   ôðar huerigin,
    ne sulic barn ne sulic bôcan.   Hêt that thar te bedu fôrin
    threa man fon thero thiodu,   hêt sie thenkean uuel,
    huan êr sie gisâuuin ôstana   up sîðogean
595 that godes bôcan gangan,   hêt sie garuuuian sân,
    hêt that uui im folgodin,   sô it furi uurði,
    uuestar oƀar thesa uueroldi.   Nu is it al giuuârod sô,
    cuman thurh craft godes: the cuning is gifôdit,
    giboran bald endi strang: uui gisâhun is bôcan skînan
600 hêdro fon himiles tunglun,   sô ic uuêt, that it hêlag drohtin,
    marcoda mahtig selƀo.   Uui gisâhun morgno gihuilikes
    blîcan thana berhton sterron,   endi uui gengun aftar them
        bôcna herod
    uuegas endi uualdas huuîlon.

§9. Herod's Threat

630 Thô gifragn ic that sân aftar thiu   slîðmôd cuning
    thero uuârsagono uuord   them uurekkiun sagda,
    thea thar an elilendi   erlos uuârun
    ferran gifarana,   endi he frâgoda aftar thiu,
    huan sie an ôstaruuegun   êrist gisâhin
635 thana cuningsterron cuman,   cumbal liuhtien
    hêdro fon himile.   Sie ni uueldun is im thô helen eouuiht,
    ac sagdun it im sôðlîco.   Thô hêt he sie an thana sîð faran,
    hêt that sie ira ârundi   al undarfundin
    umbi thes kindes cumi,   endi the cuning selƀo gibôd
640 suîðo hardlico,   hêrro Iudeono
    them uuîsun mannun,   êr than sie fôrin uuestan forð,
    that sie im eft gicûðdin,   huar he thana cuning scoldi

Hêliand

    sôkean at is selðon; quað that he thar uueldi mid is gisîðun tô
    bedan te them barne.   Than hogda he im te banon uuerðan
645 uuâpnes eggiun.   Than eft uualdand god
    thâhte uuið them thinga: he mahta athengean mêr,
    gilêstean an thesum liohte: that is noh lango skîn,
    gicûðdid craft godes.   Thô gengun eft thiu cumbl forð
    uuânum undar uuolcnun.   Thô uuârun thea uuîson man
650 fûsa te faranne: giuuitun im forð thanan
    balda an bodskepi: uueldun that barn godes
    selbon sôkean.   Sie ni habdun thanan gisîðeas mêr,
    bûtan that sie thrie uuârun: uuissun im thingo giskêð,
    uuârun im glauue gumon,   the thea geba lêddun.

§10. The Flight to Egypt

    Thô uuarð sân aftar thiu uualdandes,
700 godes engil cumen   Iosepe te sprâcun,
    sagde im an suuefne   slâpandium an naht,
    bodo drohtines,   that that barn godes
    slîðmôd cuning   sôkean uuelda,
    âhtean is aldres;   'nu scaltu ine an Aegypteo
705 land antlêdean   endi undar them liudiun uuesan
    mid thiu godes barnu   endi mid theru gôdan thiornan,
    uunon undar themu uuerode,   untthat thi uuord cume
    hêrron thînes,   that thu that hêlage barn
    eft te thesum landscepi   lêdian môtis,
710 drohtin thînen.'   Thô fon them drôma ansprang
    Ioseph an is gestseli,   endi that godes gibod
    sân antkenda: giuuêt im an thana sîð thanen
    the thegan mid theru thiornon,   sôhta im thiod ôðra

§10. The Flight to Egypt

      oƀar brêdan berg: uuelda that barn godes
715 fiundun antfôrian.   Thô gifrang aftar thiu
      Erodes the cuning,   thar he an is rîkea sat
      that uuârun thea uuîson man   uuestan gihuuorƀan
      ôstar an iro ôðil   endi fôrun im ôðran uueg:
      uuisse that sie im that ârundi   eft ni uueldun
720 seggian an is selðon.   Thô uuarð im thes an sorgun hugi,
      môd mornondi,   quað that it im thie man dedin,
      heliðos te hônðun.   Thô he sô hriuuig sat,
      balg ina an is briostun, quað that he is mahti betaron râd,
      ôðran githenkien: 'nu ic is aldar can,
725 uuêt is uuintergitalu: nu ic giuuinnan mag,
      that he io oƀar thesaro erðu   ald ni uuirðit,
      hêr undar thesum heriscepi.'   Thô he sô hardo gibôd,
      Erodes oƀar is rîki,   hêt thô is rinkos faran
      cuning thero liudio,   hêt that sie kinda sô filo
730 thurh iro handmagen   hôƀdu binâmin,
      sô manag barn umbi Bethleem,   sô filo sô thar giboran
          uurði,
      an tuêm gêrun atogan.   Tionon frumidon
      thes cuninges gisîðos.   Thô scolda thar sô manag kindisc man
      sueltan sundiono lôs.   Ni uuarð sîð noh êr
735 giâmarlîcara forgang   iungaro manno,
      armlîcara dôð.   Idisi uuiopun,
      môdar managa,   gisâhun iro megi spildian:
      ni mahte siu im nio giformon,   thoh siu mid iro faðmon tuêm,
      iro êgan barn   armun bifengi,
740 liof endi luttil,   thoh scolda is simbla that lîf geƀan

Hêliand

    the magu for theru môdar.   Mênes ni sâhun,
    uuîties thie uuamscaðon: uuâpnes eggiun
    fremidun firinuuerc mikil.   Fellun managa
    maguiunge man.   Thia môdar uuiopun
745 kindiungaro qualm.   Cara uuas an Bethleem,
    hofno hlûdost: thoh man im iro herton an tuê
    sniði mid suerdu,   thoh ni mohta im gio sêrara dâd
    uueröan an thesaro uueroldi,   uuîƀun managun,
    brûdiun an Bethleem: gisâhun iro barn biforan
750 kindiunge man,   qualmu sueltan
    blôdag in iro barmun.   Thie banon uuîtnodun
    unsculdige scole: ni biscriƀun giouuiht
    thea man umbi mênuuerk: uueldun mahtigna,
    Krist selƀon aquellian.   Than habde ina craftag god
755 gineridan uuið iro nîðe,   that inan nahtes thanan
    an Aegypteo land   erlos antlêddun,
    gumon mid Iosepe   an thana grôneon uuang,
    an erðono beztun,   thar ên aha fliutid,
    Nîlstrôm mikil   norð te sêuua,
760 flôdo fagorosta.   Thar that friðubarn godes
    uuonoda an uuilleon,   antthat uurd fornam
    Erodes thana cuning,   that he forlêt eldeo barn,
    môdag manno drôm.   Thô scolda thero marca giuuald
    êgan is erƀiuuard: the uuas Archelâus
765 hêtan, heritogo   helmberandero:
    the scolda umbi Hierusalem   Iudeono folkes,
    uuerodes giuualdan.   Thô uuarđ uuord cuman
    thar an Egypti   eðiliun manne,
    that he thar te Iosepe,   godes engil sprac,
770 bodo drohtines,   hêt ina eft that barn thanan

§10. The Flight to Egypt

lêdien te lande. 'nu haƀad thit lioht afgeƀen', quaðhe,
'Erodes the cuning;   he uuelde is âhtien giu,
frêson is ferahas.   Nu maht thu an friðu lêdien
that kind undar euua cunni,   nu the cuning ni liƀod,
775 erl oƀarmôdig.'   Al antkende
Iosep godes têcan: geriuuide ina sniumo
the thegan mit thera thiornun,   thô sie thanan uueldun
bêðiu mid thiu barnu: lêstun thiu berhton giscapu,
uualdandes uuillion,   al sô he im êr mid is uuordun gibôd.

§11. John the Baptist

Giuuêt im thô gangan,   al sô Jordan flôt
uuatar an uuilleon,   endi them uueroda allan dag,
875 aftar them landscepi them liudiun cûðda,
that sie mid fastunniu   firinuuerc manag,
iro selƀoro   sundea bôttin,
'that gi uuerðan hrênea', quað he.   'Heƀanrîki is
ginâhid manno barnun.   Nu lâtad eu an euuan môdseƀon
880 euuar selƀoro   sundea hreuuan,
lêdas that gi an thesun liohta fremidun,   endi mînun lêrun
   hôrd
uuendeat aftar mînun uuordun.   Ic eu an uuatara scal
gidôpean diurlîco,   thoh ic euua dâdi ne mugi,
euuar selƀaro   sundea alâtan,
885 that gi thurh mîn handgiuuerc   hluttra uuerðan
lêðaro gilêsto: ac the is an thit lioht cuman,
mahtig te mannun   endi undar eu middiun stêd,
— thoh gi ina selƀun   gisehan ni uuillean —,
the eu gidôpean scal   an euues drohtines namon

Hêliand

890 an thana hâlagon gêst. ...

Erlos managa
bi them lêrun thô,   liudi uuândun,
905 uueros uuârlîco,   that that uualdand Krist
selƀo uuâri,   huuanda he sô filu sôðes gisprac,
uuâroro uuordo.   Thô uuarð that sô uuîdo cûð
oƀar that forgeƀana land   gumono gihuuilicum,
seggiun at iro selðun: thô quâmun ina sôkean tharod
910 fon Hierusalem   Iudeo liudio
bodon fon theru burgi   endi frâgodun, ef he uuâri that
    barngodes
'that hêr lango giu', quâðun sie,   'liudi sagdun,
uueros uuârlîco,   that he scoldi an thesa uuerold cuman'.
Iohannes thô gimahalde   endi tegegnes sprac
915 them bodun baldlîco: 'ni bium ic', quað he, 'that barn
    godes,
uuâr uualdand Krist,   ac ic scal im thanan uueg rûmien,
hêrron mînumu.'   Thea heliðos frugnun,
thea thar an them ârundie   erlos uuârun,
bodon fon thero burgi: 'ef thu nu ni bist that barn godes,
920 bist thu than thoh Elias,   the hêr an êrdagun
uuas undar thesumu uuerode?   He is uuiscumo
eft an thesan middilgard.   Saga ûs huuat thu manno sîs!
Bist thu ênig thero,   the hêr êr uuâri
uuîsaro uuârsaguno?   Huuat sculun uui them uuerode fon thi
925 seggean te sôðon?   Neo hêr êr sulic ni uuarð
an thesun middilgard   man ôðar cuman
dâdiun sô mâri.   Bihuuî thu hêr dôpisli
fremis undar thesumu folke,   ef thu tharo forasagono
ênhuuilic ni bist?'   Thô habde eft garo
930 Iohannes the gôdo   glau anduuordi:

§11. *John the Baptist*

    'Ic bium forabodo   frâon mînes,
lioƀes hêrron;   ic scal thit land recon,
thit uuerod aftar is uuillion.   Ic hebbiu fon is uuorde mid me
stranga stemna,   thoh sie hêr ni uuillie forstandan filo
935 uuerodes an thesaro uuôstunni.   Ni bium ic mid uuihti gilîc
drohtine mînumu: he is mid is dâdiun sô strang,
sô mâri endi sô mahtig — that ic thes uuirðig ni bium,
that ic môti an is giscuoha,   thoh ic sî is scalc êgan,
940 an sô rîkiumu drohtine   thea reomon antbindan:
sô mikilu is he betara than ic.   Nis thes bodon gimaco
ênig oƀar erðu,   ne nu aftar ni scal
uuerðan an thesaro uueroldi.   Hebbiad euuan uuillion tharod,
liudi euuan gilôƀon: than eu lango scal
945 uuesan euua hugi hrômag;   than gi helligithuuing,
forlâtad lêðaro drôm   endi sôkead eu lioht godes,
upôdes hêm,   êuuig rîki,
hôhan heƀenuuang.   Ne lâtad euuan hugi tuuîflien!'

§12. The Baptism of Christ

    Iohannes stôd,
dôpte allan dag   druhtfolc mikil,
uuerod an uuatere   endi ôk uualdand Krist,
980 hêran heƀencuning   handun sînun
an allaro baðo them bezton   endi im thar te bedu gihnêg
an cneo craftag.   Krist up giuuêt
fagar fon them flôde,   friðubarn godes,
liof liudo uuard.   Sô he thô that land ofstôp,
985 sô anthlidun thô himiles doru,   endi quam the hêlago gêst
fon them alouualdon   oƀane te Kriste:
— uuas im an gilîcnissie   lungres fugles,

Hêliand

  diurlîcara dûbun — endi sat im uppan ûses drohtines ahslu,
  uuonode im obar them uualdandes barne. Aftar quam thar
    uuord fon himile
990 hlûd fon them hôhon radura en grôtta thane hêleand
    selbon,
  Krist, allaro cuningo bezton, quað that he ina gicoranan
    habdi
  selbo fon sînun rîkea, quað that im the sunu lîcodi
  bezt allaro giboranaro manno, quað that he im uuâri allaro
    barno liobost.

§13. THE TEMPTING OF CHRIST

1020 Sô gefragn ic that Iohannes thô gumono gihuuilicun,
  loboda them liudiun lêra Kristes,
  hêrron sînes, endi hebenrîki
  te giuuinnanne, uuelono thane mêston,
  sâlig sinlîf. Thô he im selbo giuuêt
1025 aftar them dôpislea, drohtin the gôdo,
  an êna uuôstunnea, uualdandes sunu;
  uuas im thar an thero ênôdi erlo drohtin
  lange huuîla; ne habda liudeo than mêr,
  seggeo te gisîðun, al sô he im selbo gicôs:
1030 uuelda is thar lâtan coston craftige uuihti,
  selbon Satanasan, the gio an sundea spenit,
  man an mênuuerk: he consta is môdsebon,
  uurêðan uuilleon, huuô he thesa uuerold êrist,
  an them anginnea irminthioda
1035 bisuêc mit sundiun, thô he thiu sinhîun tuuê,
  Adaman endi Êuan, thurh untreuua

§13. The Tempting of Christ

    forlêdda mid luginun,   that liudio barn
    aftar iro hinferdi   hellea sôhtun,
    gumono gêstos.   Thô uuelda that god mahtig,
1040 uualdand uuendean   endi uuelda thesum uuerode forgeƀen
    hôh himilrîki: bethiu he herod hêlagna bodon,
    is sunu senda.   That uuas Satanase
    tulgo harm an is hugi: afonsta heƀanrîkies
    manno cunnie: uuelda thô mahtigna
1045 mid them selƀon sacun   sunu drohtines,
    them he Adaman   an êrdagun
    darnungo bedrôg,   that he uuarð is drohtine lêð,
    besuuêc ina mid sundiun — sô uuelda he thô selƀan dôn
    hêlandean Krist.   Than habda he is hugi fasto
1050 uuið thana uuamscaðon,   uualdandes barn,
    herte sô giherdid: uuelda heƀenrîki
    liudiun gilêstean.   Uuas im the landes uuard
    an fastunnea   fiortig nahto,
    manno drohtin,   sô he thar mates ni antbêt;
1055 than langa ni gidorstun im   dernea uuihti,
    nîðhugdig fiund,   nâhor gangan,
    grôtean ina geginuuarðan: uuânde that he god ênfald,
    forûtar mancunnies uuiht   mahtig uuâri,
    hêleg himiles uuard.   Sô he ina thô gehungrean lêt,
1060 that ina bigan bi thero menniski   môses lustean
    aftar them fiuuartig dagun,   the fiund nâhor geng,
    mirki mênscaðo: uuânda that he man ênuald
    uuâri uuissungo,   sprac im thô mid is uuordun tô,
    grôtta ina the gêrfiund: 'ef thu sîs godes sunu', quað he,
1065 'bihuuî ni hêtis thu than uuerðan,   ef thu giuuald haƀes,
    allaro barno bezt,   brôd af thesun stênun?
    Gehêli thînna hungar.'   Thô sprac eft the hêlago Crist:

Hêliand

      'ni mugun eldibarn', quað he,   'ênfaldes brôdes,
      liudi libbien,   ac sie sculun thurh lêra godes
1070 uuesan an thesaro uueroldi   endi sculun thiu uuerc frummien,
      thea thar uuerð ad ahlûdid   fon thero hêlogun tungun,
      fon them galme godes: that is gumono lîf
      liudeo sô huilicon,   sô that lêstean uuili,
      that fon uualdandes   uuorde gebiudid.'
1075 Thô bigan eft niuson   endi nâhor geng
      unhiuri fîund   ôðru sîðu,
      fandoda is frôhan.   That friðubarn tholode
      uurêðes uuilleon   endi im giuuald forgaf,
      that he umbi is craft mikil   coston môsti
1080 lêt ina thô lêdean   thana liudscaðon,
      that he ina an Hierusalem   te them godes uuîha,
      alles oƀanuuardan,   up gisetta
      an allaro hûso hôhost,   endi hoscuuordun sprac,
      the gramo thurh gelp mikil: 'if thu sîs godes sunu', quað he,
1085 'scrîd thi te erðu hinan.'

§14. Jesus Returns to Galilee

      Uuas im an them sinuueldi   sâlig barn godes
      lange huîle,   untthat im thô lioƀora uuarð,
      that he is craft mikil   cûðien uuolda,
      uueroda te uuillion.   Thô forlêt he uualdes hlêo,
1125 ênôdies ard   endi sôhte im eft erlo gemang,
      mâri meginthioda   endi manno
      geng im thô bi Iordanes staðe: thar ina Iohannes antfand,
      that friðubarn godes,   frôhan sînan,
      hêlagana heƀencuning,   endi them heliðun sagda,

§14. Jesus Returns to Galilee

1130 Iohannes is iungurun, thô he ina gangan gesah:
'thit is that lamb godes, that thar lôsean scal
af thesaro uuîdon uuerold uurêða sundea,
mancunneas mên, mâri drohtin,
cuningo craftigost.' Krist im forð giuuêt
1135 an Galileo land, godes êgan barn,
fôr im te them friundun, thar he afôdit uuas,
tîrlîco atogan, endi talda mid uuordun
Krist undar is cunnie, cuningo rîkeost,
huuô sie scoldin iro selƀoro sundea bôtean,
1140 hêt that sie im iro harmuuerc manag hreuuan lêtin,
feldin iro firindâdi: 'nu is it all gefullot sô,
sô hîr alde man êr huuanna sprâcun,
gehêtun eu te helpu heƀenrîki:
nu is it giu ginâhid thurh thes neriandan craft: thes môtun
  gi neotan forð,
1145 sô huue sô gerno uuili gode theonogean,
uuirkean aftar is uuilleon.' Thô uuarð thes uuerodes filu,
thero liudeo an lustun: uurðun im thea lêra Cristes,
sô suôtea them gisîðea. He began im samnon
gumono te iungoron, gôdoro manno,
1150 uuordspâha uueros. Geng im thô bi ênes uuatares staðe,
thar thar habda Iordan aneƀan Galileo land
ênna sê geuuarhtan. Thar he sittean fand
Andreas endi Petrus bi them ahastrôme,
bêðea thea gebrôðar, thar sie an brêd uuatar
1155 suuîðo niudlîco netti thenidun,
fiscodun im an them flôde. Thar sie that friðubarn godes
bi thes sêes staðe selƀo grôtta,
hêt that sie im folgodin, quað that he im sô filu uuoldi

Hêliand

       godes rîkeas forgeƀen;   'al sô git hîr an Iordanes strôme
1160 fiscos fâhat,   sô sculun git noh firiho barn
       halon te incun handun,   that sie an heƀenrîki
       thurh inca lêra   lîðan môtin,
       faran folc manag.'   Thô uuard frômôd hugi
       bêðiun them gibrôðrun: antkendun that barn godes,
1165 lioƀan hêrron: forlêtun al saman
       Andreas endi Petrus,   sô huuat sô sie bi theru ahu habdun,
       geuunstes bi them uuatare: uuas im uuilleo mikil,
       that sie mid them godes barne   gangan môstin,
       samad an is gisîðea,   scoldun sâliglîco
1170 lôn antfâhan: sô dôt liudeo sô huuilic,
       sô thes hêrron uuili   huldi githionon,
       geuuirkea is uuilleon.   Thô sie bi thes uuatares staðe
       furðor quâmun,   thô fundun sie thar ênna frôdan man
       sittean bi them sêuua   endi is suni tuuêne,
1175 Iacobus endi Iohannes: uuârun im iunga man.
       Sâtun im thâ gesunfader   an ênumu sande uppen,
       brugdun endi bôttun   bêðium handun
       thiu netti niudlîco,   thea sie habdun nahtes êr
       forsliten an them sêuua.   Thar sprac im selƀo tô
1180 sâlig barn godes,   hêt that sie an thana sîð mid im
       Iacobus endi Iohannes,   gengin bêðie,
       kindiunge man.   Thô uuârun im Kristes uuord
       sô uuirðig an thesaro uueroldi,   that sie bi thes uuatares
               staðe
       iro aldan fader   ênna forlêtun,
1185 frôdan bi them flôde,   endi al that sie thar fehas êhtun,

§14. Jesus Returns to Galilee

nettiu endi neglitskipu,   gecurun im thana neriandan Krist
hêlagna te hêrron,   uuas im is helpono tharf
te githiononne: sô is allaro thegno gehuuem,
uuero an thesero uueroldi.   Thô giuuêt im the uualdandes
      sunu
1190 mid them fiuuariun forð,   endi im thô thana fîfton gicôs
Krist an ênero côpstedi,   cuninges jungoron,
môdspâhana man: Mattheus uuas he hêtan,
uuas im ambahteo   eðilero manno,
scolda thar te is hêrron   handun antfâhan
1195 tins endi tolna;   treuua habda he gôda,
âðalandbâri: forlêt al saman
gold endi silubar   endi geba
diurie meðmos,   endi uuarđ im ûses drohtines man;
côs im the cuninges thegn   Crist te hêrran,
1200 milderan meðomgebon,   than êr is mandrohtin
uuâri an thesero uueroldi: feng im uuôðera thing,
langsamoron râd.

§15. The Sermon on the Mount

Thô giuuêt im mahtig self
an ênna berg uppan,   barno rîkiost,
1250 sundar gesittien,   endi im selbo gecôs
tuuelibi getalda,   treuuafta man,
gôdoro gumono,   thea he im te iungoron forð
allaro dago gehuuilikes,   drohtin uuelda
an is gesîðskepea   simblon hebbean.
1255 Nemnida sie thô bi naman   endi hêt sie im thô nâhor
      gangan,
Andreas endi Petrus   êrist sâna,

Hêliand

```
         gebrôðar tuuêne,    endi bêðie mid im,
         Iacobus endi Iohannes:    sie uuârun gode uuerðe;
         mildi uuas he im an is môde;    sie uuârun ênes mannes suni
1260  bêðie bi geburdiun;    sie côs that barn godes
         gôde te iungoron    endi gumono filu,
         mâriero manno:    Mattheus endi Thomas,
         Iudasas tuuêna    endi Iacob ôðran,
         is selbes suuiri:    sie uuârun fon gisustruonion tuuêm
1265  cnôsles cumana,    Krist endi
         gôde gadulingos.    Thô habda thero gumono thar
         the neriendo Krist    niguni getalde,
         treuuafte man:    thô hêt he ôc thana tehandon gangan
         selbo mid them gisîðun:    Sîmon uuas he hêtan;
1270     hêt ôc Bartholomeus    an thana berg uppan
         faran fan them folke âðrum    endi Philippus mid im,
         treuuafte man.    Thô gengun sie tuuelibi samad,
         rincos te theru rûnu,    thar the râdand sat,
         managoro mundboro,    the allumu mancunnie
1275     uuið hellie gethuuing    helpan uuelde,
         formon uuið them ferne,    sô huuem sô frummien uuili
         sô lioblîka lêra,    sô he them liudiun thar
         thurh is giuuit mikil    uuîsean hogda.
```

§16. Admonitions

```
         Thô umbi thana neriendon Krist    nâhor gengun
1280  sulike gesîðos,    sô he im selbo gecôs,
         uualdand undar them uuerode.    Stôdun uuîsa man,
         gumon umbi thana godes sunu    gerno suuîðo,
```

§16. Admonitions

    uueros an uuilleon: uuas im thero uuordo niud,
    thâhtun endi thagodun,   huuat im thero thiodo drohtin,
1285 uueldi uualdand self uuordun cûðien,
    thesum liudiun te lioƀe.   Than sat im the landes hirdi
    geginuuard for them gumun,   godes êgan barn:
    uuelda mid is sprâcun   spâhuuord manag
    lêrean thea liudi,   huuô sie lof gode
1290 an thesum uueroldrîkea   uuirkean scoldin.
    Sat im thô endi suuîgoda   endi sah sie an lango,
    uuas im hold an is hugi   hêlag drohtin,
    mildi an is môde,   endi thô is mund antloc,
    uuîsde mid uuordun   uualdandes sunu
1295 manag mârlîc thing   endi them mannum sagde
    spâhun uuordun,   them the he te theru sprâcu tharod,
    Krist alouualdo,   gecoran habda,
    huuilike uuârin allaro   irminmanno
    gode uuerðoston   gumono cunnies;
1300 sagde im thô te sôðan,   quað that thie sâlige uuârin,
    man an thesoro middilgardun,   thie hêr an iro môde uuârin
    arme thurh ôdmôdi: 'them is that êuuana rîki,
    suuîðo hêlaglîc   an heƀanuuange
    sinlîf fargeƀen.'   Quað that ôc sâlige uuârin
1305 mâđmundie man: 'thie môtun thie mârion erðe,
    ofsittien that selƀe rîki.'   Quað that ôc sâlige uuârin,
    thie hîr uuiopin iro uuammun dâdi; 'thie môtun eft uuillion
        gebîdan,
    frôfre an iro frâhon rîkia.   Sâlige sind ôc, the sie hîr
        frumono gilustid,
    rincos, that sie rehto adômien. Thes môtun sie uuerðan an
        them rîkia drohtines

Hêliand

1310 gifullit thurh iro ferhton dâdi: sulîcoro môtun sie frumono bicnêgan,
    thie rincos, thie hîr rehto adômiad, ne uuilliad an rûnun besuuîcan
    man, thar sie at mahle sittiad. Sâlige sind ôc them hîr mildi uuirðit
    hugi an heliðo briostun: them uuirðit the hêlego drohtin,
    mildi mahtig selbo. Sâlige sind ôc undar thesaro managon thiudu
1315 thie hebbiad iro herta gihrênod: thie môtun thane hebenes uualdand
    sehan an sînum rîkea.' Quað that ôc sâlige uuârin,
    'thie the friðusamo undar thesumu folke libbiod endi ni uuilliad êniga fehta geuuirken,
    saca mid iro selboro dâdiun: thie môtun uuesan suni drohtines genemnide,
    huuande he im uuil genâdig uuerðen; thes môtun sie niotan lango
1320 selbon thes sînes rîkies.' Quað that ôc sâlige uuârin
    thie rincos, the rehto uueldin, 'endi thurh that tholod rîkioro manno
    heti endi harmquidi: them is ôc an himile eft
    godes uuang forgeben endi gêstlîc lîf
    after te êuuandage, sô is io endi ni cumit,
1325 uuelan uunsames.' Sô habde thô uualdand Crist
    for them erlon thar ahto getalda
    sâlda gesagda; mid them scal simbla gihuue
    himilrîki gehalon, ef he it hebbien uuili
    ettho he scal te êuuandaga aftar tharbon
1330 uuelon endi uuillion, sîðor he these uuerold agibid,

§16. Admonitions

erðlîbigiscapu,   endi sôkit im ôðar lioht
sô liof sô lêð,   sô he mid thesun liudiun hêr
giuuercod an thesoro uueroldi,   al sô it thar thô mid is
    uuordun sagde
Crist alouualdo,   cuningo rîkiost
1335 godes êgen barn   iungorun sînun:
'Ge uuerđat ôc sô sâlige', quað he,   'thes iu saca biodat
liudi aftar theson lande   endi lêð sprecat,
hebbiad iu te hosca   endi harmes filu
geuuirkiad an thesoro uueroldi   endi uuîti gefrummiad
1340 felgiad iu firinsprâka   endi fiundscepi,
lâgniad iuuua lêra,   dôt iu lêðes filu
harmes thurh iuuuen hêrron.   Thes lâtad gi euuan hugi
    simbla,
lîf an lustun,   huuand iu that lôn stendit
an godes rîkia garu,   gôdo gehuuilikes,
1345 mikil endi managfald: that is iu te mêdu fargeƀen,
huuand gi hêr êr biforan   arƀid tholodun,
uuîti an thesoro uueroldi.   Uuirs is them ôðrun,
giƀiðig grimmora thing,   them the hêr gôd êgun,
uuîdan uuorolduuelon: thie forslîtit iro uunnia hêr;
1350 geniudot sie genôges   sculun eft narouuaro thing
aftar iro hinferdi   heliðos tholoian.
Than uuôpian thar uuanscefti,   thie hêr êr an uunnion sîn,
libbiad an allon lustun,   ne uuilliad thes farlâtan uuiht,
mêngithâhtio,   thes sie an iro môd spenit,
1355 lêðoro gilêstio.   Than im that lôn cumid,
uƀil arƀetsam,   than sie is thane endi sculun
sorgondi gesehan.   Than uuirðid im sêr hugi,
thes sie thesero uueroldes sô filu   uuillean fulgengun,

Hêliand

      man an iro môdseƀon.   Nu sculun gi im that mên lahan,
1360 uuerean mid uuordun,   al sô ic giu nu geuuîsean mag,
      seggean sôðlîco,   gesîðos mîne,
      uuârun uuordun,   that gi thesoro uueroldes nu forð
      sculun salt uuesan,   sundigero manno,
      bôtian iro baludâdi,   that sie an betara thing,
1365 folc farfâhan   endi forlâtan fiundes giuuerk,
      diuƀales gedâdi,   endi sôkean iro drohtines rîki.
      Sô sculun gi mid iuuuon lêrun   liudfolc manag
      uuendean aftar mînon uuilleon.   Ef iuuuar than auuirðid
            huuilic,
      farlâtid thea lâra,   thea he lêstean scal,
1370 than is im sô them salte,   the man bi sêes staðe
      uuîdo teuuirpit: than it te uuihte ni dôg,
      ac it firiho barn   fôtun spurnat,
      gumon an greote. Sô uuirðid them, the that godes uuord scal
      mannun mârean: ef he im than lâtid is môd tuuehon,
1375 that he ne uuillea mid hluttro hugi   te heƀenrîkea
      spanen mid is sprâcu   endi seggean spel godes,
      ac uuenkid thero uuordo,   than uuirðid im uualdand gram,
      mahtig môdag,   endi sô samo manno barn;
      uuirðid allun than   irminthiodun,
1380 liudiun aleđid,   ef is lêra ni dugun.'

§17. Hearing the Sermon

Sô sprac he thô spâhlîco   endi sagda spel godes,
lêrde the landes uuard   liudi sîne
mid hluttru hugi. Heliðos stôdun,
gumon umbi thana godes sunu   gerno suîðo,

§17. Hearing the Sermon

1385 uueros an uuilleon: uuas im thero uuordo niud,
thâhtun endi thagodun,   gihôrdun thero thiodo drohtin
seggean êu godes   eldibarnun;
gihêt im heƀenrîki   endi te them helið un sprac:
'ôc mag ic iu seggean,   gesîðos mîna,
1390 uuârun uuordun,   that gi thesoro uueroldes nu forð
sculun lioht uuesan   liudio barnun,
fagar mid firihun   oƀar folc manag,
uulitig endi uunsam: ni mugun iuuua uuerk mikil
biholan uuerðan,   mid huuilico gi sea hugi cûðeat:
1395 than mêr the thiu burg ni mag,   thiu an berge stâð,
hôh holmkliƀu   biholen uuerðen,
uurisilîc giuuerc,   ni mugun iuuua uuord than mêr
an thesoro middelgard   mannum uuerðen,
iuuua dâdi bidernit.   Dôt, sô ic iu lêriu:
1400 lâtad iuuua lioht mikil   liudiun skînan,
manno barnun,   that sie farstandan iuuuan môdseƀon,
iuuua uuerc endi iuuuan uuilleon,   endi thes uualdand god
mit hluttro hugi,   himiliscan fader,
loƀon an thesumu liohte,   thes he iu sulica lêra fargaf.
1405 Ni scal neoman lioht, the it haƀad,   liudiun dernean,
te hardo behuuelƀean,   ac he it hôho scal
an seli settean,   that thea gesehan mugin
alla gelîco,   thea thar inna sind,
helið os an hallu. Than hald ni sculun gi iuuua hêlag uuord
1410 lâtad iuua lioht mikil   liudiun skînan,
manno barnun,   that sie farstandan iuuuan môdseƀon,
iuuua uuerc endi iuuuan uuilleon,   endi thes uualdand god
mit hluttro hugi,   himiliscan fader,
loƀon an thesumu liohte,   thes he iu sulica lêra fargaf,

Hêliand

1415 tulgo uuîse man   uuordun gesprâcun,
     than sie thana aldan êuu   erlos heldun,
     endi ôc sulicu suuîðor,   sô ic iu nu seggean mag,
     alloro gumono gehuuilic   gode thionoian,
     than it thar an them aldom   êuua gebeode.

§18. Swearing Oaths

     Ôc is an them êo gescriban
     uuârun uuordun,   sô gi uuitun alle,
     that mîðe mênêðos   mancunnies gehuuilic,
1505 ni forsuerie ina selbon,   huuand that is sundie te mikil,
     farlêdid liudi   an lêðan uueg.
     Than uuilleo ic iu eft seggean,   that sân ni suerea neoman
     ênigan êðstaf   eldibarno,
     ne bi himile themu hôhon,   huuand that is thes hêrron stôl,
1510 ne bi erðu thar undar,   huuand that is thes alouualdon
     fagar fôtscamel,   nec ênig firiho barno
     ne suuerea bi is selbes hôbde,   huuand he ni mag thar ne
          suuart ne huuît
     ênig hâr geuuirkean,   bûtan sô it the hêlago god
     gemarcode mahtig;   bethiu sculun mîðan filu
1515 erlos êðuuordo.   Sô huue sô it ofto dôt,
     sô uuirðid is simbla uuirsa, huuand he imu giuuardon ni mag.
     Bithiu scal ic iu nu te uuârun   uuordun gebeodan,
     that gi neo ne suerien   suuîðoron êðos,
     mêron met mannun,   bûtan sô ic iu mid mînun hêr
1520 suuîðo uuârlico   uuordun gebiudu:
     ef man huuemu saca sôkea,   biseggea that uuâre,
     queðe iâ, gef it sî,   geha thes that uuâr is,

§18. Swearing Oaths

queðe nên, af it nis,　　lâta im genôg an thiu;
sô huat sô is mêr oƀar that　　man gefrummiad,
1525　sô cumid it al fan uƀile　　eldibarnun,
that erl thurh untreuua　　ôðres ni uuili
uuordo gelôƀian.

§19. The Lord's Prayer

'Hêrro the gôdo', quað he, 'ûs is thînoro huldi tharf,
te giuuirkenne thînna uuilleon,　　endi ôc thînoro uuordo sô self,
1590　alloro barno bezt,　　that thu ûs bedon lêres,
iungoron thîne,　　sô Iohannes duot,
diurlîc dôperi,　　dago gehuuilicas
is uuerod mid uuordun,　　huuô sie uualdand sculun,
gôdan grôtean.　　Dô thîna iungoron sô self:
1595　gerihti ûs that gerûni'.　　Thô habda eft the rîkeo garu
sân aftar thiu,　　sunu drohtines,
gôd uuord angegin:　　'Than gi god uuillean', quað he,
'uueros mid iuuuon uuordun　　uualdand grôtean,
allaro cuningo craftigostan,　　than queðad gi, sô ic iu lêriu:
1600　Fadar ûsa　　firiho barno,
thu bist an them hôhon　　himila rîkea,
geuuîhid sî thîn namo　　uuordo gehuuilico.
Cuma thîn　　craftag rîki.
Uuerða thîn uuilleo　　oƀar thesa uuerold alla,
1605　sô sama an erðo,　　sô thar uppa ist
an them hôhon　　himilo rîkea.
Gef ûs dago gehuuilikes râd,　　drohtin the gôdo,
thîna hêlaga helpa,　　endi alât ûs, heƀenes uuard,
managoro mênsculdio,　　al sô uue ôðrum mannum dôan.

Hêliand

1610 Ne lât ûs farlêdean   lêða uuihti
     sô forð an iro uuilleon,   sô uui uuirðige sind,
     ac help ûs uuiðar allun   ubilon dâdiun.
     Sô sculun gi biddean,   than gi te bede hnîgad
     uueros mid iuuuom uuordun,   that iu uualdand god
1615 lêðes alâte   an leutcunnea.

§20. Lilies of the Field

     Huuat, gi that bi thesun fuglun mugun
     uuârlîco undaruuitan,   thea hîr an thesoro uueroldi sint,
     farad an feðarhamun: sie ni cunnun ênig feho uuinnan,
1670 thoh gibid im drohtin god   dago gehuuilikes
     helpa uuiðar hungre.   Ôc mugun gi an iuuuom hugi marcon,
     uueros umbi iuuua geuuâdi,   huô thie uurti sint
     fagoro gefratohot,   thea hîr an felde stâd,
     berhtlîco geblôid: ne mahta the burges uuard,
1675 Salomon the cuning,   the habda sinc mikil,
     mêðomhordas mêst,   thero the ênig man êhti,
     uuelono geuunnan   endi allaro geuuâdeo cust, —
     thoh ni mohte he an is lîbe,   thoh he habdi alles theses
         landes geuuald,
     auuinnan sulic geuuâdi,   sô thiu uurt habad,
1680 thiu hîr an felde stâd   fagoro gegariuuit,
     lilli mid sô lioflîcu blômon: ina uuâdid the landes uualdand
     hêr fan hebenes uuange.   Mêr is im thoh umbi thit heliðo
         cunni
     liudi sint im lioboron mikilu,   thea he im an thesumu lande
         geuuarhte,

§20. Lilies of the Field

uualdand an uuilleon sînan.   Bethiu ne thurƀon gi umbi
    iuuua geuuâdi sorgon,
1685 ne gornot gi umbi iuuua gegariuui te suuîðo: god uuili is
    alles râdan
helpan fan heƀenes uuange, ef gi uuilliad aftar is huldi
    theonon.

§21. Pearls Before Swine

Ne sculun gi suînum teforan
iuuua meregrîton macon   ettho mêðmo gestriuni,
hêlag halsmeni,   huuand siu it an horu spurnat,
suluuiad an sande: ne uuitun sûƀreas geskêđ,
fagaroro fratoho.

§22 Bad Tree, Bad Fruit

Huuand gi uuitun,   that eo an thorniun ne sculun
uuînberi uuesan   eftha uuelon eouuiht,
fagororo fruhteo,   nec ôc figun ne lesad
heliðos an hiopon.   That mugun gi undarhuggean uuel,
1745 that eo the uƀilo bôm,   thar he an erðu stâd,
gôden uuastum ne giƀid,   nec it ôc god ni gescôp,
that the gôdo bôm   gumono barnun
bâri bittres uuiht,   ac cumid fan alloro bâmo gehuilicum
sulic uuastom te thesero uueroldi,   sô im fan is uurteon
    gedregid,
1750 ettha berht ettha bittar.

§23. The Narrow Gate

'Ôc scal ic iu uuîsean, huuô hîr uuegos tuêna
liggead an thesumu liohte, thea farad liudeo barn,
al irminthiod. Thero is ôðar sân
uuîd strâta endi brêd, — farid sie uuerodes filu,
1775 mancunnies manag, huand sie tharod iro môd spenit,
uueroldlusta uueros — thiu an thea uuirson hand
liudi lêdid, thar sie te farlora uueröad,
heliðos an helliu, thar is hêt endi suart,
egislîc an innan: ôði ist tharod te faranne
1780 eldibarnun, thoh it im at themu endie ni dugi.
Than ligid eft ôðar engira mikilu
uueg an thesoro uueroldi, ferid ina uuerodes lût,
fâho folcskepi: ni uuilliad ina firiho barn
gerno gangan, thoh he te godes rîkea,
1785 an that êuuiga lîf, erlos lêdea.
Than nimad gi iu thana engean: thoh he sô ôði ne sî
firihon te faranne, thoh scal he te frumu uueröan
sô huuemu sô ina thurhgengid, sô scal is geld niman,
suuîðo langsam lôn endi lîf êuuig,
1790 diurlîcan drôm. Eo gi thes drohtin sculun,
uualdand biddien, that gi thana uueg môtin
fan foran antfâhan endi forð thurh gigangan
an that godes rîki. He is garu simbla
uuiðar thiu te geƀanne, that man ina gerno bidid,
1795 fergot firiho barn. Sôkead fadar iuuuan
up te themu êuuinom rîkea: than môtun gi ina aftar thiu
te iuuuoru frumu fîðan. Cûðead iuuua fard tharod
at iuuuas drohtines durun: than uueröad iu andôn after thiu,

§23. *The Narrow Gate*

    himilportun anthlidan,   that gi an that hêlage lioht,
1800 an that godes rîki   gangan môtun,
    sinlîf sehan.

§24. A House upon Sand

        Ôc scal ic iu seggean noh
    far thesumu uuerode allun   uuârlîc biliðï
    that alloro liudeo sô huilic   sô thesa mîna lêra uuili
    gehaldan an is herton   endi uuil iro an is hugi athenkean,
1805 lêstean sea an thesumu lande,   the gilîco duot
    uuîsumu manne,   the giuuit haƀad,
    horsca hugiskefti,   endi hûsstedi kiusid
    an fastoro foldun   endi an felisa uppan
    uuêgos uuirkid,   thar im uuind ni mag,
1810 ne uuâg ne uuatares strôm   uuihtiu getiunean,
    ac mag im thar uuið ungiuuidereon   allun standan
    an themu felise uppan,   huand it sô fasto uuarð
    gistellit an themu stêne: anthaƀad it thiu stedi niðana,
    uureðid uuiðar uuinde,   that it uuîcan ni mag.
1815 Sô duot eft manno sô huilic, sô thesun mînun ni uuili
    lêrun hôrien   ne thero lêstien uuiht,
    sô duot the unuuîson   erla gelîco,
    ungeuuittigon uuere,   the im be uuatares staðe
    an sande uuili   selihûs uuirkean,
1820 thar it uuestrani uuind   endi uuâgo strôm,
    sêes ûðeon teslâad;   ne mag im sand endi greot
    geuureðien uuið themu uuinde,   ac uuirðid teuuorpan than,
    tefallen an themu flôde,   huand it an fastoro nis
    erðu getimbrod.   Sô scal allaro erlo gehues

1825 uuerc gethîhan   uuiðar thiu, the hi thius mîn uuord frumid
     haldid hêlag gebod.'

§25. Lambs among Wolves

He im thô bêðiu befal
ge te seggennea   sînom uuordun,
huuô man himilrîki   gehalon scoldi,
1840 uuîdbrêdan uuelan,   gia he im geuuald fargaf,
that sie môstin hêlean   halte endi blinde,
liudeo lêfhêdi,   legarbed manag,
suâra suhti,   giac he im selƀo gebôd,
that sie at ênigumu manne   mêde ne nâmin,
1845 diurie mêðmos: 'gehuggead gi', quað he, — 'huand iu is
     thiu dâd cuman,
that geuuit endi the uuîsdôm,   endi iu thea geuuald fargiƀid
alloro firiho fadar,   sô gi sie ni thurƀun mid ênigo feho
     côpon,
mêdean mid ênigun mêðmun, — sô uuesat gi iro mannun forð
an iuuuon hugiskeftiun   helpono mildea,
1850 lêread gi liudio barn   langsamna râd,
fruma forðuuardes;   firinuuerc lahad,
suâra sundeo.   Ne lâtad iu siloƀar nec gold
uuihti thes uuirðig,   that it eo an iuuua geuuald cuma,
fagara fehoscattos: it ni mag iu te ênigoro frumu huuergin,
1855 uuerðan te ênigumu uuilleon. . . .
                      Nu ic iu sendean scal
aftar thesumu landskepie   sô lamb undar uulƀos:
1875 sô sculun gi undar iuuua fîund faren,   undar filu theodo,
undar mislîke man.   Hebbead iuuuan môd uuiðar them
sô glauuan tegegnes,   sô samo sô the gelouuo uurm,

§25. Lambs among Wolves

nâdra thiu fêha,   thar siu iro nîðskepies,
uuitodes uuânit,   that man iu undar themu uuerode ne mugi
1880 besuîcan an themu sîðe.

§26. Entering Heaven

1915 Ne cumat thea alle te himile,   thea the hîr hrôpat te me manno te mundburd.   ...

1940 Ef sie than sô sâliga thurh iro selboro dâd
uuerðan ni môtun,   that sie iuuua uuerc frummien,
lêstien iuuua lêra,   than gi fan them liudiun sân,
farad fan themu folke,   — the iuuua friðu huuirbid
eft an iuuuoro selboro sîð, —   endi lâtad sie mid sundiun forð,
1945 mid baluuuercun bûan   endi sôkiad iu burg ôðra,
mikil manuuerot,   endi ne lâtad thes melmes uuiht
folgan an iuuuom fôtun,   thanan the man iu antfâhan ne uuili,
ac scuddiat it fan iuuuon scôhun,   that it im eft te scamu uuerðe,
themu uuerode te geuuitskepie,   that iro uuillio ne dôg.
1950 Than seggeo ic iu te uuârun,   sô huan sô thius uuerold endiad
endi the mâreo dag   obar man farid
that than Sodomoburg,   thiu hîr thurh sundeon uuarð
an afgrundi   êldes craftu,
fiuru bifallen,   that thiu than habad friðu mêran,
1955 mildiran mundburd,   than thea man êgin,
the iu hîr uuiðaruuerpat   endi ne uuilliad iuuua uuord frummien.

§27. Water to Wine

M anagoro drohtin
2000 geng imu thô mid is iungoron,   godes êgan barn,
an that hôha hûs,   thar the heri dranc,
thea Iudeon an themu gastseli: he im ôc an them gômun uuas,
giac he thar gecûðde,   that he habda craft godes,
helpa fan himilfader,   hêlagna gêst,
2005 uualdandes uuîsdôm.   Uuerod blîðode,
uuârun thar an luston liudi atsamne,
gumon gladmôdie.   Gengun ambahtman,
skenkeon mid scâlun,   drôgun skîriane uuîn
mid orcun endi mid alofatun;   uuas thar erlo drôm
2010 fagar an flettea,   thô thar folc undar im
an them benkeon sô bezt   blîðsea afhôbun,
uuârun thar an uunneun.   Thô im thes uuînes brast,
them liudiun thes lîðes: is ni uuas farlêbid uuiht
huergin an themu hûse,   that for thene heri forð
2015 skenkeon drôgin,   ac thiu scapu uuârun
lîðes alârid.   Thô ni uuas lang te thiu
that it sân antfunda   frîo scôniosta,
Cristes môder: geng uuið iro kind sprecan,
uuið iro sunu selbon,   sagda im mid uuordun,
2020 that thea uuerdos thô mêr   uuînes ne habdun
them gestiun te gômun.   Siu thô gerno bad,
that is the hêlogo Crist   helpa geriedi
themu uuerode te uuilleon.   Thô habda eft is uuord garu
mahtig barn godes   endi uuið is môder sprac:
2025 'huat is mi endi thi', quað he,   'umbi thesoro manno lîð,

§27. Water to Wine

umbi theses uuerodes uuîn?   Te huî sprikis thu thes, uuîf, sô filu
manos mi far thesoro menigi?   Ne sint mîna noh
tîdi cumana.'   Than thoh gitrûoda siu uuel
an iro hugiskeftiun,   hêlag thiorne,
2030 that is aftar them uuordun   uualdandes barn,
hêleandoro bezt   helpan uueldi.
Hêt thô thea ambahtman   idiso scôniost,
skenkeon endi scapuuardos,   thea thar scoldun thero scolu
    thionon,
that sie thes ne uuord ne uuerc   uuiht ne farlêtin,
2035 thes sie the hêlogo Crist   hêtan uueldi
lêstean far them liudiun.   Lârea stôdun thar
stênfatu sehsi.   Thô sô stillo gebôd
mahtig barn godes,   sô it thar manno filu
ne uuissa te uuârun,   huô he it mid is uuordu gesprac:
2040 he hêt thea skenkeon thô   skîreas uuatares
thiu fatu fullien,   endi he thar mid is fingrun thô,
segnade selƀo   sînun handun,
uuarhte it te uuîne   endi hêt is an ên uuêgi hladen,
skeppien mid ênoro scâlon,   endi thô te them skenkeon
    sprac,
2045 hêt is thero gesteo,   the at them gômun uuas
themu hêroston   an hand geƀan,
ful mid folmun,   themu the thes folkes thar
geuueld aftar themu uuerde.   Reht sô hi thes uuînes gedranc,
sô ni mahte he bemîðan,   ne hi far theru menigi sprac
2050 te themu brûdigumon,   quað that simble that bezte lîð
alloro erlo gehuilic   êrist scoldi
geƀan at is gômun: 'undar thiu uuirðid thero gumono hugi
auuekid mid uuînu,   that sie uuel blîðod,
druncan drômead.   Than mag man thar dragan aftar thiu

Hêliand

2055 lîhtlîcora lîð: sô ist thesoro liudeo thau.

Than habas thu nu uunderlîco uuerdskepi thînan
gemarcod far thesoro menigi: hêtis far thit manno folc
alles thînes uuînes that uuirsiste
thîne ambahtman êrist brengean,
2060 geban at thînun gômun. Nu sint thîna gesti sade,
sint thîne druhtingos druncane suîðo,
ist thit folc frômôd: nu hêtis thu hîr forð dragan
alloro lîðo lofsamost, thero the ic eo an thesumu liohte gesah
huuergin hebbean. Mid thius scoldis thu ûs hindag êr
2065 gebon endi gômean: than it alloro gumono gehuilic
gethigede te thanke.'

§28. Reward and Punishment

Thô sprac eft uualdand Crist,
2125 the gumo uuið is iungoron, quað that hi an Iudeon huergin
undar Israheles aboron ne fundi
gemacon thes mannes, the io mêr te gode
an themu landskepi gelôbon habdi,
than hluttron te himile: 'nu lâtu ic iu thar hôrien tô,
2130 thar ic it iu te uuârun hîr uuordun seggeo,
that noh sculun elitheoda ôstane endi uestane,
mancunnies cuman manag tesamne,
hêlag folc godes an hebenrîki:
thea môtun thar an Abrahames endi an Isaakes sô self
2135 endi ôc an Iacobes, gôdoro manno,
barmun restien endi beðiu getholegean,
uuelon endi uuilleon endi uuonotsam lîf,

§28. Reward and Punishment

     gôd lioht mid gode.   Than scal Iudeono filu,
     theses rîkeas suni   berôƀode uuerðen,
2140 bedêlide sulicoro diurðo,   endi sculun an dalun thiustron
     an themu alloro ferristan   ferne liggen.
     Thar mag man gehôrien   heliðos quîðean,
     thar sie iro torn managˆ   tandon bîtad;
     thar ist gristgrimmo   endi grâdag fiur,
2145 hard helleo gethuing,   hêt endi thiustri,
     suart sinnahti   sundea te lône,
     uurêðoro geuurhteo,   sô huemu sô thes uuilleon ne haƀad,
     that he ina alôsie,   êr hi thit lioht ageƀe,
     uuendie fan thesoro uueroldi.

§29. Raising the Dead

2180   ...   thô sâhun sie thar ên hrêo dragan,
     ênan lîflôsan lîchamon   thea liudi fôrien,
     beran an ênaru bâru   ût at thera burges dore,
     maguiungan man.   Thiu môder aftar geng
     an iro hugi hriuuig   endi handun slôg,
2185 carode endi cûmde   iro kindes dôđ,
     idis armscapan;   it uuas ira ênag barn:
     siu uuas iru uuidouua,   ne habda uunnea than mêr,
     biûten te themu ênagun sunie   al gelâten
     uuunnea endi uuillean,   anttat ina iru uurð benam,
2190 mâri metodogescapu.   Megin folgode,
     burgliudeo gebrac,   thar man ina an bâru drôg,
     iungan man te graƀe.   Thar uuarð imu the godes sunu,
     mahtig mildi   endi te theru môder sprac,
     hêt that thiu uuidouua   uuôp farlêti,
2195 cara aftar themu kinde: 'thu scalt hîr craft sehan,

Hêliand

    uualdandes giuuerc: thi scal hîr uuilleo gestanden,
    frôfra far thesumu folke: ne tharft thu ferah caron
    barnes thînes.'   Thuo hie ti thero bâron geng
    iac hie ina selbo anthrên,   suno drohtines,
2200 hêlagon handon,   endi ti them heliðe sprak,
    hiet ina sô alaiungan   upp astandan,
    arîsan fan theru restun.   Thie rinc up asat,
    that barn an thero bârun: uuarð im eft an is briost cuman
    the gêst thuru godes craft,   endi hie tegegnes sprac,
2205 the man uuið is mâgos.   Thuo ina eft thero muoder bifalah
    hêlandi Crist an hand: hugi uuarð iro te frôbra,
    thes uuîbes an uuunneon   huand iro thar sulic uuilleo
        gistuod.
    Fell siu thô te fuotun Cristes   endi thena folco drohtin
    loboda for thero liudeo menigi,   huand hie iro at sô liobes
        ferahe
2210 mundoda uuiðer metodigisceftie: farstuod siu that hie uuas
        the mahtigo drohtin
    the hêlago, thie himiles giuualdid,   endi that hie mahti
        gihelpan managon,
    allon irminthiedon.

§30. Calming the Storm

    Thuo uuas thar uuerodes sô filo
    allaro elithiodo cuman   te them êron Cristes
    te sô mahtiges mundburd.   Thuo uuelda hie thar êna meri
        lîðan,
    the godes suno mid is iungron   aneban Galilealand,
2235 uualdand ênna uuâgo strôm.   Thuo hiet hie that uuerod
        ôðar

§30. Calming the Storm

forđuuerdes faran,   endi hie giuuêt im fahora sum
an ênna nacon innan,   neriendi Crist,
slâpan sîðuuôrig.   Segel upp dâdun
uuederuuîsa uueros,   lietun uuind after
2240 manon oƀar thena meristrôm,   unthat hie te middean
   quam,
uualdand mid is uuerodu.   Thuo bigan thes uuedares craft,
ûst up stîgan,   ûðiun uuahsan;
suang gisuerc an gimang: thie sêu uuarð an hruoru,
uuan uuind endi uuater;   uueros sorogodun,
2245 thiu meri uuarð sô muodag,   ni uuânda thero manno nigên
lengron lîƀes.   Thuo sia landes uuard
uuekidun mid iro uuordon   endi sagdun im thes uuedares
   craft,
bâdun that im ginâðig   neriendi Crist
uurði uuið them uuatare: 'eftha uui sculun hier te uunder-
   quâlu
2250 sueltan an theson sêuue.'   Self upp arês
thie guodo godes suno   endi te is iungron sprak,
hiet that sia im uuedares giuuin   uuiht ni andrêdin:
'te huî sind gi sô forhta?' quathie.   'Nis iu noh fast hugi,
gilôƀo is iu te luttil.   Nis nu lang te thiu,
2255 that thia strômos sculun   stilrun uuerðan
gi thit uuedar uunsam.'   Tho hi te them uuinde sprac
ge te themu sêuua sô self   endi sie smultro hêt
bêðea gebârean.   Sie gibod lêstun,
uualdandes uuord: uueder stillodun,
2260 fagar uuarð an flôde.   Thô bigan that folc undar im,
uuerod uundraian,   endi suma mid iro uuordun sprâkun,
huilic that sô mahtigoro   manno uuâri,

Hêliand

    that imu sô the uuind endi the uuâg   uuordu hôrdin,
    bêðea is gibodskepies.   Thô habda sie that barn godes
2265 ginerid fan theru nôdi: the naco furðor skreid,
    hôh hurnidskip;   heliðos quâmun,
    liudi te lande,   sagdun lof gode,
    mâridun is megincraft.   Quam thar manno filu
    angegin themu godes sunie;   he sie gerno antfeng,
2270 sô huene sô thar mid hluttru hugi   helpa sôhte;
    lêrde sie iro gilôbon   endi iro lîchamon
    handun hêlde: nio the man sô hardo ni uuas
    gisêrit mid suhtiun: thoh ina Satanases
    fêknea iungoron   fiundes craftu
2275 habdin undar handun   endi is hugiskefti,
    giuuit auuardid,   that he uuôdiendi
    fôri undar themu folke,   thoh im simbla ferh fargaf
    hêlandeo Crist,   ef he te is handun quam,
    drêf thea diublas thanan   drohtines craftu,
2280 uuârun uuordun,   endi im is geuuit fargaf,
    lêt ina than hêlan   uuiðer hetteandun,
    gaf im uuið thie fiund friðu,   endi forð giuuêt
    an sô huilic thero lando,   sô im than leobost uuas.

§31. THE SOWER AND THE SEED

    He stôd imu thô bi ênes uuatares staðe,
    ni uuelde thô bi themu gethringe   obar that thegno folc
2380 an themu lande uppan   thea lêra cûðean,
    ac geng imu thô the gôdo   endi is iungaron mid imu,
    friðubarn godes,   themu flôde nâhor
    an ên skip innan,   endi it scalden hêt
    lande rûmor,   that ina thea liudi sô filu,

§31. The Sower and the Seed

2385 thioda ni thrungi.　　Stôd thegan manag,
　　　uuerod bi themu uuatare,　　thar uualdand Crist
　　　oƀar that liudio folc　　lêra sagde:
　　　'huat, ik iu seggean mag', quaðhe,　　'gesîðos mîne,
　　　huô imu ên erl bigan　　an erðu sâian
2390 hrêncorni mid is handun.　　Sum it an hardan stên
　　　oƀanuuardan fel,　　erðon ni habda,
　　　that it thar mahti uuahsan　　eftha uurteo gifâhan,
　　　kînan eftha biclîƀen,　　ac uuarð that corn farloren,
　　　that thar an theru lêian gilag.　　Sum it eft an land bifel,
2395 an erðun aðalcunnies:　　bigan imu aftar thiu
　　　uuahsen uuânlîco　　endi uurteo fâhan,
　　　lôd an lustun:　　uuas that land sô gôd,
　　　frânisco gifehod.　　Sum it eft bifallen uuarð
　　　an êna starca strâtun,　　thar stôpon gengun,
2400 hrosso hôfslaga　　endi heliðo trâda;
　　　uuarð imu thar an erðu　　endi eft up gigeng,
　　　bigan imu an themu uuege uuahsen;　　thô it eft thes uuerdos
　　　　　farnam,
　　　thes folkes fard mikil　　endi fuglos alâsun,
　　　that is themu êcsan uuiht　　aftar ni môste
2405 uuerðan te uuillean,　　thes thar an thene uueg bifel.
　　　Sum uuarð it than bifallen,　　thar sô filu stôdun
　　　thiccero thorno　　an themu dage;
　　　uuarð imu thar an erðu　　endi eft up gigeng,
　　　kên imu thar endi cliƀode. Thô slôgun thar eft crûd an
　　　　　gimang,
2410 uueridun imu thene uuastom:　　habda it thes uualdes hlea
　　　forana oƀarfangan,　　that it ni mahte te ênigaro frumu
　　　　　uuerðen,

Hêliand

ef it thea thornos sô thringan môstun.'
Thô sâtun endi suîgodun gesîðos Cristes,
uuordspâha uueros: uuas im uundar mikil,
2415 be huilicun biliðiun that barn godes
sulic sôðlîc spel seggean bigunni.

§32. INTERPRETATION

Than brêdid an thes breostun that gibod godes,
2475 thie luƀigo gilôbo, sô an themu lande duod
that korn mid kîðun, thar it gikund haƀad
endi imu thiu uurð bihagod endi uuederes gang,
regin endi sunne, that it is reht haƀad.
Sô duod thiu godes lêra an themu gôdun manne
2480 dages endi nahtes, endi gangid imu diuƀal fer,
uurêða uuihti endi the uuard godes
nâhor mikilu nahtes endi dages,
anttat sie ina brengead, that thar bêð iu uuirðid
ia thiu lêra te frumu liudio barnun,
2485 the fan is môðe cumid, iac uuirðid the man gode;
haƀad sô giuuehslod te thesaro uueroldstundu
mid is hugiskeftiun himilrîkeas gidêl,
uuelono thene mêstan: farid imu an giuuald godes,
tionuno tômig. Treuua sind sô gôda
2490 gumono gehuilicumu, sô nis goldes hord
gelîk sulicumu gilôƀon. Uuesad iuuuaro lêrono forð
mancunnie mildie; sie sind sô mislîka,
heliðos gehugda: sum haƀad iro hardan strîd,
uurêðan uuillean, uuancolna hugi,
2495 is imu fêknes ful endi firinuuerko.

80

§32. Interpretation

      Than biginnid imu thunkean,   than he undar theru thiodu stâd
      endi thar gihôrid   oƀar hlust mikil
      thea godes lêra,   than thunkid imu, that he sie gerno forð
      lêstien uuillie;   than biginnid imu thiu lêra godes
2500 an is hugi hafton,   anttat imu than eft an hand cumid
      feho te gifôrea   endi fremiði scat.
      Than farlêdead ina   lêða uuihti,
      than he imu farfâhid   an fehogiri,
      aleskid thene gilôƀon: than uuas imu that luttil fruma,
2505 that he it gio an is hertan gehugda,   ef he it halden ne uuili.
      That is sô the uuastom,   the an themu uuege began,
      liodan an themu lande: thô farnam ina eft thero liudio fard.
      Sô duot thea meginsundeon   an thes mannes hugi
      thea godes lêra, ef he is ni gômid uuel;
2510 elcor bifelliad sia ina   ferne te boðme,
      an thene hêtan hel,   thar he heƀencuninge
      ni uuirðid furður te frumu,   ac ina fîund sculun
      uuîtiu giuuaragean.

§33. The Wheat in the Field

2580   Thô sprak im eft iro hêrro angegin,
      mâri mahtig Crist: 'that is', quað he, 'mannes sunu:
      ik selƀo bium that, thar sâiu,   endi sind thesa sâliga man
      that hluttra hrêncorni,   thea mi hêr hôread uuel,
      uuirkead mînan uuillean;   thius uuerold is the akkar,
2585 thit brêda bûland   barno mancunnies;
      Satanas selƀo   is that, thar sâid aftar
      sô lêðlîca lêra: haƀad thesaro liudeo sô filu,

Hêliand

    uuerodes auuardid,   that sie uuam frummead,
    uuirkead aftar is uuilleon;   thoh sculun sie hêr uuahsen forð
2590 thea forgriponon gumon,   sô samo sô thea gôdun man,
    anttat mûdspelles megin   oƀar man ferid,
    endi thesaro uueroldes.   Than is allaro accaro gehuilic
    gerîpod an thesumu rîkea: sculun iro regangiscapu
    frummien firiho barn.   Than tefarid erða:
2595 that is allaro beuuo brêdost;   than kumid the berhto drohtin
    oƀana mid is engilo craftu,   endi cumad alle tesamne
    liudi, the io thit lioht gisâun,   endi sculun than lôn antfâhan
    uƀiles endi gôdes.   Than gangad engilos godes,
    hêlage heƀenuuardos,   endi lesat thea hluttron man
2600 sundor tesamne,   endi duat sie an sinscôni,
    hôh himiles lioht,   endi thea ôðra an hellia grund,
    uuerpad thea faruuarhton   an uuallandi fiur;
    thar sculun sie gibundene   bittra logna,
    thrâuuerk tholon,   endi thea ôðra thioduuelon
2605 an heƀenrîkea,   huîtaro sunnon
    liohtean gelîco.   Sulic lôn nimad
    uueros uueldâdeo.   Sô hue sô giuuit êgi,
    gehugdi an is hertan,   ettha gihôrien mugi,
    erl mid is ôrun,   sô lâta imu thit an innan sorga,
2610 an is môdseƀon,   huô he scal an themu mâreon dage
    uuið thene rîkeon god   an reðiu standen
    uuordo endi uuerko   allaro, the he an thesaro uueroldi giduod.
    That is egislîcost   allaro thingo,
    forhtlîcost firiho barnun,   that sie sculun uuið iro frâhon mahlien,

§33. The Wheat in the Field

2615 gumon uuið thene gôdan drohtin: than uueldi gerno gehue
    uuesan,
allaro manno gehuilic   mênes tômig,
slîðero sacono.   Aftar thiu scal sorgon êr
allaro liudeo gehuilic,   êr he thit lioht afgeƀe,
the than êgan uuili   alungan tîr,
2620 hôh heƀenrîki   endi huldi godes.'

§34. Herodias' Daughter Dances

Thô uurðun an themu gêrtale   Iudeo cuninges
tîdi cumana,   sô thar gitald habdun
2730 frôde folcuueros,   thô he gifôdid uuas,
an lioht cuman.   Sô uuas thero liudio thau,
that that erlo gehuilic   ôƀean scolde,
Iudeono mid gômun.   Thô uuarð thar an thene gastseli
megincraft mikil   manno gesamnod,
2735 heritogono an that hûs,   thar iro hêrro uuas
an is kuningstôle.   Quâmun managa
Iudeon an thene gastseli;   uuarð im thar gladmôd hugi,
blîði an iro breostun: gisâhun iro bâggeƀon
uuesan an uunneon.   Drôg man uuîn an flet
2740 skîri mid scâlun,   skenkeon huurƀun,
gengun mid goldfatun: gaman uuas thar inne
hlûd an thero hallu,   heliðos drunkun.
Uuas thes an lustun   landes hirdi,
huat he themu uuerode mêst   te uunniun gifremidi.
2745 Hêt he thô gangan forð   gêla thiornun,
is brôder barn,   thar he an is benki sat
uuînu giuulenkid,   endi thô te themu uuîƀe sprac;

grôtte sie fora themu gumskepie endi gerno bad,
that siu thar fora them gastiun gaman afhôƀi
2750 fagar an flettie: 'lât thit folc sehan,
huô thu gelînod haƀas liudio menegi
te blîðseanne an benkiun; ef thu mi thera bede tugiðos,
mîn uuord for thesumu uuerode, than uuilliu ik it hêr te uuârun gequeðen
liahto fora thesun liudiun endi ôk gilêstien sô,
2755 that ik thi than aftar thiu êron uuilliu,
sô hues sô thu mi bidis for thesun mînun bâguuiniun.

§35. The Death of John

Thô uuîsde siu aftar iro uuilleon, hêt that siu uuihtes than êr
ni gerodi for themu gumskepie, biûtan that man iru Iohannes
2775 an theru hallu innan hôƀid gâƀi
alôsid af is lîchamon. That uuas allun them liudiun harm,
them mannun an iro môde, thô sie that gihôrdun thea magað sprekan;
sô uuas it ôk themu kuninge: he ni mahte is quidi liagan,
is uuord uuendien: hêt thô is uuêpanberand
2780 gangen fan themu gastseli endi hêt thene godes man
lîƀu bilôsien. Thô ni uuas lang te thiu,
that man an thea halla hôƀid brâhte
thes thiodgumon, endi it thar theru thiornun fargaf,
magað for theru menigi: siu drôg it theru môder forð.
2785 Thô uuas êndago allaro manno
thes uuîsoston, thero the gio an thesa uuerold quâmi,
thero the quene ênig kind giƀâri,
idis fan erle, lêt man simla then ênon biforan,
the thiu thiorne gidrôg, the gio thegnes ni uuarð

§35. *The Death of John*

2790 uuîs an iro uueroldi,   biûtan sô ine uualdand god
fan heƀenuuange   hêlages gêstes
gimarcode mahtig: the ni habde ênigan gimacon huergin
êr nec aftar.   Erlos huurƀun,
gumon umbi Iohannen,   is iungaron managa,
2795 sâlig gesîði,   endi ine an sande bigrôƀun,
leoƀes lîchamon: uuissun that he lioht godes,
diurlîcan drôm   mid is drohtine samad,
upôdas hêm   êgan môste,
sâlig sôkean.

§36. Jesus Walks on Water

Thô telêt that liuduuerod   aftar themu lande allumu,
2900 tefôr folc mikil,   sîðor iro frâho giuuêt
an that gebirgi uppan,   barno rîkeost,
uualdand an is uuilleon.   Thô te thes uuatares staðe
samnodun thea gesîðos Cristes,   the he imu habde selƀo
   gicorane,
sie tuelîƀi thurh iro treuua gôda: ni uuas im tueho nigiean,
2905 neƀu sie an that godes thionost   gerno uueldin
oƀar thene sêo sîðon.   Thô lêtun sie suîðean strôm,
hôh hurnidskip   hluttron ûðeon,
skêðan skîr uuater.   Skrêd lioht dages,
sunne uuarð an sedle;   the sêolîðandean
2910 naht neƀulo biuuarp;   nâðidun erlos
forðuuardes an flôd;   uuarð thiu fiorðe tid
thera nahtes cuman   — neriendo Crist
uuarode thea uuâglîðand —:   thô uuarð uuind mikil

Hêliand

    hôh uueder afhaben: hlamodun ûðeon,
2915 strôm an stamne; strîdiun feridun
    thea uueros uuiðer uuinde, uuas im uurêð hugi,
    sebo sorgono ful: selbon ni uuândun
    lagulîðandea an land cumen
    thurh thes uuederes geuuin. Thô gisâhun sie uualdand Krist
2920 an themu sêe uppan selbun gangan,
    faran an fâðion: ni mahte an thene flôd innan,
    an thene sêo sincan, huand ine is selbes craft
    hêlag anthabde. Hugi uuarð an forhtun,
    thero manno môdsebo: andrêdun that it im mahtig fîund
2925 te gidroge dâdi. Thô sprak im iro drohtin tô,
    hêlag hebencuning, endi sagde im that he iro hêrro uuas
    mâri endi mahtig: 'nu gi môdes sculun
    fastes fâhen; ne sî iu forht hugi,
    gibâriad gi baldlîco: ik bium that barn godes,
2930 is selbes sunu, the iu uuið thesumu sêe scal,
    mundon uuið thesan meristrôm.'

§37. Saint Peter's Keys

    Diurlîco scalt thu thes lôn antfâhen,
    hluttro habas thu an thînan hêrron gilôbon, hugiskefti sind
        thîne stêne gelîca,
    sô fast bist thu sô felis the hardo; hêten sculun thi firiho
        barn
    sancte Pêter: obar themu stêne scal man mînen seli uuirkean,
3070 hêlag hûs godes; thar scal is hîuuiski tô
    sâlig samnon: ni mugun uuið them thînun suîðeun crafte

§37. Saint Peter's Keys

    anthebbien hellie portun.   Ik fargibu this himilrîceas
        slutilas,
    that thu môst aftar mi   allun giuualda
    kristinum folke;   kumad alle te thi
3075 gumono gêstos;   thu habe grôte giuuald,
    huene thu hêr an erðu   eldibarno
    gebinden uuillies: themu is bêðiu giduan,
    himilrîki biloken,   endi hellie sind imu opana,
    brinnandi fiur;   sô huene sô thu eft antbinden uuili,
3080 antheftien is hendi,   themu is himilrîki,
    antloken liohto mêst   endi lîf êuuig,
    grôni godes uuang.   Mid sulicaru ik thi gebu uuilliu
    lônon thînen gilôbon.   Ni uuilliu ik, that gi thesun liudiun
        noh,
    mârien thesaru menigi,   that ik bium mahtig Crist,
3085 godes êgan barn.   Mi sculun Iudeon noh,
    unsculdigna   erlos binden,
    uuêgean mi te uundrun   — dôt mi uuîties filo —
    innan Hierusalem   gêres ordun,
    âhtien mînes aldres   eggiun scarpun,
3090 belôsien mi lîbu.   Ik an thesumu liohte scal
    thurh ûses drohtines craft   fan dôde astanden
    an thriddiumu dage.'

§38. THE TRANSFIGURATION

    Thô imu thar te bedu gihnêg,
    thô uuarð imu thar uppe   ôðarlîcora
    uuliti endi giuuâdi: uurðun imu is uuangun liohte
3125 blîcandi sô thiu berhte sunne: sô skên that barn godes,
    liuhte is lîchamo: liomon stôdun

Hêliand

    uuânamo fan themu uualdandes barne;   uuarð is geuuâdi sô huît
    sô snêu te sehanne.   Thô uuarð thar seldlîc thing
    giôgid aftar thiu: Elias endi Moyses
3130 quâmun thar te Criste   uuið sô craftagne
    uuordun uuehslean.   Thar uuarð sô uunsam sprâka,
    sô gôd uuord undar gumun,   thar the godes sunu
    uuið thea mârean man   mahlien uuelde,
    sô blîði uuarð uppan themu berge: skên that berhte lioht,
3135 uuas thar gard gôdlic   endi grôni uuang,
    paradise gelîc.   Petrus thô gimahalde,
    helið hardmôdig   endi te is hêrron sprac,
    grôtte thene godes sunu: 'gôd is it hêr te uuesanne,
    ef thu it gikiosan uuili,   Crist alouualdo,
3140 that man thi hêr an thesaru hôhe   ên hûs geuuirkea,
    mârlîco gemaco   endi Moysese ôðer
    endi Eliase thriddea: thit is ôdas hêm,
    uuelono uunsamost.'   Reht sô he thô that uuord gesprak,
    sô tilêt thiu luft an tuê: lioht uuolcan skên,
3145 glîtandi glîmo,   endi thea gôdun man
    uulitiscôni beuuarp.   Thô fan themu uuolcne quam
    hêlag stemne godes   endi them heliðun thar
    selbo sagde,   that that is sunu uuâri,
    libbiendero liobost: 'an themu mi lîcod uuel
3150 an mînun hugiskeftiun.   Themu gi hôrien sculun,
    fulgangad imu gerno.'

§39. Fishing for Coins

3200   . . .   hêt thô thene is mârean thegan,
    Sîmon Petrus   an thene sêo innen

§39. Fishing for Coins

```
       angul uuerpen:    'suliken sô thu thar êrist mugis
       fisk gifâhen', quað he,   'sô teoh thu thene fan themu flôde
          te thi,
       antklemmi imu thea kinni:   thar maht thu under them
          kaflon nimen
3205   guldine scattos,   that thu fargelden maht
       themu manne te gimôdea    mînen endi thînen
       tinseo sô huilican,   sô he ûs tô sôkid.'
       He ni thorfte imu thô aftar thiu   ôðaru uuordu
       furðor gibioden:    geng fiscari gôd,
3210   Sîmon Petrus,    uuarp an thene sêo innen
       angul an ûðeon    endi up gitôh
       fisk an flôde    mid is folmun tuêm,
       teklôf imu thea kinni    endi undar them kaflun nam
       guldine scattos:    dede al, sô imu the godes sunu
3215   uuordun geuuîsde.   Thar uuas thô uualdandes
       megincraft gimârid,   huô scal allaro manno gehuilic
       suîðo uuilleiendi    is uueroldhêrron
       sculdi endi scattos,   thea imu geskeride sind,
       gerno gelden:    ni scal ine fargûmon eouuiht
3220   ni farmuni ine an is môde,   ac uuese imu mildi an is hugi,
       thiono imu thiolîco:    an thiu mag he thiodgodes
       uuillean geuuirkean   endi ôk is uueroldhêrron
       huldi habbien.
```

§40. The Rich Man and Lazarus

```
3295         Sah imu aftar thô
       Krist alouualdo,   quað it thô thar he uuelde,
       te them is iungarun geginuuardun,   that uuâri an godes rîki
       unôði ôdagumu manne    up te comanne:
```

Hêliand

    'ôður mag man olbundeon,   thoh he sî unmêt grôt,
3300 thurh nâðlan gat,   thoh it sî naru suîðo,
     sâftur thurhslôpien,   than mugi cuman thiu siole te himile
     thes ôdagan mannes,   the hêr al haƀad
     giuuendid an thene uueroldscat   uuilleon sînen,
     môdgithâhti,   endi ni hugid umbi thie maht godes.'
3305 Imu anduuordiade   êrthungan gumo,
     Sîmon Petrus,   endi seggean bad
     leoƀan hêrron: 'huat sculun uui thes te lône nimen', quað he,
     'gôdes te gelde,   thes uui thurh thîn iungardôm
     êgan endi erƀi   al farlêtun
3310 hoƀos endi hîuuiski   endi thi te hêrron gicurun,
     folgodun thînaru ferdi: huat scal ûs thes te frumu uuerðan,
     langes te lône?'   Liudeo drohtin
     sagde im thô selƀo: 'than ik sittien kumu', quað he,
     'an thie mikilan maht   an themu mârean dage,
3315 thar ik allun scal   irminthiodun
     dômos adêlien,   than môtun gi mid iuuuomu drohtine thar
     selƀon sittien   endi môtun thera saca uualdan:
     môtun gi Israhelo   eðilifolcun
     adêlien aftar iro dâdiun: sô môtun gi thar gidiuride uuesen.
3320 Than seggiu ik iu te uuâran: sô hue sô that an thesaru
         uueroldi giduot,
     that he thurh mîna minnea   mâgo gesidli
     liof farlêtid,   thes scal hi hêr lôn niman
     tehan sîðun tehinfald,   ef he it mid treuuon duot,
     mid hluttru hugi.   Oƀar that haƀad he ôk himiles lioht,
3325 open êuuig lîf.'   Bigan imu thô aftar thiu
     allaro barno bezt   ên biliði seggian,
     quað that thar ên ôdag man   an êrdagun

§40. The Rich Man and Lazarus

uuâri undar themu uuerode: 'the habde uuelono genôg,
sinkas gisamnod   endi imu simlun uuas
3330 garu mid goldu   endi mid godouuebbiu,
fagarun fratahun   endi imu so filu habde
gôdes an is gardun   endi imu at gômun sat
allaro dago gehuilikes: habde imu diurlîc lîf,
blîtzea an is benkiun.   Than uuas thar eft ên biddiende man,
3335 gilêbod an is lîchamon,   Lazarus uuas he hêten,
lag imu dago gehuilikes   at them durun foren,
thar he thene ôdagan man   inne uuisse
an is gestseli   gôme thiggean,
sittien at sumble,   endi he simlun bêd
3340 giarmod thar ûte: ni môste thar in cuman,
ne he ni mahte gebiddien,   that man imu thes brôdes tharod
gidragan uueldi,   thes thar fan themu diske niðer
antfel undar iro fôti: ni mahte imu thar ênig fruma
     uuerðen
fan themu hêroston, the thes hûses giuueld,   biûtan that
     thar gengun is hundos tô,
3345 likkodun is lîkuundon,   thar he liggiandi
hungar tholode;   ni quam imu thar te helpu uuiht
fan themu rîkeon manne.   Thô gifragn ik that ina is
     reganogiscapu,
thene armon man   is êndago
gimanoda mahtiun suîð,   that he manno drôm
3350 ageben scolde.   Godes engilos
antfengun is ferh   endi lêddun ine forð thanen,
that sie an Abrahames barm   thes armon mannes
siole gisettun: thar môste he simlun forð
uuesan an uunniun.   Thô quâmun ôk uurdegiscapu,
3355 themu ôdagan man   orlaghuîle,

Hêliand

    that he thit lioht farlêt: lêðа uuihti
    besinkodun is siole   an thene suarton hel,
    an that fern innen   fîundun te uuillean,
    begrôƀun ine an gramono hêm.   Thanen mahte he thene
        gôdan scauuon,
3360 Abraham gesehen,   thar he uppe uuas
    lîƀes an lustun,   endi Lazarus sat
    blîði an is barme,   berht lôn antfeng
    allaro is armôdio,   endi lag the ôdago man
    hêto an theru helliu,   hriop up thanen:
3365 'fader Abraham', quað he,   'mi is firinun tharf,
    that thu mi an thînumu môdseƀon   mildi uuerðes,
    lîði an thesaru lognu: sendi mi Lazarus herod,
    that he mî gefôrea   an thit fern innan
    caldes uuateres.   Ik hêr quic brinnu
3370 hêto an thesaru helliu: nu is mi thînaro helpono tharf,
    that he mi aleskie   mid is lutticon fingru
    tungon mîne,   nu siu têkan haƀad,
    uƀil arƀedi.   Inuuidrâdo,
    lêðaro sprâka,   alles is mi nu thes lôn cumen.'

§41. Workers in the Vineyard

    Than uualdandi Crist
3445 mênda im thoh mêra thing,   thoh hie oƀar that manno folc
    fan them uuîngardon sô   uuordon sprâki,
    huô thar unefno   erlos quâmun,
    uueros te them uuerke.   Sô sculun fan thero uueroldi duon
    manncunnies barn   an that mârio lioht,
3450 gumon an godes uuang: sum biginnit ina giriuuan sân
    an is kindiski,   haƀit im gicoranan muod,

§41. Workers in the Vineyard

uuilleon guodan,   uueroldsaca mîðit,
farlâtit is lusta;   ni mag ina is lîkhamo
an unspuod farspanan: spâhiða lînot,
3455 godes êu,   gramono forlâtit,
uurêðaro uuillion,   duot im sô te is uueroldi forð,
lêstit sô an theson liohte,   antthat im is lîƀes cumit,
aldres âƀand;   giuuîtit im than uppuuegos:
thar uuirðit im is araƀedi   all gilônot,
3460 fargoldan mid guodu   an godes rîkie.
That mêndun this uuuruhteon,   thia an them uuîngardon
âdro an ûhta   arƀidlîco
uuerc bigunnun   endi thuruuuonodon forð,
erlos unt âƀand.   Sum thar ôc an undern quam,
3465 habda thuo farmerrid,   thia moraganstunda
thes daguuerkes forduolon;   sô duot doloro filo,
gimêdaro manno;   drîƀit im mislîc thing
gerno an is iuguði,   — haƀit im gelpquidi
lêða gilînot   endi lôsuuord manag —,
3470 antthat is kindiski   farcuman uuirðit,
that ina after is iuguði   godes anst manot
blîði an is brioston;   fâhit im te beteron than
uuordon endi uuercon,   lêdit im is uuerold mid thiu,
is aldar ant thena endi: cumit im alles lôn
3475 an godes rîkie,   gôdaro uuerko.

§42. Going to Jerusalem

Quað that sie thô te Hierusalem   an that Iudeono folc
lîðan scoldin: 'thar uuirðid all gilêstid sô,
gefrumid undar themu folke,   sô it an furndagun

Hêliand

uuîse man be mi   uuordun gesprâkun.
3525 Thar sculun mi farcôpon   undar thea craftigon thiod
heliðos te theru hêri;   thar uuerðat mîna hendi gebundana,
faðmos uuerðad mi thar gefastnod;   filu scal ik thar githoloian,
hoskes gihôrien   endi harmquidi,
bismersprâka   endi bihêtuuord manag;
3530 sie uuêgeat mi te uundron   uuâpnes eggiun,
bilôsiad mi lîbu: ik te thesumu liohte scal
thurh drohtines craft   fan dôde astanden
an thriddeon dage.   Ni quam ik undar thesa theoda herod
te thiu, that mîn eldibarn   arbed habdin,
3535 that mi thionodi thius thiod: ni uuilliu ik is sie thiggien nu,
fergon thit folcskepi,   ac ik scal imu te frumu uuerðen,
theonon imu theolîco   endi for alla thesa theoda geben
seole mîne.   Ik uuilliu sie selbo nu
lôsien mid mînu lîbu,   thea hêr lango bidun
3540 mankunnies manag,   mînara helpa'.

§43. The Blind Men

Thar uuas sô mahtiglîc
biliði gibôknid,   thar the blindon mann
3590 bi themu uuege sâtun,   uuîti tholodun,
liohtes lôse: that mênid thoh liudio barn,
al mancunni,   huô sie mahtig god
an themu anaginne thurh is ênes craft
sinhîun tuê   selbo giuuarhte,
3595 Adam endi Êvan: fargaf im upuuegos,
himilo rîki;   ac thô uuarð im the hatola te nâh,
fîund mid fêknu   endi mid firinuuerkun,
bisuêk sie mid sundiun,   that sie sinscôni

§43. The Blind Men

lioht farlêtun: uurðun an lêðaron stedi,
3600 an thesen middilgard   man faruuorpen,
tholodun hêr an thiustriu   thiodarƀedi,
uunnun uuracsîðos,   uuelon tharƀodun:
fargâtun godes rîkies,   gramon theonodun,
fîundo barnun;   sie guldun is im mid fiuru lôn
3605 an theru hêton helliu.   Bethiu uuârun siu an iro hugi blinda
an thesaru middilgard,   menniscono barn,
huand siu ine ni antkiendun,   craftagne god,
himilisken hêrron,   thene the sie mid is handun giscôp,
giuuarhte an is uuillion.   Thius uuerold uuas thô sô
        farhuerƀid,
3610 bithuungen an thiustrie,   an thiodarƀidi,
an dôðes dalu: sâtun im thô bi theru drohtines strâtun
iâmarmôde,   godes helpe bidun:
siu ni mahte im thô êr uuerðen,   êr than uualdand god
an thesan middilgard,   mahtig drohtin,
3615 is selƀes sunu   sendien uueldi
that he lioht antluki   liudio barnun,
oponodi im êuuig lîf,   that sie thene alouualdon
mahtin antkennien uuel,   craftagna god.
Ôk mag ik giu gitellien,   of gi thar tô uuilliad
3620 huggien endi hôrien,   that gi thes hêliandes mugun
craft antkennien,   huô is kumi uurðun
an thesaru middilgard   managun te helpu,
ia huat he mid them dâdiun   drohtin selƀo
manages mênde,   ia behuiu thiu mârie burg
3625 Hiericho hêtid,   thiu thar an Iudeon stâd
gimacod mid mûrun: thiu is aftar themu mânen ginemnid,
aftar themu torhten tungle: he ni mag is tîdi bemîðen,
ac he dago gehuilikes   duod ôðerhueðer,

uuanod ohtho uuahsid.   Sô dôd an thesaro uueroldi hêr,
3630 an thesaru middilgard   menniscono barn ...

§44. Entering Jerusalem

Thô gesah uualdand Krist
the gôdo te Hierusalem,   gumono bezta,
3685 blîcan thene burges uual   endi bû Iudeono,
hôha hornseli   endi ôk that hûs godes,
allaro uuîho uunsamost.   Thô uuel imu an innen
hugi uuið is herte: thô ni mahte that hêlage barn
uuôpu auuîsien,   sprak thô uuordo filu
3690 hriuuiglîco   — uuas im is hugi sêreg—:
'uuê uuarð thi, Hierusalem', quað he,   'thes thu te uuârun ni uuêst
thea uurðegiskefti,   the thi noh giuuerðen sculun,
huô thu noh uuirðis behabd   heries craftu
endi thi bisittiad   slîðmôde man,
3695 fiund mid folcun.   Than ni habas thu friðu huergin,
mundburd mid mannun: lêdiad thi hêr manage tô
ordos endi eggia,   orlegas uuord,
farfioth thîn folcskepi   fiures liomon,
these uuîki auuôstiad,   uuallos hôha
3700 felliad te foldun: ni afstâd is felis nigiean,
stên oḃar ôðrumu,   ak uuerðad thesa stedi uuôstia
umbi Hierusalem   Iudeo liudeo,
huand sie ni antkenniad,   that im kumana sind
iro tîði tôuuardes,   ac sie habbiad im tuîflien hugi,
3705 ni uuitun that iro uuîsad   uualdandes craft'.

§45. A Thane's Duty

Thuo ên thero tueliƀio,
Thuomas gimâlda — uuas im githungan mann,
diurlîc drohtines thegan —: 'ne sculun uui im thia dâd
    lahan, quathie,
3995 'ni uuernian uui im thes uuillien, ac uuita im uuonian mid,
thuoloian mid ûsson thiodne: that ist thegnes cust,
that hie mid is frâhon samad fasto gistande,
dôie mid im thar an duome. Duan ûs alla sô,
folgon im te thero ferdi: ni lâtan ûse fera uuið thiu
4000 uuihtes uuirðig, neƀa uui an them uuerode mid im,
dôian mid ûson drohtine. Than lêƀot ûs thoh duom after,
guod uuord for gumon.'

§46. Judgment Day

4045   'All hebbiu ik gilôƀon sô', quað siu,
'that it sô giuuerðan scal, sô huan sô thius uuerold endiod,
endi the mâreo dag ôƀar man ferid,
that he than fan erðu scal up astanden
an themu dômes daga, than uuerðad fan dôđe quica
4050 thurh maht godes mankunnies gehuilic,
arîsad fan restu.' Thô sagde rîkeo Krist
theru idis alomahtig oponun uuordun,
that he selƀo uuas sunu drohtines,
bêðiu ia lîf ia lioht liudio barnon
4055 te astandanne: 'nio the sterƀen ni scal,
lîf farliosen, the hêr gilôƀid te mi:
thoh ina eldibarn erðu bithekkien,
diapo bidelƀen, nis he dôd thiu mêr:

Hêliand

       that flêsk is bifolhen,   that ferha is gihalden,
4060 is thiu siola gisund.'   Thô sprak imu eft sân angegin
       that uuîf mid iro uuordun: 'ik gilôƀiu that thu the uuâro
           bist', quað siu
       'Krist godes sunu: that mag man antkennien uuel,
       uuiten an thînun uuordun,   that thu giuuald haƀes
       thurh thiu hêlagon giscapu   himiles endi erðun.'

§47. Raising Lazarus

4065 Thô gefragn ik that thar thero idisio quam   ôðar gangan
       Maria môdkarag: gengun iro managa aftar
       Iudeo liudi.   Thô siu themu godes barne
       sagde sêragmôd,   huat iru te sorgun gistôd
       an iro hugi harmes: hofnu kûmde
4070 Lazaruses farlust,   liaƀes mannes,
       griat gornundi,   antat themu godes barne
       hugi uuarð gihrôrid: hête trahni
       uuôpu auuellun,   endi thô te themu uuîƀun sprac,
       hêt ina thô lêdien,   thar Lazarus uuas
4075 foldu bifolhen.   Lag thar ên felis bioƀan,
       hard stên behliden.   Thô hêt the hêlago Crist
       antlûcan thea leia,   that he môsti that lîk sehen,
       hrêo scauuoien.   Thô ni mahte an iro hugi mîðan
       Martha for theru menegi,   uuið mahtigne sprak:
4080 'frô mîn the gôdo', quað siu,   'ef man thene felis nimid,
       thene stên antlûkid,   than uuâniu ik that thanen stank
           kume,
       unsuôti suek,   huand ik the seggian mag
       uuârun uuordun,   that thes nis giuuand ênig,

§47. Raising Lazarus

    that he thar ni bifolhen uuas   fiuuuar naht endi dagos
4085 an themu erðgraƀe.'   Anduuordi gaf
    uualdand them uuîƀe: 'huat, ni sagde ik the te uuârun êr',
        quað he,
    'ef thu gilôƀien uuili,   than nis nu lang te thiu,
    that thu hêr antkennien scalt   craft drohtines,
    the mikilon maht godes?'   Thô gengun manage tô,
4090 afhôƀun harden stên.   Thô sah the hêlago Crist
    up mid is ôgun,   ôlat sagde
    themu the these uuerold giscôp,   'thes thu mîn uuord
        gihôris', quað he,
    'sigidrohtin selƀo;   ik uuêt that thu sô simlun duos,
    ac ik duom it be thesumu grôton   Iudeono folke,
4095 that sie that te uuârun uuitin,   that thu mi an these uuerold
        sendes
    thesun liudiun te lêrun.'   Thô he te Lazaruse hriop
    starkaru stemniu   endi hêt ina standen up
    ia fan themu graƀe gangan.   Thô uuarð the gêst kumen
    an thene lîchamon: he bigan is lið i hrôrien,
4100 antuuarp undar themu giuuêdie: uuas imo sô beuunden thô
        noh,
    an hrêobeddion bihelid.   Hêt imu helpen thô
    uualdandeo Krist.   Uueros gengun tô,
    antuundun that geuuâdi.   Uuânum up arês
    Lazarus te thesumu liohte: uuas imu is lîf fargeƀen,
4105 that he is aldarlagu   êgan môsti,
    friðu forðuuardes.   Thô fagonadun bêðea,
    Maria endi Martha: ni mag that man ôðrumu
    giseggian te sôðe,   huô thea gesuester tuô
    mendiodun an iro môde.   Maneg uundrode

Hêliand

4110 Iudeo liudio, thô sie ina fan themu graƀe sâhun
 sîðon gesunden, thene the êr suht farnam
 endi sie bidulƀun diapo undar erðu
 lîƀes lôsen: thô môste imu libbien forð
 hêl an hêmun. Sô mag heƀenkuninges,
4115 thiu mikile maht godes manno gehuilikes
 ferahe giformon endi uuið fiundo nîđ
 hêlag helpen, sô huemu sô he is huldi fargiƀid.

§48. Jesus as Threat

 Than uuas eft thes uuerodes sô filu,
 sô môdstarke man: ni uueldun the maht godes
 antkennien kûðlîco, ac sie uuið is craft mikil
 uunnun mid iro uuordun: uuârun im uualdandes
4125 lêra sô lêða: sôhtun im liudi ôðra
 an Hierusalem, thar Iudeono uuas
 hêri handmahal endi hôƀidstedi,
 grôt gumskepi grimmaro thioda.
 Sie kûðdun im thô Kristes uuerk, quâðun that sie quickan sâhin
4130 thene erl mid iro ôgun, the an erðu uuas,
 foldu bifolhen fiuuuar naht endi dagos,
 dôd bidolƀen, antat he ina mid is dâdiun selƀo,
 mid is uuordun auuekide, that he môsti these uuerold sehan.
 Thô uuas that sô uuiđeruuord uulankun mannun,
4135 Iudeo liudiun: hêtun iro gumskepi thô,
 uuerod samnoian endi uuarƀos fâhen,
 meginthioda gimang, an mahtigna Krist

§48. Jesus as Threat

riedun an rûnun: 'nis that râd ênig', quâðun sie,
'that uui that githoloian: uuili thesaro thioda te filu
4140 gilôƀien aftar is lêrun. Than ûs liudi farad,
an eoridfolc, uuerðat ûsa oƀarhoƀdun
rinkos fan Rûmu. Than uui theses rîkies sculun
lôse libbien etha uui sculun ûses lîƀes tholon,
heliðos ûsaro hôƀdo.' Thô sprak thar ên gihêrod man
4145 oƀar uuarf uuero, the uuas thes uuerodes thô
an theru burg innan biscop thero liudio
— Kaiphas uuas he hêten; habdun ina gicoranen te thiu
an theru gêrtalu Iudeo liudi,
that he thes godes hûses gômien scoldi,
4150 uuardon thes uuîhes —: 'mi thunkid uunder mikil', quað he,
'mâri thioda, — gi kunnun manages giskêđ —
huî ge that te uuârun ni uuitin, uuerod Iudeono,
that hêr is betera râd barno gehuilicumu,
that man hêr ênne man aldru bilôsie
4155 endi that he thurh iuuua dâdi drôreg sterƀe,
for thesumu folcskepi ferah farlâte,
than al thit liuduuerod farloren uuerðe.'

§49. Apocalypse

Thô the rîkio sprak,
hêr heƀencuning — hôrdun the ôðra —:
4280 'ik mag iu gitellien', quað he, 'that noh uuirðid thiu tîd kumen,
that is afstanden ni scal stên oƀar ôðrumu,
ac it fallid ti foldu endi fiur nimid,
grâdag logna, thoh it nu sô gôdlîc sî,

Hêliand

  sô uuîslîco giuuarht, endi sô dôd all thesaro uueroldes
   giscapu,
  teglîdid grôni uuang.' ...
  Ik mag iu thoh gitellien, huilic hêr têcan biforan
  giuuerðad uunderlîc, êr than he an these uuerold kume
4310 an themu mâreon daga: that uuirðid hêr êr an themu
   mânon skîn
  iac an theru sunnun sô same; gisuerkad siu bêđiu,
  mid finistre uuerðad bifangan; fallad sterron,
  huît heƀentungal, endi hrisid erðe,
  biƀod thius brêde uuerold — uuirðid sulicaro bôkno filu —:
4315 grimmid the grôto sêo, uuirkid thie geƀenes strôm
  egison mid is ûðiun erðbûandiun.
  Than thorrot thiu thiod thurh that gethuing mikil,
  folc thurh thea forhta: than nis friðu huergin,
  ac uuirðid uuîg sô maneg oƀar these uuerold alla
4320 hetelîc afhaben, endi heri lêdid
  kunni oƀar ôðar: uuirðid kuningo giuuin,
  meginfard mikil: uuirðid managoro qualm,
  open urlagi — that is egislîc thing,
  that io sulik morð sculun man afhebbien —,
4325 uuirðid uuôl sô mikil oƀar these uuerold alle,
  mansterƀono mêst, thero the gio an thesaru middilgard
  suulti thurh suhti: liggiad seoka man,
  driosat endi dôiat endi iro dag endiad,
  fulliad mid iro ferahu; ferid unmet grôt
4330 hungar hetigrim oƀar heliðo barn,
  metigêdeono mêst: nis that minniste
  thero uuîteo an thesaru uueroldi, the hêr giuuerðen sculun
  êr dômes dage. Sô huan sô gi thea dâdi gisehan

§49. Apocalypse

giuuerðen an thesaro uueroldi,   sô mugun gi than te uuâran
   farstanden,
4335 that than the lazto dag   liudiun nâhid ...
   Uuacot gi uuarlîco: iu is uuiscumo
   duomdag the mâreo   endi iuues drohtines craft,
   thiu mikilo meginstrengi   endi thiu mârie tîd,
4355 giuuand thesaro uueroldes.   Fora thiu gi uuardon sculun,
   that he iu slâpandie   an suefrestu
   fârungo ni bifâhe   an firinuuercun,
   mênes fulle.   Mûtspelli cumit
   an thiustrea naht,   al sô thiof ferid
4360 darno mid is dâdiun,   sô kumid the dag mannun,
   the lazto theses liohtes,   sô it êr these liudi ni uuitun,
   sô samo sô thiu flôd deda   an furndagun,
   the thar mid lagustrômun   liudi farteride
   bi Nôeas tîdiun,   biûtan that ina neride god
4365 mid is hîuuiskea,   hêlag drohtin,
   uuið thes flôdes farm: sô uuarð ôk that fiur kuman
   hêt fan himile,   that thea hôhon burgi
   umbi Sodomo land   suart logna bifeng
   grim endi grâdag,   that thar nênig gumono ni ginas
4370 biûtan Loth êno: ina antlêddun thanen
   drohtines engilos   endi is dohter tuâ
   an ênan berg uppen: that ôðar al brinnandi fiur
   ia land ia liudi   logna farteride:
   sô fârungo uuarð that fiur kumen,   sô uuarð êr the flôd sô
      samo:
4375 sô uuirðid the lazto dag.   For thiu scal allaro liudio gehuilic
   thenkean fora themu thinge;   thes is tharf mikil
   manno gehuilicumu: bethiu lâtid iu an iuuuan môd sorga.

§50. Washing Feet

Than uuisse that friðubarn godes
4495 uuâr uualdand Krist, that he these uuerold scolde,
ageƀen these gardos endi sôkien imu godes rîki,
gifaren is faderôdil. Thô ni gisah ênig firiho barno
mêron minnie, than he thô te them mannun ginam,
te them is gôdun iungaron: gôme uuarhte,
4500 sette sie suâslîco endi im sagde filu
uuâroro uuordo. Skrêd uuester dag,
sunne te sedle. Thô he selƀo gibôd,
uualdand mid is uuordun, hêt im uuater dragan
hluttar te handun, endi rês thô the hêlago Crist,
4505 the gôdo at them gômun endi thar is iungarono thuôg
fôti mid is folmun endi suarf sie mid is fanon aftar,
druknide sie diurlîca. Thô uuið is drohtin sprak
Sîmon Petrus: 'ni thunkid mi thit sômi thing', quað he,
'frô mîn the gôdo, that thu mîne fôti thuahes
4510 mid them thînun hêlagun handun.' Thô sprak imu eft is
    hêrro angegin,
uualdand mid is uuordun: 'ef thu is uuillean ni haƀes', quað he,
'te antfâhanne, that ik thîne fôti thuahe
thurh sulica minnea, sô ik thesun ôðrun mannun hêr
dôm thurh diurða, than ni haƀes thu ênigan dêl mid mi
4515 an heƀenrîkea.' Hugi uuarð thô giuuendid
Sîmon Petruse: 'thu haƀa thi selƀo giuuald', quað he,
endi mînes hôfdes sô sama, handun thînun,
thiadan, te thuahanne, te thiu that ik môti thîna forð
huldi hebbian endi heƀenrîkies
4520 sulic gidêli, sô thu mi, drohtin, uuili
fargeƀen thurh thîna gôdi.'

§51. Jesus Identifies the Betrayer

4575   Nu seggiu ik iu te uuâran hêr,
that uuili iuuuar tuelibio ên treuuana suîkan,
uuili mi farcôpon undar thit kunni Iudeono,
gisellien uuiðer silubre, endi uuili imu thar sinc niman,
diurie mêðmos, endi geben is drohtin uuið thiu,
4580 holdan hêrran. That imu thoh te harme scal,
uueröan te uuîtie; be that he thea uurdi farsihit
endi he thes arbedies endi scauuot,
than uuêt he that te uuâran, that imu uuâri uuôðiera thing,
betera mikilu, that he io giboran ni uurði
4585 libbiendi te thesumu liohte, than he that lôn nimid,
ubil arbedi inuuidrâdo.'
Thô bigan thero erlo gehuilic te ôðrumu scauuon,
sorgondi sehan; uuas im sêr hugi,
hriuuig umbi iro herta: gehôrdun iro hêrron thô
4590 gornuuord sprekan. Thea gumon sorgodun,
huilican he thero tuelibio te thiu tellien uueldi,
sculdigna scaðon, that he habdi thea scattos thar
gethingod at theru thiod. Ni uuas thero thegno ênigumu
sulikes inuuiddies ôði te gehanne,
4595 mêngithâhtio — antsuok thero manno gehuilic —,
uurðun alle an forhtun, frâgon ne gidorstun,
êr than thô gebôknide baruuirðig gumo,
Sîmon Petrus — ne gidorste it selbo sprekan —
te Iohanne themu gôdon: he uuas themu godes barne
4600 an them dagun thegno liobost,
mêst an minniun endi môste thar thô an thes mahtiges
    Kristes

Hêliand

    barme restien   endi an is breostun lag,
    hlinode mid is hôbdu: thar nam he sô manag hêlag gerûni,
    diapa githâhti,   endi thô te is drohtine sprac,
4605 began ina thô frâgon: 'hue scal that, frô mîn, uuesen',
        quað he,
    'that thi farcôpon uuili,   cuningo rîkeost,
    undar thînaro fiundo folc?   Ûs uuâri thes firiuuit mikil,
    uualdand, te uuitanne.'   Thô habde eft is uuord garu
    hêleando Crist: 'seh thi, huemu ik hêr an hand gebe
4610 mînes môses for thesun mannun: the habed mêngithâht,
    birid bittran hugi;   the scal mi an banono geuuald,
    fiundun bifelhen,   thar man mînes ferhes scal,
    aldres âhtien.'   Nam he thô aftar thiu
    thes môses for them mannun   endi gaf is themu
        mênscaðen,
4615 Iudase an hand   endi imu tegegnes sprac
    selbo for them is gesîðun   endi ina sniumo hêt
    faran fan themu is folke: 'frumi sô thu thenkis', quað he,
    'dô that thu duan scalt: thu ni maht bidernien leng
    uuilleon thînan.   Thiu uurd is at handun,
4620 thea tîdi sind nu ginâhid.'   Sô thô the treulogo
    that môs antfeng   endi mid is mûðu anbêt,
    sô afgaf ina thô thiu godes craft,   gramon in geuuitun
    an thene lîchamon,   lêða uuihti,
    uuarð imu Satanas   sêro bitengi,
4625 hardo umbi is herte,   sîður ine thiu helpe godes
    farlêt an thesumu liohte.   Sô is thena liudio uuê,
    the sô undar thesumu himile scal   hêrron uuehslon.

§52. Jesus In Gethsemane

Thô hiet hie is iungron thar
bîdan uppan themo berge,   quað that hie ti bedu uueldi
an thiu holmclibu   hôhor stîgan;
4735 hiet thuo thria mid im   thegnos gangan,
Iacobe endi Iohannese   endi thena guodan Petruse,
thrîstmuodian thegan.   Thuo sia mid iro thiedne samad
gerno gengun.   Thuo hiet sia thie godes suno
an berge uppan   te bedu hnîgan,
4740 hiet sia god gruotian,   gerno biddian,
that he im thero costondero   craft farstôdi,
uurêðaro uuilleon,   that im the uuiðersaco,
ni mahti the mênscaðo   môd gituîflean,
iak imu thô selbo gihnêg   sunu drohtines
4745 craftag an kniobeda,   kuningo rîkeost,
forðuuard te foldu: fader alothiado
gôdan grôtte,   gornuuordun sprac
hriuuiglîco: uuas imu is hugi drôbi,
bi theru menniski   môd gihrôrid,
4750 is flêsk uuas an forhtun: fellun imo trahni,
drôp is diurlîc suêt,   al sô drôr kumid
uuallan fan uundun.   Uuas an geuuinne thô
an themu godes barne   the gêst endi the lîchamo:
ôðar uuas fûsid   an forðuuegos,
4755 the gêst an godes rîki,   ôðar giâmar stôd,
lîchamo Cristes: ni uuelde thit lioht ageben,
ac drôbde for themu dôðe.   Simla he hreop te drohtine forð
thiu mêr aftar thiu   mahtigna grôtte,
hôhan himilfader,   hêlagna god,
4760 uualdand mid is uuordun: 'ef nu uuerðen ni mag', quað he,

Hêliand

'mankunni generid, ne sî that ik mînan geƀe
lioƀan lîchamon for liudio barn
te uuêgeanne te uundrun, it sî than thîn uuilleo sô,
ik uuilliu is than gicoston: ik nimu thene kelik an hand,
4765 drinku ina thi te diurðu, drohtin frô mîn,
mahtig mundboro. Ni seh thu mînes hêr
flêskes gifôries. Ik fullon scal
uuilleon thînen: thu haƀes geuuald oƀar al.'
Giuuêt imu thô gangen, thar he êr is iungaron lêt
4770 bîdan uppan themu berge; fand sie that barn godes
slâpen sorgandie: uuas im sêr hugi,
thes sie fan iro drohtine dêlien scoldun.
Sô sind that môdthraca manno gehuilicumu,
that he farlâtan scal liaƀane hêrron,
4775 afgeƀen thene sô gôdene.

§53 THE CAPTURE OF CHRIST

4810   Uuîsde im Iudas,
gramhugdig man; Iudeon aftar sigun,
fiundo folcscepi; drôg man fiur an gimang,
logna an liohtfatun, lêdde man faklon
brinnandea fan burg, thar sie an thene berg uppan
4815 stigun mid strîdu. Thea stedi uuisse Judas uuel,
huar he thea liudi tô lêdean scolde.
Sagde imu thô te têkne, thô sie thar tô fôrun
themu folke biforan, te thiu that sie ni farfengin thar,
erlos ôðren man: 'ik gangu imu at êrist tô' quað he,
4820 'cussiu ine endi queddiu: that is Crist ƀo
Thene gi fâhen sculun folco craftu,
binden ina uppan themu berge endi ina te burg hinan

§53. The Capture of Christ

lêdien undar thea liudi: he is lîƀes haƀad
mid is uuordun faruuerkod.'   Uuerod sîðode thô,
4825 antat sie te Criste   kumane uurðun
grim folc Iudeono,   thar he mid is iungarun stôd,
mâri drohtin: bêd metodogiscapu,
torhtero tîdeo.   Thô geng imu treulôs man,
Iudas tegegnes   endi te themu godes barne
4830 hnêg mid is hôƀdu   endi is hêrron quedde,
custe ina craftagne   endi is quidi lêste,
uuîsde ina themu uuerode,   al sô he êr mid uuordun gehêt.
That tholode al mid githuldiun   thiodo drohtin,
uualdand thesara uueroldes   endi sprak imu mid is uuordun tô
4835 frâgode ine frôkno: 'behuî kumis thu sô mid thius folcu te
    mi,
behuî lêdis thu mi sô these liudi tô   endi mi te thesare lêðan
    thiode
farcôpos mid thînu kussu   under thit kunni Iudeono,
meldos mi te thesaru menegi?'   Geng imu thô uuið thea man
    sprekan,
uuið that uuerod ôðar   endi sie mid is uuordun fragn,
4840 huene sie mid thiu gisîðiu   sôkean quâmin
sô niudlico an naht,   'so gi uuillean nôd frummien
manno huilicumu.'   Thô sprak imu eft thiu menegi
    angegin,
quâðun that im hêleand thar   an themu holme uppan
geuuîsid uuâri,   'the thit giuuer frumid
4845 Iudeo liudiun   endi ina godes sunu
selƀon hêtid.   Ina quâmun uui sôkean herod,
uueldin ina gerno bigeten: he is fan Galileo lande,
fan Nazarethburg.'   Sô im thô the neriendio Crist
sagde te sôðan,   that he it selƀo uuas,

Hêliand

4850 sô uurðun thô an forhtun folc Iudeono,
uurðun underbadode, that sie under bac fellun
alle efno sân, erðe gisôhtun,
uuiðeruuardes that uuerod: ni mahte that uuord godes,
the stemni antstandan: uuârun thoh sô strîdige man,
4850 ahliopun eft up an themu holme, hugi fastnodun,
bundun briostgithâht, gibolgane gengun
nâhor mid nîðu, anttat sie thene neriendion Crist
uuerodo biuurpun. Stôdun uuîse man,
suîðo gornundie giungaron Kristes
4860 biforan theru dereƀeon dâdi endi te iro drohtine sprâkun:
'uuâri it nu thîn uuillio', quâðun sie, 'uualdand frô mîn,
that sie ûs hêr an speres ordun spildien môstin
uuâpnun uunde, than ni uuâri ûs uuiht sô gôd,
sô that uui hêr for ûsumu drohtine dôan môstin
4865 beniðiun blêka'. Thô gibolgan uuarð
snel suerdthegan, Sîmon Petrus,
uuell imu innan hugi, that he ni mahte ênig uuord sprekan:
sô harm uuarð imu an is hertan, that man is hêrron thar
binden uuelde. Thô he gibolgan geng,
4870 suîðo thrîstmôd thegan for is thiodan standen,
hard for is hêrron: ni uuas imu is hugi tuîfli,
blôð an is breostun, ac he is bil atôh,
suerd bi sîdu, slôg imu tegegnes
an thene furiston fiund folmo crafto,
4875 that thô Malchus uuarð mâkeas eggiun,
an thea suîðaron half suerdu gimâlod:
thiu hlust uuarð imu farhauuan, he uuarð an that hôƀid
uund,

§53. The Capture of Christ

    that imu herudrôrag   hlear endi ôre
    beniuundun brast: blôd aftar sprang,
4880 uuell fan uundun.   Thô uuas an is uuangun scard
    the furisto thero fiundo.   Thô stôd that folc an rûm:
    andrêdun im thes billes biti.   Thô sprak that barn godes
    selƀo te Sîmon Petruse,   hêt that he is suerd dedi
    skarp an skêđia: 'ef ik uuiđ thesa scola uueldi', quađ he,
4885 'uuiđ theses uuerodes geuuin   uuîgsaca frummien,
    than manodi ik thene mâreon   mahtigne god,
    hêlagne fader   an himilrîkea,
    that he mi sô managan engil herod   oƀana sandi
    uuîges sô uuîsen,   sô ni mahtin iro uuâpanthreki
4890 man adôgen: iro ni stôdi gio sulic megin samad,
    folkes gifastnod,   that im iro ferh aftar thiu
    uuerđen mahti.   Ac it haƀad uualdand god,
    alomahtig fader   an ôđar gimarkot,
    that uui githoloian sculun,   sô huat sô ûs thius thioda tô
4895 bittres brengit: ni sculun ûs belgan uuiht,
    uurêđean uuiđ iro geuuinne;   huand sô hue sô uuâpno nîđ,
    grimman gêrheti   uuili gerno frummien,
    he suiltit imu eft   suerdes eggiun,
    dôit im bidrôregan: uui mid ûsun dâdiun ni sculun
4900 uuiht auuerdian.'   Geng he thô te themu uundon manne,
    legde mid listiun   lîk tesamne,
    hôƀiduundon,   that siu sân gihêlid uuarđ,
    thes billes biti ...
            Uuerod Iudeono
    gripun thô an thene godes sunu,   grimma thioda,
4915 hatandiero hôp,   huurƀun ina umbi
    môdag manno folc   — mênes ni sâhun —,
    heftun herubendium   handi tesamne,

faðmos mid fitereun. Im ni uuas sulicaro firinquâla
tharf te githolonne, thiodarƀedies,
4920 te uuinnanne sulic uuîti, ac he it thurh thit uuerod deda,
huand he liudio barn lôsien uuelda,
halon fan helliu an himilrîki,
an thene uuîdon uuelon.

§54. Peter Denies His Lord

4940   Thô sie te dale quâmun
fan themu berge te burg, thar iro biscop uuas,
iro uuîhes uuard, thar lêddun ina uulanke man,
erlos undar ederos. Thar uuas êld mikil,
fiur an frîdhoƀe themu folke tegegnes
4945 geuuarht for themu uuerode: thar gengun sie im uuermien tô,
Iudeo liudi, lêtun thene godes sunu
bîdon an bendiun. Uuas thar braht mikil,
gêlmôdigaro galm. Iohannes uuas êr
themu hêroston cûð: bethiu môste he an thene hof innan
4950 thringan mid theru thioda. Stôd allaro thegno bezto,
Petrus thar ûte: ni lêt ina the portun uuard
folgon is frôen, êr it at is friunde abad,
Iohannes at ênumu Iudeon, that man ina gangan lêt
forð an thene frîdhof. Thar quam im ên fêkni uuîf
4955 gangan tegegnes, thiu ênas Iudeon uuas,
iro theodanes thiuu, endi thô te themu thegne sprac
magad unuuânlîc: 'huat, thu mahtis man uuesan', quað siu,
'giungaro fan Galilea, thes the thar genouuer stêd
faðmun gifastnod.' Thô an forhtun uuarð
4960 Sîmon Petrus sân, slac an is môde,
quað that he thes uuîƀes uuord ni bikonsti
ni thes theodanes thegan ni uuâri:

§54. Peter Denies His Lord

mêđ is thô for theru menegi, quað that he thena man ni antkendi:
'ni sind mi thîne quidi kûðe,' quað he;   uuas imu thiu craft godes,
4965 the herdislo fan themu hertan.   Huarabondi geng
forð undar themu folke,   antat he te themu fiure quam;
giuuêt ina thô uuarmien.   Thar im ôk ên uuîf bigan
felgian firinsprâka: 'hêr mugun gi,' quað siu, 'an iuuuan fîund
  sehan:
thit is gegnungo   giungaro Kristes,
4970 is selbes gesîð.'   Thô gengun imu sân aftar thiu
nâhor nîðhuata   endi ina niudlîco
frâgodun fîundo barn,   huilikes he folkes uuâri:
'ni bist thu thesoro burgliudio,' quâðun sie;   'that mugun uui an
  thînumu gibârie gisehen,
an thînun uuordun endi an thînaru uuîson,   that thu theses uuerodes
  ni bist,
4975 ac thu bist galilêisk man.'   He ni uuelda thes thô gehan eouuiht,
ac stôd thô endi strîdda   endi starkan êð
suîðlîco gesuôr,   that he thes gesîðes ni uuâri.
Ni habda is uuordo geuuald: it scolde giuuerðen sô,
sô it the gemarcode,   the mankunnies
4980 faruuardot an thesaru uueroldi.   Thô quam imu ôk an themu uuarbe tô
thes mannes mâguuini,   the he êr mid is mâkeo giheu,
suerdu thiu scarpon,   quað that he ina sâhi thar
an themu berge uppan,   'thar uui an themu bômgardon
hêrron thînumu   hendi bundun,
4985 fastnodun is folmos.'   He thô thurh forhtan hugi
forlôgnide thes is liobes hêrron,   quað that he uueldi uuesan thes
  lîbes scolo,
ef it mahti ênig thar   irminmanno
giseggian te sôðan,   that he thes gesîðes uuâri,
folgodi theru ferdi.   Thô uuarð an thena formon sîð
4990   hanocrâd afhaben.   Thô sah the hêlago Crist,
barno that bezte,   thar he gebunden stôð,

Hêliand

    selƀo te Sîmon Petruse,   sunu drohtines
    te themu erle oƀar is ahsla.   Thô uuarð imu an innan sân,
    Sîmon Petruse   sêr an is môde,
4995 harm an is hertan   endi is hugi drôƀi,
    suîðo uuarð imu an sorgun,   that he êr selƀo gesprak:
    gihugde thero uuordo thô;   the imu êr uualdand Krist
    selƀo sagda,   that he an theru suartan naht
    êr hanocrâdi   is hêrron scoldi
5000 thrîuuo farlôgnien.   Thes thram imu an innan môd
    bittro an is breostun,   endi geng imu thô gibolgan thanen
    the man fan theru menigi   an môdkaru,
    suîðo an sorgun,   endi is selƀes uuord,
    uuamscefti uueop,   antat imu uuallan quâmun
5005 thurh thea hertcara   hête trahni,
    blôdage fan is breostun.

§55. The Fate of a Bad Thane

B e thiu nis mannes bâg   mikilun bitherƀi,
5040 hagustaldes hrôm: ef imu thiu helpe godes
    gesuîkid thurh is sundeon,   than is imu sân aftar thiu
    breosthugi blôðora,   thoh he êr bihêt spreca,
    hrômie fan is hildi   endi fan is handcrafti,
    the man fan is megine.   That uuarð thar an themu mâreon
        skîn,
5045 thegno bezton,   thô imu is thiodanes gisuêk
    hêlag helpe.   Bethiu ni scoldi hrômien man
    te suîðo fan imu selƀon,   huand imu thar suîkid oft
    uuân endi uuilleo,   ef imu uualdand god,
    hêr heƀenkunig   herte ni sterkit.

§56. Pilate

Thô uuas thero dâdio hrôm
Iudeo liudiun,   huat sie themu godes barne mahtin
sô haftemu mêst,   harmes gefrummien.
Beuurpun ina thô mid uuerodu   endi ina an is uuangon
    slôgun,
5115 an is hleor mid iro handun   — al uuas imu that te hosce
    gidôen —,
felgidun imu firinuuord   fiundo menegi,
bismersprâka.   Stôd that barn godes
fast under fiundun: uuârun imu is faðmos gebundene,
tholode mid githuldiun,   sô huat sô imu thiu thioda tô
5120 bittres brâhte: ni balg ina neouuiht
uuið thes uuerodes geuuin.   Thô nâmon ina uurêðe man
sô gibundanan,   that barn godes,
endi ina thô lêddun,   thar thero liudio uuas,
there thiade thinghûs.   Thar thegan manag
5125 huurƀun umbi iro heritogon.   Thar uuas iro hêrron bodo
fan Rûmuburg,   thes the thô thes rîkeas giuueld:
kumen uuas he fan themu kêsure,   gesendid uuas he under
    that cunni Iudeono
te rihtienne that rîki,   uuas thar râdgeƀo:
Pilatus uuas he hêten;   he uuas fan Ponteo lande
5130 cnôsles kennit.

§57. The Death of Judas

Thô an sorgun uuarð
5145 Iudases hugi, thô he ageban gisah
is drohtin te dôðe, thô bigan imu thiu dâd aftar thiu
an is hugea hreuuan, that he habde is hêrron êr
sundea lôsen gisald. Nam imu thô that silubar an hand,
thrîtig scatto, that man imu êr uuið is thiodane gaf,
5150 geng imu thô te them Iudiun endi im is grimmon dâd,
sundeon sagde, endi im that silubar bôd
gerno te agebanne: 'ik hebbiu it sô griolîco', quað he,
'mines drohtines drôru gicôpot,
sô ik uuêt that it mi ni thîhit.' Thiod Iudeono
5155 ni uueldun it thô antfâhan, ac hêtun ina forð aftar thiu
umbi sulica sundea selbon ahton,
huat he uuið is frâhon gefrumid habdi:
'thu sâhi thi selbo thes', quâðun sie; 'huat uuili thu thes nu
  sôken te ûs?
Ne uuît thu that thesumu uuerode!' Thô giuuêt imu eft
  thanan
5160 Iudas gangan te themu godes uuîhe
suîðo an sorgun endi that silubar uuarp
an then alah innan, ne gidorste it êgan leng;
fôr imu thô sô an forhtun, sô ina fiundo barn
môdage manodun: habdun thes mannes hugi
5165 gramon undergripanen, uuas imu god abolgan
that he imu selbon thô sîmon uuarhte,
hnêg thô an herusêl an hinginna,

uuarag an uurgil   endi uuîti gecôs,
hard hellie gethuing,   hêt endi thiustri,
5170 diap dôđes dalu,   huand he êr umbi is drohtin suêk.

§58. Christ before Pilate

Thô sprak eft the kêsures bodo
5210 uulank endi uurêðmôd,   thar he uuið uualdand Krist
reðiode an them rakude: 'ni bium ik theses rîkies hinan',
    quað he,
'Giudio liudio,   ni gadoling thîn,
thesaro manno mâguuini,   ac mi thi thius menigi bifalah,
agâƀun thi thîna gadulingos mi,   Iudeo liudi,
5215 haftan te handun.   Huat haƀas thu harmes giduan,
that thu sô bittro scalt   bendi tholoian,
qualm undar thînumu kunnie?'   Thô sprak imu eft Krist
    angegin,
hêlendero bezt,   thar he giheftid stôd
an themu rakude innan: 'nis mîn rîki hinan', quað he,
5220 'fan thesaru uueroldstundu.   Ef it thoh uuâri sô,
than uuârin sô starkmôde   uuiðer strîdhugi,
uuiðer grama thioda   iungaron mîne,
sô man mi ni gâƀi   Iudeo liudiun,
hettendiun an hand   an herubendiun
5225 te uuêgeanne te uundrun.   Te thiu uuarð ik an thesaru
    uueroldi giboran,
that ik geuuitscepi giu   uuâres thinges
mid mînun kumiun kûðdi.   That mugun antkennien uuel
the uueros, the sind fan uuâre kumane: the mugun mîn
    uuord farstanden,
gilôƀien mînun lêrun.'

§59. Christ before Herod

Erodes biheld thar
craftagne kuningdôm, sô ina imu the kêsur fargaf,
the rîkeo fan Rûmu, that he thar rehto gehuilic
gefrumidi undar themu folke endi friðu lêsti,
5255 dômos adêldi. He uuas ôk an themu dage selƀo
an Hierusalem mid is gumscepi,
mid is uuerode at themu uuîhe: sô uuas iro uuîse than,
that sie thar thia hêlagun tîd haldan scoldun,
pascha Iudeono. Pilatus gibôd thô,
5260 that then hafton man heliðos nâmin
sô gibundanan, that barn godes,
hêt that sie ina Erodese, erlos brâhtin
haften te handun, huand he fan is heriscepi uuas,
fan is uuerodes geuuald. Uuîgand frumidun
5265 iro hêrron uuord: hêlagne Krist
fôrdun an fiteriun for thena folctogun,
allaro barno bezt, thero the io giboren uurði
an liudio lioht; an liðubendiun geng,
antat sie ina brâhtun, thar he an is benkia sat,
5270 cuning Erodes: umbihuarf ina craft uuero,
uulanke uuîgandos: uuas im uuilleo mikil,
that sie thar selƀon Crist gisehen môstin;
uuândun that he im sum têkan thar tôgean scoldi
mâri endi mahtig, sô he managun dede
5275 thurh is godcundi Iudeo liudeon.
Frâgoda ina thuo thie folccuning firiuuitlîco
managon uuordon, uuolda is muodseƀon
forð undarfindan, huat hie te frumu mohti
mannon gimarcon. Than stuod mahtig Crist,
5280 thagoda endi tholoda: ne uuolda them thiedcuninge,

§59. Christ before Herod

Erodese ne is erlon   antsuôr geban
uuordo nigênon.   Than stuod thiu uurêða thiod,
Iudeo liudi   endi thena godes suno
uuurrun endi uuruogdun,   anthat im uuarð the uueroldcuning
5285 an is hugi huoti   endi all is heriscipi,
farmuonstun ina an iro muode: ne antkendun maht godes,
himiliscan hêrron,   ac uuas im iro hugi thiustri,
baluuues giblandan.

§60. The Second Hearing before Pilate

Thuo huarf im eft thie heritogo   an that hûs innan
5340 te thero thingstedi,   thrîstion uuordon
gruotta thena godes suno   endi frâgoda, huat hie gumono
      uuâri:
'huat bist thu manno?' quathie.   'Te huî thu mi sô thînan
      muod hilis,
dernis diopgithâht?   Uuêst thu that it all an mînon duome
      stêd
umbi thînes lîbes gilagu?   Mi thi hebbiat thesa liudi
      fargeban,
5345 uuerod Iudeono,   that ik giuualdan muot
sô thik te spildianne   an speres orde,
sô ti quellianne an crûcium,   sô quican lâtan,
sô hueðer sô mi selbon   suotera thunkit
te gifrummianne mid mînu folcu.'   Thuo sprac eft that
      friðubarn godes;
5350 'uuêst thu that te uuâron', quathie,   'that thu giuuald obar
      mik
hebbian ni mohtis,   ne uuâri that it thi hêlag god
selbo fargâbi?   Ôc hebbeat thia sundeono mêr,

Hêliand

    thia mik thi bifulhun   thuru fiondscipi,
    gisaldun an sîmon haftan.'

§61. Pilate's Offer

    Thiu uurd nâhida thuo,
5395 mâri maht godes   endi middi dag,
    that sia thia ferahquâla   frummian scoldun.
    Than lag thar ôc an bendion   an thero burg innan
    ên ruof reginscaðo,   thie habda under them rîke so filo
    morðes girâdan   endi manslahta gifrumid,
5400 uuas mâri meginthiof: ni uuas thar is gimaco huergin;
    uuas thar ôc bi sînon   sundion giheftid,
    Barrabas uuas hie hêtan;   hie after them burgion uuas
    thuru is mêndâdi   manogon gicûðid.
    Than uuas landuuîsa   liudio Iudeono,
5405 that sia iâro gihuem   an godes minnia
    an them hêlagon dage   ênna haftan mann
    abiddian scoldun,   that im iro burges uuard,
    iro folctogo   ferah fargâbi.
    Thuo bigan thie heritogo   thia hêri Iudeono,
5410 that folc frâgoian,   thar sia im fora stuodun,
    hueðeron sia thero tueio   tuomian uueldin,
    ferahes biddian: 'thia hier an feteron sind
    haft undar theson heriscipie?'   Thiu hêri Iudeono
    habdun thuo thia aramun man   alla gispanana,
5415 that sia themo landscaðen   lîf abâdin,
    githingodin them thioƀe,   thie oft an thiustria naht
    uuam giuuarahta,   endi uualdand Crist
    quelidin an crûcie.   Thuo uuarð that cûð oƀar all,

§61. *Pilate's Offer*

huô thiu thiod haƀða duomos adêlid. Thuo scoldun sia thia
    dâd frummian,
5420 hâhan that hêlaga barn. That uuarð them heritogen
sîð or te sorgon, that hie thia saca uuissa,
that sia thuru nîðscipi neriendon Crist,
hatoda thiu hêri, endi hie im hôrda te thiu
uuarahta iro uuillion: thes hie uuîti antfeng,
5425 lôn an theson liohte endi lang after,
uuôi sîðor uuann, sîðor hie thesa uuerold agaf.

§62. SATAN'S ATTEMPT AND PILATE'S WIFE

Thuo uuarð thes thie uurêðo giuuaro, uuamscaðono mêst,
Satanas selƀo, thuo thiu seola quam
Iudases an grund grimmaro helliun —
5430 thuo uuissa hie te uuâren, that that uuas uualdand Crist,
barn drohtines, that thar gibundan stuod;
uuissa thuo te uuâron, that hie uuelda thesa uuerold alla
mid is henginnia hellia githuinges,
liudi alôsian an lioht godes.
5435 That uuas Satanase sêr an muode,
tulgo harm an is hugie: uuelda is helpan thuo,
that im liudio barn lîf ne binâmin,
ne quelidin an crûcie, ac hie uuelda, that hie quic liƀdi,
te thiu that firio barn fernes ne uuurðin,
5440 sundiono sicura. Satanas giuuêt im thuo
thar thes heritogen hîuuiski uuas
an thero burg innan. Hie thero is brûdi bigann,
thera idis opanlîco unhiuri fîond
uuunder tôgian, that sia an uuordhelpon
5445 Criste uuâri, that hie muosti quic libbian,

Hêliand

    drohtin manno   — hie uuas iu than te dôðe giscerid —
    uuissa that te uuâron,   that hie im scoldi thia giuuald
        biniman,
    that hie sia oƀar thesan middilgard   sô mikila ni haƀdi,
    oƀar uuîda uuerold.   That uuîf uuarð thuo an forahton,
5450 suîðo an sorogon,   thuo iru thiu gisiuni quâmun
    thuru thes dernien dâd   an dages liohte,
    an helið helme bihelid.   Thuo siu te iru hêrren anbôd,
    that uuîf mid iro uuordon   endi im te uuâren hiet
    selƀon seggian,   huat iro thar te gisiunion quam
5455 thuru thena hêlagan mann,   endi im helpan bad,
    formon is ferhe: 'ik hebbiu hier sô filo thuru ina
    seldlîkes giseuuan,   sô ik uuêt, that thia sundiun sculun
    allaro erlo gihuem   uƀilo githîhan,
    sô im fruocno tuo   ferahes âhtið.'
5460 Thie segg uuarð thuo an sîðe,   antat hie sittian fand
    thena heritogon   an huaraƀe innan
    an them stênuuege,   thar thiu strâta uuas
    felison gifuogid.   Thar hie te is frôhon geng,
    sagda im thes uuîƀes uuord.   Thuo uuarð im uurêð hugi,
5465 them heritogen,   — huar huarƀoda an innan —,
    giblôðit briostgithâht: uuas im bêðies uuê,
    gie that sea ina sluogin   sundia lôsan,
    gie it bi them liudion thuo   forlâtan ne gidorsta
    thuru thes uuerodes uuord.   Uuarð im giuuendid thuo
5470 hugi an herten   after thero hêri Iudeono,
    te uuerkeanne iro uuillion: ne uuardoda im nieuuiht
    thia suârun sundiun,   thia hie im thar thuo selƀo gideda.
    Hiet im thuo te is handon dragan   hluttran brunnion,
    uuatar an uuêgie,   thar hie furi them uuerode sat,

§62. Satan's Attempt and Pilate's Wife

5475 thuôg ina thar for thero thioda   thegan kêsures,
      hard heritogo   endi thuo fur thero hêri sprac,
      quað that hie ina thero sundiono thar   sicoran dâdi,
      uurêðero uuerco: 'ne uuilliu ik thes uuihtes plegan',
         quathie,
      'umbi thesan hêlagan mann,   ac hleotad gi thes alles,
5480 gi uuordo gie uuerco,   thes gi im hêr te uuîtie giduan.'

§63. Pilate's Soldiers Take Jesus

Ageban uuarð thar thuo furi them Iudeon   allaro gumono
   besta
hettendion an hand,   an herubendion
narauuo ginôdid,   thar ina nîðhuata,
5490 fîond antfengun: folc ina umbihuarf,
mênscaðono megin.   Mahtig drohtin
tholoda githuldion,   sô huat sô im thiu thioda deda.
Sia hietun ina thuo fillian,   êr than sia im ferahes tuo,
aldres âhtin,   endi im undar is ôgun spiuuun,
5495 dedun im that te hoske,   that sia mid iro handon slôgun,
uueros an is uuangun   endi im is giuuâdi binânum,
rôbodun ina thia reginscaðon,   rôdes lacanes
dedun im eft ôðer an   thuru unhuldi;
hietun thuo hôbidband   hardaro thorno
5500 uuundron uuindan   endi an uualdand Crist
selbon settean,   endi gengun im thia gisîðos tuo,
queddun ina an cuninguuîsu   endi thar an knio fellun,
hnigun im mid iro hôbdu: all uuas im that te hoske giduan,
thoh hie it all githolodi,   thiodo drohtin,
5505 mahtig thuru thia minnia   manno cunnies.
Hietun sia thuo uuirkian   uuâpnes eggion

Hêliand

    heliðos mid iro handon   hardes bômes
    craftiga crûci   endi hietun sie Cristan thuo,
    sâlig barn godes   selƀon fuorian,
5510 dragan hietun sie ûsan drohtin,   thar hie bedrôragad scolda
    sueltan sundiono lôs.

§64. The Crucifixion

Thuo sia thar an griete   galgon rihtun,
    an them felde uppan   folc Iudeono,
    bôm an berege,   endi thar an that barn godes
5535 quelidun an crûcie: slôgun cald îsarn,
    niuua naglos   nîðon scarpa
    hardo mid hamuron   thuru is hendi endi thuru is fuoti,
    bittra bendi: is blôd ran an erða,
    drôr fan ûsan drohtine.   Hie ni uuelda thoh thia dâd uurecan
5540 grimma an them Iudeon,   ac hie thes god fader
    mahtigna bad,   that hie ni uuâri them manno folke,
    them uuerode thiu uureðra: 'huand sia ni uuitun, huat sia
        duot', quathie.
    Thuo thia uuîgandos   giuuâdi Cristes,
    drohtines dêldun, dereƀia man,   ...
5545 thes rîken girôbi.   Thia rincos ni mahtun
    umbi thena selƀon ...   samuuurdi gesprecan,
    êr sia an iro huaraƀe   hlôtos uuurpun,
    huilic iro scoldi hebbian   thia hêlagun pêda,
    allaro giuuâdio uunsamost.   Thes uuerodes hirdi
5550 hiet thuo, the heritogo,   oƀar them hôƀde selƀes
    Cristes an crûce scrîƀan,   that that uuâri cuning Iudeono,
    Iesus fan Nazarethburh,   thie thar neglid stuod
    an niuuon galgon   thuru nîðscipi,

§64. The Crucifixion

    an bômin treo.   Thuo bâdun thia liudi
5555 that uuord uuendian,   quâðun that hie im sô an is uuilleon
        sprâki,
    selbo sagdi,   that hie habdi thes gisîðes giuuald,
    cuning uuâri obar Iudeon.   Thuo sprac eft thie kêsures
        bodo,
    hard heritogo: 'it ist iu sô obar is hôbde giscriban,
    uuîslîco giuuritan,   sô ik it nu uuendian ni mag.
5560 Dâdun thuo thar te uuîtie   uuerod Iudeono
    tuêna fartalda man   an tuâ halba
    Cristes an crûci: lietun sia qualm tholon
    an them uuaragtreuue   uuerco te lône,
    lêðaro dâdio.   Thia liudi sprâcun
5565 hoscuuord manag   hêlagon Criste,
    grôttun ina mid gelpu: sâuuun allaro gumono then beston
    quelan an themo crûcie: 'ef thu sîs cuning obar all' quâðun sia,
    'suno drohtines,   sô thu habis selbo gisprocan,
    neri thik fan thero nôdi   endi nîðes atuomi,
5570 gang thi hêl herod;   than uuelliat an thik helið o barn,
    thesa liudi gilôbian.'   Sum imo ôk lastar sprac
    suîðo gêlhert Iudeo,   thar hie fur them galgon stuod:
    'uuah uuarð thesaro uueroldi', quathie,   'ef thu iro scoldis
        giuuald
    Thu sagdas that thu mahtis an ênon dage   all teuuerpan
5575 that hôha hus   hebancuninges,
    stênuuerco mêst   endi eft standan giduon
    an thriddion dage,   sô is elcor ni thorfti bithîhan mann
    theses folkes furðor.   Sînu huô thu nu gifastnod stês,
    suîðo gisêrid: ni maht thi selbon uuiht
5580 balouues gibuotian.'   Thuo thar ôc an them bendiun sprac

Hêliand

    thero theoƀo ôðer,   all sô hie thia thioda gihôrda,
    uurêðon uuordon   — ne uuas is uuillio guod,
    thes thegnes githáht —:   'ef thu sîs thiodcuning', quathie,
    'Crist, godes suno,   gang thi thann fan them crûce niðer,
5585 slôpi thi fan them sîmon   endi ûs samad allon
    hilp endi hêli. Ef thu sîs heƀancuning,
    uualdand thesaro uueroldes,   giduo it then an thînon uuercon scîn,
    mâri thik fur thesaro menigi.'   Thuo sprac thero manno ôder
    an thero henginna,   thar hie giheftid stuod,
5590 uuan uuunderquâla: 'bihuî uuilt thu sulic uuord sprecan,
    gruotis ina mid gelpu?   stês thi hier an galgen haft,
    gibrôcan an bôme.

§65. The Death of Jesus

Thuo uuarð thar an middian dag   mahti têcan
uuundarlîc giuuaraht   oƀar thesan uuerold allan,
thuo man thena godes suno   an thena galgon huof,
Crist an that crûci: thuo uuarð it cûð oƀar all,
5625 huô thiu sunna uuarð gisuorkan: ni mahta suigli lioht
scôni giscînan,   ac sia scado farfeng,
thimm endi thiustri   endi sô githrusmod neƀal.
Uuarð allaro dago druoƀost,   duncar suîðo
oƀar thesan uuîdun uueruld,   sô lango sô uualdand Crist
5630 qual an themo crûcie,   cuningo rîkost,
ant nuon dages.   Thuo thie neƀal tiscrêd,
that gisuerc uuarð thuo tesuungan,   bigan sunnun lioht
hêðron an himile.   Thuo hreop upp te gode

§65. The Death of Jesus

    allaro cuningo craftigost,   thuo hie an themu crûcie stuod
5635 faðmon gifastnot: 'fader alomahtig', quathie,
    'te huî thu mik sô farlieti,   lieƀo drohtin,
    hêlag heƀancuning,   endi thîna helpa dedos,
    fullisti sô ferr?   Ik standu under theson fiondon hier
    uundron giuuêgid.'   Uuerod Iudeono
5640 hlôgun is im thuo te hosce: gihôrdun then hêlagun Crist,
    drohtin furi them dôđe   drincan biddian,
    quað that ina thurstidi.   Thiu thioda ne latta,
    uuerêða uuiðarsacon: uuas im uuilleo mikil,
    huat sia im bittres tuo   bringan mahtin.
5645 Habdun im unsuôti   ecid endi galla
    gimengid thia mênhuaton;   stuod ênn mann garo,
    suîðo sculdig scaðo,   thena habdun sia giscerid te thiu,
    farspanan mid sprâcon,   that hie sia an êna spunsia nam,
    lîðo thes lêðosten,   druog it an ênon langa scafte,
5650 gibundan an ênon bôme   endi deda it them barne godes,
    mahtigon te mûðe.   Hie ankenda iro mirkiun dâdi,
    gifuolda iro fêgnes: furðor ni uuelda
    is sô bittres anbîtan,   ac hreop that barn godes
    hlûdo te them himiliscon fader: 'ik an thina hendi befilhu', quathie,
5655 'mînon gêst an godes uuillion;   hie ist nu garo te thiu,
    fûs te faranne.'   Firio drohtin
    gihnêgida thuo is hôƀid,   hêlagon âðom
    liet fan themo lîkhamen.   Sô thuo thie landes uuard
    sualt an them sîmon,   sô uuarð sân after thiu
5660 uundartêcan giuuaraht,   that thar uualdandes dôđ
    unqueðandes sô filo   antkennian scolda,
    gifuolian is êndagon: erða biƀoda,

Hêliand

       hrisidun thia hôhun bergos,   harda stênos cluƀun,
       felisos after them felde,   endi that fêha lacan tebrast
5665 an middien an tuê,   that êr managan dag
       an themo uuîhe innan   uuundron gistriunid
       hêl hangoda   — ni muostun heliðo barn,
       thia liudi scauuon,   huat under themo lacane uuas
       hêlages behangan: thuo mohtun an that horð sehan
5670 Iudio liudi —   graƀu uuurðun giopanod
       dôdero manno,   endi sia thuru drohtines craft
       an iro lîchamon   libbiandi astuodun
       upp fan erðu   endi uuurðun giôgida thar
       mannon te mârðu.   That uuas sô mahtig thing,
5675 that thar Cristes dôð   antkennian scoldun,
       so filo thes gifuolian,   thie gio mid firihon ne sprac
       uuord an thesaro uueroldi.   Uuerod Iudeono
       sâuuun seldlîc thing,   ac uuas im iro slîði hugi
       sô farhardod an iro herten,   that thar io sô hêlag ni uuarð
5680 têcan gitôgid,   that sia trûodin thiu bat
       an thia Cristes craft,   that hie cuning oƀar all,
       thes uuerodes uuâri.   Suma sia thar mid iro uuordon
            gisprâcun,
       thia thes hrêuues thar   huodian scoldun,
       that that uuâri te uuâren   uualdandes suno,
5685 godes gegnungo,   that thar an them galgon sualt,
       barno that besta.   Slôgun an iro briost filo
       uuôpiandero uuîƀo: uuas im thiu uuunderquâla
       harm an iro herten   endi iro hêrren dôð
       suîðo an sorogon.   Than uuas sido Iudeono,
5690 that sia thia haftun thuru thena hêlagon dag   hangon ni
            lietin

§65. The Death of Jesus

     lengerun huîla,   than im that lîf scriði,
     thiu seola besunki: slîðmuoda mann
     gengun im mid nîðscipiu nâhor,   thar sô beneglida stuodun
     theoƀos tuêna,   tholodun bêðia
5695 quâla bi Criste: uuârun im quica noh than,
     untthat sia thia grimmun   Iudeo liudi
     bênon bebrâcon,   that sia bêðia samad
     lîf farlietun,   suohtun im lioht ôðer.
     Sia ni thorftun drohtin Crist   dôðes bêdian
5700 furðor mid ênigon firinon: fundun ina gifaranan thuo iu:
     is seola uuas gisendid   an suoðan uueg,
     an langsam lioht,   is lîði cuolodun,
     that fera uuas af them flêske.   Thuo geng im ên thero
          fîondo tuo
     an nîðhugi,   druog negilid sper
5705 hard an is handon,   mid heruthrummeon stac,
     liet uuâpnes ord   uuundun snîðan,
     that an selƀes uuarð   sîdu Cristes
     antlocan is lîchamo.   Thia liudi gisâuun,
     that thanan bluod endi uuater   bêðiu sprungun,
5710 uuellun fan thero uuundun,   all sô is uuillio geng
     endi hie habda gimarcod êr   manno cunnie,
     firiho barnon te frumu: thuo uuas it all gifullid sô.

§66. The Burial

Sô thuo gisêgid uuarð   seðle nâhor
     hêdra sunna   mid heƀantunglon
5715 an them druoƀen dage,   thuo geng im ûses drohtines thegan
     — uuas im glau gumo,   iungro Cristes

Hêliand

    managa huîla, sô it thar manno filo
    ne uuissa te uuâron, huand hie it mid is uuordun hal
    Iudeono gumscipie: Ioseph uuas hie hêtan,
5720 darnungo uuas hie ûses drohtines iungro: hie ni uuelda
        thero farduanun thiod
    folgon te ênigon firinuuercon, ac hie bêd im under them
        folke Iudeono,
    hêlag himilo rîkies — hie geng im thuo uuið thena heri-
        togon mahlian,
    thingon uuið thena thegan kêsures, thigida ina gerno,
    that hie muosti alôsian thena lîkhamon
5725 Cristes fan themo crûcie, thie thar giquelmid stuod
    thes guoden fan them galgen endi an graf leggian,
    foldu bifelahan. Im ni uuelda thie folctogo thuo
    uuernian thes uuillien, ac im giuuald fargaf,
    that hie sô muosti gifrummian. Hie giuuêt im thuo forð
        thanan
5730 gangan te them galgon, thar hie uuissa that godes barn,
    hrêo hangondi hêrren sînes,
    nam ina thuo an thero niuuun ruodun endi ina fan naglon
        atuomda,
    antfeng ina mid is faðmon, sô man is frôhon scal,
    lioƀes lîchamon, endi ina an lîne biuuand,
5735 druog ina diurlîco — sô uuas thie drohtin uuerð —,
    thar sia thia stedi haƀdun an ênon stêne innan
    handon gihauuuan, thar gio heliðo barn
    gumon ne bigruoƀon. Thar sia that godes barn
    te iro landuuîsu, lîco hêlgost
5740 foldu bifulhun endi mid ênu felisu belucun
    allaro graƀo guodlîcost

§67. The Resurrection

Thuo uuurðun thar giscerida   fan thero scolu Iudeono
uueros te thero uuahtu: giuuitun im mid iro giuuâpnion
     tharod
te them graƀe gangan,   thar sia scoldun thes godes barnes
hrêuues huodian.   Uuarð thie hêlago dag
5765 Iudeono fargangan.   Sia oƀar themo graƀe sâtun,
uueros an thero uuahtun   uuânamon nahton,
bidun undar iro bordon,   huan êr thie berehto dag
oƀar middilgard   mannon quâmi,
liudon te liohte.   Thuo ni uuas lang te thiu,
5770 that thar uuarð the gêst cuman   be godes crafte,
hâlag âðom   undar thena hardon stên
an thena lîchamon.   Lioht uuas thuo giopanod
firio barnon te frumu: uuas fercal manag
antheftid fan helldoron   endi te himile uueg
5775 giuuaraht fan thesaro uueroldi.   Uuânom upp astuod
friðubarn godes,   fuor im thar hie uuelda,
sô thia uuardos thes   uuiht ni afsuoƀun,
derƀia liudi,   huan hie fan them dôðe astuod,
arês fan thero rastun.   Rincos sâtun
5780 umbi that graf ûtan,   Iudeo liudi,
scola mid iro scildion.   Scrêd forðuuardes
suigli sunnon lioht.   Sîðodun idisi
te them graƀe gangan,   gumcunnies uuîf,
Mariun munilîca: habdun mêðmo filo
5785 gisald uuiðer salƀum,   siluƀres endi goldes,
uuerðes uuiðer uuurtion,   sô sia mahtun auuinnan mêst,
that sia thena lîchamon   lioƀes hêrren,

Hêliand

     suno drohtines,   salƀon muostin,
     uuundun uuritanan.   Thiu uuîf soragodun
5790 an iro seƀon suîðo,   endi suma sprâcun,
     huie im thena grôtan stên   fan themo graƀe scoldi
     gihuereƀian an halƀa,   the sia oƀar that hrêo sâuuun
     thia liudi leggian,   thuo sia thena lîchamon thar
     befulhun an themo felise.   Sô thiu frî haƀdun
5795 gegangen te them gardon,   that sia te them graƀe mahtun
     gisehan selƀon,   thuo thar suôgan quam
     engil thes alouualdon   oƀana fan radure,
     faran an feðerhamon,   that all thiu folda an scian,
     thiu erða dunida   endi thia erlos uuurðun
5800 an uuêkan hugie,   uuardos Iuðeono,
     bifellun bi them forahton: ne uuândun ira fera êgan,
     lîf lengerun huîl.   Lâgun tha uuardos,
     thia gisîðos sâmquica: sân upp ahlêd
     thie grôto stên fan them graƀe,   sô ina thie godes engil
5805 gihueriƀida an halƀa,   endi im uppan them hlêuue gisat
     diurlîc drohtines bodo.   Hie uuas an is dâdion gelîc,
     an is ansiunion,   sô huem sô ina muosta undar is ôgon
         scauuon
     sô bereht endi sô blîði   all sô blicsmun lioht;
     uuas im is giuuâdi   uuintarcaldon
5810 snêuue gilîcost.

Commentary to the Readings

Comments on individual sections of readings from the *Hêliand* are marked with §. The intention of the comments is not to be exhaustive but rather to indicate points of cultural and historical interest.[1] Translations of German citations have been provided (except for those in a few footnotes). A bibliography is appended. Biblical quotes are from *The New English Bible with the Apocrypha* (Oxford University Press, Cambridge University Press: 1970).[2]

Abbreviations used below are: **Gmc**. – Germanic; **IE** – Indo-European; **l**. – line(s); **MDu** – Middle Dutch; **MHG** – Middle High German; **OE** – Old English; **OI** – Old Icelandic; **OIr** – Old Irish; **OHG** – Old High German; **ON** – Old Norse; **OS** – Old Saxon; **PGmc**. – Primitive Germanic.

---

[1] My thanks go to Klaus Gantert and to G. Ronald Murphy for their comments on my comments and to my anonymous critics in classes at Harvard University and Indiana University. Very special thanks go to members of classes at the University of Massachusetts, particularly to Antonio Ornelas, for many corrections and improvements..

[2] See Behagel *Heliand und Genesis* (Altdeutsche Textbibliothek 4) for correspondences between the *Hêliand* and the OHG *Tatian*.

Hêliand

§1. Introduction

Lines 1 to 85a

The *Hêliand* opens not with an epic admonition to harken to the words of an omniscient speaker in the first person but rather obliquely assigns the telling to the Four who were chosen where many had failed. (Later an anonymous narrator breaks in; see the comment to §43 for epic admonition. An attempt has been made to identify the narrator and putative author of the *Hêliand*, but with no convincing result.[3]) The Latin *Praefatio B* that most likely once was appended to the *Hêliand*[4] alludes to Caedmon, who wrote the first Christian poem, and the first complete poem to survive in OE. As in the story of Caedmon's divine inspiration composed by the English monk Bede (673-735) but written in Latin, the Four Evangelists 'had strength from God, help from heaven, the Holy Spirit, power from Christ' (*thia habdon maht godes, / helpa fan himila, hêlagna gêst, / craft fan Criste*) — a string of phrases well intended to link ancient associations and emotional responses of old words to new concepts. Here we are told that many made the effort to 'recount the mystery' (*reckean that girûni*) that the mighty Christ worked wonders among men with works and words. The word *reckean* in the sense 'recount' is in parallel with other allusions in older literature to the ability of the wise to retell the story of creation (cf. *Beowulf* 90-91: *Sægde se þe cuþe / frumsceaft fira feorran reccan* 'said he, who was able to recount the origin of men'). The unusual, then modern, aspect is the reference to the evangelists (the 'wiser' ones) who, instead of composing orally, wanted to write 'brightly in book' to praise the teachings of Christ that they may 'raise with holy voice the good message' (*that sea scoldin ahebbean hêlagaro stemnun / godspell that guoda*). Here we have the *Legitimation der Buchdichtung* equating the written word with oral transmission of sacred knowledge.

The words that the Four Evangelists use to tell of their dear Lord (*drohtin diurie*) liken Him to the esteemed leader of faithful

---

[3] See von Weringha (1965), Veenbaas (1992), Klein (1992), and Hofstra (1992).
[4] See The Dating of the *Hêliand* and the *Praefatio* in THE WORK for more on the introduction.

§. 1

followers, an image that recurs throughout the *Hêliand*.⁵ He can stand against strife (*strîd uuiðerstande*), for He has a strong disposition (*huand hie habda starkan hugi*) and is an almighty Leader in battle (*aðalordfrumo alomahtig*). This last phrase constitutes one of the shortest alliterating lines in the whole of the *Hêliand*, which serves to highlight its importance.

We thus find old words that had been used in ancient Germanic and pre-Christian Saxon culture now assigned new meanings for the purposes of the Christian mission.⁶ Some of these words were perhaps used only in poetry to lead the audience into familiar mythic or heroic realms of epic story-telling. If Christ is *drohtin*, what does that imply? The term *drohtin* originated in the Migration Period (ca. 3rd to 7Th centuries A.D.) and designated the head of a troop known by the Latin word *comitatus*. In a discussion of the figure of Satan in the West Saxon *Genesis B* Doane (1991) characterizes him as an early *drohtin*:

> In the comitatus a petty lord ... operates with a band of freely sworn but loosely committed followers for his own advantage in a situation of universal competition and equality among war bands. In this older system, from the point of view of the [*drohtin*], there are no upward-looking hierarchies, only downward-linking bonds depending on personal and shifting loyalties. Instead of one great complex system of interlocking and irrevocable responsibilities into which every member of society fits in an ascending pyramidical structure culminating in a central monarch, a concept which it was the concern of Charlemagne and his successors to instill and promote, Satan retrogressively conceives of a multitude of petty hierarchies, each self-sufficient, self-justifying, and opportunistic. In the

---

⁵ Cf. the theological interpretation of Saint Boniface: "In den karolingischen Musterkatechesen, die als Predigten des heiligen Bonifatius überliefert sind (PL 89,842 bis 872), ist es einfach Gott, der aus der Jungfrau geboren wurde und für uns in den althochdeutschen Dichtungen, vor allem im Heliand, begegnet, wo auch das germanische Heldenideal das Bild mitbestimmt. Christ ist der Gott-König, dem man die Gefolgschaft leistet, die man ihm in der Taufe zugeschworen hat" [In the Carolingian model catechisms, which have been preserved as sermons of Saint Boniface (PL 89,842 to 872), it is only God Who was born of the virgin and Whom we meet in the OHG poetical monuments, (but) above all in the Heliand, where the Germanic heroic ideal plays a part in defining the image. Christ is the God-King to Whom one owes obedience which one promises to Him in baptism] (Jedin, 1965: 360-361).

⁶ The purposes of the Christian mission allowed for use of the vernacular. Cf. the *Monsee Fragments* on OHG territory.

ideology of the Carolingians, such a Tacitean model excludes its adherents from ideal polity and real power. Satan is, in fact, a picture of just such a petty lord in rebellion; in particular he would have fit among the contemporary Saxons, who traditionally recognized no king and whose aristocrats with their pretensions of independence perennially plagued the Carolingians (p. 123).

For a Christian theology in which the Trinity is a central concept, Christ as *drohtin* is conceptually also the head of a "downward-linking" hierarchy. The matter of "freely sworn but loosely committed followers" and their place in a Carolingian polity, not to speak of negative associations inherent in the term *drohtin*, would clearly need – and in the *Hêliand* received – correction through the message of the gospel. Worldly terms received an added dimension when redefined and semantically adjusted to the new way of thinking that includes the divine that stands beyond this world.[7]

Among these older words is also certainly *aðalordfrumo*, which by the time of composition of the *Hêliand* may through semantic shift have faded in its literal meaning as an ancient military term. Historically, the word *aðal* meant, among other things, 'main; chief, head', while the latter part literally meant '[spear]point hurler' or the like, once probably descriptive of the position of the *drohtin* at the head of his troops. (One can't help feeling that it would be of critical importance to know what the OS understanding of this word in the 9th century was, but that is alas beyond our ken.) The culturally-embedded term *aðalordfrumo* was appropriated by the author of the *Hêliand* in order to endorse and lend an awe-inspiring aura to the Christian Creator, whose words had the power to defeat ('fell') works of evil (*firinuuerc fellie*) – as Boniface famously felled the sacred oak near Geismar in 724 and Charlemagne the Saxon world-pillar *Irmensûl* in 772 – or subdue the enmity of foes (*eftho fiundo nîð*), but here He is also called 'generous and good' (*mildean endi guodan*). The Four were to 'write with their fingers, set down, and sing, and proclaim' (l. 32-33) that which Murphy (1992) translates from l. 38 to 42a as "all the things which the Ruler spoke from the beginning, when He, by His own power, first made the world and formed the whole universe with one word. The heavens and the earth and all that is contained within them, both inorganic and organic,

---

[7]See Cathey (1999) '*Interpretatio Christiana Saxonica*: redefinition for re-education.'

everything, was firmly held in place by the Divine words" (p. 4). The notion that one powerful Ruler, designated in native terms as *aðalordfrumo*, had created the world and what was beyond was new to the Saxons, whose gods were subject to the final destruction, a *ragnarǫk*, of this world. The new feature is that God stands outside the universe and is not subject to it.

Schützeichel glosses the OHG reflex *ortfrumo* as 'Urheber, Schöpfer'. Ilkow points out that the weak masculine form *ordfruma* in OE glossed Latin *origo* and was employed to mean 'origin' in Aelfric, and he refers to the etymology of *frumo* (cognate with Latin *primus*), asserting that here it could have meant something like 'Urheber des Anfangs,' a Prime Mover.

> Die in der ae. Dichtung häufigen Fürstenkenningar mit dem Grundwort *-fruma* ... lassen schließen, daß auch das Komp. ae. *ord-fruma*, as. *ord-frumo*, ahd. *ort-frumo* ursprünglich ein Kenning der Dichtersprache war. Dafür spricht auch die Anwendung von ae. *Ord-fruma* ... auf *Ecgþēow* in Beow. 263: *wæs mīn fæder gecȳþed / æþele ordfruma Ecgþēow hāten*. Wie die letztgenannte Stelle zeigt, scheint die syntaktische Phrase, aus der sich das as. Komp. *aðal-ordfrumo* entwickelt hat, dem Formelschatz der gemeinwestgerm. Dichtersprache angehört zu haben[8] (p. 37).

The adjective *alomahtig* in the half-line *aðalordfrumo alomahtig is*, on the other hand, not necessarily an ancient religious or military term but rather most likely a loan translation from Latin *omnipotens*. Ilkow states,

> "Das Adjektiv *alo-mahtig* wird in Hel. und Gen. als Epitheton in Verbindung mit *god* und *fader* ... gebraucht, die substantivierte Form wird nur auf Christus bezogen. Es deckt sich bedeutungsmäßig vollkommen mit dem schon in der biblischen Schrift häufig gebrauchten *omnipotens*, das u.a. im ersten Artikel des apostolischen Glaubensbekenntnisses enthalten ist:

---

[8] The frequent kennings for kings in OE poetry with the base in *-fruma* ... allow the conclusion that the compound noun OE *ord-fruma* ... was originally a kenning used in poetry. The use of OE *ord-fruma* for *Ecgþēow* in Beow. 263: *wæs mīn fæder gecȳþed / æþele ordfruma Ecgþēow hāten* also speaks for this view. As this latter example shows, the syntactical phrase, out of which the OS compound *aðal-ordfrumo* developed, seems to have belonged among the formulae of common West Germanic poetry.

Hêliand

> *Credo in Deum, patrem omnipotentem*"[9] (p. 46).

(Note, however, that in the OI *Landnámabók* the cognate of *alo-mahtig* is used when the god Thor is called *hinn almátki áss* 'the almighty god.')

Another Christian loan translation but from Greek via Latin and with subsequent folk-etymological change is *godspell* in l. 25. Ilkow summarizes,

> Eine direkte Lehnübersetzung aus gr. εὐαγγέλιον (daraus lat. *evangelium*) 'die gute Botschaft' ist ae. *gŏd-spell*. Wäre diese Entlehnung im Ahd. vor sich gegangen, dann müßte das ahd. Komp. **guot-spell* lauten. Im Ae. dagegen konnte das lange ō der Stammsilbe lautgesetzlich verkürzt werden; dadurch fiel der erste Teil in der Lautung mit *god* 'Gott' zusammen und das Komp. wurde volksetymologisch in 'Gottes Botschaft' umgedeutet[10] (p. 150).

The ubiquitous adjective *hêlag*, as for example in l. 7 (*hêlag uuord godes*), whose modern English reflex is 'holy', was already an ancient Germanic word with special sanctified meaning. Jente comments,

> Germ. Grdf. **hailaga* 'heilig' eigentlich 'glückbringend'. Stammverwandt sind germ. **haili–z* n. 'gute Vorbedeutung, Glück' (vgl. anord. *heill*, ags. *hǣl* 'gute Vorbedeutung, Glück', as. *hêl*, ahd., mhd. *heil* 'Glück, Heil') und germ. **haila-* adj. 'heil, gesund' .... Welchem von diesen beiden Stämmen germ. **hailaga-* näher steht, ist nicht festzustellen .... In allen germ. Sprachen tritt das Wort frühzeitig im christlichen Sinne 'sacer, sanctus' auf; im Anord. konnte aber *heilagr* auch auf die heidnischen Götter bezogen werden. Eine Bedeutung 'geweiht' schon in heidnischer Zeit läßt sich nicht nur auf Grund der lat. Übersetzung 'sacer' vermuten, sondern sie wird auch durch

---

[9] The adjective *alo-mahtig* is used in the Hêliand and Genesis as an epithet in connection with *god* and *fader*. The nominal form is used only for Christ. In meaning it coincides completely with the word *omnipotens* frequently used in the Bible, and appears in the first article of the Apostolic Creed: *Credo in Deum, patrem omnipotentem.*

[10] OE *gŏd-spell* is a direct loan translation from Greek εὐαγγέλιον (thence Latin *evangelium*) 'good news.' If this loan had gone through OHG, the compound would have been **guot-spell*. In OE, on the other hand, the long ō of the root syllable would have been shortened; because of this the first part coincided in pronunciation with *god* 'God' and the compound was understood as 'God's news.'

§. 1

den gewiß sehr alten Namen *hāligmōnað* für einen Monat, in dem den Göttern Opfer gebracht wurden, wahrscheinlich gemacht.[11] (p. 37).

Polomé says of *hêlag*,

> Germanic *hailagaz* involves the concepts of 'salvation,' health, physical and bodily wholeness – i.e. it is oriented towards man and focuses on human dependence on divine care. If Germanic religion is a belief in divine powers ruling the cosmos they organized and implied the idea that man's very existence is in their hands, the gods are undoubtedly entitled to worship and sacrifice, but the distance between man and god is definitely less than in the classical world. ... [T]he pre–Christian concept of **hailag-* stresses this 'life-insuring' power of Germanic religion (p. 88).

The "'life-insuring' power of Germanic religion" was guaranteed to the king by blood-right (*Blutheiligtum*) of accession transferred to a Christian basis. Miller writes:

> The right of the Carolingians to the kingship was ... a blood-right based on their adoption by St. Peter and their role as guarantors of victory and divine favor, a role proper to the members of the new dynasty owing both to their personal qualities and to their relationship to the supernatural through their patron, St. Peter (p. 139).

The word *hêlag* for 'holy' was a usage from the northern, Irish and Anglo-Saxon, mission. Because of the heathen connotations which the word must at least originally have conveyed, the reflexes of **hailagaz* were avoided in a mission posited by some to have been led by Goths to southern Germany, where reflexes of *wîh* were used, e.g. OS *the hêlago gêst* vs. OHG *der wîho âtum* for *spiritus sanctus* 'the Holy Spirit.' See Dick (p. 468 ff.) for an investigation into historical connections between *drohtin*, *hêlag*, and *hêliand*.

The *Hêliand* instructs its audience that the power of Christ, the

---

[11] The Germanic form **hailaga* 'holy' actually meant 'luck-bringing.' Related to it are Gmc. **haili–z* neut. 'good omen, luck' (cf. ON *heill*, OE *hl* 'good omen, luck', OS *hêl*, OHG, MHG *heil* 'luck, prosperity') and Gmc. **haila-* adj. 'sound, healthy' ... It cannot be determined which of these two stems was closer related to Gmc. **hailaga–*. The word appears very early in all Germanic languages in the sense of 'sacer, sanctus'; ON *heilagr* could also refer to heathen gods. The meaning 'hallowed' can be posited for the heathen period not only on the basis of the Latin translation 'sacer,' but it is also likely because of the very old name *hāligmōnað* for a month in which sacrifices were made to the gods.

Hêliand

best of Healers (*hêlandero bestan*), has come to this world for the help of many (*an thesan middilgard managon te helpun*) against the 'enmity of fiends' (*uuið fiundo nîð*) and the 'bewitching, paralyzing enchantment of hidden ones' (*uuið dernero duualm*). See also the commentary to §13 regarding the 'hidden ones.'

In order to tell His story the author of the *Hêliand* needed to impart biblical history in terms the Saxons could understand, so they are told that the 'Chieftain God' (*drohtin god*) had given the lands of the Jews, the greatest of realms, to the 'people of Romans', and had strengthened the hearts of their army (*habda them heriscipie herta gisterkid*) so that Herod could be installed as ruler. The 'helmeted troops (*helmgitrôsteo*) from Rome's stronghold had subdued every people and won the realm' (l. 56 to 59a). Among the richly descriptive and intimidating words of war is *hildiscalc* (l. 68), which is usually glossed as 'Kriegsknecht' or 'Krieger'. More likely this term denotes a thrall compelled to serve as a warrior. Ilkow points out (p. 208) that this is not merely a poetic word but part of the general vocabulary, as it has an OHG counterpart in *hiltiscalh* "mit der Bedeutung 'leibeigener Knecht'."[12] The situation of the listeners was not entirely unlike that of the Jews in that the military means employed by Charlemagne and the *Capitulatio de partibus Saxoniae* of 797 (see THE EXTERNAL HISTORY) served to subjugate the Saxons.

Herod was chosen as king in Jerusalem over that people, dispatched by the caesar in Rome. Here he is called *kuning* and *thiodan* (l. 62 and 63), and it is said that he was 'chosen as king.' Ilkow elucidates,

> Wie wir aus der Vita des angelsächsischen Missionars Lebuin erfahren, hatten sich bei den Sachsen die republikanische Verfassung noch im 8. Jh. erhalten, höchste entscheidende Landesgewalt war die Markloer Stammesversammlung; einen König kannten sie nicht. Vor Einführung des Königtums war also bei den germanischen Stämmen die Landesgemeinde Träger der Staatsgewalt. Aber diese konnte einen Beamten an die Spitze des Stammes stellen und ihm den Befehl im Kriege ... übertragen. ... Eine rein germanische Bezeichnung für 'König' ist got. *þiudans* zu *þiuda* 'Volk', ebenso ae. *þēoden*, as. *thiodan*[13] (p. 246-247).

---

[12] with the meaning 'thrall'

[13] As we know from the Vita of the OE missionary Lebuin, the republican form of government lasted into the 8th century. The highest authority was the assembly at Marklo; they had no king. Before the introduction of kingship the local council

§. 1

Generally *kuning* is used in the *Hêliand* to indicate 'leader, chieftain' as, for example, in *heancuning* in l. 91, but note that James and John chose Christ as king in the Germanic way in l. 1185–1186 (cf. commentary to §14).

Herod was not of that people (*Hie ni uuas thoh mid sibbeon bilang / aƀaron Israheles, eðiligiburdi, / cuman fon iro cnuosle*). The phrase *fan iro cnuosle* means 'from their family' more closely than 'from their people'. (In l. 297 Mary is called *aðalcnôsles uuîf* 'a woman of noble kin', as she is from the line of David; cf. the commentary to §4.)

The *Hêliand* uses the word *heritogon* to state that dukes were put into place over each district. Ilkow has a long article on this word in which he says, *inter alia*,

> Der Ausdruck *Herzog* wird zufrühst auf altfränkischem Boden historisch greifbar und erscheint hier an eine militärisch-staatspolitische Einrichtung des Merowinger-reiches geknüpft. ... Im Hel. bezieht sich *heri-togo* zunächst in der Mehrzahl auf Statthalter römischer Provinzen, die aber militärisches Oberhaupt in ihrem Regierungsbereich waren[14] (p. 202).

The word *heritogo* used in the *Hêliand* to designate the governors of Roman provinces was coined to denote leaders set in place over the Saxons by Charlemagne. It is perhaps worth pondering what impact these words of war and occupation in the *Hêliand* may have had on the Saxons, who had recently been subdued by the Franks.

---

held the highest authority. But this council could place a leader at the head of the state and give him command in the case of war. A purely Germanic designation for 'king' is Gothic *þiudans* from *þiuda* 'folk' and similarly OE *þēoden*, as. *thiodan*.

[14] The word *Herzog* is attested earliest on Old Franconian territory and appears here in connection with a military-political institution of the Merovingian realm. ... In the Hêliand *heri-togo* refers generally to officials of the Roman provinces, who were the military commanders in their areas of government.

Hêliand

§2. Elizabeth's Child

Lines 119b to 158
(Luke 1:5-25)

Heralding the birth of John the Baptist the Angel Gabriel introduces himself as God's attendant, standing ever present before Him (*Ik ... gio for goda standu, anduuard for them alouualdon*). Ilkow comments on *alouualdo*, which he views as another pre-Christian term with a new usage,

> Wie uns scheint, [ist] das Nomen agentis *alo-waldo* ... eine urgerm. Fürstenbezeichnung ...[15] (p. 48).

The reason for this conclusion is that elsewhere in early Gmc. there are near cognates, formed as present participles instead of as *n*-stem *nomina agentis*, to *alouualdo* in Gothic (*allwaldands*), OI (*allsvaldandi*), OE (*ealwealdend*), and OHG (*alawaltenti*).

The Angel Gabriel is dispatched to make known to the couple Zacharias, a faithful and devout priest, and Elizabeth, that a child will be born to her in spite of her age (*fon thîneru alderu idis*) and that he will have the name John (l. 133–135a). This child will be wise in words (*uuordun spâhi*), a Germanic virtue and compliment of highest praise (cf. l. 237–238, 563, 572, 1150, 1381, 2414, and elsewhere with other locutions, e.g. 567 *gôd-sprâkea gumon*). The power of God has decreed that never in his life shall John taste wine (*uuîn*) nor fruit wine (*lîð*) and that he will be the companion of the Heavenly King. The prohibition against drinking wine applied to Nazirites, persons who were "to be set apart from others in the service of God. ... The obligation was either for life or for a defined time" (Smith, p. 600; cf. also *Nya Testamentet*, p. 138). Gabriel then commands that Zacharias and Elizabeth should rear the child in fidelity (*tuhin thurh treuua*) and that he should receive the name John.

Zacharias regrets that it is all too late for them to accomplish (*It is unc al te lat sô te giuuinnanne*) what God (through Gabriel) commands. They were, after all, twenty years old when he chose her as

---

[15] It seems to us that the agent noun *alo-waldo* is an ancient Germanic designation for ruler.

§. 2

his wife, and they have lived together for seventy more years as companions on the same bench and in the same bed (*gibenkeon endi gibeddeon*) without producing an inheritor. Their eyesight is now almost gone, their flesh weak. Zacharias does not believe what the angel tells him (*sô thu mid thînun uuordun gisprikis*). For his disbelief he is rendered mute until the prophesy is fulfilled.

The episode is true to Luke 1:5-25, but with embellishment. The detail concerning Zacharias' life with Elizabeth is an expansion of Luke 1:18 ("Zachariah said to the angel, 'How can I be sure of this? I am an old man and my wife is well on in years.'"). A clearly Germanic manner of expression is included in the phrase 'thus have the fates, the "measurer" marked' (*sô habed im uurdgiscapu, metod gimarcod*), which is set in redundant juxtaposition to 'the power of God' (*maht godes*). That is, the authority of the pre-Christian concepts of those forces which preordain the course of one's life are equated here with the might of the single Christian God.

Lochrie (1986) remarks regarding OE, "The perplexing relationship between man's knowledge and his *wyrd*, or that which happens through God's providence, is explored more extensively in Alfred's translation of Boethius' *De Consolatione Philosophiae*. Alfred defines *wyrd*: ... *þæt þæt we wyrd hata, þæt bið Godes weorc þæt he ælre dæg wyrc* ... 'What we call Wyrd is God's work which he does all day....'."

To *metod*, the 'measurer', Ilkow notes,

> Im Hel. wirkt ... *metod* durchwegs in christlichem Sinn. Die alte heidnische Vorstellung einer zumessenden Schicksalsmacht ist in den christlichen Glauben an Gott als den obersten Messer und Richter und das von ihm zugemessene oder verhängte Schicksal übergegangen[16] (p. 293).

Lochrie (1986) states, "Like *Judgment Day I*, *The Wanderer* and *The Seafarer* predispose us to a philosophical resignation before the inexorability of fate. The Seafarer's stoicism takes its strength from his perception of man's thought before God's [*meotud*'s] *wyrd*: *Wyrd bið swiþre, meotud meahtigra þonne ænges monnes gehygd* ('Wyrd is stronger, God mightier, than any man's thought')" (p. 210). Another juxtaposition occurs, for example, in the OE poem

---

[16] In the Hêliand *metod* is used without exception in the Christian sense. The old heathen idea of a measuring power of fate was transformed in Christian belief into God as the highest Surveyor or Judge and into the fate that was dealt out by Him.

Hêliand

Judith (154-155): *ēow ys Metod blīðe, cyninga Wuldor* (' God is gracious to you, the Glory of kings').

The redefinition of *metod* as *maht godes* in l. 128 made this transfer of belief overt even to those who perhaps were not yet converted. (Cf. also the notes on *uurd* in §10 and on *metodogiscapu* in §29.) The method of redefinition through comparison and/or variation (*metod* = *maht godes*) in order to imprint old concepts with new, Christian meanings is used throughout the *Hêliand*.[17] In lines presented so far we see the following examples, among others: *lêra Cristes* = *hêlag uuord godes* (10–11); *stark* = *mildi endi guod* (29–30); *uurdgiscapu* = *metod* = *maht godes* (127–128); *gibod godes* = *formon uuordu* (217–218); etc. Such redefinitions are, however, not used consistently, as below in l. 197, where the ancient, pre-Christian term *wurdigiscapu* is used for the time set for the birth of John and in the raising of the Widow's Son (cf. §29).

§3. The Birth of John

Lines 192b to 242
(Cf. Luke 1:12-24, 59-65; 80)

Luke 1:24 describes the conception of John and adds that Elizabeth lived for five months in isolation, which is reflected in the *Hêliand* by l. 196–197 where it is said that she awaited *uurdigiscapu* 'the fates' (l. 196–197), which likely meant that she was waiting for a 'good birth'. Ilkow says regarding this expression,

> Wir ... möchten ... auf eine Heliandstelle aufmerksam machen, in der vielleicht Spuren eines alten Nornenglaubens nachklingen. Elisabeth erwartet die 'Fügung des Schicksals', d.h. die Geburt ihres Kindes. ... Nordischen Nachweisen zufolge bestimmen die Nornen nicht nur die Geschicke des Lebens und den Eintritt des Todes, sie erscheinen auch als eine Art von Geburtshelferinnen, treten also mit jedem Menschen bereits zu seiner Geburtsstunde in Beziehung. In christlicher Form hat sich der Mythus von den drei Wehemüttern bis heute im deutschen Volksglauben bewahrt.

---

[17]Cf. footnote 7.

§. 3

> ... Es ist nicht ausgeschlossen, daß uns in der formelhaften Phrase des Hel[iand]D[ichters] *bêd that uuîf uurdigiscapu* ein Nachklang an die Vorstellung der Norne(n) als Geburtshelferin(nen) erhalten ist[18] (p. 437).

While Elizabeth waited the birth of John the Baptist, the winter passed and the year's count changed. Ilkow points out that this passage may reflect a change in the calendar that was imposed by Charlemagne:

> [D]as Jahr begannen [die Germanen] mit dem Winter und wendeten den Namen dieser Jahreszeit zur Bezeichnung des ganzen Jahres an (vgl. *winter-gital*). ... In vorchristlicher Zeit überwog der 1. Oktober (Ende der Weidezeit); die Westgoten übernahmen nach römischem Muster den 1. Januar (*Kalendae Januariae*, Beschneidung Christi); Franken, Alemannen und Langobarden bevorzugten den 1. März, während unter Karl dem Großen der 25. März (Mariä Verkündigung) das Jahr eröffnete. Diesen letztgenannten Jahresbeginn scheint der HelD vor Augen gehabt zu haben, als er den Zeitverlauf zwischen der Empfängnis und der Geburt Johannes des Täufers folgendermaßen beschrieb: ... 'der Winter ging zu Ende, es ging des Jahres Zahl dahin', d.h. es ging die laufende Jahreszahl, das (Kalendar–)Jahr zu Ende, indem am 25. März der Jahreswechsel eintrat, und im folgenden Sommer (am 24. Juni) wurde Johannes geboren[19] (pp. 146-147).

---

[18] We want to note a place in the Hêliand with perhaps a reminiscence of a belief in norns. Elizabeth awaits the 'workings of fate,' i.e., the birth of her child. ... According to Nordic custom the norns determine not only the fortunes of life and time of death, but they appear also as a kind of birth helpers and thus come into contact with every person in the hour of birth. In Christian form the myth of the three midwives has been retained up to this day in German popular belief. ... It cannot be excluded that in the formulaic phrase *bêd that uuîf uurdigiscapu* used by the author of the Hêliand there is a remembrance of the three norns as helpers at birth.

[19] The Germanic peoples began the year with winter and used the name of this season as a designation for the whole year (cf. *winter-gital*). ... In pre-Christian time it was predominately October 1st (end of the grazing season); the West Goths took over January 1st in the Roman fashion (*Kalendae Januariae*, Circumcision of Christ); the Franks, Alemanns, and Langobards preferred March 1st, while the year began under Charlemagne on March 25th (the Annunciation of Mary). The author of the Hêliand seems to have had the latter in mind when he described the time between the conception and the birth of John the Baptist as follows: 'the winter ended and the year's count with it,' i.e. the (calendar)year ended as the change of year occurred on March 25th, and in the following summer (on June 24th) John was born.

Hêliand

The expected baby is described as *erƀiuuard, suîðo godcund gumo ... barn an burgun* 'an inheritor, a very divine man, a child of *burgun*.' This last description seems dissonant with the first and the second. The first was important in Germanic society, as an inheritor was and is of importance in most agrarian societies.[20] The second phrase fits the biblical context, but the word *burg* seems rather odd here. The word meant 'hill-top fortification,' and its inhabitants evidently had a special status. Ilkow remarks,

> Städte in unserem Sinne gibt es nämlich erst seit dem 12. Jh., und unter 'Burg' verstehen wir die sog. 'Herrenburg', die ein weltlicher Herrscher als Stütze seiner Macht anlegen läßt. Mit dem Bau derartiger Burgen begann auf germ. Gebiet Karl der Große. ... Was bezeichnet nun 'Burg' ursprünglich? ... Schon in vorchristlicher Zeit gelangt das germ. Wort, wohl durch Vermittlung eines nordbalkanischen Volkes, als πύργς ins Griechische, das schon bei Homer 'Schutzwehr, Befestigung' bedeutet... . Wie die in lat. Form überlieferten Ortsnamen *Asciburgium* und *Teutoburgium* beweisen, bezeichnete das germ. Wort ursprünglich die sog. 'Volks- oder Fluchtburg', die für den Fall der Kriegsnot angelegt, in friedlichen Zeiten aber nur von wenigen Menschen bewohnt war. Solche Burgen legte man gerne auf der Hochfläche eines Berges an (vgl. *an theru hôhon burg* v. 4187 ähnlich 2176, 4367). In der deutschen Geschichte begegnen einander beide Burgformen zur Zeit der Eroberung Sachsens durch Karl den Großen. Die Sachsenburgen, die ihm Widerstand leisteten und zum Teil noch erhalten sind, wie die Eresburg, die Sifiburg oder die Brunsburg bei Höxter, waren alte 'Volksburgen'. Sie waren auf hohen ebenen Bergkuppen gelegen und von riesigen Wallringen mit einem Durchmesser von 400 bis 1000 m umgeben (vgl. *burges uual* v. 3085). ... [D]er HelD. betrachtet die Städte Palästinas als solche[21] (pp. 78-80).

---

[20] Cf. *arbeo laosa* in the OHG *Hildebrandslied* and its interpretation by Schwab (1972) as a legal term.

[21] Cities in our sense have existed only since the 12th century. With 'burg' we understand the so-called 'Herrenburg,' which a political ruler had built to support his power. Charlemagne began the construction of such fortifications on Germanic territory. ... What did 'burg' mean originally? ... Already in pre-Christian time the Germanic word arrived as πύργς in Greek, likely intermediated by a north Balkan people. Homer used the word as 'fortification'. ... As the place names *Asciburgium* and *Teutoburgium* show in their Latinized forms, the Germanic word originally meant 'protective fort' built for flight in case of war but during peace time occupied by very few people. They were commonly sited on tops of mountains (cf. *an theru hôhon burg* in verse 4187 and similarly 2176, 4367). In German history both types of fortifications existed during Charlemagne's campaign against the Saxons. The *Sachsenburgen* which

§. 3

Kellermann (1967) writes,

> Strategische Bedeutung innerhalb einer großräumigen politischen Planung erlangten [die Rundburgen] erst seit der Entstehung des Frankenreiches.[22] In Anlehnung an römische Traditionen wurden nun die Burgen zu Stützpunkten einer Besatzungsmacht in den einzelnen Stammesgebieten, waren mit Truppen belegt und bildeten zugleich die Missionszentren des Christentums[23] (columns 1536-1537).

Thus, according to these views of the meaning of *burg*, the phrase *barn an burgun* imparts a special status to the Child, as only certain privileged people lived within the protective walls. Doane, however, disagrees with the above and states,

> Ilkow (78-80) argues that in OS poetry *burg* meant neither 'city' nor 'castle,' because the former did not exist in Germany until the twelfth century, and the latter not until carolingian times. It means, he says, 'hillfort' for temporary emergency use. But the use of *burg* to translate *civitas* was well established in OS and OE poetry: the [*Hêliand*] poet knows the difference between *civitas* and *castellum: uueldin im te Emaus that castel* (Vulg. 'castellum') *suocan* (5959) ...; in *Genesis A burg* is the usual poetic word for *civitas* while *ceaster* ... is prosaic. The [Vatican *Genesis*] poet shows what his concept of a city is in lines 255, 287: a collection of houses, each man dwelling in his own house (pp. 350-351).

When the year's number changed (gêres gital) and the winter passed, John was born ('came into the light of humanity'). The *Hêliand* inserts a long section on the appearance of the baby, which offers a contrast to the description of Zacharias and Elizabeth in l. 150b to 156a but also continues the Germanic heroic tradition of describing striking physical attributes of remarkable achievers at birth, here in

---

offered resistance to him and which are in part still extant (the Eresburg, the Sifiburg, or the Brunsburg by Höxter) were old 'protective forts.' They were on high, level mountain tops surrounded by gigantic circular walls with a diameter of 400 to 1000 m (cf. *burges uual* in l. 3085). ... The author of the Hêliand views the cities of Palestine as such.

[22] Cf. the circular fortress of the Avars. "Charlemagne ... takes the treasure of the Avars, which ... is stored in their central fortress, the "ring," and ... shares it with his vassals and the pope" (Scholz, p. 12).

[23] The round fortifications achieved strategic importance in political planning only after the foundation of the realm of the Franks. Following Roman tradition the fortifications were occupied by troops as barracks of an occupying power and simultaneously served as missionary centers of Christianity.

service of the idea that such a beautiful child could only have come through a command of God (*gibod godes*). Compare, for example, Byock (p. 37) for a description of the also quite unusual birth of Volsung, whereby the mother is unable to give birth although pregnant. When the child is cut from her after six years, he was "big, strong, and daring in what were thought to be tests of manhood and prowess. He become the greatest of warriors ... ." His twin son and daughter, Sigmund and Signy, were also "in all things ... the foremost and the finest looking of the children of King Volsung, though all the other sons were imposing." Another example would be Egill Skallagrímsson, who although not beautiful, exhibited great physical attributes at an early age. Jones translates, "He was called Egil. ... When he was three years old he was as big and strong as other boys who were six or seven. He was a talker from the first, and clever with words" (p. 85). Especially the latter remark is of interest, as being 'word wise' also emerges as a characteristic of leadership in the *Hêliand*.

The shock of giving the baby the unconventional name John would have been as great with the OS audience as it was in the biblical setting. The Bible states that "neighbors and relatives" wanted to name the child Zacharias, but Elizabeth responded that he should be called John (Luke 1:58-59). The Saxons were doubtless keenly aware that the giving of names to Germanic heroes or nobles must continue the patronym in the prescribed manner, either by alliteration or by other variation of constituent part (cf. Schramm, p. 37 f.). Hadubrand, for example, could more easily be identified as Hildebrand's son in the *Hildebrandlied* by means of the alliteration that followed from the father's name to the son's. The non-Germanic name John, or Johannes, was certainly foreign to that tradition. Störmer (1973) states in regard to early name-giving:

> Daß die germanischen Namen – meist zweistämmig und auffallend lang –, welche den deutschen Namenschatz beherrschten, zum größten Teil ausgesprochen kriegerisch sind, ist von der germanistischen Forschung schon lange erkannt worden. Es kann kein Zweifel sein, daß es sich bei diesen Namen um mythische Leitbilder handelt, die noch magische Kraft hatten. Auf dem Glauben an diese Kraft des Namens beruhte eben der Wunsch, mit dem spezifischen Namen dem Kinde jenes Heil zu schenken, das der Name birgt. ... Neben dem Kriegerischen tritt besonders auch die germanische Götterwelt in den deutschen Namen hervor. Natürlich dürfte die Bedeutung dieser Götterweltnamen im Frühmittelalter bereits etwas säkurlarisiert oder umgedeutet worden sein, wenigstens im Bereich des Bewußten. ... Daß aber im Bereich des Un-

§. 3

> bewußten, Volkstümlichen, Traditionellen 'Heidnisches' und Christliches unvermischt vor allem in der unreflektierten Bauernwelt des Brauchtums bis in unser Jahrhundert nebeneinander herlaufen, vermag die Volkskunde heute auf breiter Basis zu beweisen[24] (pp. 31-32).

Störmer states further:

> Wir dürfen kaum annehmen, daß die adeligen Eltern – wenn sie überhaupt allein den Namen ihres Kindes wählten – völlig beliebig in der Wahl des Namens walten konnten. Das Frühmittelalter ist keineswegs eine Zeit, in der es ausgeprägten Individualismus gibt. Der Bedeutungsgehalt des Namens des jungen menschen mußte offenbar im Rahmen der Familie oder der Sippe eingebettet sein; d.h. der Name mußte zur Tradition der adeligen Familie oder Sippe gehören[25] (p. 37).

In the *Hêliand* Elizabeth validates the choice of name as being ordained in the previous year (*fernun gêre*) by the 'teaching of God' (*godes lêrun*), which stands in redundant apposition to the native concept of 'a command by the word of the first [leader, commander]' (*formon uuordu gibod*). Additional narrative is added to the *Hêliand* when 'an audacious (*gêlhert*) man' objects that no person in 'our kith or kin' (*aðalboranes ûses cunnies eftho cnôsles*) had ever had such a name and says, 'Let's give him some other pleasant name and let him enjoy it!' Again a man of wise speech (*the frôdo man, the thar consta filo mahlian*) is enlisted to turn the argument. Ilkow points out that the term *aðalboran* may originally

---

[24] The fact that Germanic names – most of them containing two stems and strikingly long – for the most part expressly describe the qualities of warriors has been recognized for a long time. There can be no doubt that these names reflect mythological concepts which still had magical power. Belief in this power of the name reveals the desire to give to the child with that specific name the good omen inherent in the name. ... Aside from qualities of the warrior, names were embued with the world of Germanic gods. Naturally the meanings of these names from Germanic religion were already secularized or reinterpreted in the early medieval period, at least consciously. ... In the realm of the unconscious, however, popular, traditionally "heathen" and Christian coexisted side-by-side in unreflective rural usage up to our century, as folkloristic study can document on a broad basis.

[25] We can scarcely suppose that parents from the nobility – even if they could choose the name of their child by themselves – would have freedom to select a name completely arbitrarily. The early middle ages were by no means a time in which there was pronounced individualism. The semantics of the name of the young person must clearly have had to fit within the framework of the family or kinship group, i.e., the name had to belong to the tradition of the noble family or kinship group.

have designated the heir of an *ôðal* 'home property' but seems to be an honorific in the *Hêliand*. All paragons are 'of noble descent': "Bei allen Menschen, mit denen wir fühlen und die uns vorbildlich erscheinen sollen, beton[t] der HelD, daß sie edler Abkunft sind"[26] (p. 34).

Zacharias is incapable of speaking, so the *frôdo man* advised that they ask him what the child should be called by giving him a *bôk* and having him *bi bôcstabon brêf geuuirkean, namon giscrîban* (l. 230), *uurîtan uuîslîco uuordgimerkiun* (l. 233). Ilkow comments on the history of books,

> Lat. *caudex, cōdex* (zu *cudēre* 'schlagen') entwickelt aus der Grundbedeutung 'geschlagener Baum, Klotz' über 'gespaltenes Holz, Brett' die Bedeutung 'Holztafel, Schreibtafel'. Eine ähnliche Entwicklungsgeschichte hat der germ. Ausdruck 'Buch'. Bekanntlich ritzten die Germanen ihre Runen in Holz oder Metall. Man verwendete Eschen- oder Buchenholz, und nannte die Schreibtafel nach letzterem schlechthin 'Buch'; diese Bedeutung hat as. *bôk* in Hel. 232[27] (p. 66).

Note that Zacharias is here advised to *wrîtan* 'write' (German *ritzen* 'scratch, carve') with *uuordgimerkiun* 'word marks' as would be done on a wooden slat.

---

[26] The author of the Hêliand stresses that all people with whom we empathize and who should seem ideal to us are of noble descent.

[27] Latin *caudex, cōdex* (cf. *cudēre* 'strike') developed from the basic meaning of 'felled tree, block of wood' via 'split wood, board' the meaning 'wooden tablet, writing tablet.' German 'Buch' underwent a similar development. It is known that early Germanic scribes scratched their runes in wood or metal. Ash or beech wood was used, and the writing tablets were known simply as 'book,' [a word related to 'beech']; *bôk* in l. 232 of the *Hêliand* has this meaning.

§4. Mary's Child

Lines 243 to 330a
(cf. Luke 1:26-36, 38; Matthew 1:18-21)

The author of the *Hêliand* prefaces this section with the information that God Almighty wanted to send his own Son hither to earth to redeem humankind from punishment.

Again Gabriel, the 'trusted, reliable messenger' (*uuisbodo*), appears. Some read *uuîsbodo* 'wise messenger' here, but Ilkow argues for *uuisbodo*, saying, "Ein Bevollmächtigter des Königs war dessen besonderer Vertrauter, ein Mann, auf den sich der König verlassen konnte, dessen er gewiß war, daher *wis-bodo*"[28] (p. 421 f.). This may be in analogy to the *missi* sent out by Charlemagne to carry out his orders. Myers states, "The *missi dominici* ... had responsibility for making the counts and assistant judges familiar with new royal capitularies" (p. 134).

This time Gabriel comes to Mary, who was spoken for by Joseph (*sea ên thegan habda, Ioseph gimahlit*), who had 'bought her as wife,'[29] to announce the miraculous conception of Jesus. Mary's credentials are established for the OS audience as being a 'lovely maiden' (*munilîca magað*), a 'handsome (well-grown) lady' (*thiorna githigan*), a 'praiseworthy woman' (*diurlîc uuîf*), a 'woman of distinguished family' (*aðalcnôsles uuîf*), and a 'lady associated with a vow' (*anthêti* 'promised, pledged' cf. OHG *antheizo* 'vow') to Joseph and to God. Ilkow (p. 36) states,

> Wie Vilmar (S. 53) ausführt, ist der an as. *knôsal* geknüpfte Begriff enger als der durch *kunni* ausgedrückte. Während *kunni* dem Begriff *thiod* 'Volk' nahesteht und in unserer Sprache ... am besten durch 'Stamm' wiedergegeben wird, entspricht *knôsal* etwa unserem Begriff 'Familie'. Maria wird im

---

[28] An agent of the king was his special confidant, a man whom the king could rely on, of whom he was sure, and for this reason a *wis-bodo*.

[29] Doan (1991:324) points out that "[t]he custom of concluding a marriage by 'brideprice' was universal in the old Germanic laws: the *lex Saxonum* (40) sets it at 300 solidi."

Hêliand

Hel. als *aðalcnôsles uuîf* v. 297 bezeichnet, denn sie entstammt dem Geschlecht Davids.[30]

In addition to the wording in Luke 1:28-33 the angel tells Mary that she is 'dear to your Lord,' and 'worthy to the Ruler (Wielder),' for she has 'understanding/intelligence/wit' (*giuuit*)[31]. He assures her that he is not there to tempt or to deceive her (*ne quam ic thi te ênigun frêson herod, ne dragu ic ênig drugithing*), detail again beyond that provided in biblical sources in order to allay any tendency to view Gabriel as a trick-playing elf, wight, or other 'hidden being' (cf. the commentary for §36 and the disciples' reaction to the sight of Jesus walking on water).

The child shall bear not the incomprehensible foreign name Jesus, as stipulated in Luke 1:31, but rather the Saxon name *hêliand* 'Savior'. (The name 'Jesus' was itself a word for 'savior'; cf. *Die Bibel*, note to Matthew 1:21: "Der Name Jesus (Jeschua) wird hier als 'Retter', 'Erlöser' gedeutet.")[32]

To Mary's question as to how she can conceive a child when she has known no man, the angel replies with an eloquent paraphrase of Luke 1:35, "The Holy Spirit will come to you from the meadow of heaven through the power of God. From there the child shall be given to this world. The power of the Wielder shall overshadow you with light from the highest King of Heaven" (l. 275-279a). Particularly interesting here are the words *heƀanuuang* 'meadow of heaven' and *skimo*. The former was likely not to be taken literally but certainly familiar to the audience as poetical diction and was chosen for metrical purposes, even though *heƀanuuang* seemingly harkens to a pre-Christian concept of paradise. Ilkow points to a similar usage in Wulfila's translation of the Bible into Gothic and says,

> Aus Wulfilas Anwendung von got. *waggs* ... ergibt sich, daß dem germ. Wort der Begriff einer lieblichen, lustvollen Aue, einer 'Aue der Wonne' innegewohnt haben muß ... . Mit Recht weist Vilmar (S. 22) darauf hin, daß für die alten Ger-

---

[30] As Vilmar (p. 53) explains, the concept associated with OE *knôsal* is narrower than the one associated with *kunni*. While *kunni* is close to the concept *thiod* 'people' and can best be rendered with 'tribe,' *knôsal* corresponds approximately to our concept 'family.' Maria is called *aðalcnôsles uuîf* in l. 297, for she is from the kinship of David.

[31] Doane (1991) characterizes OE *gewit* thus: "The purpose of *gewit* was the understanding of obligation of service" (p. 121).

[32] The name Jesus (Jeschua) is interpreted here as 'Savior, Redeemer.'

§. 4

manen die stillen, freundlichen grünen Waldwiesen Orte der Freude und des Friedens waren, im Gegensatz zu der finsteren tiefen Waldwüste, dem Ort des Schreckens, wilder Tiere und geflüchteter Verbrecher (vgl. *sinweldi*)[33] (pp. 183-184).

See the commentary to §14 for *sinuueldi*.

The usage of *skimo* ('luster, light') is a circumlocution of *lioht* which in the *Hêliand* repeatedly alludes to life.[34] (cf. 1. 199, 372, 578, etc.).

At l. 288 the anonymous story teller breaks the frame of narration with the insertion *Sô gifragn ik* ('Thus I learned'), which both suddenly adds the perspective of an outside observer and overburdens what otherwise would be a reasonably proper alliterative line. This seemingly unnecessary intrusion likely served the purpose of adding the authority of a witness to the improbable story being told.

In this section, as throughout the *Hêliand* the words *hugi*, *môd*, and *seo* overlappingly and – for us confusingly – denote certain qualities of emotion, thought, and feeling. The word *hugi* has cognates like Gothic *hugjan* 'think', OI *hugr* 'mind; mood, heart, temper', Swedish (*komma i*) *håg* 'remember', Middle Dutch *gehogen* 'remember', OHG *hukkan* 'think', OE *hyge* 'thought; intention; courage, pride', OS *huggean* 'think', etc. all referring to what we regard to be a capacity of cognition, remembrance, and so forth, but also of emotion. Ilkow says,

> Als Bezeichnung geistiger Tätigkeit oder Fähigkeit erscheint *hugi* in Wendungen wie: *that uuas fruod gumo, habda ferahtan hugi* v. 73 – oder: *thoh he spâhan hugi* v. 173 / *bâri an is breostun*. Die letzte Stelle enthält gleichzeitig eine der vielen überlieferten Formeln, in denen uns jene alte Anschauung entgegentritt, nach der die Brust bzw. das Herz nicht nur als Sitz der Gefühle und des Willens galt, sondern auch der Geisteskräfte[35] (pp. 228-229).

---

[33] From Wulfila's usage of Gothic *waggs* .. we conclude that the concept of a lovely, pleasurable meadow, a 'meadow of joy' must have been inherent in the meaning of the word. Vilmar (p. 22) correctly points out that for the ancient Germanic peoples the quiet, friendly, green forest meadows were places of happiness and peace in contrast with the dark, deep woodland wastes, the place of terror, wild animals, and lurking criminals (cf. *sinweldi*).

[34] Cf. the gloria painted about the heads of saints and other holy persons.

[35] As an indicator of mental activity or ability *hugi* appears in expressions like *that uuas fruod gumo, habda ferahtan hugi* ['that was an experienced man (who) had a devout mind'] in l. 73 – oder: *thoh he spâhan hugi/ bâri an is breostun* ['though he had a wise mind in his breast'] in l. 173 . This citation contains simultaneously

Hêliand

The word *môd* has cognates in Gothic *moþs* 'anger', English *mood*, German *Mut* 'courage', and etc. denoting a spirit of rage, or disquietude ('moody'), of emotional agitation, and/or of certain aspects of aggression. Ilkow says further,

> Der Germane trennte ... nicht, wie wir es gewohnt sind, den im menschlichen Körper angenommenen Sitz der Gemütsregungen vom Sitz der Denkkraft. Das Herz bzw. die Brust als der Teil des Körpers, der das Herz umschließt, galt ihm als Sitz aller Geistes-, Gefühls- und Willensregungen... Der Germane kannte also eine Art 'Körperseele' ... Zur Bezeichnung der Kräfte dieser Seele diente ihm u.a. *môða- in erster Linie auf die Gemüts- und Willensregungen Anwendung. Besonders weit verbreitet ist bei den Letzteren in den altgerm. Sprachen die Bezeichnung des 'Zornes' ... . Wie in der übrigen altgerm. Überlieferung (und noch engl. *mood*), dient *môd* im Hel. zunächst der Bezeichnung einer seelischen Stimmung[36] (p. 299).

Cf. also §53 for more on the 'corporeal soul' (Körperseele).

The word *seƀo* is isolated with no modern cognates, although its internal history can be reconstructed. Flowers says,
"PIE *sap-: 'to taste; perceive' > PGmc *saf- (with i-*umlaut*) in nominal and verbal constructions. Evidence for the original Germanic *sāf- is limited to the preterite forms OHG *suob* and MDu. *besoef* 'tasted, perceived.' Possible cognates are Lat. *sapio*: 'taste, discern,' Arm. *ham*: 'taste,' OIr. *sāir*: 'experienced, clever.' However, the etymology remains difficult" (p. 128).[37]

> one of the many attested formulae in which we encounter the old view that the breast or the heart is not only the site of feelings and will but also of mental ability.

[36] The ancient Germanic peoples did not – as we are accustomed to do – separate the assumed site of emotions from that of mental activity. The heart, or breast as a part of the body which surrounds that heart, was thought to be the origin of all mental, emotional, and volitional impulses... A sort of 'corporeal soul' was imagined ... The word *môða–* served to designate the powers of this soul primarily as regards emotions and intentions. The meaning 'anger' is especially wide-spread in the older Germanic languages ... As in other ancient Germanic records (and still in English 'mood') *môd* served in the *Hêliand* to indicate a mental and emotional state.

[37] Ilkow (p. 302): "Dem ... schwachen Maskulinum germ. *seƀan- steht ein in den westgerm. Sprachen in Präfixverbindungen verbreitetes Verbum *saƀjan zur Seite. As. *af-sebbian, an-sebbian* und *bi-sebbian* sind in den Bedeutung-en 'bemerken, wahrnehmen' überliefert. Dagegen ist uns in mhd. *ent-sebben* (sic)

§. 4

The angel admonishes Mary not to have an irresolute or indecisive *hugi*. Mary's *hugi* was turned to God's task and to His will. Her *hugi* does not doubt. The narrator 'learned' that Mary accepted the commandment of God *mid leohtu hugi endi mid gilôƀon gôdun*. Upon learning of Mary's pregnancy Joseph's *hugi* (= *môd* here) was thrown into confusion. Joseph even begins to think in his *hugi* how he will be rid of Mary. Gabriel comes to Joseph in a dream and tells him not to judge her too harshly, which shows *hugi* here as a verbal stem. Lastly in this section, Mary is admonished not to let her *hugi* doubt nor her *môdgithâht* (a compound containing *môd* along with a word for 'thought') doubt (*Ne lât thu thi thînan hugi tuîflien, / merrean thîna môdgithâht*).

As we see, *môd* as a concept is commingled with *hugi*, perhaps overlapping with it. Joseph's *môd was giuuorrid* 'confused' (cognate with German *verwirren*.) Joseph began to think about these matters in his *môd*. The angel came to Joseph in a dream and called upon him to 'hold her well, love her in his *môd*.'

As noted above, the seat of thought and emotion was not in the head, as in the modern concept, but in the breast. Mary understood in her breast ([*in*] *ira breostun*) and in her *seƀo* that the power of the

[*entseben*, 'mit dem geschmacke wahrnehmen': Lexer] eine ältere Bedeutungsschicht dieser Wortsippe enthalten. Wie die Verwendung des mhd. Verbums zeigt, haben sich aus 'mit dem Geschmack' dann 'mit den Sinnen (überhaupt) wahrnehmen' durch Wendung ins Geistige die Bedeutungen 'erkennen, innnewerden' entwickelt. Germ. *seƀan- bezeichnete also ursprünglich die 'Wahrnehmung durch den Geschmackssinn', dann die 'sinnliche Wahrnehmung überhaupt', dann die 'geistige Einsicht' und 'Erkenntnis', schließlich wurde der Ausdruck ähnlich *hugi* und *môd* auf jede Regung des Seelenlebens übertragen... Außergerm. vergleichen sich lat. *sapa* 'eingemachter Most, Mostsyrup' und *sapiō, –ere*, das, nicht unähnlich mhd. *ent-sebben*, aus 'schmecken, nach etwas riechen' die Bedeutungen 'weise sein, einsichtig sein' entwickelt hat." [The PGmc. weak masculine *seƀan is a counterpart to the verb *saƀjan, widely attested as a prefixed verb in West Germanic languages. Old Saxon *af-sebbian*, *an-sebbian* and *bi-sebbian* have the meanings 'notice, perceive.' An older layer of meaning is retained on the other hand in the MHG *ent-sebben* (sic) [entseben 'perceive by taste': Lexer]. As usage of the MHG verb shows, the meanings 'recognize, become aware' developed through transition into the spiritual realm from 'perceive by taste' then 'perceive with the senses (generally)'. PGmc *seƀan- thus originally meant 'perception through taste', then 'sensory perception generally,' then 'spiritual insight' and 'realization'. As with *hugi* and *môd* the expression finally included every aspect of spiritual life... Outside of Germanic languages, Latin *sapa* 'fruit wine, fruit syrup' and *sapiō, –ere* developed the meanings 'be wise, insightful' from 'taste, smell like', similarly to MHG *ent-sebben*.]

Hêliand

Almighty had impregnated her. (*Uuard the hêlago gêst, / that barn an ira bôsma; endi siu ira breostun forstôd / iac an ire sebon selbo, sagda them siu uuelda, / that sie habde giôcana thes alouualdon craft / hêlag fon himile*). The conflation of what apparently were once separate categories of emotion and/or thought is indicated by the compound noun *môdsebo* (compare *môdgithâht* above) occurring in l. 241, 539, and elsewhere). See also the commentary on §53 for what Ilkow terms the *Körperseele*. Murphy (1992) points out in his footnote 37 that this passage conflicts with orthodox theology from earliest Christian time which separates the Holy Spirit from the Father and the Son as the third part of the Trinity, not as born with the incarnation of the Son. Murphy speculates that this confusion may rest in a misunderstanding of the phrase *et incarnatus est de Spiritu Sancto* "He was made flesh by the Holy Spirit" or perhaps of the Annunciation as depicted in Luke.

Again the ability to speak well and persuasively is employed as a mark of nobility of manner and of person. The angel has his word(s) at the ready (*uuord garu*), and Mary is prepared to accept them 'according to your words.'

While Mary was telling all to whom she wanted that she had been impregnated by the 'holy power of the Almighty from heaven' (293b-295a), Joseph was confused and knew nothing of the happy news (*blîði gibodskepi*). His concern was to protect her, not betray her to the multitudes, as he feared for her life (304b-312a). The idea of danger from fellow citizens because of a pregnancy would have been new to the audience of the *Hêliand*. For that reason the Old Law of the Hebrews (*then aldon êu, Ebreo folkes*) had to be explained in l. 308 to 312a. (See Leviticus 20:10 and Deuteronomy 22:22-29.)

§5. THE BIRTH OF JESUS

Lines 339 to 374a
(Luke 2:1-6)

The Roman ruler Octavian Augustus commanded all citizens of the Imperium Romanum to return to their home districts in order to be registered in the tax roles. The explanation of this edict is couched in terms comprehensible to the audience and interesting for us. The order (*ban endi bodskepi*) came from the Roman caesar (*kêsur*) to certain rulers (kings) with seats (of power) over districts

§. 5

(*fon them kêsure cuningo gihuilicun*, / *hêmsitteandiun*) as far as his dukes (*heritogon*) held sway over the people. Murphy (1992) points out that the author of the *Hêliand* emended Luke:

> By eliminating the name of the specific governor given in Luke's gospel (Lk 2:2-3: *when Quirinius was governor of Syria*) and by making the statement on governorships a general statement in the plural, the author has created the possibility of his audience identifying closely with his story, since the occupied country of the Saxons was ruled by military legates (*missi*) sent from 'Caesar' in Aix-la-Chapelle[38] (Footnote 22).

Thus, under Murphy's (1992) reading, the author of the *Hêliand* wanted to be sure that any analogy between the Roman occupation of Jewish lands and Charlemagne's of Saxon lands would be quite obvious. The payment of (church) taxes was a serious matter.

The term *hêmsittiandi* is, as Ilkow puts it, "der 'Einheimische' im Gegensatz zum *eli-lendi*, dem 'Ausländer'"[39] (p. 197). The men outside of their home districts (*alla thea elilendiun man*) should return home. (The Three Wise Men are called *elilendi uueros* in l. 632.) The people should seek their family property (*iro ôðil*) and the site of their home court (*handmahal*), perhaps the legal entity where the swearing of oaths was valid. Ilkow says,

> Im Hel. wird also *hand-mahal* ... etwa in der Bedeutung 'Versammlungsstätte' gebraucht. Diese Bedeutung wird durch das Grundwort von *hand-mahal* ausgedrückt, wie auch got. *maþl* die 'Versammlungsstätte' bezeichnet. Das Vorderglied dagegen scheint im Gebrauch des Komp. durch den HelD keine deutlich erkennbare Funktion auszuüben. Dagegen überliefert uns mlat. *anth-mallum*, das die 'zuständige Gerichtsstätte' bezeichnet, seine ursprüngliche Bedeutung[40] (p. 173).

Meyer sees the *handmahal* as having arisen from the marker of the 'local court' (*Hausgericht*), "das ja seit alters ein Kreuzpfahl an

---

[38] Now the German city Aachen, where Charlemagne resided.

[39] the 'native' in contrast with *eli-lendi*, the 'foreigner'

[40] In the Hêliand *hand-mahal* ... is used in the meaning 'assembly site.' This meaning is expressed by the basic component of *hand-mahal* as also in Gothic *maþl*, which indicates 'assembly site.' The first component seems to have no clearly recognizable function in the usage of the Hêliand poet. On the other hand Middle Latin *anth-mallum*, which means the 'designated place of jurisdiction,' retains the original meaning.

Hêliand

der Gerichtsstelle war."[41] This pre-Christian symbol of the court site where oaths were confirmed by the touching of the cross-shaped pole and the raising of the hand to a higher power would presumably have been familiar to the audience of the *Hêliand* and provided a further connection between old practice and the new significance of the cross.[42]

The concepts behind the OS words used to explain why Joseph and Mary went to Bethlehem are not biblical but were enlisted as translation equivalents or as loanwords (like *kêsur*) to retell the story. The taxation was carried out by officials (*bodon*) with impressive credentials, namely the skills of literacy; they were 'book-eloquent' (*bôkspâhi*) and wrote in documents (*brêf scriƀun*). The tax officials thus also fulfilled basic modern requirements of writing (and reading), which qualified them as 'eloquent' men.

One can only imagine the difficulties inherent in describing Roman law and customs in the Near East for an audience in North Germany in the 800's, but there may have been a similar practice on Saxon territory. Ilkow (p. 80) cites Dionysius of Halicarnassus' description of the Roman Emperor Servius Tullius' (577–534) establishment of massive circular fortifications for protection of the rural population in which scribes were always present to keep lists of who belonged to the fortification and who was required to pay taxes. The Saxon *burg* was at least a similar construction used for protection of the rural population; cf. commentary to §3.

In Bethlehem was the throne (*stôl*) of the famous one (*thes mâreon*), of the noble king, of David the good, who long was able to hold the *hôhgisetu*. This latter term is a synonym for *stôl* in the sense of 'throne' but is plural in form. Saxons would have had different mental images than we would on hearing these words.

Ilkow says,
> Den Plural der Form as. *hôh-gisetu* ('das Hochgestühle') möchte ich mit dem Umstand zusammenbringen, daß der meist geräumige Hochsitz nicht bloß einem, sondern oft mehreren Teilhabern an Gewalt oder Erbe diente, so der *hēah-setl* im Beowulf, der vom König, seiner Gemahlin und dem Mitregenten eingenommen wird (Beow. 642, 1164ff.) (p. 220). Der bei den Germanen in Gebrauch gelangte erhöhte Ehrensitz geht historisch auf die spätrömische *sella curulis* ...

---

[41]that since ancient times was a cross-shaped post on the site of the court (p. 116).

[42]For a summary of scholarship on *handmahal* see Schmidt-Wiegand.

§. 5

zurück. Der älteste uns erhaltene germ. Thron, der Faltstuhl König Dagoberts (in Paris), ist nach dem Vorbild der *sella aurea* Diokletians angefertigt[43] (pp. 220; 249).

The imitation of the Roman *sella aurea* and perhaps even of the custom itself of having a special seat for the one or those in power to whom honor was due may also have been an import that played into the Germanic concept of god-given holiness by 'blood right' (*Blutheiligtum*).

Again the narrator breaks in (l. 367) to tell that he learned there (*thar gifragn ic*) that the 'bright fates' (*thiu berhtun giscapu*) and the 'might of God' decreed (*gimanodun*) that a son would be given to Mary on that journey (*an them sîða*). The most powerful of kings, the strongest of men (*barno strangost*), the renowned (*the mâreo*) would come into the 'light of men' as prophesied in days of yore by images (*biliði*)[44] and many signs (*filu bôcno*).

§6. Signs of Jesus' Birth

Lines 386b to 426
(Luke 2:8-15)

In this telling of the familiar Christmas story, the shepherds were watching in fields by night, but here they herded not sheep but horses. The first element of the compound noun *ehuscalcos* contains a reflex of the Indo-European word for horse, cognate with OE *eoh*, Latin *equus*, Greek ἵππος (*hippos*), etc. The latter part is the word for 'servant, thrall' as in the word *hildiscalc* 'warrior ['battle-*scalc*'] in l. 68 or as *scalc* in l. 939. (The other word for horse, *wiggi* in l.

---

[43] The plural form of OS *hôh-gisetu* ('the high seating') can be connected with the circumstance that the most commodious high seat served not merely one but often several persons sharing power, as with the *hēah-setl* in Beowulf which was used by the king, his spouse, and the co-regent ... The raised seat of honor as borrowed by the Germanic peoples goes back to the late Roman *sella curulis*. The oldest Germanic throne still in existence, the folding chair of King Dagobert (in Paris), was made on the pattern of the *sella aurea* used by Diocletian.

[44] Kluge-Seebold indicates under the entry for *Bild* that the root *bil*- indicated "'(über-, ungewöhnliche) Kraft, Wunderkraft' ['(superior, unusual power, miraculous power')]" and that "[d]emgemäß bedeutet asächs. *biliði* zunächst 'Wunder(zeichen)', dann erst 'Bild, Abbild; Gleichnis'... [accordingly, Old Saxon *biliði* first means 'miracle, miraculous sign' and only then 'picture, image; parable']."

Hêliand

389, is an ancient circumlocution cognate with Latin *veho* 'carry, bear', Sanskrit *vahyá-* 'fit for travel', OI *vigg* 'horse', etc.) Ilkow cites Lauffer, who notes that the *Hêliand* reflects Luke 2:8 without reference to *noctis* 'by night,' because the OS word *ehuscalcos* in l. 388 alone would indicate the time involved.

Ilkow goes on to say,

> Im Gegensatz zu den anderen Weidetieren kamen die Pferde, soweit es sich um Arbeitstiere handelt erst gegen Abend hinaus auf die Weide und blieben dort über Nacht. [Lauffer erwähnt], daß die Nachtweide die Zeit der Spukgeschichten war und daß das Wunder der Engelserscheinung den Sachsen in diesem Rahmen besonders anschaulich gemacht sei[45] (pp.93-94).

The cleaving of the air and the appearance of the 'light of God' gloriously through the clouds along with the arrival of the 'mighty angel of God' petrified the shepherds with fear. The angel spoke to them and admonished them that they ought not 'dread anything of evil from the light' (*uuiht ne antdrêdin lêðes fon them liohta*) but that he would tell them of the 'great power: now Christ is born' (l. 398-399), a 'joy to the kin of man' (*mendislo manno cunneas*) and 'advantage (or 'advancement') for all people' (l. 402-403). The *liohta* and the overpowering appearance of the angel has a counterpart in l. 5804b to 5810a, where the angel is described as being in white (*uuas im is giuuâdi uuintarcaldon / snêuue gilîcost*) and bathed in light as bright as lightening (*all sô blicsmun lioht*). It is possible that the image of this figure and that of the angels, that fair host of God (*fagar folc godes*), wending their way through the clouds (*uundun thurh thiu uuolcan*) may contain a reference to valkyries, *dísir*, swanmaidens, and similar flying figures in Germanic mythology.

The form *fîðan* 'find' in l. 404 is the expected Saxon reflex of Proto-Germanic **finþan-* with the elision of a nasal consonant before

---

[45] In contrast to other grazing animals horses, if they were work animals, came out onto the meadows in the evening and stayed there over night. (Lauffer mentions) that the time of nocturnal grazing was the time for ghost stories and that the miracle of the angels' appearance was made quite clear to the Saxons within this context.

§. 6

a spirant and the co-occurring lengthening of the preceding vowel. Generally, however, the form is *findan*, a back formation on the verbal parts with retained *n*, e.g. *fundan* 'gefunden' (see A BRIEF OUTLINE OF OLD SAXON GRAMMAR, §2.4c and Holthausen §§191, 435).

§7. JESUS IN THE TEMPLE

Lines 503b to 531a
(Luke 2:36-38)

The aged widow Anna recognized by the arrival of the child in the temple that the salvation of the Savior (*neriandas ginist*) had neared, just as the written documentation (*opera manuum: handgiuuerc*, cf. Ilkow [pp. 167-169]) in the book of holy men had taught (l. 529-531). She announced that 'joyful news' (*uuilspel*) to the people in the temple. Here we see the nomen agentis for 'savior', in the form of the nominalized present participle *neriand* from the weak verb *nerian* 'rescue, save' that was in semantic competition with *hêliand*, the nominalized present participle of the weak verb *hêlian* 'heal'. (The former is, however, deverbal with the Indo-European *o*-grade of a stem *nes-/*nos- that also occurs in the strong verb *ginesan* 'recover, be saved', while the latter is deadjectival from *hêl* 'hale, whole, healthy', both weak *jan*-verbs.) The word for 'salvation' *ginist* also contains the historical root *nes- that appears in *ginesan* and in *nerien*.

The temple was described as *alah*, which previously had meant 'cult site' or 'heathen place of worship' in OS. Polomé says,

> Gothic *alhs*, OE *ealh*, OS *alah* 'temple' must originally have designated [a sacred enclosure], as their etymological links with OE *ealʒian* 'protect, defend' and Old Lithuanian *alkas*, *alkà* '(sacred) grove' suggest; Tacitus (*Germania*, Chapter 9) tells us, the Germanic people would not confine their gods within walls ..., but rather consecrate woods and groves to them (p. 83).

This word has clearly undergone a shift of function in the same way that the heathen temple itself was refitted for Christian worship. (Note the circumlocutions *uuîh* in l. 519, *godes uuîh ... allaro hûso hôhost* in l. 1081-1083 and *hêlag hûs godes* in l. 3070 for 'church'; cf. Feist under *alhs*.) The latter phrase obviously means 'holy house

Hêliand

of God', which seems benign enough. One can speculate, however, that *hêlag hûs godes* perhaps had similar connotations with *alah* (cf. Ilkow, pp. 410-412), once denoting shrines consecrated to heathen gods, and know for certain that the designation *uuîh* (cognate with ON *vé*, OE *wêoh*, OHG *wîh*, etc.) did. The words *alah* and *wîh* seem to occur in free variation. Markey (1972) writes:

> Interestingly enough, *kirika* does not occur in *Hel.*, though it is attested from contemporaneous lesser texts. ... Due to their usage in a Christian context very little may be ascertained about the use of OS *alah* and *wîh* as pagan terms. However, one might infer that, together with their interpretive circumlocutions, they were employed to the exclusion of *kirika* or the like to indicate the Christian incorporation of pagan ideals and to interpret the new faith in familiar terms, rather than in novel, possibly obscure, foreign learned vocabulary (p. 370).

§8. THE THREE WISE MEN

Lines 537b to 603b
(Matthew 2:1-6)

The three very wise men (*suîðo glauua gumon*) came from the east following a bright beacon a long way across the land, seeking with a pure heart (*mid hluttru hugi*) the Child of God. While Matthew 2 speaks only of Herod's having heard of the arrival of the three wise men, here we read that 'God's fates drove them' (*dribun im godes giscapu*) to Herod, whose court knew nothing of the birth of Christ (l. 538b-541b). There they found the 'king (Herod) who spoke with grim words' (*slîðuurdean kunig*) 'wrathful with his men' (*môdagna mid is mannun*).

The adjective *slîðuurdi* seems to capture the essence of a conniving, untrustworthy, malicious personality. The first element is cognate to Gothic *sleidjai* [nom. pl.] 'bad, dangerous', *sleiþa* 'harm'; OI *slîðr* 'malevolent, terrible'; OHG *slîdîc* 'angry, terrible'. With Indo-European 'movable-*s*' and *o*-grade ablaut (cf. Prokosch, p. 45 and pp. 120 ff.) these words would be formed from the same stem as found in OS *lêð*, OI *leiðr*, OE *lâð* (Modern English 'loath'), OHG *leid* 'evil, malevolent' (cf. Feist under **sleiþs*). The second part of

§. 8

the compound is the adjectival form of *uuord* 'word'.

The *Hêliand* embellishes the biblical account with, among other things, a conversation between the three wise men and Herod, who wished to know their errand ('whether you are carrying wound gold as a gift to any men'.) and why they had come from afar on their *uuracsîð* (path of exile). The reference to 'wound gold' is to the Germanic practice of gift giving, whereby men of lower stature gave gifts to men of high stature in order to secure protection (see also the comment to *bâggebo* in §34). Herod remarks (l. 557b-558a), 'I can see that you are of noble birth of a good family.' Perhaps Herod thought the wise men were royalty coming to pay homage to him.

Instead, the wise men speak in an extensive emendation to the words of Matthew of a man of their own people 'so wise of speech' (*thar ni uuarð sîðor ênig man / sprâkono sô spâhi*) that he could 'relate the word of God' (*rekkien spel godes*), for 'the Lord of people had given to him that he might hear the words of the Wielder from earth' (l. 573–574)[46]. Here again we see a reference to the ancient wisdom of those who *cuþe frumsceaft fira feorran reccan* (*Beowulf* 90-91). A word of interest to us in the Germanic context of leadership and the giving of wise help is *spâhi*. In the *Hêliand* this word seems to mean something like 'experienced in communication', as it usually occurs with *uuord* 'word', *bôk* 'book', etc. When the Angel Gabriel descends as a messenger of God to announce the birth of John the Baptist, he says that the child will be *uuordun spâhi* (l. 125) 'experienced with words, eloquent'. When Zacharias, who has been rendered mute 'yet had wise thought' (l. 173b–174a), is asked what the child will be named, a book (perhaps a beech slat) is brought to him, and he is told to 'write wisely with wordmarks,' after which he thought (l. 235b), wrote John's name, and then 'spoke with his word(s) very eloquently' (*spâhlîco*, [l. 237–238a]). He then again possessed his power of speech, his wit and normal way and manner.

When the three men from the east following the star of Bethlehem appear at Herod's court and are described as *uuordspâhe uueros* (l. 563) 'word-wise men,' they tell how they knew of the impending birth of Christ, for 'A long time ago there were noble men, men of good speech (*gôdsprâka* [l. 567]), who promised so much good and help in truthful words (*uuârun uuordun* [l. 569]) from the King of Heaven. At that time there was a wise man, a man of experience and

---

[46] Compare also l. 188–189, where 'the people understood that [Zacharias] had himself seen something of the divine' as he emerged from the temple.

great wisdom (*frôd endi filuuîs* [l. 570]) – this was long ago – our ancestor there in the East.' The word *frôd* is the Germanic word for 'wise'.[47] In Germanic antiquity the term *filu-uuîs*, like OI *fjǫlvitr*, meant not 'wise' but rather 'prescient,' and *uuîs* itself meant more than 'wise.' Ilkow says, "[*weise*] bezeichnet ... 'kundig, erfahren' im Wahrsagen oder Traumdeuten, mit geheimem oder überirdischem Wissen oder Können begabt"[48] (p. 423). The three wise men relate that there had never since been any man who spoke so wisely (*sprâkono sô spâhi* [l. 572]), who was able to interpret God's speech (*rekkien spel godes* [l. 572]), because the Lord of man had granted him the ability to hear the Ruler's words up above from down on earth. For this reason, 'the man's knowledge was great in his mind' (l. 575). The repetition of words indicating eloquence is dense: 'well-spoken'; 'with true words'; 'senior and very wise'; 'of phrases so experienced'; 'he could interpret God's message'; and 'great intelligence'. The ability to perceive knowledge from the gods above and interpret it to those below was, indeed, in early Germanic societies a kingly attribute.[49]

The wise old man prophesied before he 'gave up the property, the crowd of relatives, left the tumult of life to seek the other light' (i.e. before he died) that 'a wise king, renowned and mighty [and] of best birth, the child of God' (*uuîscuning mâri endi mahtig ... hes bezton giburdies .. barn godes*) would come to rule this world, earth and heaven, to eternity (l. 582b–586). He further prophesied that on the same day 'a white heavenly star' (*himiltungal huît*) would rise and guide three men from that people. The Three Wise Men say that he ordered that 'we follow it' (*hêt that uui im folgodin*) 'such that it may be in front, west over this world' (*sô it furi uurði, / uuestar obar thesa uueroldi*). And thus they followed that beacon 'for a long while on paths through forests' (*uuegas endi uualdas huuîlon*), a distinctly Germanic landscape fraught with threat by wolf or brigand in deep woodland districts. Murphy (1999) sees in the journey of the Three Wise Men the proto-journey of seeking and finding the Holy Grail with later analogues in Wolfram's *Parzival* and writes, "By

[47] Cf. Cathey (1995).

[48] (*weise*) means ... 'knowledgeable, experienced' in prophesy or interpretation of dreams, endowed with secret or supernatural knowledge or ability.

[49] Myers (1982: 4) states that for the earliest period "we find traces of two distinct types of kings. ... One was a tribal embodiment in a sacred person, the other a warrior ruler. The first was needed in order to deal with the gods effectively, the second for the reason of needing one man's leadership in battle."

making the Magi into Germanic warriors the nature of the warrior's quest is changed from seeking treasure to seeking Christ in Bethlehem" (p. 22 f.)

§9. Herod's Threat

Lines 630 to 654
(Matthew 2:1-11)

The anonymous narrator again breaks in to tell the audience 'Then I found out' (*Thô gifragn ic*) that soon thereafter Herod, the 'evil-hearted' (*sliðmôd*) king, directed the three wandering expatriots (*uurekkiun*) to tell him the name of the town where the Child would be born and to return later and tell him exactly where to seek the Child in His lodging (*sôkean at is selðon*). The narrator relates that Herod planned to murder the Child, 'Then he intended to kill him with edges of a weapon' (*Than hogda he im te banon uuerðan / uuâpnes eggiun.*) Here we are even given a description of the thoughts of God, who considered the matter (*thâhte uuid them thinga*). He decided that Christ should accomplish more in this world, which is still in evidence, the revealed power of the Christian God (l. 645– 648a). Murphy (1992) comments: "In other words, the Christian God is depicted here as thinking about frustrating the normal procedure of fate, and then deciding to do it" (Footnote 39).

The wise men were 'eager to travel' (*fûsa te faranne*). They had no companions, other than that there were three of them together, and they revealed nothing to Herod.

Hêliand

§10. The Flight to Egypt

Lines 699b to 779
(Matthew 2:13-22)

This section faithfully renders Matthew 2:13-22 but with considerable embellishment. The geography of the flight is explained to the Saxon audience, including crossing the mountainous Sinai to the home of another people (l. 713b–714a) to the land of the Egyptians, to that green pasture (*an thana grôneon uuang*), to the best of earths, where a certain water flows, the great Nile north to the sea, the fairest of floods (l. 754b–760a).

After the wise men had returned to their 'ancestral homes in the east' (*ôstar an iro ôðil*) without informing Herod as to the whereabouts of the Child, the evil king became depressed (*uuarð im thes an sorgun hugi, / môd mornondi*), thinking that the wise men had scorned him (*that it im thie man dedin, / heliðos te hônðun*). Herod is described in this passage as *ôbarmôdig*, an accusation of the sin of *superbia* in terms of the new Christian teaching.[50] Again here the *Hêliand* expands on the words of Matthew (2:16) for dramatic and pathetic effect in l. 727b to 754a. Women weep; mothers see their sons destroyed, never again to be held dear and little in their two arms; the evildoers (*uuamskaðon*) saw nothing of crime (*mên*) nor of punishment but furthered the great sinful deed with weapon's edges; the lamentation of mothers was heard throughout Bethlehem, as though one cut their hearts in two with a sword; many brides in Bethlehem saw their children suffer death bloody on their bosoms; the killers murdered the guiltless, wanted to kill mighty Christ Himself.

God provided for the rescue of Christ from the enmity of the evildoers (l. 754b–755a) by sending angels to Joseph in a dream, directing the flight to Egypt, where they are to stay until the word of the Lord comes to lead the Holy Child back 'to this land' (l. 699b–709). The Holy Family lived there in grace until 'fate' (*uurd*) took Herod the king so that he left the children of men, the 'grim' (*môdag*) one left the 'clamor of men' (*manno drôm*). In commenting

---

[50] See Hempel, p. 85.

§. 10

on the OE *Judgment I*, Lochrie (1986) states with respect to the grim-minded (*gromhydig*) man,

> It is the quality of these men's thoughts and of their cognition which distinguishes them and ultimately determines their judgment. The *gromhydig* man, who never thinks the truth in his heart, instead rejects his Lord and seeks hell. He does not know, the poet warns us, the 'dark creation' which eternally awaits him because he is mired in the present. The *gromhydig* man is blinded by his wrath, and his thoughts are therefore turned to evil and destruction (p. 203).

Archelâus, the duke of 'helmet bearing soldiers' (*heritogo helmberandero*), was to have 'power over the district' (*marca giuuald*).

Jesus is called *friðubarn* in this passage, one of twenty occurrences of this locution. Ilkow comments,

> Das Komp. wurde in den bisherigen Wörterbüchern und Glossaren fälschlich als 'Frieden bringendes Kind' oder 'Friedenskind' gedeutet. Vom Standpunkt der Bibel wäre die Bildung eine[r] Kenning dieser Bedeutung durchaus zu rechtfertigen ... Doch ist nicht zu vergessen, daß der biblische Begriff *pax* – ähnlich as. *friðu* – auch die Bedeutungen des Schutzes, der Sicherheit und gottgewollten Ordnung beinhaltet. Der *princeps pacis* ist nicht nur ein Fürst des Friedens, sondern auch ein Herrscher, der seinen Untertanen Schutz und Sicherheit gewährt. Professor Starck [*Speculum* 1, 458] bemerkt zu unserem Komp.: 'To the ancient Saxons Jesus must have appealed rather as a protector than a bringer of peace. Thus *friðubarn* would better be rendered *Schutzkind*.' ... Wenn der HelD in Christus den Schutzherrn der Menschheit sieht, hebt er eine Seite hervor, die natürlich auch in der Bibel begründet ist[51] (pp. 136-137).

---

[51] This nominal compound was interpreted in previous dictionaries and glossaries incorrectly as "peace-bringing child' or 'child of peace.' From the standpoint of biblical knowledge the formation of a kenning with this meaning would be justified. ... But it should not be forgotten that the biblical concept *pax* – similar to OS *friðu* – also contains the meanings of protection, of security, and of divine order. The *princeps pacis* is not only a prince of peace but also a ruler who gives protection and security to his subjects. Prof. Starck ... notes: 'To the ancient Saxons Jesus must have appealed rather as a protector than a bringer of peace.' Thus *friðubarn* would better be rendered *Schutzkind*' [protective child]. If the

Compare also the emphasis on help and protection in the *Hêliand*'s version of the Lord's Prayer. (Cf. §19.)

§11. JOHN THE BAPTIST

Lines 873 to 890b, 903b to 948
(Luke 3:3; Matthew 3:2, 11; John 1:20-27)

This section, in accord with Luke 3:3, begins with a strongly Christian message of atonement for sins through fasting and of purification from evil (*lêðes*) 'that ye have done in this light' (*that gi an thesun liohta fremidun*). John spoke such truth (*huuanda he sô filu sôðes gisprac, uuâroro uuordo*) that the people believed him to be the Promised One, but he denied it, saying that he was merely the herald (*forabodo*) who would prepare the way for Him (*ic scal im thana uueg rûmien*). Then they thought he must be Elijah, who in days of yore was among the people (*the hêr an êrdagun / uuas undar thesumu uuerode*, cf. John 1:21), but John had a clever answer (*glau anduuordi*) to those who demanded to know who he was (l. 930). Again here verbal acuity is a trait associated with powerful men of authority.

On the other hand, these verses lend themselves well to usage of Germanic images of subordination before the commander, as we see in the untying of the shoe. John is nothing like his Lord (*Ni bium ic mid uuihti gilic / drohtine mînumu*), for His deeds are so strong, so renowned, and so mighty. Even though he may be His Own servant (*thoh ic sî is scalc êgan*), John is not worthy even to loosen the shoe thongs of 'so powerful a lord' (*sô rîkiumu drohtine*).

The section ends with the admonition to turn your wills, your faith and trust (*euuan gilobon*) thither, for then shall you escape the confinement of hell (*helligithuuing*) and the clamor of evil ones (*lêðaro drôm*), and your spirit (*hugi*) shall long be happy. The concept of 'hell' predates Christianity, but at first it had no presentiment of punishment. Ilkow says,

> author of the Hêliand sees in Christ the Protector of mankind, he emphasizes an aspect, which is naturally also founded in the Bible.

§. 11

> Das Gemeinsame an der germanischen Unterwelt und der christlichen Hölle – zumindest nach mittelalterlicher Auffassung – ist, daß beide nicht etwa als geistige oder symbolische Begriffe, sondern als ganz konkret gedachte Örtlichkeiten aufgefaßt werden; der Unterschied liegt darin, daß die germ. Unterwelt nicht als Ort des Schreckens und der Bestrafung galt[52] (p. 186).

The concept of 'confinement' was also likely a pre-Christian notion that had to do with being captured by or otherwise forced by death. Ilkow says further,

> Bei as. *githwing*, ahd. *gidwing*, die mit ablautend ahd. *gidwang* 'Zusammenpressung, Bedrängnis, Not' zu der germ. Verbalwurzel **þweng-* '(mit der Faust) zusammenpressen' gehören ..., schwingt dagegen die konkrete Vorstellung einer körperlichen Ungemach noch deutlich mit[53] (p. 188).

The better place indicated by 'thither' (*Hebbiad euuan uuillion tharod*) is further defined in redundant emphasis as the light of God, the 'home properties above' (*upôdes hêm*), the eternal realm, and the 'high meadow of heaven' (*hebenuuang*), which we have seen before in l. 275, 325, 411, 414, and perhaps as an allusion thereto in l. 757, where the flight to Egypt is described as *an thana grôneon uuang, / an erðono beztun*. The *Hêliand* often associates the reward of faith with the acquisition of property.

---

[52] The aspect common to the Germanic underworld and Christian hell – at least in the medieval imagination – is that both are understood not as spiritual or symbolic concepts but rather as quite concrete locations; the difference is that the Germanic underworld was not thought of as a place of terror and punishment.

[53] In OS *githwing*, OHG *gidwing*, which along with ablauting OHG *gidwang* 'being squeezed together, distress, peril' belong to the Germanic verbal root **þweng-* 'press together (with the hand),' ... the concrete idea of bodily discomfort is still clearly present.

§12. The Baptism of Christ

Lines 975b to 994
(Luke 3:21-22; Matthew 3:14 f.; John 1:32-34)

This section retells the story of Christ's baptism by John, but it contains phraseology that would likely have led the Saxon audience to identify the Holy Spirit descending from heaven in the 'form of a powerful bird' (*an gilîcnisse lungres fugles*) and alighting on 'our Lord's shoulder' (*uppan ûses drohtines ahslu*) with other famous birds on the shoulders of a god. Murphy (1989) comments:

> In placing the powerful white dove not just above Christ, but right on his shoulder, the *Heliand* author has portrayed Christ, not only as the Son of the All-Ruler, but also as a new Woden. ... With this image, Christ becomes a Germanic god, one into whose ears the Spirit of the Almighty whispers. ... The vivid picture of Christ with the dove on his shoulder offers both a comforting similarity to the old high god and a reassuring difference as well. The *Heliand* suggests that when the Saxons were being baptized by force in the River Lippe, the twilight of the old gods had come; but now that the almighty God stood among the people – a recognizable figure – with the familiar divine bird on his shoulders, they had not been abandoned (pp. 79-80).

§13. The Tempting of Christ

Lines 1020 to 1085a
(Matthew 4:2-10; Mark 1:12-13; Luke 4:1-13)

The Tempting of Christ takes place in a *uuôstunnia* 'wasteland, desert' (l. 1026), yet at the end we see Him emerge from the *uualdes hlêo* 'the shelter of the forest' (l. 1124) in the *sinuueldi* 'great (eternal) woods' (l. 1121); cf. *Hebanuuang* above in §4 and *sinuueldi* below in §14. It seems that the notion of 'wasteland' evoked the image of the perilous and dark forest to the Saxon audience. Moreover, we can speculate that a period of banishment to the 'eternal forest' could possibly have had reference to initiation or "coming-of-age" rites practiced in early pre-Christian times. It must

§. 13

be admitted that such a supposition is impossible to underpin with more than somewhat vague and circumstantial evidence to such practice, e.g. the testing of Sinfjotli in the forest. Cf. Byock, p. 45.

Christ lets Himself be tempted by *craftige uuihti*, which for the Saxons were elf-like beings that kept to the woods, demons[54]. In a statement likely still valid for the time and territory under consideration here, Hillgarth states,

> The extent to which men's minds were dominated by demons is difficult for us to realize. In these centuries [350-750] every-one, pagan and Christian alike, believed in the existence of demons. Demons were in the air you breathed, the water you drank, and the meat you ate. The Christian John Cassian in the early fifth century tells us 'that ... it is fortunate for men that they are not permitted to see them' (p. 12).

While the notion of temptation was foreign to the pre-Christian ethos, here the *craftige uuihti* are redefined for the Saxon audience in Christian terms as *selƀon Satanasan* (l. 1031). The image of the devil lurking to tempt is, of course, ubiquitous in Christian writings from the earliest time, e.g. in the *Ionae Vitae Columbani Liber Primus* from the 7th Century, cited by Wolfram (1982: 411), where we find Columban invisibly but perilously under siege: *tandem contra eum antiquus hostis loetifera tela laxare* "Da begann der alte Feind, todbringende Geschosse gegen ihn bereitzustellen"[55], and in the *Hêliand* we see the devil defined as *gêrfiund*, literally 'spear-fiend'. The word *uuiht* was in the pro-cess of undergoing a semantic shift from the notion of 'wight, hidden being' perhaps kin to dwarfs, elves, trolls, etc. to the meaning 'thing'. Line 1055 alludes to 'hidden beings' (*dernea wihti*), and in the Lord's Prayer (l. 1610) one asks for protection from the tempting of *lêða uuihti*. Elsewhere the word has a quite neutral meaning, as in l. 935, where John says that he is 'in nothing equal to my Lord' (*Ni bium ic mid uuihti gilîc / drohtine mînumu*). In the *Hêliand* the term *uuiht* has both meanings.

---

[54] Regarding the early church, Alfred Burns (p. 145) writes, "... it never occurred to the Christians raised in the mythological environment to question the existence of the Olympian gods. Instead they resorted to downgrading them to manifestations of the forces of evil; thus the Greek *daimones* became demons."

[55] Then the old fiend began to make ready death-bringing projectiles against him.

Hêliand

§14. JESUS RETURNS TO GALILEE

Lines 1121 to 1202a
(Matthew 4:18-22; 9:9; Luke 5:27-28)

After His confrontation with Satan Jesus is depicted as emerging from a great forest (*an them sinuueldi ... uualdes hlêo ... ênôdies ard* [l. 1121, 1126-1127]). The word *sinuueldi* conjures a dark, dangerous wood where 'hidden beings' lurk. Ilkow says,

> Die altwestgerm. Sprachen verknüpfen das Wort noch nicht mit dem Bild unseres gehegten und gepflegten Forstes; wie Kl[uge]-Götze betont, können as. ahd. *wald* auch 'Wildnis' bedeuten ... Während des Mittelalters gilt der Wald als ein unwirtlicher Ort, wo wilde Tiere hausen und böse Geister ihr Wesen treiben, und wo sich der Mensch nur ungerne aufhält[56] (pp.358-359).

The biblical text has no mention of the landscape other than to say that Jesus came to the sea coast, "he went and settled at Capernaum on the Sea of Galilee" beyond the Jordan (Matthew 4:13-14). The *Hêliand*, following John 1:29, lets John the Baptist meet Christ at the bank of the Jordan. John announces to his own disciples, when he saw Him walking there: "'Look,' he said, 'there is the Lamb of God; it is He who takes away the sin of the world' (l. 1127b-1134a). Here Jesus meets His own first disciples and first begins to preach (Matthew 4:17). The *Hêliand* motivates His departure from the *sinuueldi* and His proselytizing with the remark that "He would rather make known His great power" (l. 1122b-1123).

Jesus begins here to gather His disciples, described as *uuordspâha uueros* 'well spoken men' themselves endowed with the persuasive leadership quality of eloquence. The first two are Andrew

---

[56] The ancient West Germanic languages do not yet associate the word with the image of our well-tended forest; As Kluge-Götze stresses, OS, OHG *wald* can also mean 'wilderness' ... During the medieval period the forest is viewed as an inhospitable place where wild animals dwell and evil spirits linger, and where people only reluctantly stay.

§. 14

and Peter, who are fishing along the stream in the manner of Saxons. Murphy (1992) remarks in connection with *thenidun* 'stretched out':

> Apparently Saxon fishermen did not 'cast' their nets when fishing ... but must either have staked the nets out in the current or used seining techniques. Peter and Andrew are described as sitting on the sand (a difficult position to cast nets from!) ... James and John are described as repairing nets cut open 'the night before'. The author seems to have been aware of night fishing with nets stretched between stakes (weirs) in the current (Footnote 62).

James and John (*Iacobus endi Iohannes*) left their father and their property, which consisted of *nettiu endi neglitskipu* 'nets and nailed ships'. Presumably a ship constructed using nails was commonly known among the Saxons as a quite fine type of vessel. (A point of comparison, although of a rather older and perhaps longer ship for the open sea, would be the Nydam boat from Schleswig, which dates from the middle of the 4th century. It is a high-prowed, lapstrake boat with nailed joints and can be viewed in the Danish National Museum in Copenhagen. See, for example, Oxenstierna, p. 23 f., Almgren, p. 248 f., or Marstrander, p. 18-19.)

One word, *gesunfader* in l. 1176 is worthy of special note because of the similar compound *sunufatarungo* in the *Hildebrandlied*. The latter word has been taken to mean 'son and father' or 'the family including father and son'.[57]

Notice here in l. 1185–1186 that James and John *gecurun im thana neriandan Krist ... te hêrron* ('They chose for themselves the Saving Christ ... as Lord'), not the other way around. Early Germanic society provided for the election of leaders (cf. Chaney, p. 16 f.), and this is a reflection of that practice. Christ was for them furthermore 'the more generous jewel giver' (*milderan mêðomgeƀon*). Ilkow comments,

> ... *mêðom-giƀo* ist wie *bôg-geƀo* eine Fürstenkenning der westgerm. Dichtersprache. Die Anwendung dieser Fürstenbezeichnung auf Christus besagt nicht, daß der HelD, wie

---

[57] Ilkow says, "*gisun-fader* bedeutet nämlich nicht 'Sohn und Vater', sondern, wie schon Schmeller ... richtig erklär[t], '*filii cum patre*, die Söhne und der Vater'. ... Das Präfix *gi-* scheint also ... schon vor der Composition dem Vorderglied angehört zu haben" (p. 148) [*gisun-fader* does not mean 'son and father' but rather, as Schmeller already correctly explains, '*filii cum patre* 'the sons and the father.' ... The prefix *gi-* seems thus to have been associated with the first element of the compound before its composition.]

Hêliand

> früher behauptet wurde, den Erlöser als einen germ. Gefolgsherrn darstellen wollte. Die Übertragung des germ. Ausdrucks auf Christus kann unter dem Einfluß ähnlicher kirchlicher Vorbilder stattgefunden haben. Die biblische Schrift stellt Gott in zahlreichen Wendungen als den 'Geber der Menschheit' dar, die kirchenlat. Literatur bezeichnet ihn öfter als *dator* oder *largitor*[58] (p. 278).

Note also the commentary to §34, where King Herod is characterized as a *bâggebo* at l. 2738.

§15. The Sermon on the Mount

Lines 1248b to 1278
(Matthew 5:1)

The author of the *Hêliand* regroups the disciples in front of their Lord and names them one-by-one. Matthew 5:1 states merely, "And seeing the multitudes, he went up into a mountain; and when he was set, his disciples came unto him."

Here the numinous quality of Christ, *mahtig self*, is stressed along with the faithful qualities of the Twelve *treuuafta man, gôde gadulingos* who went to council with the Helping One (*rincos to theru rûnu, thar the râdand sat*). The pre-Christian concept of receiving wise help from one's lord against one's enemies is retained,

---

[58] *mêðom-gebo* is like *bôg-gebo* a kenning for 'ruler' in West Germanic poetical language. The use of this designation applied to Christ does not mean that the author of the Hêliand, as earlier had been maintained, meant to portray the Redeemer as a Germanic leader. The transfer of the Germanic expression to Christ may have taken place under the influence of similar ecclesiastical models. The Bible presents God in many expressions as the 'Giver of mankind,' and ecclesiastical Latin literature characterizes Him often as *dator* or *largitor*.

§. 15

but in place of warlike advice Jesus counsels forbearance, which is to say that his appearance as *râdand* 'counselor' forces a radical change in the meaning of the word. This *râdand* is there to help all mankind against the forces of hell. Note too that *râd* instead of 'bread' (OS *brôd*) is beseeched in the Lord's Prayer at l. 1607 (cf. §19).

§16. ADMONITIONS

Lines 1279 to 1380
(Matthew 5:2-10; Luke 6:20-23)

In Luke (6:17) we read that Jesus goes down from a mountain and speaks to the crowd. The *Hêliand* follows Matthew 5:1 instead, where Christ takes the disciples with him up onto a mountain, where He speaks the Beatitudes. The latter is more in keeping with the tradition of the *drohtin* and his followers (*rincos*) going with their Lord to secret counsel (*gengu ... te theru rûnu* [l. 1272–1273]), as we saw in §15. However, the words of the Beatitudes would be quite untraditional *râd* as compared to the kind of followers a Saxon *drohtin* would have been familiar with.

Especially the seventh Beatitude (Matthew 5:9) would likely have been puzzling to the Saxon mind set: "Blessed are the peacemakers, for they shall be called the children of God." The *Hêliand* nuances this by stating instead (l. 1316b–1320a), as Murphy (1992) translates:

> He said that those too were fortunate 'who live peacefully among the people and do not want to start any fights or court cases by their own actions, they will be called the Chieftain's sons for He will be gracious to them, they will long enjoy His kingdom' (p. 46).

This modifies Matthew 5:9 (How blest are the peacemakers; God shall call them his sons) by the implied maintenance of property rights through not bringing a court case (*saca*). It was in the local Germanic assembly that proper settlement of disagreements was possible through procedures which could yield legal sanction to duel against or otherwise try to gain compensation from an opponent. The result could be long-lasting vendettas between kinship groups. (Note Amira, pp. 161-162: "Der altgermanische Rechtsgang [Prozeß] beruhte auf folgenden Prinzipien. Der Prozeß ist ein Kampf ..., worin

Hêliand

der Gegner den andern zu überwinden hat. ... Des Klägers Tätigkeit ist Angriff ..., die des Beklagten Abwehr ... ."[59] See also the survey of the semantics of Germanic *sakan and *sôkian in Freudenthal, p. 146 f.)

But not only that: the disciples were admonished to count themselves blessed in suffering scorn, loathsome words, and punishment from the court cases brought upon them by others, for Jesus' followers would have their reward prepared in heaven (l. 1336–1347a). The disciples would be the "salt of the earth" (*thesoro uueroldes ... salt*) to heal the evil deeds of sinful men, *bôtian iro baludâdi*. Ilkow establishes the basic meaning of Germanic *balwa- as 'Quälerei' ['torment'] and says further,

> Wenn *balwa- mit des Menschen Streben, Willen oder Gemüt in Beziehung gebracht wird, bezeichnet es eine Absicht zu quälen, bedeutet also soviel wie 'Arglist, Tücke, Bosheit'. ... Die Verallgemeinerung von 'Arglist, Tücke' zu 'Sünde' vollzieht sich unter dem Einfluß des Christentums. ... Die Alliteration mit dem Stamm *bat-, *bôt-, der in gewissem Sinn den Gegenbegriff von *balwa- ausdrückt, nämlich 'relativ nützlich' gegenüber 'schädlich', [hat] einerseits die Ethisierung von *balwa-, anderseits dessen Verwendung in der Stabreimdichtung gefördert....[60] (p. 56).

Murphy (1992) remarks:

> The *Heliand* author transforms the salt analogy of the gospel from one of discipleship as having a 'taste-improvement' role for the world, to a medical one ... as a (painful) antiseptic for improving the condition of wounds. The disciples are thus given a much more active (if more abrasive) role in the *Heliand* (Footnote 82).

The compound *erðlîbigiscapu* at l. 1331 is also of some interest. Ilkow says,

---

[59] Ancient Germanic justice was based on the following principles: the case is a battle ..., in which the plaintiff must beat the other person. The task of the plaintiff is attack ..., that of the defendant defense.

[60] If *balwa- is brought into association with human striving, will, or disposition, it denotes an intention to torment and thus means as much as 'guile, deception, malice.' ... Generalizing from 'guile, malice' to 'sin' occurs under the influence of Christianity. ... The alliteration with the stem *bat-, *bôt-, which in a certain sense expresses the opposite of *balwa-, namely 'relative useful' as opposed to 'injurious,' has promoted on the one hand the ethical cleansing of *balwa- and on the other hand its use in alliterative poetry.

§. 16

Wie der Gebrauch von *erðlibi-giskapu* als Gegenpol zum christlichen Ewigkeitsbegriff zeigt, verwendet der Dichter dieses Komp. in ausgesprochen christlichem Sinn. Es ist auch nur in ausgesprochen christlichem Sinn möglich, denn der Begriff des irdischen Daseins wurde erst in christlicher Zeit als Gegensatzbegriff zum 'ewigen Dasein nach dem Tode' entwickelt. Das Vorderglied *erð-lîf halte ich für eine Lehnübersetzung nach kirchenlat. *vita terrena*. ... Notker verwendet [das althochdeutsche] *erd-lib* als Gegensatzbegriff zu *himil-lib*: *vita caelestis*[61] (p. 113).

Christ told the disciples of the 'eight good fortunes' that await the faithful. (Cf. Murphy 1992:44 f.) Those to whom good fortune is not given will suffer the pain of hell and *narouuaro thing after iro hinferdi* (l. 1350-1351). Doane (1991) comments, "Here *narouuaro* seems to mean 'confining,' hence causing a sense of helplessness, anxiety" (p. 346).[62]

§17. HEARING THE SERMON

Lines 1381 to 1419
(Matthew 5:14-18)

We know from Einhard that "Charlemagne ordered that the laws of all the peoples under his power, which up to then had been

---

[61] As the use of *erðlibi-giskapu* opposing the Christian concept of eternity shows, the author uses this nominal compound in a pronounced Christian sense. It is also possible only in a pronounced Christian sense, because the concept of earthly existence was developed only in Christian times as a concept of 'eternal existence after death.' The first element *erð-lîf I consider a loan translation from Church Latin *vita terrena* ... Notker uses [OHG] *erd-lib* as the opposite of *himil-lb*: *vita caelestis*.

[62] Cf. *gethwing* (footnote 53).

transmitted by oral tradition, should be copied down in writing" (Riché p. 132), and Jesus' appearance here is like that of a Germanic law-speaker with his retinue listening in respectful silence (l. 1381-1387). The disciples are the 'light of the world' (*thesoro uueroldes ... lioht*) that shines over many peoples and cannot be hidden any more than can the city on a hill. The 'city' is something special here, a *burg* quite impressive to the Saxons. It is called *uurisilîk giuuerc* 'gigantic construction'; cf. Genzmer, p. 320, who translates this phrase as *mächtige Bauwerk der Riesen* 'mighty edifice of giants' and relates it to autochthonic mythology; Middle Dutch has the reflex *vreselijc* 'fear-inspiring', Modern Dutch 'dreadful, terrible'; cf. also the comments on *burg* in §3.

The notion of proclaiming the law for instruction of the people returns in the latter part of this excerpt. The disciples should spread the holy word so that people understand and carry it out as when in ancient days very wise men spoke the 'old law' (l. 1409b-1419). It is known that the law was proclaimed at annual assemblies in three-year cycles in Scandinavia, and perhaps that was also the case in Saxon tradition. Note OI *lǫgsǫgumaðr*, OHG *ēsago*, Old Frisian *âsega*, and OS *êosago* 'lawspeaker, Gesetzes-ausleger'. (Cf. Grimm, Vol. II, p. 394 f.) Here Christ clearly reveals a new Law for the Jews — but also for the Saxons.

§18. Swearing Oaths

Lines 1502b to 1527a
(Matthew 5:33-37)

These passages from Matthew are elaborated with detail from Germanic law, which would naturally be the *êo* the audience of the *Hêliand* would know. Matthew has nothing of *mênêð* or the swearing of false oaths (*forsuerie*), but proof of an assertion under Germanic law was based solely on oath-taking and/or on eye-witness corroboration. Proof of innocence by oath was directed at the opponent (not to an impartial officer of the court), who received the oath by repeating it in the so-called *êdstaf* (l. 1508; cf. Amira, p. 166 f.) Ilkow says,

§. 18

> Auch zum Abnehmen des Eides dient der Stab. Der germanische Eidgang besteht nämlich aus dem Sprechen des Eides, der an bestimmte Worte gebunden ist, und dem Antasten des Gegenstandes, auf den geschworen wird. Der eidabnehmende Richter hält den Stab in einer Hand und sagt die Eidesformel vor. Das Abnehmen des Eides heißt daher auch 'den Eid staben' ...[63] (p. 91).

Such oaths were binding and sworn to by higher powers. For that reason the author of the *Hêliand* proscribes false oaths or the receiving of oath-sworn testimony. Murphy (1992) remarks:

> The nobles of the warrior class among Franks and Saxons often legally 'proved' their innocence in court simply by swearing an oath that they were not guilty of the charge. The author makes the gospel passage intelligible by pointing out what must have been a fact under the system of Germanic law: if too many guilty earls establish their innocence through frequent false oaths, then the system will lose its credibility. Any earl will not believe another's word of honor because of the frequency of incidents of *untreuua*. Thus the gospel system is presented as not only simpler, but as restoring faith in Germanic *treuua* (Footnote 85).

Matthew 5:34-35 warns that one should not swear oaths by high heaven, for there is God's throne, nor by the earth below, for that is His footstool. This striking image is commented on by Ilkow:

---

[63] The staff serves also to administer an oath. Germanic oath-taking consists of speaking the oath, which is tied to specific words, and touching an object on which one swears the oath. The judge administering the oath holds the staff in one hand and recites the oath. The administration of the oath is thus also 'to stave the oath.'

Hêliand

> Das biblische Gleichnis vom Himmel als dem Thron und der Erde als dem Fußschemel Gottes müßte den Germanen besonders einleuchten, denn schon in altgerm. Zeit war der Hochsitz ... meistens mit einem Fußschemel versehen. ... Auch in karolingischer Zeit und später ist der untere Teil von Hochsitzen, aber auch von gewöhnlichen Sesseln und Stühlen recht hoch und erfordert als Stütze eine Fußbank, die entweder fest mit dem Sitzgerät verbunden oder nur als angeschobenes Möbel erscheint... Der Fußschemel diente nicht nur dem Zweck würdevoller Repräsentation beim Thron, sondern auch einem praktischen Zweck, dem Schutz gegen den kalten Zimmerboden[64] (p. 134).

§19. THE LORD'S PRAYER

Lines 1588 to 1615a
(Matthew 6:5-15; Luke 11:2-4)

One of the disciples expresses desire for the *huldi* of their Lord (as admonished in the gnomic verse in l. 1170 to 1172a) and of His words in order that they might work His will. Greene defines *huldi* as "the disposition of God toward his worshipers which is to be brought about by the latters' service" (p. 155). A disciple asks to be taught to pray, as John the Baptist taught his disciples (cf. Luke 11:1). Christ Himself should reveal that secret (*gerûni*: cf. l. 3, 1273, 4138, and 4603).

The most striking word in this version of the Lord's Prayer is certainly *râd* 'teaching, counsel; help, support; gain, profit' in l. 1607 in place of the expected *brôd* (which does occur in l. 1066, 1068, and 3341). There is a shift of emphasis from use of a concrete substance to stand for a more abstract concept ('bread' as exemplum of general life support) to a straightforward plea for help. The disciples in the role of thanes of their *drohtin* would have primary interest in obtaining counsel and help in return for their services to a worldly lord, and here we see the old concept in that specific

---

[64] The biblical parable of heaven as the throne and the earth as the footstool of God must have seemed plausible to the ancient Germanic peoples, since in Germanic times the high seat ... was usually provided with a footstool. ... In the Carolingian period and later the lower part of the high seat, but also of normal seats and chairs, was quite high and required a support for the feet either as part of the seat or a piece of furniture pushed up to it. ... The footstool served not only the purpose of lending dignity to the throne but also a practical purpose of protection against the cold floor.

context. In an analogous manner the might of God offers *helpa fan himila* (l. 11), and God's power came through Christ to this earth as help to the many (l. 49-51; note l. 521, 568, 1143, 1187, 1608, etc. for similar usages). The next line (1608) serves to define this application of *râd* as *thîna hêlaga helpa*.[65]

Before the request for 'help against all evil deeds,' the prayer asks that 'evil beings' or 'loathsome wights/things' not mislead us. The phrase *lêða uuihti* as the embodiment of lurking yet personified danger from unseen 'wights' occurs with some frequency as a remembrance of Germanic traditions. Note in this connection *slîðuurdi* in the commentary to §8, the commentary to §13, and l. 2502, 3356, and 4623 along with *dernea uuihti* in l. 1055.

§20. LILIES OF THE FIELD

Lines 1667b to 1686
(Matthew: 6:26-31)

This poetical passage speaks of the birds in their feather-coats (*feðarhamun*) and of the splendidly decorated (*fagoro gefratohot*) worts (*uurti*) standing in the field. The word for 'lily' occurs here rather as a definition of *uurt*, the plant familiar to the Saxon audience, and it is the *lilli* that the 'ruler of the land' (*landes uualdand*) clothes.

The birds are given that which is requested of God in the Lord's Prayer in place of 'bread,' namely *helpa*, against hunger. Likewise will God grant help (*is alles râdan, helpan fan heƀenes uuange*) that people may be clothed 'if ye are willing to serve according to his *huldi*' (l. 1685b to1686), cf. l. 1588: *ûs is thînoro huldi tharf*. The Lord's *huldi* proceeds from the 'meadow of heaven,' defined in l. 947 as *upôdes hêm, êuuig rîki*, which can be rendered as 'the world of property above, the eternal realm', again using a pre-Christian notion which immediately is redefined in Christian terms.

---

[65]Cf. Cathey (1995).

§21. PEARLS BEFORE SWINE

Lines 1720b to 1724a (Matthew 7:6)

This short passage is remarkable in its retelling of Matthew 7:6, which says "Do not give dogs what is holy; do not throw your pearls to the pigs: they will only trample on them, and turn and tear you to pieces." Here not only pearls are cast before the swine but also a 'treasure of jewels' (*mêðmo gestriuni*) and a (or the) 'holy necklace' (*hêlag halsmeni*).

The word *merigrîta* for 'pearl' is a loanword – most likely from Latin *margarita* (in turn from Greek *margarítes*), compare OE *meregrot, -grêot*, OHG *merigreoz* 'Meergries'. The loanword has been folk-etymologized into the OS (OE, OHG, etc.) constituents *meri* 'ocean' and *grîta*, cf. *griota* 'kernel, grit' (see the summary of views in Ilkow, p. 290-291). The folk etymology notwithstanding, the word is here further redefined as the 'treasure of precious objects, or jewels' and, most interestingly, as 'holy necklace.'

Ilkow (p. 166) cites Heyne, who views *halsmeni* as a medicinal amulet worn around the neck: "Die ... am Halsband angebrachten Anhängsel dienten häufig als Amulette, denen man die Kraft zuschrieb, böse Geister und Krankheiten zu bannen".[66] Ilkow remarks that the Christian cross later replaced the heathen amulet and believes that was likely what the author of the *Hêliand* had in mind.

Another association perhaps still present in the memory of the audience could be to the goddess Freyja and her *Brisingamen*, described as a costly necklace. Freyja is also has to do with swine. In the Norse *Hyndlaljóð* Freyja rides on a boar called *Hildisvín*, and she has the nickname *Sýr* 'Sow'. Derolez also terms *Brisingamen* an amulet, which was put around the waist to ease birth (p. 182). Klaeber (1941) comments on *Brôsinga mene* in l. 1199 of *Beowulf* that "we judge that Hâma had robbed Eormenrîc of the famous collar" (p. 178). (See also Brodersen, pp. 103-109.) The point here is that a 'holy necklace' well known to the Saxons from Germanic mythology was something valuable which never would be defiled.

The *Hêliand* omits mention of "giving that which is holy unto the dogs," perhaps because a reference to offerings of ritually pre-

---

[66] The pendants on a necklace were often used as amulets to which the power to ban evil spirits and sickness was ascribed.

§. 21

pared meat could be read into that phrase, and the author of the *Hêliand* found all reminders of the same abhorrent. The prohibition introduced by Christian missionaries against the consumption of horse meat can be understood in the same way (cf. Bökönyi, p. 300).

§22 BAD TREE, BAD FRUIT

Lines 1741b to 1750a
(Matthew 7:16-18)

The biblical verses speak of grapes on thorns and of figs on thistles. Here we have *uuînberi an thorniun*, which corresponds well, but *figun an hiopun* 'figs on briers'. Again here it seems that considerations of alliteration carried the day in l. 1743-1744. (OS *thistil* is attested but does not occur in the *Hêliand*.)

Matthew 7:17-18 tell us that a good tree produces good fruit and that a bad tree brings forth bad fruit. A good tree can produce no bad fruit nor a bad tree good fruit. In the *Hêliand* the warning is of 'the evil tree' and that 'where it stands on earth' it never gives good growth (*uuastum*). The good tree was not created by God such that it might 'bear anything bitter.' The specific warning concerning the nature of the fruit ('bright' or 'bitter' depending upon what it 'draws from its roots') is an expansion on the biblical text. Although there is no further evidence for the assumption, it is tempting to conjecture that this may be a reference to the World Tree, known best from Nordic sources harkening to pre-Christian traditions, as the World Tree had three roots, one at the well from which Woden drank in order to obtain wisdom (cf. Young, pp. 42-43). The Saxon *Irmensûl* was also a World Tree (cf. Hammerbacher, 1984).

§23. THE NARROW GATE

Lines 1771 to 1801a
(Matthew 7:13-14)

From these two verses in Matthew the author of the *Hêliand* constructs a long passage. The worldly multitudes (*uuerodes filu ... uueroldlusta uueros*) choose the path onto which their hearts urge them (*tharod iro môd spenit*). This is the broad path that 'leads many people on the worse (which is to say the left) hand' (*thiu an thea*

Hêliand

uuirson hand liudi lêdid), while the few (*uuerodes lût, fâho folkskepi*) take the path that is more narrow by far (*engira mikilu uueg*). The conditions in hell at the end of the *uuîd strâta endi brêd* are depicted in graphic terms (*hêt endi suart, egislîc an innan*), and it is easy for the children of men to travel thither. God is, however, ever ready to help men who ask that they might start the narrow path from the beginning and go forth to the end in the realm of God (l. 1790b-1795a). 'Ye should announce your journey thither at your Lord's doors, and the portals of heaven will be opened that ye might enter the Holy Light and see eternal life.'

Murphy (p.c.) speculates that this luminous image may be a Christian reinterpretation of the rainbow bridge (*bifrǫst*) over which (in this version) humans pass from Midgard, the earth, to the home of the gods at the end of the world (*ragnarǫk*), as depicted in Nordic apocalyptic visions. Davidson (1964) says, "In Norse mythology ... we find the image of a bridge that links the worlds. This may be fragile and steeply poised above the abyss, as thin as a needle or a sword-edge, so that only the man with tremendous mantic power may cross it. ... We also hear of the bridge *Bifrǫst*, a rainbow span of three colours ... which linked earth and heaven. Over this the gods rode each day, and Snorri connects it with the Milky Way" (p. 193).

This passage is important in reinforcing the idea of a hot, dark hell as a place of punishment after this life. Germanic notions of an afterlife may, among others, be reflected in the phrase *grôni uuang* 'green meadow' which describes fruitful abodes (l. 3135-3136a: *uuas thar gard gôdlîc endi grôni uuang, paradise gelîc*) and in its variants *hebenes uuang* (l. 1682) and *grôni godes uuang* (l. 3082). In another Nordic tradition the land of the dead lay to the north, where cold and darkness reign. (See Derolez, p. 269 f., for a brief summary of visions of the afterworld.)

§24. A House upon Sand

Lines 1801b to 1826a
(Matthew 7:24-27; Luke 6:47-49)

This familiar parable of the house on rock and the house on sand is here stated in a manner that bespeaks the audience's familiarity with the seacoast. Phrases like *uuind ni mag, / ne uuâg ne uuatares strôm* (1809b - 1810a) or – in the case of the unwise man

§. 24

who – *im be uuatares staðe / an sande uuili selihûs uuirkean, / thar it uuestrani uuind endi uuâgo strôm, sêes ûðeon teslâad* (1818b - 1821a) employ a graphic vocabulary of the northern seacoast. The image of the house of the foolish man subjected to the ravages of waves beaten high by the westerly wind is cast in vocabulary indicative of real experience with the local Saxon geography.

§25. LAMBS AMONG WOLVES

Lines 1837b to 1855a, 1873b to 1880a
(Matthew 10:7-9, 16-17)

The disciples are sent on their way "like sheep among wolves" to make known that the kingdom of heaven is near, to heal the sick, to wake the dead, to cleanse lepers, and to drive out evil spirits with the admonition that they should be as "wary as serpents, innocent as doves" (Matthew 10:16). They should be generous in th*eir intentions (an* iuuuon hugiskeft*iun helpono* mildea), pr*oclaim eternal gain/help (lêread ... langsamna râd) and further advantage (fruma forðuuardes),* and say how one might attain heaven, the expansive property (*huuô man himilrîki gehalon scoldi, / uuîdbrêdan uuelan*). The emphasis is first on the self-denial of the disciples, who should take no payment, but second on the self-interest of those to be converted to seize the advantage and to gain the wide and broad realm of heaven, the weal, the property.

In sending the disciples as lambs among wolves, the danger is actually in the encounter with enemies (*fiund*) and various kinds of men (*mislîke man*). Throughout the *Hêliand* there seems to be a reflexive suspicion against strangers who are not, in this reference, Saxons (cf. Herod's reaction to the Wise Men and the constant reference to the enmity of the Jews).

Whereas Matthew speaks of being as "wary as serpents," here we find a quite specific reference to 'the yellow snake, the colorful adder' (*the gelouuo uurm, nâdra thiuu fêha*). According to Steward (1971) candidates for 'the yellow snake' occurring in northern Germany may be the Aesculapian Snake (*Natrix longissima*), which is reported to have occurred as far north as Denmark, the Grass Snake (*Natrix natrix natrix*), and, most likely, the Adder (*Vipera berus berus*), the same word historically as OS *nâdra*. However, none of the above is said to be completely yellow, although that color is

185

Hêliand

striking even as part of a pattern (perhaps indicated by *thiuu fêha*), and yellow is a universal danger sign in nature (cf. bees, wasps, etc.). Adders, moreover, like to lie in sunny spots, even in the tops of bushes, and males engage in so-called combat dances "in which they oppose or chase each other with the front parts of their bodies raised vertically, and try to push each other over" (Steward, p. 163 f.). Such behavior, if observed by the Saxons, would probably have made a strong impression. Beyond this, we can also note that the robes of Judas Iscariot in medieval art were yellow. Another, more mundane factor is also at work here. As Gantert (p.c.) points out that "allein das Adjektiv 'gelu' mit dem biblisch vorgegebenen 'glau' alliteriert. Mit anderen Worten, metrisch reagiert zwar 'glau' auf 'gelu', das den Hauptstab trägt, aber übersetzungstechnisch muß der Dichter das Wort 'glau' schreiben und braucht einen Stab dazu, das heißt, die Abhängigkeit dreht sich hier um."[67] That is, for the sake of alliterating with the biblically mandated word 'glau' a word like 'gelu' had to be used, and perhaps the presence of yellowish snakes on Saxon territory made the rhyme logical.

§26. ENTERING HEAVEN

Lines 1915 to 1916a and 1940 to 1956
(Matthew 7:21, 10:14-15)

Here the lessons of the Good Tree and the Bad Tree (cf. §23) and the sending out of the disciples are continued. Not all who cry out to Christ as Protector (*mundburd*) will come into heaven. If they cannot become blessed (*sâliga*) through their own works in that they hear and heed the teachings of the disciples, then they should be abandoned and the disciples should continue on their way in search of receptive souls.

---

[67][T]he adjective 'gelu' alone alliterates with the biblically required 'glau.' In other words, 'glau' reacts metrically to 'gelu,' which carries the main stress, but for translating the author must write the word 'glau' and needs an alliteration for it. The dependency turns on this.

§. 26

One interesting aspect of this section is the clause *endi the mâreo dag oƀar man farid*, which finds a similar locution in the OHG *Muspilli*, l. 55: *verit denne stuatago in lant* 'then the day of judgment fares into the land.' Corresponding to OHG *muspilli*, the OS reflex *mûtspelli* (also spelled *mûdspelli*) occurs in l. 2591 *anttat mûdspelles megin oƀar man ferid, endi thesaro uueroldes* ('until the sons of *mûdspelli* fare over men, the end of this world') and l. 4358 *mûtspelli cumit an thiustrea naht, al sô thiof ferid* ('*mûtspelli* comes in the dark night, just as a thief fares'), indicating a commonality of image. The *Muspilli* and *Hêliand* are roughly contemporary works from around the year 830. See Kartschoke (1994: 136f.) for a summary of attempts to analyze the word 'muspilli' and also the commentary to §33.

§27. WATER TO WINE

Lines 2000 to 2065a
(John 2:2-10)

Again the author expands on the biblical story to enliven it for the Saxon audience. The Marriage at Cana is elaborated with phrases descriptive of Saxon drinking, and, in fact, the marriage is not much mentioned. God's Own Child was in that high hall (*that hôha hûs*) where the soldiers drank in the banquet hall (*thar the heri dranc ... an themu gastseli*), where men were of good cheer (*blîðode*, cf. *blîði* 'cheerful') and happy of spirit (*gladmôdie*). Servants drew pure wine with bowls (*scâlun*), jugs (*orcun*), and ale mugs (*alofatun*), all words picked for purposes of alliteration in their respective lines. (One suspects that maybe not even the Saxons would serve *skîrianne uuîn* in ale mugs.) The clamor of men (*erlo drôm*) was fair in the hall (*fagar an flettea*), and the men among themselves (*folk under im*) let cheer rise from the benches, were in bliss (*uuârun thar an uunneun*).

The northern Germanic hall typically had a long fire down the middle with raised platforms along the sides and ends on which men sat, ate, and slept. These were the 'benches' (cf. the illustration of a reconstruction of an interior of the Viking period in Almgren, p. 170). The description of the drinking and the cheer may have to do with a phrase found below in l. 3339: *sittian at sumble*. Bauschatz (1982) says,

Hêliand

> Those participating come together and sit, usually within a chieftain's hall. ... The *symbel* is a kind of feast. It is solemn in the sense of having deep significance and importance, but it is not essentially dour. Thus in *Beowulf* (611-12), in the poem's first description of the events at Hrothgar's *symbel*, we hear that ... 'There was laughter of the men, noise sounded, / the words were winsome'. ... With respect to the *symbel*, only three types of activity are central: drinking (and its related actions such as the passing of the drinking cup), speech making (with related recitation and singing), and gift giving (p. 72 f.).

In the *Hêliand*, following John 2:3, they drink until the scoops are empty of wine (*thiu scapu uuârun lîðes alârid*). The word *lîð* here refers to Germanic fruit or apple wine (cf. Todd, p. 79). Glob (1969:35) describes *lîð* as "half way between beer and a fruit wine. Barley and the wild plants cranberry and bog myrtle were used in its manufacture. The alcoholic content may have been increased by the addition of honey." After the famous collocation between Mary and Jesus (John 2:3-4: "The wine gave out, so Jesus's mother said to him, 'They have no wine left.' He answered, 'Your concern, mother, is not mine. My hour has not yet come.'"), the mother of Christ ordered the pourers and 'scoopwards' (*skenkeon endi scapuuardos*) to serve the crowd and trusted that Christ would help. Indeed, here we see Christ bless the wine with his fingers and hands and bid that the 'full' (cup) be brought to the most noble (*themu hêroston*) who ruled over the people, 'according to the innkeeper' (*aftar themu uuerde*). The blessing of the wine is biblical, but the manner of its being done is reminiscent of an episode in chapter 44 of *Egils saga* (*Signaði Bárðr fullit, fekk síðan ǫseljunni* 'Bard blessed the cup and gave it then to the ale-bearer). Murphy (1992) points out,

> The author gives great weight to the words and actions of Christ by making it important in the text that no one learn these secret magic words! Since God's words create ..., they are performative words, and can act of themselves. It seems clear that the Saxon audience would love to learn (and use!) the formula for changing clear water into apple wine, and the author has to go to great lengths to explain how the followers of Christ do not know these powerful runes – both Mary and Jesus are made to take explicit means to see that the words and actions are kept quiet (Footnote 102).

§. 27

Immediately upon drinking the miraculous wine the host cannot avoid criticizing the serving of the poor wine before the best wine (*that bezte lîð*) so that 'the spirit of the men will be awakened with wine that they may well become happy and clamor drunkenly' (l. 2052b-2054a). That a good host should draw on the 'lighter wine' only after serving the best wine is explained for the Saxon audience as being the 'custom of those people' (*sô ist thesoro liudeo thau*). But now 'your guests are satiated and your followers (*druhtingos*) are very drunk, the people are happy in spirit' (l. 2060b-2062a).

§28. Reward and Punishment

Lines 2124b 2149a
(Matthew 8:11-12)

The centurion feels himself unworthy of a visit by Christ in his house, where his servant lies in great pain but says that Christ's word will suffice to heal him (Matthew 8:5-10). The author of the *Hêliand* uses the following passages to portray the horrors of hell, the 'outer darkness' where those without faith will lament and gnash their teeth. They will be cast into the darkest dales and lie in the farthest *fern* of all. Here the loanword *fern* (from Latin *inferno*) in l. 1276 receives definition as being *an dalun thiustron*, where one can hear men cry out (*quiðean*), where they 'bite with teeth their great anger' (*thar sie iro torn manag tandon bîtad* [l. 2143]: cf. *farterian* and *torn*, OHG *zeren* 'destroy'), there is greedy fire and grinding fury (*gristgrimmo*), the hard constraint (*gethuing*) of hell, hot and dark, black eternal night. The word *gristgrimmo* is another way of saying that they *tandon bîtad*. Ilkow says,

> Das Komp. *grist-grimmo* bezeichnet ... das 'Knirschen der Zähne'. Das Wort ist Nomen actionis zu ahd. *gris(t)grim(m)on* '*stridere*', vgl. *cristcrimmod zaneo* '*stridere dentium*' ... Das zweite Glied gehört natürlich zu germ. **grem-* 'knirschen' (vgl. *gram-*, *grim-*)[68] (p. 163).

The prospect of posthumous punishment was likely a new concept for the Saxon audience. Ilkow comments,

---

[68] The compound *grist-grimmo* characterizes ... the 'gnashing of teeth.' The word is a nomen actionis to OHG *gris(t)grim(m)on* '*stridere*', cf. *cristcrimmod zaneo* '*stridere dentium*' ... The second element naturally belongs with Gmc. **grem-* 'gnash' (cf. *gram-*, *grim-*).

Hêliand

Das dem Lat. entlehnte Wort bezeichnet, in verkürzter und unverkürzter Form [(*in*)*fern*], stets die Hölle in ihrem neuen, spezifisch jüdisch-christlichen Sinn als Ort des Feuers und der ewigen Verdammnis, nicht im Sinn von 'Totenreich, Vorhölle' ... Die Anwendung des zweiten Kompositionsgliedes -*dal* [in *fern-dalu* 'Täler, Abgründe der Hölle' ... *Thô giuuêt im the mênscaðo, / suuîðo sêragmôd Satanas thanan, / fiund undar ferndalu* v. 1115] zur Bezeichnung der Hölle, wozu auch das Simplex dient: *an dalun thiustron* v. 2140, *diop dôðes dalu* v. 5170 ... mag mit vorchristlich-germanischen Vorstellungen zusammenhängen. Als *Hermóðr* zu *Baldr* gesandt wurde, ritt er neun Nächte lang durch dunkle, tiefe Täler: *dǫkkva dala ok djúpa*. Nun bezeichnet 'Tal' besonders in alter Sprache nicht nur das zwischen Anhöhen gelegene Tiefland im Gegensatz zu Berg und Hügel, sondern ganz allgemein die 'Niederung, Vertiefung', auch die 'wilde Schlucht' (vgl. r.-ksl. *dolb* 'Grube, tiefes Loch, Schlucht'). Dem entspricht bedeutungsmäßig ein gr.-lat. *barathrum* 'Abgrund, Schlund', ein Synonym von gr.-lat. *abyssus* (vgl. *af-grundi, helli-grund*), das schon vorchristlich auf die Unterwelt und kirchensprachlich auf die Hölle angewendet wird: ... Im niederrheinischen Marienlob aus dem 13. Jh. ist von einem '*hellischen dal*' die Rede[69] (p. 124).

---

[69] The word borrowed from Latin in abbreviated and full form ([in]fern) means hell in its new, specifically Judeo-Christian sense as a place of fire and eternal damnation, not in the sense of 'realm of the dead, purgatory' ... The use of the second element of the compound -*dal* [in *fern-dalu* 'valleys, abyss of hell' ...] to designate hell, whereby the simplex (*an dalun thiustron* l. 2140, *diop dôðes dalu* l. 5170) also serves, ... may have to do with pre-Christian Germanic ideas. When *Hermóðr* was sent to *Baldr*, he rode nine nights long through dark, deep valleys: *dǫkkva dala ok djúpa*. Now especially in the older language 'valley' means not only the low land between heights in contrast with mountain and hill but quite generally 'low-lying area, hollow' and also 'wild ravine' (cf. Old Church Slavonic *dolъ* 'pit, deep hole, ravine'). Greek-Latin *barathrum* 'abyss, chasm' corresponds to it in meaning, a synonym for Greek-Latin *abyssus* (cf. *af-grundi, helli-grund*) that in pre-Christian time was used for the underworld and in ecclesiastical language for hell. ... In the Low Rhenish *Marienlob* from the 13th century there is reference to a '*hellischen dal.*'

§29. Raising the Dead

Lines 2180b to 2212a
(Luke 7:12-17)

The only child of a widow, her son, has died, and Christ finds the body being borne from the gate of the city. Whereas in Luke 7:14 Jesus merely says 'Weep not,' the further description depicts how the mother brought her hands together, sorrowed, lamented, and mourned in gestures evidently known among the Saxons. The fates (*uurð*), the *mâri metodogescapu*, have taken her son. The Son of God was touched by a feeling of generosity (*uuarð imu ... mahtig mildi*) and demonstrated power to the widow, the works of the Wielder (*thu scalt hîr craft sehen, uualdandes giuuerc*). She fell to the feet of Christ and praised Him before the crowd, for He protected for her such a dear life against fate (*uuiðer metodigisceftie*). Fate was immutable in Germanic tradition; even the gods were subject to fated demise (cf. Martin, p.3). The emphasis here is on contrasting pre-Christian concepts *uurð* and *metodogescapu* to the actions of Christ in His invocation of *craft ... uualdandes giuuerc* in order to resurrect the dead boy. When Christ approached the bier, he touched the boy with his hands. Murphy (1992) says:

> Scripture has that He touched the stretcher (Lk.7:13-14). In the Saxon text, the pronoun refers to the boy. The touching of the dead 'with holy hands' in a Germanic context (taboo in a Hebrew one) seems to add a much more magical tone to the scene, parallel to the changing of water into wine in the author's reinterpretation of the Marriage Feast at Cana (Footnote 106).

The resurrection of the son overjoyed the mother (*hugi uuarð iro te frôbra*). She fell to the feet of Christ and praised Him before the people, for He had saved for her so dear a life against the workings of fate (*Fell siu thô te fuotun Cristes endi thena folco drohtin / loboda for thero liudeo menigi, huand hie iro at sô liobes ferahe / mundoda uuiðer metodigisceftie*). According to Ilkow (p. 196) the word *frôbra*, which in OS meant 'help, support,' was reinterpreted by the English mission to mean 'consolatio' in the *Hêliand*.

Hêliand

See the commentary to §2 for Ilkow on *metod*. He says about *metodigiskaft*,

> Wenn Kienles Vermutung (S. 88f.) zutrifft, wäre in der Schicksalsbezeichnung *giskapu* noch ... die uralte Bedeutung des Verbalstammes 'durch Behauen formen, bilden'; das zugrunde liegende Bild des schaffenden Künstlers sei hier auf die Schicksalsgöttin übertragen, die bei der Geburt des Menschen gleichsam dessen zukünftiges Leben formt. ... Ebenso wirkt *metod(o)-giskapu*, wie auch das synonyme *metodi-giskaft*, als Bezeichnung einer von Gott gelenkten Macht[70] (p. 294).

§30. CALMING THE STORM

Lines 2231b to 2283
(Matthew 8:23-34; Mark 4, 35-41 and 5:1-10; Luke 8:22-31)

As in the House upon Sand (§24) the author of the *Hêliand* here again shows intimate knowledge of maritime conditions (or at least of their formulaic expression in traditional poetic diction) and evinces great skill as a poet. The lines describing the wind and waves caused by the blowing up of the storm virtually plunge and heave when read aloud. For an analysis of the testing of the disciples' faith through these vividly written weather events, see Swisher (pp. 232-238).

Christ calmed the waves and the weather became fair. The 'high horned ship' of Saxon construction familiar to the audience proceeded to land. Such ships with prominent prows are well known from archeological finds in southern Scandinavia and northern Germany. (See, for example, Ellmers or Marstrander for illustrations

---

[70] If Kienle's supposition (p. 88 f.) is correct, *giskapu* in the meaning of fate would still have the ancient meaning of the verbal stem 'form by hewing, sculpt'; the image of the creative artist would be transferred to the goddess of fate, who at the birth of a person molds the future life. ... Likewise *metod(o)-giskapu*, as also the synonymous *metodi-giskaft*, serves as a designation for power controlled by God.

inter alia of the Nydam ship from the 4th C and the Kvalsund boat from the 7th C.)

Upon landing many came toward Christ, and He willingly received whoever with pure heart sought help. Following Mark and/or Luke, the author of the *Hêliand* tells of the driving out of spirits from the man possessed, whom Satan's deceitful disciples had in hand (*undar handun*) by the power of the fiend (*fiundes craftu*).

See also Henrotte (1992).

§31. THE SOWER AND THE SEED

Lines 2378b to 2416
(Matthew 13:1-9; Mark 4:1-9; Luke 8:4-9)

Luke tells us that Jesus seated himself in a boat because the people on the bank became too many. The *Hêliand* tells us that He did not want to proclaim His teachings to the throng, so He and the disciples all got in a boat and had it pushed away from the shore, so that the people did not crowd Him.

In the familiar parable of the sower and the seed, the *Hêliand* follows most closely Luke, who mentions the trampling of the seed. Matthew and Mark speak only of the birds eating the seed. Here the seed falls on a hard road (*an êna starca strâta*) where footsteps (*stôpon*) went and the hoofbeat of horses and the treading of people (*hrosso hôfslaga endi heliðo trâda*) threaten. An aspect of Saxon geomorphy is inserted with the seeds in the thorns, where the shelter of the forest (*uualdes hlea*) grows to cover them over.

The biblical story ends with the injunction that those with ears should hear, an admonishment to the listening crowd. The *Hêliand* directs our attention instead to the disciples, wordwise men themselves, who like Germanic followers of a *drohtin* sit in impressed and respectful silence at the wisdom and eloquence of their Leader.

§32. INTERPRETATION

Lines 2474 to 2513a
(Matthew 13:18-23; Mark 4:13-20; Luke 8:11-15)

The Saxon audience is presented with more lessons than those indicated by the three biblical citations, which say that as the seed which falls on good earth, so does the word of God prosper and grow day and night in the good man. Here the fates (*uurð*) and course of the weather, rain and sun, favor this seed.

For the Saxons it was also important that an understanding of the teachings of God kept the devil and evil spirits at a distance (*endi gangid imu diuƀal fer / uurêða uuihti*) and that God's Protector (*the uuard godes*) comes ever closer (*[gangid] mikilu nâhor*) day and night. Murphy (1992) translates *the uuard godes* as "the protection of God" (p. 82), which seems to make better sense, although, strictly speaking, *uuard* means 'Beschützer; protector' and the like.

The good man changes to heaven's share and fares empty of sin into the kingdom of God, the greatest of prosperities (*uuelono thene mêstan*). The keeping of faith is good for every man (*Treuua sind sô gôda / gumono gehuilicumu*). A hoard of gold is not equal to such belief (l. 2489b-2491a). The teachings of God may remain with the man of inconstant spirit (*uuancolna hugi*) until worldly goods (*fremiði scat*) allow 'evil things' or 'beings' (*lêða uuihti*) to seduce him and he is ensnared in greed for property (*he imu farfâhid an fehogiri*). The danger is that main sins (*meginsundeon*) may propel him to the bottom of hell where fiends would strangle (?) him with punishment (*ac ina fiund sculun / uuîtiu giuuaragean*). The historical precursors of the word *uuarag* in the verb meant 'strangle' and referred often to hangings. Whether this connotation was still prominent or the verb merely meant 'punish' in some way is not clear; cf. the commentaries to §57 and §64.

§33. The Wheat in the Field

Lines 2580b to 2620
(Matthew 13:37-43)

The interpretation of the parable of the wheat in the field as transmitted by Matthew speaks of the good seed and the weeds which grow together on the field. Ilkow points out that the phrase *hluttar hrênkorni* is not a translation of the Latin *bonum semen* in Matthew 13:30, as the *bonum* is rendered by *hluttar*. He says,

> Daß *hrên-korni* wirklich kein poetisches Komp., sondern ein agrartechnischer Ausdruck zumindest vornehmlich zur Bezeichnung des Weizens ist, beweisen ahd. und as. Glossen: vor allem ein Beleg im ahd. Codex Selestadiensis, wo neben anderen Getreidearten und Lebensmitteln *Triticum · reincurni weizzi* erwähnt wird. ... Die in allen germ. Sprachen enthaltenen Entsprechungen des Adjektivs ... führen ... auf ... idg. *(s)qrei-*, das in lat. *cerno* 'sichte', *crō-brum* 'Sieb' fortlebt. ... Unser Komp. *hrên-korni* ist also ... zunächst als 'gesiebtes Korn, gesiebtes Getreide' auszulegen. Nachdem das Getreide gedroschen ist, muß es sorgfältig gereinigt werden, denn je reiner das Korn ist, um so besser hält es sich, und um so weniger wird es vom Kornwurm angegriffen[71] (p. 224-225).

The sower is the Son of Man, the field the world, the good seed the sons of the realm, and the weeds the sons of evil. The enemy who sowed the weeds is Satan, the harvest is the end of the world, and the harvest workers are the angels. When the weeds are gathered together and thrown into the fire, it is the end of the world. The Son of Man will send out his angels to gather together all who have transgressed against God's commandments and throw them into the burning oven. The righteous will shine like the sun in the realm of their Father.

The *Hêliand* states that the damned and the good men will grow forth together *anttat mûdspelles megin oƀar man ferid, / endi thesaro uueroldes.* This 'power of *mûdspelli* that fares over men'

---

[71] OHG and OS glosses prove that *hrên-korni* is really not a poetic compound but a technical, agricultural expression. An attestation exists in the OHG Codex Selestadiensis, where aside from other kinds of grain and edibles *Triticum · reincurni weizzi* is mentioned. ... The cognates of the adjective, retained in all Germanic languages, derive from IE *(s)qrei-* with Latin cognates *cerno* 'I sift' and *crō-brum* 'sieve.' ... Our compound *hrên-korni* is thus to be understood primarily as 'sieved wheat, sifted grain.' After the grain is threshed it must carefully be cleaned, because the purer the grain is the better it keeps and the less it is set upon by grain worms.

reflects similar usage in OHG and in OI. The OHG *Muspilli* contains the words *prinnit mittilagart ... uerit denne stuatago in lant, / uerit mit diu uuiru uiriho uuison. / Dar ni mac denne mak andremo helfan uora demo muspilli* (verse 54 ff.). In this passage 'the earth burns' and 'the day of judgment fares into the land, fares with fire to punish men. Then one relative cannot help another before the (court of) judgment, the "Muspilli".' The OI reference is from the apocalyptic vision titled *Vǫluspá* (The Prophesy of the Seeress). Here we read in Verse 52 that the 'people of *Múspell* come over the sea, and in the OI *Lokasenna*, Verse 42, that the 'sons of *Múspell* ride over Mirk Wood.' (See Nordal.) The image of the apocalypse called '*mûdspelli / muspilli / múspell*' faring forth over men is strikingly similar in these three sources from widely separated regions.

If the setting of the OHG *Muspilli* is that of a court of judgment (cf. Kolb, pp. 2-33), so too does the *Hêliand* have a sense of the same in the admonition *sô lâta imu thit an innan sorga, / an is môdseƀon, huô he scal an themu mâreon dage / uuið thene rîkeon god an reðiu standen* (l. 2609b- 2611). Here the worry is about how one shall stand to account before 'the powerful God' on 'the famous day.' We find the same image at l. 1950 ff., where the fiery end of the world comes to Sodom, and the 'famous day' fares over men: *Than seggeo ic iu te uuârun, sô huan sô thius uuerold endiad / endi the mâreo dag oƀar man farid / that than Sodomoburg, thiu hîr thurh sundeon uuarð / an afgrundi êldes craftu, / fiuru bifallen ... .* In l. 4310 the word *mâri* occurs in a similar context: *Liudeo drohtin / sagde im thô selƀo: 'than ik sittien kumu', quað he, / 'an thie mikilan maht an themu mârean dage, / thar ik allun scal irminthiodun dômos adêlien* ..., where Christ sits in judgment 'on the famous day'. Again at l. 4047 ff. we read of the end of the world when that famous day fares over men: *sô huan sô thius uuerold endiod, / endi the mâreo dag ôƀar man ferid* 'whenever this world ends and the famous day fares over men.'

Yet another word for 'fate' alongside *uurd, metodogiscapu, metodigiscaft,* and *orlag* (cf. the commentaries to §10 and §40) occurs in this passage: *reganogiscapu*. The first element of the compound has cognates in OI *regin* 'Götter', Gothic *ragin* 'Rat, Beschluß', OE *regn-* 'mächtig' and in verbs like Gothic *rahjnan* 'ordnen'. The semantic base is the notion of 'order'. Ilkow devotes a long section to *regan(o)*, discussing various Germanic reflexes, and says,

> Es läßt sich überhaupt nicht mit Sicherheit feststellen, ob das Komp. *regan(o)-giskapu* in vorchristliche Zeit zurückgeht oder erst als poetische Formel im Variationsapparat unseres

§. 33

Dichters entstand. Mit Bestimmtheit aber kann gesagt werden, daß der im Vorderglied enthaltene Ausdruck einst eine heidnische Schicksalsmacht bezeichnete. Es ist möglich, daß diese Schicksalsbezeichnung aus dem Vorstellungskreis des Richters als des 'Anordnenden, Bestimmenden' (vgl. idg. *reg-'anordnen') gewonnen wurde (ähnlich *metod*, das vielleicht den Richter als den 'Zumessenden, Zuteilenden' bezeichnete). Im Hel. erfolgte dann (wie bei *metod*) eine Übertragung des Ausdrucks auf Gott als den obersten Richter und Weltordner, der den Lauf der Welt bestimmt und den Menschen ihr Schicksal zuteilt... . In den übrigen Komp. des Hel., in ... *regin-skaðo* ... , wirkt das Vorderglied als Intensivierungselement" (pp. 334-335). "*regan(o)-giskapu* [bezeichnet] im Hel. des Menschen Schicksal, wie es durch Gottes Willen vorherbestimmt ist. Dies tritt besonders deutlich in der Beschreibung des bevorstehenden Weltuntergangs zutage, in der es heißt, daß die Menschenkinder das (von der göttlichen Vorsehung) über sie verfügte Schicksal vollenden werden[72] (p. 336).

The passage ends with an admonition that all who aspire to *alungan tîr*, the high realm of heaven, and God's *huldi* should concern themselves with these things before giving up 'this light.' Ilkow comments to *alungan tîr*,

Die Phrase *aldar-lang tîr* 'ewiger Ruhm', die hier zur Umschreibung des Begriffs 'Himmelreich' angewendet wird, deutet auf den Formelschatz germ. Heldendichtung zurück. Tatsächlich erscheint der einzige Beleg des ae. Komp. ebenfalls in Verbindung mit *tîr*: *Hīealdorlangne tīr geslōgen æt sacce* 'Sie gewannen ewigen Ruhm in der Schlacht' (bei Brunanburg) ... Es bezeichnet ursprünglich als diesseitsgebundener Begriff eine irdische immerwährende Dauer, die allerdings nur eine relative Ewigkeit darstellt, denn sie ist mit dem Bestehen der Welt zu Ende. ... Mit dem Christentum

---

[72]It cannot be said with certainty whether the compound *regan(o)-giskapu* goes back to pre-Christian time or was coined as a poetic formulation in our poet's stock of variations. It can, however, be stated with certainty that the expression contained in the first element once pertained to a heathen power of fate. It is possible that this expression for fate (and similarly *metod*, the "measurer, distributor') was taken from the function of the judge as the one imposing 'order, certainty' (cf. IE *reg- 'arrange, order'). A transfer of the expression (also as with *metod*) to God as the highest judge and arbiter of order, who determines the course of the world and of fate for every person, occurred in the Hêliand. In other compounds like *regin-skaðo* the first element serves as an intensifier (pp. 334-335). *regan(o)-giskapu* in the Hêliand refers to human fate as predetermined by the will of God. This can clearly be seen in the description of the impending apocalypse where it is said that the children of men will fulfill the fate determined for them by divine providence.

Hêliand

> erhält der Begriff der 'immerwährenden Dauer' seinen neuen jenseitsbezogenen Gehalt ...[73] (p. 51).

The Germanic concept of the honor (OS *tîr*) of a loyal follower and the favor (*huldi*) granted in return by a leader was, of course, strictly a worldly concern but of highest value in the pre-Christian order of things. The *huldi* of God and a new concept of divine order, on the other hand, carried over into the life to come. Worldly honor was condemned as *superbia* by the Church; separation from God is the root of sin.[74] (See also §45 on the duty of a good follower and §55, l. 5039 f., where the Germanic virtue of thirst for glory and the Christian sin of *superbia* are contrasted: if the help of God is absent, no amount of fighting skill will prevent a man's heart from becoming cowardly.)

---

[73] The phrase *aldar-lang tîr* 'eternal fame,' which is used here as a circumlocution of the concept 'heavenly realm' points back to formulae used in Germanic heroic poetry. In fact, the only attestation of the OE compound occurs in connection with *tîr*: *Hīealdorlangne tīr geslōgen æt sacce* 'They won eternal fame in the battle' (of Brunanburgh) ... As a worldly concept it originally indicated long-lasting duration in this world, which of course represented only a relative eternity, because with the apocalypse it ended. ... Under Christianity the concept of 'long-lasting duration' received its new meaning for the hereafter.

[74] "Die *superbia* ist also, wie die Schrift lehrt, als Trennung von Gott der Anfang aller Sünde" [As scripture teaches, the beginning of all sin is thus *superbia* as separation from God.] (Hempel, p. 12)

§34. Herodias' Daughter Dances

Lines 2728 to 2756
(Matthew 14:6-7; Mark 6:21-22)

Herodias sought revenge against John the Baptist. John had admonished Herod Antipas (the son of king Herod the Great who had received the three wise men) not to cohabit with Herodias, as she had been the wife of Herod's brother and furthermore the granddaughter of Herod the Great. (Sexual relations with a sister-in-law are expressly forbidden in Leviticus 18:16). *Nya Testamentet* explains in a note to Matthew 14:3 "Herodias var sondotter till Herodes den store. Josefus bekräftar att Herodes Antipas övergav sin egen hustru och tog Herodias från en av sina halvbröder, som hon var gift med." [75]

Herod Antipas had John thrown into prison to please Herodias, but he feared the popular reaction if he were to have John killed. Herod Antipas asked on the occasion of his birthday celebration to let his brother's daughter by Herodias dance before him and promised that he would give her what she desired.

In treating of Matthew 14:6 the *Hêliand* expands on the following verse: "But at his birthday celebrations the daughter of Herodias danced before the guests, and Herod was so delighted that he took an oath to give her anything she cared to ask." As we see in this section (l. 2728-2733a), the custom of celebrating birthdays had to be explained to the Saxon audience. The portrayal of the celebration is, as in the Marriage at Cana, that of a Saxon drinking party in a banquet hall (*gastseli*). The mood was glad, and the guests reveled; men were drunk, and it was loud in the hall. The lord was on his royal seat (*iro hêrro uuas an is kuningstôle*), and the war leaders and their men were present (*uuarð ... megincraft mikil manno gesamnod, heritogono*). The king, Herod, is also described as *bâggeƀo* 'ring giver' derived from the custom of a ruler to present wound gold to faithful followers. Ilkow comments:

> Die genannten Fürstenbezeichnungen der Dichtung weisen

---

[75] Herodias was the granddaughter of Herodes the Great. Josefus confirms that Herodes Antipas abandoned his own wife and took Herodias from one of his half-brothers to whom she was married. (Josef was an historian born in the year 37 or 38.)

Hêliand

> auf eine alte Sitte, nach der das Verteilen von Geschenken zu den Anstandspflichten des Gefolgsherrn gehörte. Das Verhältnis zwischen dem Gefolgsherrn und seinen Gefolgsleuten fußt auf wechselseitiger Treue (vgl. *bōg-wini*). ... die gewöhnlichste Form der Belohnung aber stellte der 'Baug', der Armring, dar ...[76] (p. 64 f.).

Among "die genannten Fürstenbezeichnungen der Dichtung" Ilkow cites *Beowulf* (l. 1102) where the Danish prince Hnæf is called *bēag-gifa* and l. 3009 where Beowulf is described as the one *þē ūs bēagas gaf* ('who gave us rings').

The *Hêliand* relates that the king was inebriated along with his men, and his request for Herodias' daughter to dance and the promise to give what she requested of him was binding. A promise, an oath, or the word of a king were all normative in their power and each word must be right and be kept. The 'blind promise' made here may reflect a motif still current in later medieval literature in Germany, cf. Iwein who forgets his promise and loses his honor or King Arthur in *Iwein*, who loses his wife because of his 'blind promise' (l. 4528-4722).

§35. The Death of John

Lines 2773 to 2799a
(Mark 6:25-29)

King Herod asked the daughter of Herodias what she desired in return for her dance, and she went to ask her mother what it should be. It was the head of John the Baptist. Mark 6:26 says, "The king was greatly distressed, but out of regard for his oath and for his guests he could not bring himself to refuse her." The *Hêliand* reflects the biblical story's message and adds local color. Mark 6 does not

---

[76] The nomenclature of the ruler in poetry indicates an old custom, according to which the distribution of gifts belonged among the formal courtesies of the commander. The relationship between the commander and his followers is based on mutual loyalty (cf. *bōg-wini*). ... The 'Baug,' the arm ring, represented the most usual form of reward.

§. 35

mention the reaction of the revelers to the demand for the head of John, but the *Hêliand* tells us of their dismay (*That uuas allun them liudiun harm*). The king had to deliver John's severed head, "out of regard for his oath," or, as the *Hêliand* expresses it, *he ni mahti is quidi liagan*. Oaths were binding by Germanic law and custom and could neither be denied nor changed. (See also the commentary to §18.)

The lamentation of the last day (*êndago*) of 'the wisest of all men', save the One who was borne by the woman who never knew a thane in her world (*lêt man simla then ênon beforan, / the thiu thiorne gedrôg, the gio thegnes ni uuarð / uuîs an iro uueroldi*), is an excursus not found in Mark. While carefully excepting Christ as ultimate in its praise of the 'wisest of all men', the *Hêliand* presents John as a Germanic hero, marked for his role as if by the *metod* but here by the 'wielding God of the Holy Spirit from the meadows of heaven'. Regarding *metod* and the concept of fate Ilkow says, "Eine ... Vorstellung ist die des 'Messens', genauer des 'Zumessens' oder 'Zuteilens'. ... Klar erkennen läßt sich nur, daß das Schicksal als von höheren Gewalten 'gemessen' gedacht wurde"[77] (p. 292).

The compound *êndago* has counterparts in OE and ON. Ilkow says,

> Das an. Komp *ein-dagi* ist ein alter Rechtsausdruck ...; es bezeichnet einen 'festgesetzten Termin' ..., an dem eine Zahlung fällig ist oder sonst eine Verpflichtung erfüllt sein soll ... . Diese Verwendung des Komp. scheint der Dichtung schon in gemeingerm. Zeit bekannt gewesen zu sein. Zwar sind die an. und ae. Komp. nicht im Sinne 'Todestag' bezeugt, wohl aber die syntaktische Phrase '*einn dag[r]*' in den Fáfnismál (10,2) der Edda[78] (pp. 100-101).

Bellows' translation given below indicates that the implication of the phrase *til ens eina dags* 'the destined day' in the OI is clear:

---

[77] One ... idea is that of 'measuring,' more exactly of 'apportioning' or 'allocating.' ... It can clearly be perceived only that fate was thought of as 'measured' by a higher power.

[78] The ON compound *ein-dagi* is an old legal expression ...; it designates a 'fixed deadline' ... on which a payment is due or an obligation must be fulfilled ... . This use of the compound seems to have been used in poetry already in common Germanic time. The ON and OE compounds are not used in the sense of 'day of death,' but the syntactic phrase '*einn dag[r]*' is in the Fáfnismál (10.2) of the Edda.

Héliand

Féi ráða skal fyrða hverr	Some one the hoard shall ever hold
æ til ens eina dags;	Till the destined day shall come
þvíat einu sinni skal alda hverr	For a time there is when every man
fara til heljar heðan.	Shall journey hence to hell.

His disciples buried John in the secure knowledge that he would 'seek the light of God, the precious clamor (or dream) together with his Lord' and that he would possess *uppôdas hêm*. The phrase *uppôdas hêm* might be viewed as either a parallel expression to *uphimil* (cf. l. 2886) or perhaps as the Saxon rendering of Latin *caelestis patria* (cf. Ilkow, pp. 386-387). Its literal meaning would at one point have been something like 'the homestead of upper hereditary property.'

§36. JESUS WALKS ON WATER

Lines 2899 to 2931a
(Matthew 14:23-27; Mark 6:45-50; John 6:16-20)

The disciples set out in a boat while Jesus stayed behind. While they rowed toward the opposite shore, a wind came up and the waves rose. Matthew 14:24 says, "The boat was already some furlongs from the shore, battling with a head-wind and a rough sea." The *Héliand* makes the most of this scene, which lends itself to the OS vocabulary of seafaring on the rough North Sea. Here they let their 'high-prowed ship' (*hôh hurnidskip*) cleave 'the swift stream, the pure waves, the sheer water'. Nocturnal fog enveloped the seafarers (*sêolîðandean*), the wind increased, and the waves hammered on the stem. Murphy (1992) comments here:

> The author displays a great deal of nautical competence in this section. He knows about North-Sea fog (there is none in the biblical account), he accurately describes the high-horned, Viking-type ship and its sailing characteristics, he even knows about the danger of this type of vessel being swamped if its low sides come broadside to the waves, thus the apostles fight to keep the high bow stempost facing the oncoming waves (Footnote 132).

§. 36

The waterfarers (*lagulîðandea*) imagined they might not come to land through the weather's tumult, but Christ guarded 'the wavefarers' (*thea uuâglîðand*). These compounds in -*lîðand* belong to the common vocabulary of the North Sea, including parallel constructions in OE.

When Christ approaches them, walking on the water, they believe that they are seeing a vision. Matthew 14:26 says, "And when the disciples saw him walking on the lake, they were so shaken that they cried out in terror: 'It is a ghost!'" The disciples were very fearful, 'dreading that a mighty fiend was doing that to them as an optical illusion' (*te gidroge*). The ever-present anxiety of being set upon by *dernea uuihti* likely made this scene very frightening to the Saxon audience. (Cf. §10 and the fear of hidden beings.)

§37. Saint Peter's Keys

Lines 3066b to 3092a
(Matthew 16:18-21; Mark 3:16; Luke 6:14; John 1:42)

Peter is designated by Christ as the founder of His church on the basis of his purity of and firmness in faith: *hluttro haƀas thu an thînan hêrron giloƀon, hugiskefti sind thîne stêne gelîka, / sô fast bist thu sô felis the hardo*. The root in the name Peter means 'rock' in Greek, as does the Aramaic name Kefas, which is used instead in John 1:42 and in Paul's letters, e.g. 1 Corinthians 1:12. Matthew 16:18 says, "And I say this to you: You are Peter, the Rock; and on this rock I will build my church ..." The *Hêliand* says instead that Peter's way of thinking (*hugiskefti*) is like a stone, 'you are as firm (*fast*) as the hard rock' upon which 'one shall build my hall (*seli*), the holy house of God'. Furthermore, 'the portals of hell will not resist your great power'. Murphy (1992) points out that this reverses the biblical sense:

> The biblical metaphor is visually and militarily difficult to comprehend ... [G]ates in the North are associated with defense and are not capable of offensive ability (though they are in the Old Testament). In one stroke the author both makes the metaphor intelligible and changes it from passive to active: the gates of hell will not be able to hold out against your offensive strength (Footnote 138).

Hêliand

Peter is also given the power by Christ to consign men either to hell or heaven. Murphy (1992) comments: "... like a feudal chieftain he is visualized as having personal authority over men, to bind or free them" (Footnote 140). For one to be freed Peter will literally 'untie his hands' (*antheftien is hendi*), and the 'greatest of lights, the realm of heaven, life eternal, and God's green meadow' (l. 3080b-3082a) will be unlocked.

Matthew 16:21 says that Jesus told His disciples of the journey to Jerusalem, where He was "to be put to death and to be raised again on the third day." The *Hêliand* casts this in greater detail, depicting the impending death of Christ in terms of Germanic tradition. Like a captured *drohtin* He will be bound and tortured by the Jews and killed by 'points of spears, sharp edges', cf. l. 3085b to 3090a. Murphy (1992) surmises that,

> "Prisoners were often killed with the spear or lance, since that weapon was sacred to Woden, to whom prisoners were often 'dedicated.' The *Heliand* and its reader/listeners would have found the incident of the lance penetrating the side of the prisoner Christ particularly intelligible and moving to them" (Footnote 142).

§38. The Transfiguration

Lines 3122b to 3151a
(Matthew 17:1-8; Mark 9:2-13; Luke 9:28-36)

As Moses met God on Mount Sinai, Jesus went up onto a high mountain where he met Moses and Elijah, the two figures from the Old Testament who, according to Jewish belief in New Testament times, ascended alive to heaven (cf. *Nya Testamentet*, p. 47).

Luke 9:29 says, "And while he was praying the appearance of his face changed and his clothes became dazzling white." The *Hêliand* tells us that 'His garments were white as snow' but, as it often does, adds detail. His cheeks were as gleaming with light as the bright sun; rays stood wondrously out from Him.[79]

---

[79] Argyle in his commentary to Matthew says "Moses' face also shone after he had conversed with God (Exod. 34:29-35). Cf. also 2 Esdras in the Apocrypha (c. A.D. 100), 7:97, referring to the righteous after death: 'their face shall shine as the sun'" (p. 132).

Matthew and Mark report Jesus' conversation with Moses and Elijah, but Luke 9:31 says that they "spoke of his departure, the destiny he was to fulfil in Jerusalem." The *Hêliand* characterizes it as 'delightful talk' and the meeting as 'cheerful up on the mountain.' The light shone, there was a good field there, and a green meadow like paradise. Again the evocation of heavenly bliss is that of a shining green meadow, the springtime joy of a Saxon field. Peter calls it *ôdas hem, / uuelono uunsamost* 'the home of inheritance, most delightful of properties'. (Compare the promise of being released by Peter into *grôni godes uuang* in l. 3082 and *lioht godes and upôdas hêm* as promises of heaven in l. 2796b and 2798a, respectively.)

The light parts the sky, as in the story of the Birth of Christ (cf. l. 390b-392a), and shines resplendently down on Christ. Murphy (1992) says, "[T]he familiar and welcome image of a beam of sunlight shining down through an opening in the clouds of Northern skies is hallowed by the author, and made into an icon of divine intervention" (Footnote 146).

The Transfiguration is at the center point of the narrative, illuminated by light beaming down. Note the parallel use of beaming light as angels appear before the horse herders (l. 390 f.) to announce the birth of Christ and the parting of foggy gloom by 'sunlight, bright in the sky' (l. 5632 f.) at the Crucifixion and death of Christ. Such tripartite parallelism can only be a deliberate poetic construction to reinforce the author's religious purpose.

§39. FISHING FOR COINS

Lines 3200b to 3223a
(Matthew 17:24-27)

When Jesus and Peter returned to Capernaum, the collectors asked Peter whether his Master paid the temple tax or not. Jesus quizzed Peter as to who actually paid such a tax, the common people or their own people. Peter naturally answered that it was the common people who pay taxes. Jesus replied that since they did not want to cause offense, Peter should cast a line into the sea and take the first fish that bites. In its mouth will be a coin with which to pay the tax. The biblical account makes no more of this episode. Matthew 17:27 says, "open its mouth, and you will find a silver coin; take that and pay it in; it will meet the tax for us both." The

Hêliand

Hêliand's penchant for elaboration makes silver to gold and a coin to a hoard and describes how Peter pried open the mouth of the fish with his own two hands. The coins are here called *scattos*. Riché informs us that "[a]fter 650, [the] Frisians minted and used a silver coin, the *sceatta*, which gradually replaced the gold coinage of antiquity" (p. 3), presumably the same as indicated in the *Hêliand*. There may also be a lesson here for the Saxons and a reminder of the *Capitulatio de partibus Saxoniae* (See the EXTERNAL HISTORY).

The *Hêliand* goes on to praise the wondrous powers of the Lord (*uuas thô uualdandes megincraft gimârid*) and urges proper compliance with one's tax obligations, for in thus doing the *huldi* of one's lord is assured. Murphy (1992) comments:
"The author never encourages Saxon rebellion ... Instead of rebellion, he seems to see his hearers as being hounded like Christ and, like Peter, to be mystically associated with Christ. Then too, Saxon lords listening to the *Heliand* in their drinking halls might also not have been amused to find the singer disparaging taxes to one's 'worldly lord!'" (Footnote 150).

The *Hêliand* actually states that by paying one's tax (to the Frankish church?) the favor of one's earthly lord (Charlemagne's son and successor Louis the Pious?) will be forthcoming. The later medieval means of binding the population politically were not yet in place. Unfortunately, there is no direct evidence as to which audience(s) the *Hêliand* addressed, but from hints like this one can at least draw some tentative conclusions.

§40. THE RICH MAN AND LAZARUS

Lines 3295b to 3374
(Matthew 19:23-29; Mark 10:23-31; Luke 16:9-25)

A young man of great wealth had asked Christ how he might win eternal life. Jesus' answer was that he must sell everything and give to the poor, for then he would have riches in heaven. When he heard those words, the man's face fell and he went away with a heavy heart.

Matthew 19:27 says, "At this Peter said, 'We here have left everything to become your followers. What will there be for us?'" The Saxons were, as can be inferred from the many references to *ôðil*, *gesidli*, etc. in the *Hêliand*, ardent in their acquisition of prop-

§. 40

erty. Peter (*êrthungan gumo*) asked the dear Lord what those would have as reward who gave up their property and inheritance, their farms and family (*hoƀos endi hîuuiski*), and chose Him as Lord. (Note Peter's Germanic emphasis on their choosing Christ as Lord, not on Christ's choosing them as disciples.) Jesus' answer involves their appointment as fellow judges *an themu mârean dage* when finding will be rendered on all the great peoples (*irminthiodun*), the tribes of Israel (*Israhelo eðilifolcun*): *than môtun gi mid iuuuomu drohtine thar / selƀon sittien endi môtun thera saca uualdan*, where the phrase *saca uualdan* is straight from prose in Germanic legal codes. (Note, incidentally, that the biblical specification of the twelve tribes of Israel seems not to be of importance to the author of the *Hêliand*, who speaks merely of the 'noble formations [*folcun*] of the Israelites'.)

The one who abandons the dear dwelling place of relatives (*mâgo gesidli liof*) for the love of Christ will receive ten times tenfold reward if he does it in faith and with a pure heart. Murphy (1992) makes the point here that

> This is one of the clearest instances of what the author means by his continually repeated phrase 'with a clear mind' *mid hluttru hugi*. He sets the phrase in parallel to 'with loyalty' *mid treuuon*, and thus he paints an 'unclear mind' as a mind of uncertain or divided loyalties, one that is hedging its bets by avoiding a 'clear' commitment of feudal loyalty to its Christ-Chieftain and secretly remaining a thane to other religious chieftains. Christ is made here, in this sentence, to call on the Saxons as their feudal lord, and ask them for undivided, 'clear-minded' loyalty as a condition for their being enthroned with Him (Footnote 155).

At this logical juncture comes the story from Luke 16 about the "rich man, who dressed in purple and the finest linen, ... feasted in great magnificence every day." The *Hêliand* elaborates on the concept 'rich' to emphasize that the man in question had property (*uuelono genôg, sinkas gisamnon*) and was ever in possession of gold and precious cloths with beautiful ornamentation (*garu mid goldu endi mid godouuebbiu, / fagarun fratahun*). The word *godouuebbi* occurred in alliterative conjunction with 'gold' and indicated a kind of cloth. Ilkow, in a long article, summarizes,

> Eine Untersuchung der Heliandbelege von *godu-web(bi)* hat gezeigt, daß unser Komp. im As. nur besonders kostbare

Stoffe bezeichnet. Zu dem gleichen Ergebnis führt eine Untersuchung von an. *guð-vefr*. Genauere Bedeutungsinhalte unseres Komp. erhellen aus der ae. Übersetzungsliteratur und vor allem aus den ahd. Glossen. In ihnen übersetzt *gota-webbi* u.a. lat. *sericum* 'Seide' und *byssus* 'feines Leinen; Baumwolle'. Wir haben also damit zu rechnen, daß unser Komp. dreierlei Stoffe bezeichnen konnte: 'feines Leinen, 'Baumwolle' und 'Seide'. ... Das as. Komp. erscheint in beiden Belegen in der Formel: *mid goldu endi mid godu-webbiu*, in der ae. Version von Bedas 'Historia Ecclesiastica' findet sich: *mid golde and mid godewæbbe gefrætewod*..., in Exod. 587 *gold und godweb*, der einzige afries. Beleg lautet: *gold ende goedweb* ..., in der Liederedda findet sich: *gulli ok guðvefjun* ... Wir glauben, daß diese Alliterationsformel bereits in urgerm. Zeit bestanden haben muß. Sie enthält eine Bezeichnung kostbarster Waren, des kostbarsten Metalls und des kostbarsten Stoffgewebes. ... Wenn nun unser Komp. dem urgerm. Sprachschatz angehörte, muß es ursprünglich eine 'feine Leinwand' bezeichnet haben, denn 'Baumwolle' und 'Seide' waren den Germanen in ältester Zeit nicht bekannt. ... Wir glauben ..., daß *godu-webbi* ein 'Gewebe für einen Gott' oder 'für Götter' bezeichnete[80] (pp. 152-154).

The rich man had much produce on his farm and sat feasting every day with 'bliss on the benches' (l. 3331b-3334a) in his *gestseli*, which unlike that occupied by Joseph in l. 711 is here a banquet hall (cf. also §27 and Ilkow, pp. 140-141).
Lochrie (1986) comments on this type,

---

[80] An examination of the attestations of *godu-web(bi)* in the Hêliand shows that our compound in OS is used only for very costly cloths. An examination of ON *guðvefr* comes to the same conclusion. More exact meanings of our compound are illuminated by OE translation literature and above all by OHG glosses. In them *gota-webbi* translates Latin *sericum* 'silk' and *byssus* 'fine linen; cotton.' We can conclude that our compound could indicate three materials: 'fine linen,' 'cotton,' and 'silk.' ... The OS compound appears in both attestations in the formula: *mid goldu endi mid godu-webbiu*, in the OE version from Beda's 'Historia Ecclesiastica' there is *mid golde and mid godewæbbe gefrætewod* ..., in Exodus 587 *gold und godweb*; the only Old Frisian attestation is *gold ende goedweb*; in the Poetic Edda there is *gulli ok guðvefjun* ... We believe that this alliterative formula must have existed already in early Germanic times. It contains a characterization of the most costly wares, of the most valuable metal, and of the finest woven cloth. ... If, indeed, our compound belonged in the early Germanic vocabulary, it must originally have meant a 'fine canvass,' as 'cotton' and 'silk' were unknown in the oldest period. ... We believe that *godu-webbi* meant a 'fabric for a god' or 'for gods.'

§. 40

> Like the grim-thinking man whose thoughts are preoccupied with this world, the feaster ... is unaware of that which lies beyond the ends of this world, and worse, he is indifferent to it. He boasts and scorns holy teachings as he sits *symbelgal* 'wanton with feasting.' While the *gromhydig* man seeks hell unwittingly, the feaster will be surprised to find himself seated at Christ's left at his judgment .... Like the grim-thinking man, he is concerned only with the present (p. 203).

Lazarus was a poor, sick man stricken with sores who lay outside the door observing the rich man enjoy his feast, but the only attention he received was from the dogs who licked at his sores. One day, however, 'I found out' that the *reganogiscapu* "sovereign fates" (in Murphy's [1992] translation, p. 110) informed Lazarus of the end of his life, and God's angels conducted his soul to the bosom of Abraham, where he ever forth would dwell in joy (l. 3347b-3354a).

Likewise came the fateful machinations (*uurdegiscapu*), the time of fate (*orlaghuîle*) to the life of the rich man, and he left this light. Murphy (1992) sees these pre-Christian words as serving to "reassure the Saxons that, at the very least in history, there is a Christ-acknowledged place for fate and time in His worldview" (Footnote 158). Ilkow, quoting Kienle, comments under *orlaghwîla*,

> Im as. Komp. *orlag-hwîla* dient *orlag-*, wie gelegentlich auch *wurd*, der Bezeichnung jener Schicksalsmacht, die über das Lebensende, über den Tod des Menschen verfügt ... In einem Deutungsversuch von germ. **uz-laga-* und seinen Ableitungen müssen wir auch as. *gi-lagu* (stn. pl.) 'Schicksal' und das Komp. an. *aldr-lag* (stn.) 'Schicksal, Tod', ae. *ealdor-legu* (stf.) 'Schicksal, Tod', as. *aldar-lagu* (stn. pl.) 'die bestimmte Lebenszeit, Leben' einbeziehen. ... Germ. **laga-* gehört zu dem Verbum germ. ... *lagjan 'legen'; an. *lag* bedeutet 'was gelegt ist', Lage, Stellung', der Plural *lǫg* 'das Gesetz' ... **uz-laga-* bedeutet dann 'das was ausgelegt ist'. ... Man kann nämlich bei dem 'legen' an das Legen und Auslegen der Losstäbchen denken, das Wort also in den Vorstellungskreis der Runenpraxis einbeziehen. Die 'ausgelegten' Lose werden dem Menschen erteilt und durch sie sein künftiges Geschick. ... Das Wort *urlag* ist in ahd. Zeit sehr häufig, vor allem in den Glossen. In der übrigen Literatur wird es streng gemieden; wahrscheinlich war sein Grundcharakter zu heidnisch, um in christliche Dichtung Eingang zu finden[81] (pp. 327-328).

---

[81] In the OS compound *orlag-hwîla* the first element *orlag-*, as occasionally also *wurd*, indicates that power of fate which wields over the end of life, the death of a

Hêliand

It was not the angels who fetched the soul of the rich man but rather *lêða uuihti*, that plunged his soul into black hell, buried him in the 'home of evil spirits' (*gramono hêm*). His anguish is increased by the view which lets him see upward to Lazarus resting blissfully in the bosom of Abraham. His plea is for Abraham to send down Lazarus with cold water, for *nu is mi thînaro helpono tharf*, the Saxon appeal to the generosity of his *drohtin*. His lack of clear mind has only too late let him understand that *alles is mi nu thes lôn cumen*. The parable of Lazarus and the Rich Man has thus been turned into yet another lesson on the hazards of being out of tune with the desires of one's *drohtin*.

> person. ... In an interpretation of Gmc. **uz-laga-* and its derivations we must also include OS *gi-lagu* (str. neut. pl.) 'fate' and ON *aldr-lag* (str. neut.) 'fate, death,' OE *ealdor-legu* (str. fem.) 'fate, death,' OS *aldar-lagu* (str. neut. pl.) 'the determined period of life, life.' Gmc. **laga-* belongs with the verb **lagjan* 'lay'; ON *lag* means 'laid out, situation, position,' the plural *lǫg* 'law' ... **uz-laga-* then means 'that which has been laid out.' ... Laying brings to mind the laying out of staves or sticks for fortune-telling. This connects the word with the carving of runes. The lots are 'laid-out' for a person and therewith future fortune. ... The word *urlag* is very frequent in OHG time, above all in the glossaries. In other literature it is strictly avoided; probably its basic character was too heathen to be included in Christian poetry.

§41. Workers in the Vineyard

Lines 3444b to 3475
(cf. Matthew 20:1-16)

Jesus tells the parable of the workers in the vineyard to illustrate the proposition that the last will be first, and the first last (Matthew 19:30; 20:16). The biblical account relates the coming of the workers at various times during the day and their receiving identical pay for their varied length of workday. The *Hêliand* relates the biblical parable accurately (l. 3409- 3444a) with typical elaboration but also inserts a further explanation beyond Matthew 20:1-16.

The point of the excursus in the *Hêliand* is overtly to liken the behavior of those who are hired early in the morning to the one who in young years 'begins to prepare himself, has chosen for himself fortitude (*muod*), good will, avoids things of the world, abandons desire, learns wisdom, God's law, and rejects the demands (*uuillion*) of wroth evil spirits (*uurêdaro gramono*). If such a person continues thus to life's evening, then the paths upwards (*uppuuegos*) are open.

The foolish who have willingly engaged in different things (*mislîk thing*) in their youth, e.g. evil arrogance (*lêða gelpquidi*), still have a chance to enter heaven. It is possible that *gelpquidi* had a reference to pre-Christian ceremonial or religious rites as well, involving loud recitations, as the etymology of *gelp* indicates (cf. OE *gielpan* 'exult, talk noisily', English 'yell, yelp', a derivational variant of **galan* 'sing' which also has a reflex in English 'beguile' or in the avian name 'nightingale'; cf. also Jente §179). Hempel remarks to this word: "Germ. **gelp-* 'übermütig, prahlend, laut' gehört als Labialderivat zur weitverzweigten Familie ie. **ghel-* 'schreien, gellen'. Bedeutsam sind dabei bestimmte magische Beschwerungen in **gal(d)-* 'Zaubergesang' und in **gelp-* 'trotzige Kampfrede'"[82] (p. 49).

---

[82] Gmc. **gelp-* 'boisterous, boastful, loud' is a labial extension of the widely-attested family of IE **ghel-* 'cry, yell.' Certain magical associations are significant in **gal(d)-* 'magical song' and in **gelp-* 'defiant battle speech.'

§42. Going to Jerusalem

Lines 3521 to 3566a
(Matthew 20:17-19; Mark 10:32-34; Luke 18:31-34)

All three of these gospels are quite similar in their telling of the departure of Jesus for Jerusalem, but only Luke mentions fulfillment of the writings of the prophets. The *Hêliand* speaks of 'all being fulfilled as was spoken in days of yore by wise men' (l. 3522b-3524), which appeals to Saxon sensibilities with respect to oral tradition in the same manner as was done in similar language at l. 1415 (*tulgo uuîse man uuordun gesprâcun*) in reference to the 'old law' and also rather like the description of the *giuuittig man, / frôd endi filuuuîs* of yore (*forn*) whose prophesy guided the Three Wise Men following the Star of Bethlehem (l. 569b-576a).

Luke 18:31-33 reads, "He took the Twelve aside and said, 'we are now going up to Jerusalem; and all that was written by the prophets will come true for the Son of Man. He will be handed over to the foreign power. He will be mocked, maltreated, and spat upon. They will flog him and kill him. And on the third day he will rise again.'" The *Hêliand* describes in vivid terms the betrayal of a *drohtin* into the hands of a rival faction (l. 3525-3531a). He will be sold to that troop (*te theru hêri*), His hands bound. He will suffer scorn and words of depredation (*hoskes gihôrien endi harmquidi*), insults (*bismersprâka*: cf. English 'besmirch') and challenges (*bihêtuuord*). He will be tortured (*sie uuêgeat mi te uundron*) and killed with the edge of a weapon (*uuâpnes eggiun*). The emphasis on prophecy motivates the acceptance by the disciples of Christ's fate.

§43. The Blind Men

Lines 3588b to 3633
(Matthew 20:29-34; Mark 10:46-52; Luke 18:35-43)

In Mark and Luke there is a blind man whose faith cures his loss of vision. In Matthew there are two blind men, and the touch of Jesus serves to redeem their sight. It is this version that appealed more to the author of the *Hêliand*. The passage just prior to the one presented

§. 43

here also follows Matthew rather closely. Then, in the present passage, the *Hêliand* elaborates on the story, making the suffering of the blind men metaphoric of the casting of Adam and Eve into dark sin. God gave them 'upward paths / the realm of heavens' (*uppuuegos, / himilo rîki*), but then 'the hostile one' (*the hatola*) betrayed them with sin and they left the 'ever-beautiful light' (*sinscôni lioht*). They were driven onto the roads of exile (*uuracsîðos*) in this world, deprived of properties (*uuelon tharbodun*), served evil ones (*gramon theonodun*), and were rewarded with fire in the hot hell. The world was thus despoiled (*farhuerbid*) and constrained in darkness, heavy work, in the valley of death.

The blind men sat by the road and awaited the help of God, which they would not receive until He sent His Son into the world that He might reveal light to the children of men, eternal life. At l. 3619 the narrator turns directly to the audience and admonishes the hearers to harken to what the coming of the Lord means. He can not ignore the time set by the moon, how it wanes or waxes, nor can the children of men.

Murphy (1992) remarks,

> This is the first place where the author addresses the audience, marking the importance of this story for the meaning of the *Heliand*. He repeats his direct address again when he finishes the explanation of the story of the cure of the blind men and says, 'Listen now....' Since this sort of speaking to the audience in the epic tradition was omitted at the beginning of the *Heliand*, and first occurs at this moment, one is particularly touched at this point to have the author say *you* to the reader/hearer. ... What story in the whole gospel could have been more moving to him as he thought of himself and his Saxons – and his epic – than the scene of two by the roadside begging to be able to see 'the light' (Footnote 168).

Epic admonition that the audience should listen up and hear the story is thus postponed from the beginning of the *Hêliand* to this lesson on the importance of taking advantage of Christ's presence in the world to receive the gift of seeing the light.

§44. Entering Jerusalem

Lines 3683b to 3705
(Matthew 24:1-31; Mark 13:1-27; Luke 21:5-28)

On the entry of Jesus into Jerusalem the city is depicted as a Saxon hill fort surrounded by a stockade (*uual*). The striking phrase *hôha hornseli* in connection with the impressive view of the fortifications of the city and of the temple focuses the hearers' attention on the centrality of the place as a dwelling site of the Jews (*bû Iudeono*). R. Wolfram (1968) cites *hôha hornseli* from the *Hêliand* as a parallel to the hall Heorot in Beowulf.

> Hier ist nochmals an die Halle 'Heorot' im Beowulf zu erinnern. O. Höfler weist ... darauf hin, daß diese dänische Königshalle auch Kulthalle war. ... es ist immerhin beachtenswert, daß auf den Giebeln ansehnlicher Saalbauten zur besonderen Zier auch sonst Hirschgeweihe standen, weshalb man diese Saalbauten 'Hornsäle' (*hornseli*) nannte[83] (pp. 94-95).

Matthew 24:2 may have attracted a Germanic tradition of apocalypse involving fire, the falling of stones or of stone walls, the wolf swallowing the sun, the cleaving of the heavens and judgment of mankind. The Saxon audience may have understood the depiction of the destruction of Jerusalem in that sense (cf. Matthew 24:29). Lines 3697 to 3702 are reminiscent of apocalyptic visions in other literary monuments from the older Germanic period which may also reflect the putative Germanic tradition of the end of the world. Consider, for example, the OHG *Muspilli* 53b to 56 (*suilizot lougiu der himil, / mano vallit, prinnit mittilagart, / sten ni kistentit, verit denne stuatago in lant, / verit mit vuiru viriho uuison* : "The heavens burn with fire, the moon falls, middle-earth burns, not a stone will remain standing, the court of judgment draws nigh faring with fire and seeking men") and the OI *Vǫluspá* 52 (*Surtr ferr sunnan / með sviga lævi, / skínn af sverði / sól valtíva / grjótbjǫrg gnata, / en gífr rata, / troða halir helveg, / en himinn klofnar* : "Surt [the swarthy source of

---

[83] This reminds one again of the hall 'Heorot' in Beowulf. O. Höfler points out that this Danish royal hall was also a cult hall. ... It is in any case worth noting that antlers were affixed to the gables of noble halls, for which reason they were termed 'horned halls' (*hornseli*).

heat from below] fares from the south with the bane of switches [fire]; the sun of the battle gods shines from his sword; rocks crash, trolls tumble, men tread the way to hell, and heaven cleaves").[84]

§45. A Thane's Duty

Lines 3992b to 4002a
(cf. John 11:16)

These few lines are included in part because of the gnomic verse that is strikingly similar to a verse in the OI *Hávamál*. The *Hêliand* presents Thomas here in the image of an ideal follower of a Germanic leader, as a 'solid man' (*githungan man*), a 'prized thane of his lord' (*diurlîc drohtines thegan*), who should not deny his will (*ne sculun uui im thia dâd lahan* [where *thia dâd* refers to the determination to return to Jerusalem]) but should persevere (*ac uuita im uuonian mid*) and 'endure with our king' (*thuoloian mid ûsson thiodne*). It is the free choice (*cust*) of the thane that he stand fast with his lord and die with him. Then fame (*dôm*) will live after, good word(s) for men (or: before, in the presence of men). Here again we see the Christian problem of how to deal with the Germanic virtue of heroic glory. (One 'solution' appears in the OE *Wanderer*, where the angels maintain the honor of men in heaven.)

The OI *Hávamál* contains the verses

76	Deyr fé, deyja frændr	One's animals die, friends/kinsmen die,
	deyr sjálfr it sama;	you'll die the same;
	en orðstirr deyr aldregi	but fame never dies
	hveim er sér góðan getr.	for the one who does well for himself.
77	Deyr fé, deyja frændr	One's animals die, friends/kinsmen die,
	deyr sjálfr it sama;	you'll die the same;
	ek veit einn at aldri deyr:	I know one thing that will never die:
	dómr um dauðan hvern.	the judgment concerning every one who dies.

The words here about dying valiantly and the fame (*dôm* / *dómr*) that lives after look to be a memory from pre-Christian tradi-

---

[84] See Braune and Ebbinghaus p. 87 and Nordal pp. 135 ff. More apocalyptic visions are contained in l. 4278b to 4335 (cf. §49).

Hêliand

tion at least similar to that reflected in the *Hávamál*. Tacitus in his *Germania* (quoted by Russell [1994]) wrote,

> On the field of battle it is a disgrace to a chief to be surpassed in courage by his followers, and to the followers not to be equal to the courage of their chief. And to leave a battle alive after their chief has fallen means lifelong infamy and shame. To defend him and protect him, and to let him get the credit for their own acts of heroism, are the most solemn obligations of their allegiance. The chiefs fight for victory, the followers for their chief (119).

Murphy (1992) comments:

> This very important speech by Thomas introduces the entire recasting of the Passion and Death in Germanic 'last-stand' military terms. The *Heliand* has expanded the brief laconic statement of Thomas given in Scripture in Jn. 11:16: 'Thomas, called the Twin, said to his fellow disciples, 'Let us go, that we may die with Him'. (Footnote 186)

Note also *Beowulf*, l. 1387b-1389:

> wyrce sē þe mōte
> dōmes ǣr dēaþe; þæt bið drihtguman
> unlifgendum æfter sēlest

> Let whoever can win glory before death. When a warrior is gone, that will be his best and only bulwark (Heaney, p. 97);

Beowulf 1534-1536:

> Swa sceal man don,
> þonne he æt guðe gegan þenceð
> longumne lof; na ymb his lif cearað

> So must a man do who intends to gain enduring glory in a combat. Life doesn't cost him a thought. (Heaney, p. 107);

and *Beowulf* 2890-2891:

> Deað bið sella
> eorla gehwylcom þonne edwitlif

> A warrior will sooner die than live a life of shame. (Heaney, p. 195)[85]

---

[85] See also *Beowulf* in Hansen (1988), pp. 58-59.

§. 45

For a more general review of the topic see Frank (1990). For doubts about the historicity of this topos, see Woolf (1876). Note also the remarks on *treulogo* 'faith-breaker' in the commentary to §51.

§46. JUDGMENT DAY

Lines 4045b to 4051a
(Isaiah 26:19; John 5:28-29; 6:39-40; 11:24)

The image of the dead arising out of the earth at the Day of Judgment occurs in Isaiah and in John and is strikingly portrayed in the OHG *Muspilli* and in the *Hêliand*. Here it is in the context of the Raising of Lazarus that Jesus speaks again of the Famous Day (*the mâreo dag*; cf. l. 1951 where He refers to 'the end of the world and the famous day that fares over men'). In the *Muspilli* 'angels fare over the lands, wake the dead, direct [them] to trial; then everyone will arise from the earth, loosen himself from the burden of the grave [and] will receive again his body' (l. 79-82: *denne varant engila uper dio marha, / uuechant deota, uuîssant ze dinge. / denne scal manno gilih fona deru moltu arstên, / lossan sih ar dero leuuo vazzon: scal imo avar sîn lîp piqueman*). In the *Hêliand* mortal man will stand *an themu mâreon dage* before God in a reckoning (*an rêðiu*), l. 2610-2612. The *Muspilli* presents the same image of a scene at court: *dar scal er vora demo rihhe az rahhu stantan* 'there he will stand before the court in a reckoning' (l. 35). The Germanic *þing* 'assembly; court' serves here as the metaphorical place of judgment, but this time the Judge will deem the dead.

The faithful woman believes, and she trusts that Christ 'has power over heaven and earth through the holy fates' (l. 4061b-4064). Murphy (1992) comments here:

> ... In her enthusiasm Martha seems to have slipped back into Germanic religion, saying that Christ rules thanks to the power of fate. ... The author has intentionally inserted the word 'holy' from his Christian vocabulary and combined it with 'fate' to take the place of the expression 'the power of God.' ... In Germanic terms: when one sees Christ, one is seeing fate. 'Fate' can thus be called, as here, 'holy fate,' and eventually be identified with the will of [the Christian] God (Footnote 191).

Hêliand

In Germanic terms the fates ruled the gods too. The importance of the raising of Lazarus, more than Martha's wording, is that the incident reveals that Christ stands above and directs fate.

§47. RAISING LAZARUS

Lines 4065 to 4117
(John 11:32-44)

Mary mourns Lazarus with keening and weeping in the same manner as those mothers whose young children had been killed by Herod when he sought the baby Jesus (l. 744b-746a). Note, incidentally, that here Lazarus is buried in an earthen grave (*an themu erðgraƀe*), not the biblical cave with a stone door. The pre-Christian custom of cremation had been prohibited by an edict promulgated by Charlemagne, and the new requirement of inhumation is what is referred to. Ilkow comments,

> [D]ie Sitte der Leichenverbrennung [hält sich] bis tief in die Völkerwanderungszeit (Brünhild, Beowulf) bei Sachsen und Friesen zwischen Elbe und Ems sogar bis zur Zeit Karls des Großen, der diese Sitte im Paderborner Kapitulare (785) verbietet ... Wenn nun der Helianddichter das Grab des Lazarus ein 'Erdgrab' nennt ... das er sich allerdings, dem biblischen Bericht gemäß (J 11, 38 *erat autem spelunca et lapis superpositus erat ei*) mit einem Stein bedeckt vorstellt – dann denkt er ... an das typisch christliche Begräbnis, das den Sachsen eher neuartig als althergebracht erscheinen mußte. Im Gegensatz zu der christlichen Erdbestattung steht die heidnische Beisetzung der Asche Beowulfs an einem Grabhügel ...[86] (p. 111).

Jesus uncovered the grave and prayed to the 'Victory-Lord' (*sigidrohtin*) as a thane might petition his successful, famous, battle-

---

[86] The custom of cremation is maintained long into the Migration Period (Brunhilda, Beowulf) among Saxons and Frisians between the Elbe and Ems even up to the time of Charlemagne, who forbids the practice in the Paderborn Capitulare (785). ... The author of the Hêliand calls the grave of Lazarus an 'earth grave ... that he describes in accordance with the biblical report (John 11:38 ...) as covered with a stone. He is thinking ... of a typical Christian burial that must have seemed modern rather than traditional to the Saxons. In contrast with the Christian burial in the earth there is the heathen deposition of the ashes of Beowulf in a grave mound ... .

proven leader. Lazarus stirred, asked Christ to help him, and men went up and unwound the funeral wrappings. He then 'arose in splendor to this light' (l. 4103b-4104a). Life was given to him 'that he might own his *aldarlagu*', which is to say that he might again possess the measure of life decreed to him by the fates, cf. §40.

The passage ends with a gnomic admonition that the great might of God can foster the life-force (*ferah*) of each person and help against the enmity of fiends for those to whom he grants His *huldi*, the favor of a *drohtin* to members of his entourage.

§48. Jesus as Threat

Lines 4121b to 4157
(Matthew 26:1-5; Mark 14:1-2; Luke 22:1-2; John 11:45-53)

Jesus' resurrection of Lazarus threatened *môdstarke man*, leaders who did not want to recognize the power of God but sought to work against Him with their words. The reports from those who had seen Lazarus alive with their own eyes alarmed the Jewish leaders, and they ordered their men (*gumskepi*) to gather the people in formation (*uuerod samnoian endi uuarbos fâhen*) as at a Germanic *þing*. There they counseled in secret (*riedun an rûnun*) and determined that it would not be of help (*râd*) to tolerate that people believe in His teachings. John 11:49 says, "Then the Romans will come and sweep away our temple and our nation." The *Hêliand* says, "Then people will come at us with armies of cavalry and our overlords will be warriors from Rome. After that, we will either live dispossessed of our kingdom or we will suffer the loss of our lives, heroes, and our heads!" Murphy (1992) remarks,

> An amazing sentence – there is, of course, no mention at all of cavalry at this point, or any point, in the four gospels. Charlemagne had so developed the cavalry that the Franks possessed the best mounted forces ... in the Northern world. ... The author's deft and brief insertion of the fear of cavalry brings the speaker's words into emotional accord with the military feelings of the Saxons, and into the political fear common to both peoples, Saxon and Jewish, of being ruled by warriors 'from Rome' (Footnote 197).

The Saxons should presumably identify themselves with the Disciples here and not consider their situation to be like that of the

Hêliand

Jews but able to understand their anxiety of being overrun by a foreign force.

Caiphas, who had been chosen for that year (*an themu gêrtalu*) to care for the temple (*uuardon thes uuîhes*) argued for the loss of one life (Christ's) as against the loss of the whole people. Murphy (1992) points out that although four different pre-Christian words are used for temple, the word for pagan priest is avoided here in favor of the loanword *biscop*, asserting that "Germanic priests are not to be allowed, even by possible misunderstanding, to take the blame for killing Christ" (Footnote 198). The intent was thus to entertain and convert, not to inflame, the Saxon audience, and the more tolerable route was to ascribe the killing of Christ to a Jewish 'bishop' whose role could presumably be differentiated from that of the Catholic bishops involved in the mission to the Saxons.

§49. APOCALYPSE

Lines 4278b to 4285a; 4308 to 4335; 4352 to 4378
(Matthew 24:3-14; Mark 13:4-8; Luke 21:5-11)

Luke 21:6 quotes Jesus, Who says regarding the temple, "These things which you are gazing at – the time will come when not one stone of them will be left upon another; all will be thrown down." The *Hêliand* enlarges on this statement and adds that the green meadow will slip away (*teglîded grôni uuang*), which reminds one of the image in the OI *Vǫluspá* where the earth sinks into the sea (Verse 57: *sígr fold í mar*) only to re-emerge again from the sea 'ever green' (Verse 59: *Sér hon upp koma / ǫðru sinni / jǫrð ór ægi / iðjagroena*). Elsewhere the phrase *grôni uuang* generally occurs as a metaphor for 'heaven,' but here as with the flight to Egypt (cf. §10) the reference is strictly to the earth.

The disciples wished to know when the apocalypse would occur and what sign would foretell it. Jesus replied that many will appear with His name and claim to be Christ, saying that the time is nigh (Luke 21:7-8). First wars must come, but the end of the world will not occur immediately. Peoples will arise against peoples, earthquakes and famines will occur, and there will be mighty signs in the sky (Luke 21:10-11). Many will come to hate each other, and because God's commandments will be ignored, love will cool (Matthew 24:10-12).

§. 49

The signs which will occur *an themu mâreon daga* will have specifically to do with the darkening of the moon and sun, the falling of stars (*fallad sterron, / huît bebentungal*), the trembling of the earth (*endi hrisid erðe, / bibod thius brêde uuerold*), and the churning of the great sea which will work terror with its waves (*grimmid the grôto sêo, uuirkid thie gebenes strôm / egison mid is ûðiun*). (Compare the *Vǫluspá*: Verse 57, where the bright stars twirl from heaven; Verse 50, which tells of the earth serpent kicking up waves in a giant fury; and Verse 52, which speaks of earthquakes and the cleaving of heaven.) The *Hêliand* tells how peace will end, wars will break out, and an army will lead one kin against another (*nis friðu huergin, / ac uuirðid uuîg sô maneg obar these uuerold alla / hetelîc ahaben, endi heri lêdid / kunni obar ôðar*). (The *Vǫluspá* speaks similarly of brothers fighting and killing each other in Verse 45.) Kings will fight kings in a great campaign that will be the death of many people, open war (*uuirðid kuningo giuuin, / meginfard mikil: uuirdid managoro qualm, / open urlagi*). There will be sickness, death (*uuôl sô mikil ... mansterbono mêst*) and famine (*unmet grôt hungar hetigrim*). Sick men will fall and die (*liggiad seoka man, / driosat endi dôiat*). The end of the world is a 'certain comer' (*uuiscumo*), the famous day of judgment (*duomdag the mâreo*) and famous time (*endi thiu mârie tîd*), the end of this world (*giuuand thesaro uueroldes*).

Do not be caught sleeping, for *mûtspelli* comes in the dark of night, just as a thief goes hidden about his task (l. 4358b-4360a). Images seen in the *Hêliand* and *Vǫluspá* have analogues in the OHG *Muspilli*, where in l. 51 to 59 the mountains burn, the moon falls, not a stone remains standing, and the renowned Day of Judgment fares into the land (*verit denne stuatago in lant*). Note also *Hêliand* lines 4337 to 4355a: *duomdag the mâreo endi iuuues drohtines craft, thiu mikilo meginstrengi endi thiu mârie tîd, giuuand thesaro uueroldes*. Murphy (1992) translates *craft* as 'might' (p. 142) but Ilkow says,

> Vom Standpunkt der as. Komp. interessieren uns neben 'Körperkraft, Macht' die Bedeutungen 'Menge, Schar' ... Die Bedeutung 'Menge, Schar' wirkt in den Komp. *himil-, man-* und *megin-kraft*. ... Der Begriff der physischen Kraft oder Macht ist zunächst wohl auf eine militärische Einheit übertragen worden; vgl. *umbihuarf ina craft uuero*, v. 5270 ...[87] (p. 67).

---

[87] From the standpoint of the OS compound the meanings 'multitude, crowd' interest us in addition to 'physical power, might' ... The meaning 'multitude,

Héliand

Ilkow (p. 282) defines the variation here on *craft*, namely *meginstrengi*, in agreement with Murphy (*loc. cit.*) as 'gewaltige Macht' ('mighty power'). In l. 5270 *craft* clearly means 'crowd, mob'. The citation given above could thus be translated as 'and the troops of your Leader, the great overwhelming strength, and the renowned time, the end of this world' or as in Murphy (*loc. cit.*) "and your Chieftain's might, the force of severe strength – and the famous time, the end-turn of this world!"

§50. WASHING FEET

Lines 4494b to 4521a
(John 13:4-10)

Jesus knew that He must die, 'give up these estates/lands' (*ageƀen these gardos*) and seek His Father's ancestral property, His Father's ancestral home (*sôkien imu ... is faderôðil*), God's realm. The day 'moved west' and the sun to its 'seat'. Christ washed the feet of His disciples, but Peter thought that to be an unseemly thing. Jesus said that if he hadn't the will to receive, then he would have no dealings with Him in heaven.

The wording of this passage differs essentially from that of John 13. The *Héliand* does not mention that Satan had already commissioned Judas to betray Christ (John 13:2), although the image of sun setting in the west alludes to what is coming. The details of Jesus' changing from his robe to a linen cloth around the waist and of the conversation with Peter are missing or different in the *Héliand*. Instead of saying "I will never let you wash my feet" (John 13:8), here Peter says that it doesn't seem proper that his Lord wash his feet (l. 4508-4510). Jesus responds with a threat that Peter will not come to heaven, if he doesn't let his feet be washed. As in the biblical text Peter's mood (or mind, spirit) was changed (*Hugi uuarð thô geuuendid*), and he said, "'Then Lord ... not my feet only; wash

crowd' appears in the compound *himil-, man-,* and *megin-kraft*. ... The concept of physical power or might is probably applied primarily to a military unit; cf. *umbihuarf ina craft uuero*, l. 5270 ... .

§. 50

my hands and head as well!'" (John 13:9). The *Hêliand* has Peter say that Jesus has power to wash his head with His hands (l. 4516-4518a), but here it is 'to retain your *huldi* and to obtain such a portion of heaven as you want to give through your goodness' (l. 4518b-4521a), a depiction of the dutiful Germanic follower before his *drohtin*. Instantly Peter becomes the 'Good Thane' (cf. §45). Here it is not a question of dying for one's *drohtin* but of obeying.

§51. JESUS IDENTIFIES THE BETRAYER

Lines 4590b to 4627
(John 13:22-27; Matthew 26:20-25; Mark 14:17-21)

One of the Twelve will *treuuana swîkan*, will commit a grave breach of fidelity to his *drohtin*, and the *Hêliand* uses words to identify him that would horrify any loyal Saxon. The betrayer will sell his merciful (*hold*) leader for silver, a hoard of treasures (*sinc*), expensive jewels (*diurie mêðmos*), which act will bring him into misfortune and torture (*te harme ... te uuîtie*). The duplicitous one will know that it were better by far never to have been born than to accept such iniquitous, depraved counsel (*inuuidrâd*) when he finds out what is coming to him and 'sees the fates' (*thea uurði farsihit*).

The disciples looked nervously at one another, wondering who from among them would be counted as the guilty deceiver. John 13:23-25 says, "One of them, the disciple he loved, was reclining close beside Jesus. So Simon Peter nodded to him and said, 'Ask who it is he means.' That disciple, as he reclined, leaned back close to Jesus and asked, 'Lord who is it?'" Here the company is reclining at table, as in the Roman tradition. In John 13 we read only of the one Jesus loved most who was next to him, but John is not named, nor does his name appear in the other parallel texts — although to a reader of the Vulgate it is clear that John was meant. The *Hêliand* informs us that the disciple in question is John and portrays his inclining toward Jesus in terms of the strongest bonds between *drohtin* and a follower. John lay and inclined his head to the breast of Christ and took there 'so many a holy secret, deep thoughts' (*sô manag hêlag gerûni, diapa githâhti*) and asked how anyone could sell the most powerful of kings into the formation (*folc*) of enemies, thus casting the biblical image of the disciple's inclining as the antithesis of betrayal.

Hêliand

Jesus identifies Judas, as in the biblical account, by giving him to eat (John 13:26-27) and admonishes him to 'attain what you intend, do that which you shall do' (*frumi sô thu thenkis ... dô that thu duan scalt*) but goes on to say that 'fate is at hand, the times have now neared.' Judas is called the *treulogo* ('fidelity-liar'), which renders the concept of turning against one's *drohtin* and of breaking faith with him.

Ilkow says,

> In vorchristlicher Zeit wirkt *Treue* in erster Linie als Rechtsbegriff, der das 'Einhalten eines geschlossenen Vertrages' bezeichnet. ... Von besonderer Bedeutung ist der Treuebegriff im Vasallenverhältnis. Das Verhältnis zwischen dem Gefolgsherrn und den Gefolgsleuten fußt auf wechselseitiger Treue (vgl. *bôg-gebo*). Nach Tacitus' Bericht (Germania 4) leisteten die Gefolgsmannen ihrem Herrn bei ihrem Eintritt in die Gefolgschaft einen Treueid. Im Kriege kämpften die Gefolgsleute in unmittelbarer Umgebung ihres Herrn. Als schimpflich galt es, sein Schicksal nicht zu teilen, wenn er in der Schlacht fiel. Daher nennt der Beowulfdichter die Mannen, die ihren Gefolgsherrn beim Kampf mit dem Drachen im Stich ließen, als *trēow-logan* 'Treuebrecher' v. 2847. Auch im Hel. spiegelt das in v. 4620 auf den Verräter Judas bezogene Komp. *treu-logo* den Bruch des altgerm. Gefolgschaftsverhältnisses wider[88] (p. 375).

See also Green, p. 117-126, for *triuwa, gitriuwi*. The Christian usage of this term in the *Hêliand* was extended beyond the bonds of the retinue or of kinship, as Green points out:

> [T]he author of the *Heliand* attempts to render the Christian precept of loving one's foes more palatable or more intelligible to his audience by extending the concept of the

---

[88] In pre-Christian time *loyalty* was primarily a legal term meaning 'adherence to an agreed-to contract.' ... Of special significance is the concept of loyalty in relationship to feudal service. The relationship between the leader and the followers depends on mutual loyalty (cf. *bôg-gebo*). According to Tacitus' report (Germania 4) the followers swore an oath of allegiance to their lord upon entering the troop. In battle the followers fought in close proximity to their lord. It was viewed as humiliating not to share his fate when he fell in battle. The author of Beowulf thus calls the men who left their lord in the lurch in the battle with the dragon *trēow-logan* 'loyalty breakers' in l. 2847. The compound *treu-logo* referring to the traitor Judas in l. 4620 of the Hêliand reflects a violation of the ancient Germanic compact between leader and followers.

§. 51

kinship so as to embrace all mankind, so that he can now argue that the loyalty due to one's kinsman is no less than that which the Christian owes to any other man (1454):

> ... that gi iuuua fiund sculun
> minneon an iuuuomu môde, sô samo sô gi iuuua mâgos dôt,
> an godes namon. Dôt im gôdes filu,
> tôgeat im hluttran hugi, holda treuua,
> liof uuiðar ira lêðe   (p. 119).

Murphy (1992) translates these lines as "... that you are to love your enemies in your feelings, just as you love your family relatives, in God's name. Do a great deal of good for them, extend friendly loyalty to them with a clear mind – love versus their hatred" (p. 50). The phrase *holda treuua* was historically highly emotionally charged, indicating the inviolable quality of personal ties between *drohtin* and retinue, between members of a retinue, and among kin. As Green puts it, the term *treuua* had both "horizontal" and "vertical" bonds.

As in the biblical passage, Satan possesses Judas when he eats of the food, and 'the power of God gave him up' and evil spirits (*gramon, lêða uuihti*) entered his body. The help of God (*helpe godes*) abandoned him in this world. 'Thus is it for that one among men who under this heaven shall change his lord' (l. 4626-4627), a gnomic admonition concerning the behavior of a retainer that surely resonated strongly in the minds of the audience. It could not be expressed more strongly than that. (Compare the actions of the Good Soldier in §45.)

§52. Jesus In Gethsemane

Lines 4732b to 4775a
(Matthew 26:36-42; Luke 22:39-46; John 12:27, 18:1)

Matthew (26: 36-42) relates the Agony of Christ before his capture and crucifixion. "Jesus then came with his disciples to a place called Gethsemane. He said to them, 'sit here while I go over there to pray.' He took with him Peter and the two sons of Zebedee. Anguish and dismay came over him, and he said to them, 'My heart is ready to break with grief. Stop here, and stay awake with me.' He went on a little, fell on his face in prayer, and said 'My Father, if it is possible, let this cup pass me by. Yet not as I will, but as thou wilt.' He came to the disciples and found them asleep; and he said to Peter, 'What! Could none of you stay awake with me one hour? Stay awake, and pray that you may be spared the test. The spirit is willing, but the flesh is weak.'"

The *Hêliand* sends Jesus up high on a mountain, and the three disciples James and John and 'the good Peter, a bold thane' follow, as 'they always went eagerly with their king' as ideal followers of their commander. Here Christ not only prays but also asks His disciples to join Him in addressing (*gruotian*) God for the strength to withstand the power of tempters, the will of wroth [beings], that the opponent (*uuiðersaco*) might not bring His mind to doubt. Christ Himself fell down in prayer and greeted the Good Father of All Peoples. His flesh was weak in fear, and he cried. His tears fell, and sweat ran as blood wells from wounds (cf. Luke 22:44). The connection between blood and sweat is commented on by Beck (1978: 77): "Daneben findet auch Schweiss (*sudor*) im Bedeutungssinne von B[lut] ... Gemeint ist insbesondere das B[lut] des Jagdtieres, auch des Schlachttieres."[89] Murphy (1992) hypothesizes:

> Tears have been added by the *Hêliand* author. It is interesting that not only has none of Christ's fear of losing His life 'in battle' been suppressed, but the scene of the Agony in the Garden has been intensified by the author. Presumably, he felt the extreme realism of this part of the gospel story would be well understood by men who had already been on real battle-

---
[89] There is also sweat (*sudor*) in the meaning of blood. ... In particular the blood of a hunted animal, but also of a domestic animal for slaughter, is meant.

fields. The bloody sweat of the Agony is used by the author to draw an implicit comparison to battle wounds. ... (Footnotes 240-241)

There was a struggle between the spirit and the flesh; the one was eager for the journey while the other *drobde for themu dôðe*.

In the *Hêliand* the cup, which in the Old Testament contained a bitter drink symbolic of judgment and punishment (cf. Psalms 11 and 75), is not metaphorical but real. Jesus actually takes it in hand and drinks a toast to God and promises as a faithful thane to fulfill His will, as did the Good Soldier promise to die with and for his *drohtin* (cf. §43; see also Murphy [1989], p. 104 f.).

The scene ends with a gnomic caution on the heartbreak (*môdthraca*) that befalls every man who must give up his beloved lord (*liabane hêrron*).

§53 THE CAPTURE OF CHRIST

Lines 4810b to 4903a; 4913b to 4923a
(Matthew 26:46-53; Mark 14:42-47; Luke 22:47-51; John 18:2-12)

The author of the *Hêliand* favors here the version of the story as told in John, as the details of the torches and the naming of Peter and Malchus occur only in John 18, and only there is mention made of Judas' familiarity with the site and of the crowd's falling to the ground when Jesus said, "It is I." The statement by Judas that the soldiers should seize Jesus is, however, lacking in John and can be found instead in Matthew and Mark. The binding of Jesus is mentioned in John 18:12, but the *Hêliand* also characterizes in pre-Christian terms His awaiting the divine fortunes of brighter times (*bêd metodogiscapu / torhtero tîdeo*). The accusation of inciting to insurrection (*the thit giuuer frumid*) and the details of the confrontational men who worked up the courage to surround Him (l. 4854b-4858a) are elaborations of the *Hêliand*.

What follows is further embroidering of the biblical account. The (battle-)wise men take position in front of Christ (*Stôdun uuîse man ... biforan*) and seek a directive from their leader. 'Do you desire that they kill us here with the points of spears, [that we be] wounded with weapons? Nothing would be so good than that we could die here (be)for(e) our lord, pale with baneful wounds' (l. 4861-4865a). The hostile troops approach, after 'firming their courage' (*fastnodun hugi*) and 'binding their determination' (*bundun briostgithâht*). Ilkow comments to the latter,

> Die Komp. 1) *briost-githâht* und 2) *briost-hugi* erweisen sich als treffliche Beispiele, um uns zu zeigen, wie fern wir dem Verständnis des Bedeutungsgehalts altgerm. Wörter oft bleiben, wenn wir eine sog. 'etymologische' Übersetzung herstellen. ... Wir haben uns daran gewöhnt, entweder in dem Gehirn oder dem Kopf als dem Teil des Körpers, der das Gehirn enthält, den Sitz unserer Gedanken zu sehen, während uns das Herz oder gegebenenfalls die Brust als Sitz der Gefühle gilt. ... Im germ. Altertum wie im Mittelalter galt nämlich das Herz bzw. die Brust, der Teil des menschlichen Körpers, in dem das Herz enthalten ist, nicht nur als Sitz der Gefühle und des Wollens, sondern auch der Denkkraft. ... Das Herz bzw. die Brust gilt dem Germanen als Ursprung und Sitz aller seelisch-geistigen Kräfte. ... Wie die Verwendung von *briost* für die Gesamtheit des Seelischen und der häufige Gebrauch dieses Wortes in Verbindung mit Präpositionen wie *an, innan* ... zeigen, kannte die Vorstellungswelt der Germanen eine menschliche Seele, die man sich im Herzen bzw. in der Brust eingeschlossen dachte. Dieser vorchristliche Seelenbegriff läßt sich als 'Körperseele' bezeichnen; die 'Körperseele' ist 'die dem menschlichen Körper innewohnende Quelle aller seelischen Kräfte'... Von ihr müssen wir den platonischen Begriff der vom Körper abtrennbaren Seele, den die Germanen erst durch das Christentum kennenlernten und den sie mit den Ableitungen von germ. *saiwalō- bezeichneten, streng scheiden[90] (pp. 71-72).

---

[90] The compounds 1) *briost-githâht* and 2) *briost-hugi* are exellent examples to show us how far we often remain from understanding the meaning of ancient Germanic words when we produce a so-called 'etymological' translation. ... We have become accustomed to viewing the seat of thought either in the brain or the head as that part of the body which contains the brain, while the heart or breast is seen as the seat of emotions. In Germanic antiquity as in medieval times the heart or breast, wherein the heart is contained, was considered not only the seat of emotion and of volition but also of thought. ... The heart or breast is for the ancient Germanic peoples the origin and location of all spiritual powers. ... As the use of *briost* for the entirety of everything spiritual and the frequent use of this word in connection with prepositions like *an, innan* ... show, the imagination of the ancient Germanic people recognized a human soul which was thought to be in the heart or breast. This pre-Christian concept of the soul can be called a 'body soul'; the 'body soul' is 'the source of all spiritual powers inhabiting the human body'... We must strictly divorce it from the platonic concept of the soul as being apart from the body, which Germanic peoples became acquainted with only

§. 53

See also the commentary to §4 for *hugi* and other words having to do with what Ilkow calls the *Körperseele*.

True to Germanic ideals, Simon Peter, *snel suuerðthegan*, became swollen with anger and his *hugi* welled within him (*gibolgan uuarð ... uuell imu innan hugi*) to the point of speechlessness that anyone would dare bind his *drohtin*. He is called here *suuerðhegan*, but when the *Hêliand* was composed, not every *thegan* had a sword. Regarding *suuerðhegan* Ilkow says,

> ... *suuerð-thegan* ist eine auszeichnende Benennung, die, zur Zeit des HelD, nicht jedem *wâpan-berand* oder *hildi-skalk* beigelegt wurde. Wie Tacitus (Germania 6) berichtet, waren Schwerter bei den Germanen der Römerzeit selten gewesen, ihr Besitz war wohl ein Vorrecht der Fürsten und Edlen, und noch aus späterer Zeit verbürgt der Umstand, daß man Schwertern Namen gab, durch die sie berühmt wurden (z.B. Siegfrieds *Balmunc*), die hohe Achtung vor der Waffe und ihrem Träger[91] (p. 373).

Simon Peter went to stand in front of his lord, drew his sword, and struck toward the foremost enemy with the might of his hand (*folmo crafto*). Malchus' ear was severed (*farhauuan*), his head was wounded such that cheek and ear (*hlear endi ôre*) burst with baneful wound, blood sprang forth, welled from the wounds. The highest of the enemies was cut on his cheek.

Commenting on the word *beniuunda* 'baneful, mortal wound' Ilkow says,

> Die Bedeutungsgeschichte des Vordergliedes, das mit got. *banja*, an. *ben*, ae. *ben(n)* auf germ. **banjō* 'Wunde' führt, kommt der von *wunda* sehr nahe... Es stellt sich zu der Ver-

---

through Christianity and which they named by means of a derivation from PGmc. **saiwalō-*, a form that remains etymologically obscure.

[91] ... *suuerð-thegan* is a name of distinction that in the period during which the Hêliand was written was not given to just any *wâpan-berand* or *hildi-skalk*. As Tacitus reports in Germania 6, Germanic warriors seldom had swords during the Roman period. Their possession was restricted to rulers and nobles, and the circumstance from even later times that names were given to swords by which they became famous (for example, Siegfried's *Balmunc*), vouches for the high esteem in which the weapon and its bearer were held.

Hêliand

balwurzel **ban-* 'schlagen', bezeichnet also ursprünglich 'das (im Kampf) Geschlagene'[92] (p. 63).

Jesus responds to the wound so struck by admonishing Peter to sheathe his sharp sword. He says, "All who take the sword die by the sword" (Matthew 26:52). The *Hêliand* speaks of *uuâpno nîð* and *gêrheti*. Ilkow says,

> Wie schon Vilmar (S. 82) erkannte, leuchtet im Grundwort von *gêr-heti* eine Nebenbedeutung des Stammes 'Haß' durch, die ... vielleicht die Grundbedeutung von germ. **hatiz* war (vgl. *hetzen*), nämlich 'feindliche Verfolgung, Nachstellung' (vgl. *heti-grim*). Wie die syntaktische Phrase *uuâpno nîð* in v. 4896 (auch *nîð* kann 'Verfolgung' bedeuten) ist das in Variation zu ihr gebrauchte *gêr-heti* ein Kenning für den Begriff 'Kampf'[93] (p. 145).

The admonishment to Peter runs counter to the Germanic (or likely any other) warrior ethic. Russell (1994) quotes Max Weber, who writes,

> As a rule, the class of warrior nobles, and indeed feudal powers generally, have not readily become the carriers of a rationalistic religious ethic. The life pattern of a warrior has very little affinity with the notion of a beneficent providence, or with the systematic ethical demands of a transcendental god. ... It is an everyday psychological event for the warrior to face death and the irrationalities of human destiny. Indeed, the chances and adventures of mundane existence fill his life to such an extent that he does not require of his religion (and accepts only reluctantly) anything beyond protection against evil magic or such ceremonial rites as are congruent with his caste, such as priestly prayers for victory or for a blissful death leading directly into the hero's heaven (p. 155).

Christ's appeal to the potential of calling up to God for a host of angels offers the author of the *Hêliand* opportunity here to expand

[92] The semantic history of the first element, related to Gothic *banja*, ON *ben*, OE *ben(n)* from Gmc **banjō* 'wound,' verges on that of *wunda* ... It belongs with the verbal root **ban-* 'strike' and orginally means 'that which is struck (in battle).'

[93] As Vilmar (p. 82) already recognized, the secondary meaning of the stem 'hate' shines through in the head word of *gêr-heti*, which ... was perhaps the basic meaning of Gmc. **hatiz* (cf. German *hetzen*), namely 'hostile pursuit, stalking' (cf. *heti-grim*). As with the syntactic phrase *uuâpno nîð* in l. 4896 (*nîð* can also mean 'pursuit'), the *gêr-heti* used in variation to it is a kenning for the concept 'battle.'

§. 53

on the warlike qualities of 'many an angel' of the heavenly host, *uuîges sô uuîsen*. Men would not have been able to endure against their battle with weapons (*uuâpanthreki*), but Wielding God, the Almighty Father, had marked it otherwise. Jesus admonishes that 'we should suffer whatever this people bring that may be bitter, nothing should incite us, make us angry against their battle, for whoever furthers the hatred of weapons, grim spear-enmity, he will die by the edge(s) of the sword, die bloodied. We with our deeds should harm nothing' (l. 4894b-4900a).

The mob bound His hands with *herubendium*. The first word of this compound noun is a poetic word for sword (cf. herudrôrag 'sword-bloody' in l. 4878). What the mob bound His hands with could literally be 'sword-bonds,' but this is likely a word indicating the sort of fetters that prisoners of war were bound with, perhaps the straps that normally held the scabbard. Ellis Davidson cites archeological evidence for the scabbard having been suspended from strap over the shoulder, e.g. "On the ... scabbard ... the holders were one above the other on the same side, and ... a narrow strap could pass through one of these, then round the scabbard and over the wearer's shoulder, to return to finish at the second strap-holder" (pp. 91-92). See also in Ellis Davidson illustrations 106a-c and 109-111 for swords carried by a strap over the shoulder and Foerste (1967).

We get little help here from an etymology of *heru*. Feist (1939) cites no affirmed etymology for the Gothic cognate *hairus*. This word also has cognates in Old Icelandic, all having the poetic usage evident here. (See Cleasby-Vigfusson, p. 268.)

Ilkow, quoting E.A. Kock, holds another opinion of this word:

> [G]erm. *heru- [hat sich] im Nord- und Westgerm. nur noch als archaistischer Ausdruck der Dichtung erhalten. Ausdrücke, die in der Alltagssprache untergegangen sind, neigen dazu, Intensivierungsfunktion anzunehmen (vgl. *regan-*). Bei dem Stamm *heru-* kommt aber noch ein speziell semantischer Faktor hinzu. E.A. Kock hat festgestellt, daß Wörter, die irgendwie Beziehung zum Kriegswesen haben, ... in der germ. Stabreimdichtung als erstes Kompositionsglied häufig Bedeutungen wie 'furchtbar', 'gefährlich', oder 'grausam' annehmen und somit den Grundbegriff verstärken. ... Zu as. *heru-* sagt Kock: 'OS *heru-bendi, heru-sêl* do not combine the ideas of 'sword' and 'bond' in any manner familiar to modern thinking. In rendering *heftun heru-bendiun hendi tesamne* (Hel. 4919) or *hnêg an heru-sêl, warag an wurgil* (ibid. 5169 f.) we resort to expressions like "cruel fetters" or "horrible

Hêliand

halter.'" ... Wir glauben Kock nicht ganz folgen zu können ... Erinnern wir uns an die Etymologie unseres Wortes nhd. *Schwert*, das zunächst die 'schneidende Waffe' bezeichnet. Die *heru-bendi* sind 'eng angezogene, einschneidende' und des-wegen 'grausame Fesseln ...'[94] (pp. 204-205).

For a broader interpretation of the depiction of Christ's giving in to the enemy, see Murphy 1989 (p. 95 ff.).

§54. Peter Denies His Lord

Lines 4940b to 5005a
(Matthew 26:69-75; Mark 14:66-72; Luke 22:54-62; John 18:15,25-27)

Matthew and Mark do not mention the fire, which is described here, although Luke and John do. None claim that Peter went into the *frîdhof*. John 18:15-16 tells of the one disciple who accompanied Jesus into the enclosure while Peter waited outside. This second disciple, who knew the high priest, came back out and the (female) guard let Peter in. The author of the *Hêliand* takes this unnamed disciple to be John, 'the one that was most beloved of thanes' (l. 4599b-4601a).

Only John mentions the guard who at first would not let Peter enter, but the *Hêliand* omits the questioning of Peter by the guard and Peter's denial at that point (cf. John 18:17). After entering the courtyard, described as being 'behind fences' (*under ederos*), a 'cunning woman' (*fêkni uuîf*), servant of their king (*iro theodanes thiuu*), approached Peter. She asked whether he was a disciple of the man

---

[94] Gmc. *heru- survived in North and West Germanic only as an archaic poetical expression. Expressions which in daily speech have died out tend to assume an intensifying function (cf. *regan*-). With the stem *heru*- a special semantic factor is added. E.A. Kock established that words which have some connection to war frequently assume as the first element of a nominal compound in Germanic alliterative poetic meanings like 'terrible,' 'dangerous,' or 'horrible' and thus reinforce the basic meaning. ... Regarding OS *heru*- Kock says, 'OS. *heru-bendi*, *heru-sêl* do not combine the ideas of 'sword' and 'bond' in any manner familiar to modern thinking. In rendering *heftun heru-bendiun hendi tesamne* (Hel. 4919) or *hnêg an heru-sêl, warag an wurgil* (ibid. 5169 f.) we resort to expressions like "cruel fetters" or "horrible halter."' ... We don't believe we can entirely follow Kock here ... Let us recall the etymology of our word *Schwert*, that primarily means the 'cutting weapon'. The *heru-bendi* are 'tightly drawn-on, cutting' and therefore 'horrible fetters...'.

§. 54

from Galilee, 'the one who stands over there fastened by His hands' (*faðmun gifastnod*). Peter was filled with fear, slack of heart (*slac an is môde*), and said that he did not understand her words, that he was not the thane of the King, said that he did not know this man. Peter goes to warm himself by the fire, and another woman begins to 'perpetrate slander' (*felgian firinsprâka*) and quizzes him about his association with Jesus (cf. Luke 22:56). Thereupon 'men urging confrontation' ('whetters of treachery': *nîðhuata*) approached Peter and said, 'you are not from among the people of this city ...' (*ni bist thu thesoro burg-liudio ...*). Peter denies that he is from Galilee and swears with a strong oath that he was not one of the disciples (*endi starkan êð / suîðlîco gesuor, that he thes gesîðes ni uuâri*). Here the *Hêliand* bases its story on Matthew 26:73-74 and/or Mark 14:71, doubtless because of its mention of the oath, the faithfulness to which is a Saxon *sine qua non* in the relationship of a follower and his *drohtin*. The third denial in the version offered by the *Hêliand* is again based on John (18:26), which account brings Peter once more face-to-face with Malchus, whose ear he had earlier severed with his sword (cf. l. 4865b-4881a and 4900b-4903a). Here Peter says that he would wager his life if any could say in truth that he was one of the disciples (*quað that he uueldi uuesan thes lîbes scolo, / ef it mahti ênig thar irminmanno / giseggian te sôðan, that he thes gesîðes uuâri*). The testimony of others sworn to tell the truth before a court of judgment constituted proof of one's innocence under Germanic law, and this reference would have been obvious to the audience of the *Hêliand*.

The description of Christ *an themu bômgardon ... hendi bundun* does not, according to Ilkow (p. 70), deliberately introduce OS scenery into the biblical story; it was just that there was no other word for 'garden' than *bômgardo*.

Hêliand

§55. THE FATE OF A BAD THANE

Lines 5039-5049
(not biblical)

This little section depicts the opposite of the ethic portrayed in §43. There the correct actions of the 'Good Soldier' were set forth in a gnomic aside. Here we are told what happens to the thane whose lord has forsaken him. Murphy (1992) translates the l. 5039-5041a as "Therefore a man's boasting is not very reliable (it is merely the bragging of a young field-hand), if God's help has left him because of his sins" (p. 166). The word for 'field-hand' (*hagustald*) is interesting.

Ilkow says,

> Nach germanischem Erbrecht erhielt der erstgeborene Sohn den väterlichen Hof mit allen Rechten, die daran hafteten, sowie die väterliche Gewalt, die *Munt-* (vgl. *mund-*) über seine Geschwister. Ganz erblos gingen diese nicht aus, den jüngeren Brüdern wurde ein kleines Nebengut ..., ein 'Hag', d.h. 'ein mit einer Hecke umgebenes Grundstück', überwiesen, das zur Begründung einer eigenen Familie in der Regel nicht ausreichte. Zur Bezeichnung eines solchen 'Hagbesitzers' dienen die Komp. ahd. *haga-stalt*, mhd. *hagestalt*. ... Für das Alter des Komp. sprechen die runeninschriftlich erhaltenen urnord. Eigennamen *Hagu-staldaR* und *Hagu-staldir*. Die verschiedenen Bedeutungen, die das Wort in den einzelnen Sprachen annimmt, weisen alle auf einen Mann, der durch seine wirtschaftliche Lage am Gründen des Hausstandes behindert ist.[95] (p. 165).

---

[95] According to Germanic rights of inheritance the first-born son received the father's farm with all rights thereto accruing as well as paternal power, the *munt-* over his siblings. They did not go entirely without inheritance as the younger brothers would be given a small ancillary property ..., a 'haw,' i.e., 'a property surrounded by a hedge' that was usually not sufficient for the maintenance of a family. The compounds OHG *haga-stalt*, MHG *hage-stalt* served to name such an 'owner of a haw.' ... The age of the compound is insured by the ancient nordic personal names *Hagu-staldaR* and *Hagu-staldir* preserved in runic inscriptions. The various meanings which the word takes on in the different languages all point to a man who is prevented from founding his own homestead because of economic conditions.

§. 55

It is just such a young man who has not inherited his father's property who becomes a retainer (*thegan*) of a *drohtin* in a war band.

None of a brave man's past accomplishments will avail aught if the help of his *drohtin* is denied. Bravery crumbles to cowardice (*than is imu sân aftar thiu / breosthugi blôðora*), even though the man "might boast of his fame in battle ... and of his strength" (*hrômie fan is hildi ... fan is megine*). Ström (1948), summarizes:

> [*megin* has] its greatest use ... as appellation of inherent human power. The idea is always associated with a particular display of strength, a vigorous triumphant performance of power, an increase of health and strength of life. The loss of *megin* means impotence, illness, defeat, decline (pp. 77-78).

In §43 we saw that the Good Soldier dies with his lord and his fame lives on. Here the 'Bad Soldier' is doomed to ignominy.

§56. Pilate

Lines 5111b to 5130a
(Matthew 26:67, 27:2; Mark 14:65, 15:1; Luke 22:62-65, 23:1; John 18:28)

The *Hêliand* speaks here of the 'fame' of the deeds done by the people of the Jews, what 'they might cause of harm' to the Child of God, most greatly to the Captive. They inflicted scorn and lampooning upon him. Four times we are reminded of His being bound: *sô haftemu mest*; *Stôd that barn godes fast under fiundun*; *uuârun imu is faðmos gebundene*; and *Tho nâmon ina uurêðe man / sô gibundanan*. The concept of the captured *drohtin* bound by enemies must have been intolerable for a Saxon audience, as it signaled total disgrace and lack of the fame that would live after the 'heroic' demise of the idealized leader and his followers.

Pilate, from *Ponteo lande*, is described in terms comprehensible to the Saxons as a representative of their (the Jews') lords from Rome, dispatched by the Emperor. Pilate was the giver of counsel and aid (*râdgeo*); in other words, he was sent from Rome as a high figure of authority. Pilate 'was sent to judge ... that realm, was the *râdgebo* there' (l. 5127b-5128). Ilkow says,

> Ich halte *râdgebo* für eine alte Amtsbezeichnung der Rechtssprache. ... Die juristische Funktion des Komp. *râdgebo* kommt im Hel. ganz deutlich zum Ausdruck. Es bezeichnet hier den Herrscher in seiner Eigenschaft als Richter[96] (p. 332).

---

[96] I consider *râdgebo* to be an old designation of a legal officer. ... The legal function of the compound *râdgebo* clearly comes to the fore in the Hêliand. Here it characterizes the ruler in his function as a judge.

§57. THE DEATH OF JUDAS

Lines 5144b to 5170
(Matthew 27:3-5)

Judas rued his fate when he saw his *drohtin* delivered over to death. Matthew reports that Judas threw the silver coins into the temple and hanged himself. In the *Hêliand* we find that as a result of the withdrawal of his Lord's *helpa* angry (*môdage*) fiends (elsewhere called 'hidden ones', 'evil wights', and similar) drove him into fear, that evil spirits (*gramon*) subverted his mind and spirit (*hugi*), and that God was furious (*uuas imu god abolgan*). The betrayer then made for himself a rope (*sîmo*), bowed down on the line (*herusêl*, literally 'sword rope'; see above at §53) in hanging, strangled on the noose (*uuarg an uurgil*), and chose punishment, the hard stricture of hell, hot and dismal, the deep dale of death, for he betrayed his *drohtin*. (Cf. the commentaries to §32 and §64 for *uuarg*.)

This detailed and powerful description of the hanging of Judas is charged with an ancient set of Indo-European words and concepts having to do with binding and strangling. (Cf. Ström [1942], p. 115, ftn. 75: "Hanging did not occur as a death penalty among the Hebrews. The form of hanging that is spoken of in the Bible is a post-mortem form, an aggravation of a death penalty that had been executed in another way.") The words *sîmo* and *sêl* derive from ablaut variants of the reconstructed Indo-European root *sei-/*soi-, which means 'bind' (cf. Pokorny, p. 891). The former is clearly a word for 'rope,' while *herusêl* is probably the same strap as *herubendi* (cf. the commentary to §53).

The terms *uuarg* and *uurgil* are also from a single Indo-European source, in this case ablaut variants *worg- and *wrg- of a root meaning 'strangle' (cf. Pokorny, p. 1154). The Saxons may have been aware still of the religious significance of bound and strangled sacrifices to the gods, viz. the victims discovered preserved in Danish bogs (cf. Glob), although it must be said that the dating of those finds is some 500 to 600 years earlier than the composition of the *Hêliand*. The word *uuarg* is also a name for the wolf (note, for example, Swedish *varg* 'wolf'), the preying inhabitant of the forest, the 'strangler' and outcast, which fits this context well. Note also the alliterative phrase in OI *vargr í véum* 'wolf in the sanctuary' (Cleasby-Vigfusson, p. 680).

§58. Christ before Pilate

Lines 5209b to 5229a
(John 18:33-37)

The representative of the Roman *Caesar*, Pilate, arrogant and angry (*uulank endi uurêðmôd*), denied that he was one of the people of the Jews who had given him Christ, bound at the hands. Pilate asked what He had done that He should suffer so 'bitterly in bonds.' Christ spoke in reply 'where He stood bound in that temple.' Again the binding of Jesus is emphasized, and in l. 5224 a variant of the word for (literally but perhaps only poetically) 'sword rope' (here *herubendi* 'sword bonds') previously employed to describe the line (*herusêl*) with which Judas hanged himself is now used to refer to the killing of Christ. It may have been that Christ was imagined as having a sword at his side held by a strap, which was then used to bind His hands after He was disarmed – perhaps normal procedure when taking prisoners in Germanic battles. Oakeshott (1960) describes the swords dating from the 2nd or 3rd century A.D. found at Thorsbjerg in what is now Schleswig in Germany, one of which had "a sword-belt of thick leather 3 in. wide and 41 in. long" (94). Norman (1971) mentions another kind of strap depicted in the *Psalterium Aureum* (before 883) showing "convex round shields ...; in some cases, they are slung on the back by means of a strap" (35), and an illustration on page 36 of the same work shows a "Frankish archer of the early ninth century" with straps clearly visible across his chest, perhaps holding a quiver. The *herubendi* could have been any such straps.

Christ replies to Pilate that if He were of this world, His disciples would prove themselves so dauntless against the Jews that He would not have been delivered up in bonds to be tortured and killed. A Germanic *drohtin* whose fame would live beyond him in oral history would not find himself in such a situation.

Hêliand

§59. CHRIST BEFORE HEROD

Lines 5251b to 5288a
(Luke 23:6-11)

Herod, like Pilate, received his authority from the *kêsur* in Rome. We are told of the 'powerful kingdom' he maintained and instructed on what the proper duties of a king are: to maintain law, keep the peace, and render judgment (l. 5251b-5255a). These were also the duties of a Germanic king (cf., *inter alia*, Ganshof). Herod is here called *thiedcuning* (l. 5280), a king of all the people, as opposed to a district or 'small' king (cf. Ilkow, p. 381).

The emphasis on Jesus' being bound is continued in this passage with the phrases *then hafton man* (l. 5260), *sô gibundanan* (l. 5261), *haften te handun* (l. 5263), *an fiteriun* (l. 5266), and *an liðubendiun* (l. 5269) in close proximity to each other. King Herod sat on his 'bench', as would befit a Germanic king, and a very threatening scene ensues. Herod's men are *uuîgand* 'soldiers, warriors' who do the bidding of the leader of their formation (*folctogun*), the king. Christ is surrounded by a 'mob' (cf. commentary to §49) of *uulanke uuîgandos*, but He stood and suffered in silence. The wroth host pressed and accused Him until the *uueroldcuning* (Herod) became angry and all his men scorned Him. They did not recognize the might of God, and their spirits were dark, suffused with evil.

§60. THE SECOND HEARING BEFORE PILATE

Lines 5339 to 5354a
(John 19:7-12)

Pilate, here characterized as a 'duke' (*heritogo*) for purposes of alliteration, (re)turned to the place of assembly (*huarf im ... te thero thingstedi*). The word *thing* was well on its way to the meaning of 'thing' but still retained its older meaning of 'court; assembly' in the compounds *thingstedi* 'site of the court or assembly' (l. 3745 and 5340), *thinghûs* 'court house' (l. 5124), and in the simplex *thing* 'court' (l. 2613 and 4376).

Pilate tells Christ that he has been given the power to 'kill Him at spear point, to kill Him on the cross, or to let Him live,' whichever

§. 60

method, Germanic or Roman, seems more agreeable (*suotera* 'sweeter'). Christ responds that those who 'commended me to you, sold me to you bound on a rope.' The repetition of emphasis on binding and the associated powerlessness is palpable in this and preceding sections. The loanword *crûci* is introduced here; elsewhere the Cross is called *bôm* and *galgo*, words descriptive of Germanic execution.

Murphy (1992) comments on the binding of Christ and speculates on a Saxon parallel:

> In the New Testament account it is only mentioned twice that Christ is bound. In the *Heliand* it is repeated again and again in a spellbinding contemplative refrain. It is impossible for the audience or the reader to think of the Passion in the *Heliand* without imagining Christ standing there in chains or being led around in irons. No Saxon who had been marched off by the Christian Franks in the same manner to baptism or death could fail to be moved by the touching similarity, the mystical vision of the poet who saw his captive Saxons as Christ. (Footnote 273)

§61. Pilate's Offer

Lines 5394b to 5426
(Matthew 27:15-21)

Fate and midday drew near, *uurd* immediately redefined as the 'renowned might of God' (*mâri maht godes*).
Murphy (1992) comments:

> Fate is now clearly identified with the will of God, which, like fate of old has inexorably prespecified everything that comes to pass, including even the very time, noon on Good Friday, when the Crucifixion is destined to begin. The mention of the time, midday, brings the ancient association of the fates and time together, with their task of measuring the length of existence of any mortal being. The mention of midday thus adds a very somber and pagan tone, reminding the Germanic listener of one of the old words for the divine being: *Metod*, 'the Measurer' (Footnote 279).

Fate and midday drew near 'when they were to carry out the *ferahquâla.*' Ilkow comments to this word,

> ... *ferah* bezeichnet – neben der Bedeutung 'Seele', die das Wort erst unter christlichem Einfluß angenommen hat – das 'Leben'; es ist also Synonym von *aldar* und *lîf*, doch meint *aldar* das 'Leben als den Inbegriff einer gewissen Zeit', *lîf* die 'leibliche Existenz', während sich *ferah* zunächst auf die 'dem Leben innewohnende Kraft' bezieht ... In gewissen Wendungen und Zusammensetzungen geht der Begriff 'Leben' in den Gegenbegriff 'Lebensende, Tod' über. ... Unter 'Lebensgefahr' verstehen wir eine 'Gefahr, das Leben zu verlieren', eine 'Todesgefahr'. ... In gleicher Bedeutung ... bezieht sich das as. Komp. auf die Kreuzigung Christi ... Das Komp. gehört dem Formelschatz der gemeinwestgerm. Dichtersprache an ... [97] (p. 123).

With Christ there was also an infamous villain (*ruof reginscaðo*), Barrabas, in fetters. Barrabas is also called *landskaðo*, a 'scather of the land.' It is said that a *landskaðo* is someone 'who often in the dark of night worked evil' (l. 5416b-5417a), which reminds one of the description of *mûtspelli* 'who comes in the dark night, just as a thief fares secretly with his deeds' (l. 4358-4360a). It was the custom of the country (*landuuîsa*) that the people each year on that holy day would ask their ruler to grant clemency to one captive. They chose to release the thief and to hang that Holy Child. (*hâhan that hêlaga barn*). Ilkow (p. 254) cites a passage from Gerhard von Minden's *Magdeburger Aesop* from 1402 with a cognate of *landskaðo*, namely *lantscade* : *Ik bin ein bose zage, / ein rover unde ein dêf, / ein lantscade nemande lêf* ('I am a useless coward / a robber and a thief / a *landskaðo* dear to nobody'). Barrabas is moreover called *meginthiof*, to which Ilkow notes,

---

[97] ... *ferah* means 'life' alongside the meaning 'soul,' which the word assumed only under the influence of Christianity; it is thus a synonym for *aldar* and *lîf*, but *aldar* means 'life as embodiment of a specific time,' *lîf* 'bodily existence,' while *ferah* relates to the 'power inherent in life' ... In certain expressions and compounds the concept 'life' merges with its opposite 'end of life, death.' ... In the expression 'danger to life' we understand a 'danger of losing life,' a 'mortal danger.' ... In the same meaning ... the OS compound relates to the crucifixion of Christ ... The compound belongs among the formulae of a common Germanic language of poetry ... .

§. 61

Der Diebstahl, d.h. der heimliche Entzug fremden Eigentums, galt bei allen germ. Stämmen als die schimpflichste Missetat eines freien Mannes ... . Während Leib und Leben nur durch Geld geschützt waren, wurden Eigentumsdelikte wie das Stehlen von Pferden, von Bienen in umzäumtem Raume, und überhaupt jeder in der Nacht begangene Diebstahl, der den Wert von zwei Solidi erreichte, mit dem Tode bestraft[98] (p. 283).

Herod came to regret that he knew of this matter. For this he received punishment, a reward in this life and long after, suffered torment (*wôi*: cf. Sievers [1884], p. 111) when he gave up this world.

§62. Satan's Attempt and Pilate's Wife

Lines 5427 to 5480
(Matthew 27:19, 24-26)

Matthew 27:19 says tersely, "While Pilate was sitting in court a message came to him from his wife: 'Have nothing to do with that innocent man; I was much troubled on his account in my dreams last night.'

The author of the *Hêliand*, basing himself on Hraban's of Fulda (Rhabanus Maurus') *Comment in Matthaeum* (Liber VIII)[99], expands on the mention of the dreams and adds a remarkable tale to the biblical story. The wroth one (*thie uurēðo*), the greatest of malefactors (*uuamscaðono mêst*), Satan himself, became aware when the soul of Judas arrived at the bottom of grim hell that it was the Ruling Christ, the Child of the Lord, who there stood bound. Satan knew that He, through His hanging, would redeem souls from the stricture of hell to the light of God. Satan was afflicted of spirit (*sêr an muode*) and wanted to intervene so that the people would not take His life. Satan wanted Christ to live so that men would not be secure from sins and hell. Thereupon Satan went to where Pilate's family was, and the

---

[98]Thievery, i.e. the clandestine removal of others' property, was considered by all Germanic groups to be the worst misdeed of a free man ... . While life and limb were protected only by monetary recompense, crimes against property like stealing horses, stealing bees in enclosures, and any robbery whatever during nighttime hours that had a minimum value of two solidi were punished by death.

[99] *Patrologia Latina* 107, 1131, A-B.

uncanny fiend began to show marvels openly to Pilate's wife (*bigann, / thera idis opanlîco unhiuri fiond / uuunder tôgian*) so that she might offer words of help to Christ. The woman became frightened when visions came in the light of day through the deeds of the hidden one, concealed with a helmet.

The helmet that renders Satan invisible is reminiscent of the *tarnkappe*, a cloak of concealment, in the *Nibelungenlied* and of similar garments elsewhere in medieval literature and folklore, cf. Klaeber (1925), p. 371, and Bächtold-Stäubli Vol. 4, col. 517 and Vol. 8, col 1454. Note also *Alvissmál* 18: *Sky heita með mǫnnum ... kalla í helliu hjálm huliz* ('They are called clouds among men ... [and] are in hell called the helmet that conceals.'). Ilkow says, "Veranlassung zu diesem Glauben hatte die Nebelhülle, besonders im Gebirge, gegeben, die Gestalten plötzlich verschwinden läßt"[100] (p. 192).

Murphy (1992) writes,

> In a clever and somewhat intimidating reversal, the *Heliand* poet draws a necessary conclusion. If fate and the will of God are one, anyone who opposes fate ... opposes the will of God. Christ is fated by the will of God to be crucified at noon on Good Friday. While those who are instruments of this predetermination, Pilate and the Jewish leaders, for example, are not excused from condemnation for having cooperated in bringing it about, the only one who opposes the inevitable is Satan. Satan will not win, of course, but the author does have an explanation for the dream of Pilate's wife, the source of which is unexplained in the gospels. Even Satan makes all too human efforts to fend off what is inexorably coming to pass. (Footnote 282)

Pilate's wife sent a message to her husband in order to tell him what visions had come because of that Holy Man and asked his help to spare His life. She said "... I know that sins will increase in an evil manner (*ubilo*) for everybody (*erlo gihuem*) if His life is boldly demanded." The messenger found Pilate sitting in the crowd on the paved road (*stênuuege*) where the street was fitted with blocks. This description was sufficient to depict a Roman or other ancient paved

---

[100] The origin of this belief was the cover of fog, especially in mountains, which let figures suddenly disappear.

§. 62

road for the Saxon audience, which knew unimproved tracks and ways, and in this description the erudition of the author of the *Hêliand* is revealed. Ilkow says,

> Der HelD muß sein Augenmerk auf das *pro tribunali* 'zu Gericht, auf dem Richterstuhl' der zitierten Matthäusstelle gerichtet haben – 199,5 im Tatian, – das im vorhergehenden Tatiankapitel (198,31) mit einer genauen Ortsangabe versehen ist: J.19,13 *Pilatus ergo com audisset hos sermones, adduxit foras Ihesum et sedit pro tribunali in loco qui dicitur Litho-strotos, ebraice autem Gabatha.* Das griechische Adjektiv λιδόστωτος 'mit Steinen gepflastert', das schon Sophokles verwendet ..., und das ins Lat. entlehnt wurde, bezeichnet entweder gewöhnliches steinernes Straßenpflaster oder einen mosaikartigen Bodenbeleg aus buntem Marmor. Für unsere Untersuchung ist es maßgebend zu wissen, daß der HelD die Etymologie von gr. λιδόστωτος kennen mußte, denn er gibt uns in v. 5462-3 eine äußerst geschickte Definition[101] (p. 366).

Pilate was upset. It was woeful for Pilate both that they struck the Sinless One and that he dared not prevent it because of the wish of the people. His mood turned, and he determined to work the will of the people. Nothing warned him then of the heavy sins that he himself had committed. He bade water be brought from the pure source, and he washed himself and said that he would thereby make himself innocent of sins. Pilate continues, 'I will not be responsible for any of this ... but you take upon yourselves everything you do by way of harm to Him here.'

---

[101] The author of the Hêliand must have had in mind the *pro tribunali* 'at court, on the seat of judgment' from the cited verse in Matthew – 199.5 in Tatian – that in the preceding chapter (198.31) of Tatian has an exact citation of locality: John 19:13 ... The Greek adjective λιδόστωτος 'paved with stones,' already used by Sophocles and borrowed into Latin, indicates either normal stone paving or a mosaic covering of colored marble. For our investigation it is important to know that the author of the Hêliand must have known the etymology of λιδόστωτος, as he gives a very skilled definition in l. 5462-5463.

§63. Pilate's Soldiers Take Jesus

Lines 5487 to 5511a
(Matthew 27:27-31)

The biblical passage states that the soldiers took Christ, and in the *Hêliand* we see the full fury of the action. He suffered with patience whatever the people did to him. Again He is said to be in *herubendiun*, narrowly (tightly) restrained. They struck Him and they spat under His eyes in scorn. They hit Him on the cheeks with their hands and took His clothes. In their *unhuldi* they mocked and scorned Him. The word *unhuldi* 'infidelity' is the opposite of *holda treuua* (cf. the commentary to §51) and thus implies the opposite expected of the followers of a Germanic *drohtin*. The actions, *unhuldi*, of the mob in humiliating Christ are thus equated with betrayal of the *drohtin*. They go on to mock Him with a crown of thorns, depicted as an early Germanic *hôbidband* 'headband'. Whether the audience of the *Hêliand* knew of the custom of kings wearing crowns is open to doubt. Ilkow says, "Erst anläßlich der Kaiserkrönung zu Rom im Jahre 800 wurde Karl dem Großen der Goldreif aufs Haupt gesetzt. Seither wurde die Krönung mit der Sitte der Salbung verbunden .... Die Krönung eines Herrschers gab es bei den Germanen weder zu urgerm. noch zu urwestgerm. Zeit. Es war bei ihnen auch nicht Sitte, Haar und Stirn mit Metallreifen zu umgeben"[102] (p. 213). The men were commanded to work with their weapons a powerful cross.

---

[102] A golden diadem was set on the emperor's head for the first time on the occasion of the crowning of Charlemagne in Rome in the year 800. Since then crowning was done in addition to anointing. ... The crowning of a ruler was unknown among the Germanic peoples both in PGmc. and West Germanic time. Nor was it customary among them to enclose the hair and forehead with a metal ring.

§. 64

§64. THE CRUCIFIXION

Lines 5532 to 5592a
(Matthew 27:35-44; Mark 15:24-32; Luke 23:32-39; John 19:18-19, 23-24)

This section largely follows the scriptures. Christ was mocked by bystanders who said, "You would pull the temple down, would you, and build it in three days? Come down from the cross and save yourself, if you are indeed the Son of God" (Matthew 27:39-40). The *Hêliand*, which does not use a loanword for 'temple' calls it here *stênuuerko mêst* 'the greatest of stone constructions.' Ilkow points out that it was the Romans who introduced stone construction to Germania, where only wooden construction was known. He says,

> Das Merowingerreich kennt beide Bauarten; die fränkischen Eroberer hatten den Holzbau nach Gallien mitgebracht, und blieben auf dem Lande, wo nur immer der nötige Holzreichtum zur Verfügung stand, ihren heimatlichen Gepflogenheiten treu. ... Zunächst wurden nur Monumentalbauten, und das waren beinahe ausschließlich kirchliche Gebäude, in Stein errichtet. Auch im Zeitalter der Karolinger blieben Steinbauten ein beneidenswertes Besitztum und Vorrecht der Vermögenden; im Hel. wird nur der Tempel zu Jerusalem 'Steinbau', *stênuuerko mêst* ... genannt[103] (p. 307).

The depiction of the crucifixion mixes Germanic and Christian images. In pre-Christian times one method of ritual sacrifice involved hanging with ropes or withies on a tree or stake, while nailing to a cross is a foreign notion.[104] In criminal procedures hanging was the fate of slaves and "persons of low birth" (Ström [1942], p. 122 with sources). If Christ's death was not viewed as sacrificial, then by Saxon experience the punishment was in any case demeaning. Ström remarks (*loc. cit.*) that "One is struck by the frequency with which

---

[103] The Merovingians know both kinds of construction. The Franks, as conquerors, had brought the wooden structure to Gall and in the countryside where there was plenty of wood they remained true to their tradition. At first only monumental structures, and these were mainly ecclesiastic, were built of stone. Also in the Carolingian period stone structures were envied and restricted to people of means; in the *Hêliand* only the Temple in Jerusalem is called a 'stone structure,' *stênuuerko mêst* ...

[104] Cf. the Danish 'bog people' whose bodies date from the 3rd century A.D. See Davidson 1967:73 and 1988:62-63 and Glob 1965.

one finds hanging mentioned in older sources as a form of humiliating reprisal used against conquered enemies, thus outside the actual sphere of penal law." Another form of "humiliating reprisal" was to hang wolves (cf. *uuarg*) or, later, dogs on either side of the condemned. A Danish regulation from as late as 1688 specifies that slain wolves should be hanged on the gallows *like other thieves*: "Efter Døden vistes der Ulvene en særlig Ære, om man saa maa sige, de bleve, naar de vare præsenterede ved Tinget, ophængte i en Galge ligesom andre Tyve"[105] (Ström *op. cit.*, p. 129) . The *uuarg* as 'wolf' roamed free in the forest, like the thief a danger to all society. That this was an ancient usage is shown by the fact that Finnish borrowed Germanic *uargaz for the word 'thief,' namely *varas* (genitive *varkaan*). The word *uuaragtreo* that occurs in l. 5563 of the *Hêliand* is thus not a neologism in OS, and the two on either side of Christ are also referred to here as 'thieves': *Thuo thar ôc an them bendiun sprac / thero theoƀo ôðer*. John 18:40 says, "Barrabas was a bandit" (*erat autem Barrabas latro*). The same word 'thief-gallows,' likely for the same concept, occurs in OI, e.g. *Hamãsmál* 17: *Fram lágo brautir fundo vástigo / ok systur son sáran á meiði / vargtré vindkǫld boeiar*. Ström (1942) translates this passage as "The roads led forwards, they found the path of agony, and the nephew wounded on the gallows, wind-cold gallows, to the west of the courtyard," (p. 119, ftn. 87) wherein *vargtré* renders gallows. The Gothic translation of the Bible, five centuries older than the *Hêliand*, also uses derivations from the Germanic stem *warg- for legal terms of condemnation.

The 'cold iron, new nails' are characterized as 'bitter bonds' and as bonds in l. 5538 and 5580. Christ stands nailed on the new gallows, on the wooden tree (l. 5552b-5554a) but is also told to 'slip from the rope' in l. 5585. The other thief spoke 'at the hanging where he stood bound' and refers to Christ as *hier an galgen haft*, likely yet another allusion to ropes and binding. See also Schwab (1994: 574 f., and particularly Tafel 3 and Tafel 4) for binding on the cross.

---

[105] After death the wolves were given a special honor, if you can say that; when they were presented to the assembly, they were hanged on a gallows just like other thieves.

§. 64

Just as hanging was demeaning in Saxon criminal procedure, so was the crucifixion of criminals similarly demeaning in Roman tradition. Christ as an exemplar of Germanic leadership, the source of inspiration to his followers, is brought very low in this passage.

§65. THE DEATH OF JESUS

Lines 5621 to 5712
(Matthew 27:39-55; Mark 15:33-39; Luke 23:44-49; John 19:28-34)

Darkness fell as Christ suffered on the cross, however in the *Hêliand* the sun breaks through as He calls up to heaven asking the Almighty Father why He forsook Him, put His help so far away. 'I stand among these enemies here tortured extraordinarily' (l. 5635b to 5639a). This emphasis on *thîna helpa* and *fullisti* reflects the agony of an abandoned thane separated from the fortitude and wisdom of his *drohtin*. Murphy (1992) comments,

> Christ's plea to His Father is strengthened in the *Heliand* by being movingly recast as a captured Companion and Thane's appeal to His Chieftain, reminding Him of His obligation as a Chieftain to render help and support to a faithful Thane now in peril from the enemy. (Footnote 294)

After drinking of the bitter vinegar, He says that His spirit is eager, ready to travel, which repeats the phrase used at l. 4753b to 4755a, where He was frightened of the test to come.

It is specifically mentioned that it was the custom among the Jews not to let the corpse of the hanged remain bound longer than it took for life to leave the body (l. 5689b to 5692a). (Mark 15:32 refers to its being the eve of the Sabbath, and John 19:31 says that bodies may not remain on the cross during the Sabbath. See also Deuteronomy 21:23.) This point must be explained to the Saxons, which may indicate that they left the bodies of the hanged to decay. Ström (1942) doubts that this is an ancient practice but says "According to mediaeval legal regulations, the body of the evil-doer was to remain hanging on the gallows until it had been decomposed by weather and wind ..." (p. 126). Negative evidence to the contrary is mentioned by Ström (loc. cit.): "*Hamðismál* 17 ... tells us nothing of the practice of leaving he corpses of hanged persons suspended from the gallows. The only evidence of this from Icelandic literature ... is a miracle-story in Flateyjarbók about the hanging of an innocent per-

Hêliand

son. We are told that his family received permission to bury the corpse and take it down from the gallows, as it appears, by a special act of grace. ... Other things being equal, it is quite possible that the practice in question is of ancient origin" (footnote 114). By this passage in the *Hêliand* Christ too would perhaps in Saxon eyes have received treatment ameliorating His being hanged as a common criminal.

§66. THE BURIAL

Lines 5713 to 5741b
(Matthew 27:57-60; Mark 15:42-47; Luke 23:50-53; John 19:38-41)

Again the image of the setting sun is evoked to mark the end of life as it was when Christ understood that he must *ageben these gardos ... sôkien imu ...is faderôðil* at l. 4496-4497 (cf. §50).

Joseph of Arimathaea, a follower of Christ, asked Pilate for the body. He laid it in his own grave, which was carved into rock, and set a large stone against the entrance (Matthew 27:57-60). In the *Hêliand* Joseph went to the gallows where the body was hanging. He took the corpse from the 'new rood' and removed the nails from it. A small gnomic reminder is inserted here: [Joseph] 'took Him in his embrace, just as one should do with one's lord, the dear corpse,' which was possibly an admonishment to care for the dead after battle.

The insertion of the body into a rock cave as a means of burial had to be explained to the Saxon audience: *te iro landuuîsun, lîco hêlgost / foldu bifulhun*. Ilkow comments,

> Der HelD hält also die *spelunca*, in der Lazarus beigesetzt wurde, für eine Erdgrube. In seiner Heimat, wie überhaupt in den meisten Gebieten Deutschlands, bestattete man nämlich in Erdgruben. Nur wo steiniger Untergrund die Anlage einer Erdgrube verhinderte, wie in gewissen Alpengegenden, wurden Gräber in Felsen gehauen. Dies mag der Grund dafür sein, daß der HelD das von ihm selbst geprägte Komp. *stêngraf* 'Felsengrab' für das Grab Christi vorbehält (v. 5852). Im Gegensatz zu den 'bürgerlichen' Gräbern des Johannes und Lazarus läßt der HelD dem Heiland eine in den Augen der

§. 66

Sachsen ganz außergewönliche Bestattung zuteil werden, ein Felsengrab ... v. 5736[106] (p. 112).

See also the commentary to §47. Murphy (1992) notes:

> The *Heliand*'s depiction of the burial of Christ is a very carefully made synthesis of the Mediterranean and Germanic traditions. Though Christ is brought to a tomb hewn out of a rock as in the Bible, he is buried in the ground, in the floor of the tomb, in a Germanic earthen grave. ... The stone that sealed the entrance way to the tomb in the scriptural account is placed directly over the grave in the *Heliand*. Christ Himself is buried in the ground with a stone slab above in the old Germanic pagan style, enabling his Resurrection to be visualized as a resurrection from the soil, a Saxon Resurrection (Footnote 303).

§67. THE RESURRECTION

Lines 5761 to 5810b
(Matthew 27:62-66, 28:1-3; Mark 16:1-5; Luke 24:1-4; John 20:1-13)

Only Matthew tells of a guard assigned by Pilate to watch the grave for three days to prevent the disciples from taking the body of Christ and thereby perpetrating the fraud of faking the fulfillment of His promise of resurrection. The author of the *Hêliand*

---

[106] The author of the Hêliand thus considers the *spelunca*, in which Lazarus was buried, an earthen grave. In his home, as in most areas of Germany, burial was done in pits. Only where stony conditions obtained that prevented burial in the earth, as in certain Alpine regions, were graves hewn into rock. This may be the reason why the author of the Hêliand reserves the compound *stên-graf* (invented by him) for the grave of Christ (l. 5852). In contrast with the 'bourgeois' graves of John and Lazarus the author of the Hêliand lets the Savior have a burial which was quite extraordinary in the eyes of the Saxons — a grave hewn in rock.

Hêliand

takes considerable liberty here to describe the guard, the descent of the Holy Spirit, and the arrival of the angel of the Lord.

Men with their weapons sit over the grave in the 'brilliant nights' (*uuânamon nahton*) with their shields over them in typical warrior fashion for protection from the cold. They waited for the 'bright day' that would come over the world to men. The Holy Spirit came under the hard stone to the corpse, light was revealed for the benefit of man, many a bolt was removed from the portal of hell, and the way to heaven was wrought from this world. In glory (*uuânom*) the Peace Child of God arose and went where He wanted without the guards, the evil people, noticing anything. The guards sat outside around the grave with their shields.

The women went to the grave to anoint the body, torn with wounds, with herbs and salves, for which Mary Magdalene (*Mariun munilîca*) had sold her treasures of silver and gold. They wondered how they would turn aside the great stone before the grave. As they entered the garden an angel of the Almighty came swooshing down from heaven in his feather cloak (*thuo thar suôgan quam / engil thes alouualdon oðana fan radure, / faran an feðerhamon*). All the earth and heavens thundered (up to heaven?: *an scian* 'to the skies'? Cf. Holthausen PBB 46, 337 and Behaghel for commentary on l. 5798), and the guards were seized with fear. They did not expect to live much longer, and they lay there half alive. Regarding *feðerhamo*, which also was used in l. 1669 to describe the birds in §20, Ilkow says,

> Die nicht zu bestreitenden Beziehungen des Ausdrucks *feðarhamo* zur germ. Mythologie haben die Forschung dazu verleitet, die Engelvorstellung des HelD als eine bewußte Anlehnung an den Walkürenmythus zu erklären .... Wir dagegen sind der Auffassung, daß der HelD das Komp. *feðarhamo* gemieden hätte, wäre es zu seiner Zeit im Bewußtsein der Sachsen noch eng mit ausgesprochen heidnischen Vorstellungen verknüpft gewesen. ... Daß der HelD den Engel Gottes *an feðarhamon faran* läßt, hängt vor allem damit zusammen, daß die Engel in der karolingischen Kunst mit Flügeln dargestellt wurden. ... Der HelD wendete das Komp. *feðarhamo* auf den Engel an, da ihn die zeitgenössischen Engeldar-

§. 67

stellungen an die aus Sage und Märchen bekannten 'Federhemden' erinnern mußten[107] (pp. 118-119).

The angel of God himself rolled the great stone from the grave. The *Hêliand* describes the messenger of God here as the most impressive of figures and imbues him with heroic attributes and powerful features of nature. The angel sat upon the grave mound (*hlêuue*). He was equal in deeds and appearance to whomever could look at his face (*under is ôgun scauuon*), so bright and cheerful, just like a flash of lightening. His garb most resembled wintercold snow. The image of immaculate whiteness harkens to the Transfiguration (cf. §38), where Christ was clad in *geuuâdi sô huît / sô snêu te sehanne* (l. 3127b-3128a). We conclude with this resplendent image.

---

[107] The unarguable connection of the expression *feðar-hamo* to Germanic mythology has led scholars to explain the Hêliand author's image of angels as a conscious borrowing from the valkyrie myth. ... We are of the opinion, on the other hand, that the author of the Hêliand would have avoided the compound *feðar-hamo* if during his time there had been such a heathen connection still extant in the minds of the Saxons. ... That the author of the Hêliand lets the angel of God *feðarhamon faran* has mostly to do with the fact that angels in Carolingian art are depicted with wings. The author of the Hêliand used *feðar-hamo* in the description of angels, since contemporary depictions of angels must have reminded him of 'feather shirts' known from tales and stories.

References

Almgren, Bertil, ed. *The Viking*. (Gothenburg: Tre Tryckare, 1966).

Amira, Karl von. (4. Aufl., ergänzt von Karl August Eckhardt) *Germanisches Recht*. (Berlin: de Gruyter, 1967).

Andersson, Theodore M. 'The Caedmon Fiction in the *Heliand* Preface,' *PMLA* (1974), 278-284.

Argyle, A.W. *The Gospel According to Matthew*. (Cambridge: University Press, 1963).

Bächtold-Stäubli, Hanns, ed. *Handwörterbuch des deutschen Aberglaubens*. (Berlin: de Gruyter, 1927-1942).

Bauschatz, Paul C. *The Well and the Tree*. (Amherst: University of Massachusetts Press, 1982).

Beck, Heinrich, et al., eds. *Reallexikon der Germanischen Altertumskunde*, Vol. 3. (Berlin: de Gruyter, 1978)

Behaghel, Otto, ed. *Hêliand und Genesis*. (Altdeutsche Textbibliothek Nr. 4). (Tübingen: Niemeyer, 1984 [9th edition]).

Bellows, Henry Adams. *The Poetic Edda*. (New York: The American-Scandinavian Foundation, 1957)

Birkmann, Thomas. *Präteritopräsentia: Morphologische Entwicklungen einer Sonderklasse in den altgermanischen Sprachen*. (Tübingen: Niemeyer, 1987).

Bischoff, Bernhard. 'Die Schriftheimat der Münchener Heliand-Handschrift,' *Zeitschrift zur Geschichte der deutschen Sprache und Literatur* 101 [1979], 161.

Bischoff, Bernhard. Review of Drögereit's book *Werden und der Hêliand* in *Anzeiger für deutsches Altertum* LXVI (1952), 7-12.

Bökönyi, Sándor. 'Animals, Food' in *Dictionary of the Middle Ages*, Volume 1. (New York: Charles Scribner's Sons, 1982).

References

Braune, Wilhelm and Ernst Ebbinghaus. *Althochdeutsches Lesebuch*. (Tübingen: Niemeyer, 1962 [14th edition]).

Brodersen, Micha. 'Frejas klenodie,' *Danske Studier* 1984, 103-109.

Burns, Alfred. *The Power of the Written Word: The Role of Literacy in the History of Western Civilization* (Bern: Peter Lang, 1989).

Byock, Jesse. *The Saga of the Volsungs*. (Berkeley and Los Angeles: University of California Press, 1990).

Cathey, James E. "Die Rhetorik der Weisheit und Beredtheit im Hêliand," *Literaturwissenschaftliches Jahrbuch* 37 (1996), 31-46.

Cathey, James E. 'Give us this day our daily *râd*,' *JEGP* 94 (1995), 157-175.

Chaney, William A. *The Cult of Kingship in Anglo-Saxon England*. (Berkeley and Los Angeles: University of California Press, 1970).

Cleasby, R., Vigfusson, G., and Craigie, W. *An Icelandic-English Dictionary*, 2nd edn. (Oxford: Clarendon Press, 1957).

Cordes, Gerhard. Review of Johannes Rathofer *Der Heliand. Theologischer Sinn als tektonische Form* in *Anzeiger für deutsches Altertum* 78 (1967), 55-79.

Davidson, Hilda Roderick Ellis. *The Sword in Anglo-Saxon England: its archeology and literature*. (Oxford: Clarendon Press, 1962).

Davidson, Hilda Roderick Ellis. *Gods and Myths of Northern Europe*. (Baltimore: Penguin, 1964).

Davidson, Hilda Roderick Ellis. *Pagan Scandinavia*. (New York: Praeger, 1967).

Davidson, Hilda Roderick Ellis. *Myths and Symbols in Pagan Europe*. (Syracuse: University Press, 1988).

Derolez, R.L.M. *Götter und Mythen der Germanen*. (Wiesbaden: Verlag F. Englisch, 1976).

Dick, Ernst S. *AE. dryht und seine Sippe: Eine wortkundliche, kultur- und religionsgeschichtliche Betrachtung zur altgerman-*

ischen Glaubensvorstellung vom wachstümlichen Heil. (Münster: Verlag Aschendorff, 1965).

Die Bibel: Einheitsübersetzung. (Stuttgart, 1980).

Doane, Alger N. *The Saxon Genesis: an Edition of the West Saxon Genesis B and the Old Saxon Vatican Genesis.* (Madison, 1991).

Drögereit, Richard. 'Des Friesen Liudger Eigenkloster Werden und seine kulturelle Bedeutung im 9. Jahrhundert' in Carl Röper and Herbert Huster, eds. *Richard Drögereit Sachsen-Angelsachsen-Niedersachsen*, Vol. III, pp. 1-20 (Hamburg und Otterndorf, 1978).

Drögereit, Richard. 'Die Heimat des *Heliand*,' *Jahrbuch der Gesellschaft für niedersächsiche Kirchengeschichte* 49 (1951a), 1-18.

Drögereit, Richard. 'Die schriftlichen Quellen zur Christianisierung der Sachsen und ihre Aussagefähigkeit' in Walther Lammers, ed. *Die Eingliederung der Sachsen in das Frankenreich* (Darmstadt, 1970).

Drögereit, Richard. *Werden und der Heliand.* (Essen, 1951b).

Ellmers, Detlef. 'Die Schiffe der Angelsachsen' in *Sachsen und Angelsachsen*. Claus Ahrens, ed. (Hamburg: Veröffentlichungen des Helms-Museums Nr. 32, 1978), 495-509.

Feist, Sigmund. *Vergleichendes Wörterbuch der gotischen Sprache.* (Leiden: E.J. Brill, 1939).

Flacius Illyricus. *Catalogus testium ueritatis* (Straßburg und Basel, 1562).

Flowers, Stephen E. 'Toward an Archaic Germanic Psychology,' *Journal of Indo-European Studies* 11 (1983), 117-138.

Foerste, William 'Der römische Einfluß auf die germanische Fesselungs-Terminologie,' *Frühmittelalterliche Studien* 1 (1967) 188-199

Frank, Roberta. 'The Ideal of Men Dying with their Lord in *The Battle of Maldon*: Anachronism or *Nouvelle Vague*,' in *People and Places in Northern Europe 500-1600: Essays in Honor of Peter Hayes Sawyer.* Ian Wood and Niels Lund, eds. (The Boydell Press, 1990).

Freudenthal, Karl Fredrik. *Arnulfingisch-karolingische Rechtswörter.* (Tübingen: Neomarius Verlag, 1949).

Gallée, Johan Hendrik. *Altsächsische Grammatik.* (Halle: Niemeyer, 1910).

Ganshof, François Louis. *Frankish Institutions under Charlemagne.* (Providence: Brown University Press, 1968).

Gantert, Klaus. *Der Heliand: Eine rezeptionsästhetische Untersuchung.* (Wissenschaftliche Prüfung für das Lehramt an Gymnasien: Albert-Ludwigs-Universität, Freiburg im Breisgau, 1993.)

Genzmer, Felix. 'Heliand und Genesis,' *Zeitschrift für Religion- und Geistesgeschichte* 2 (1949-1950), 311-327.

Glob, P.V. *Mosefolket.* (København: Gyldendal, 1965).

Green, Dennis H. *The Carolingian Lord.* (Cambridge: University Press, 1965).

Grimm, Jacob. *Deutsche Rechtsaltertümer.* Volumes I and II. (Darmstadt: Wissenschaftliche Buchgesellschaft, 1974).

Hammerbacher, Hans Wilhelm. *Irminsul: das germanische Lebensbaumsymbol in der Kulturgeschichte Europas.* (Kiel: Orion-Heimreiter, 1984).

Hanson, Elaine Tuttle. *The Solomon Comples: Reading Wisdom in OE Poetry.* (Toronto: University Press, 1988).

Heaney, Seamus. *Beowulf: A New Verse Translation.* (New York: Farrar, Straus and Giroux, 2000)

Hempel, Wolfgang. *Übermuot diu alte... : Der Superbia-Gedanke und seine Rolle in der deutschen Literatur des Mittelalters.* (Bonn: Bouvier, 1970).

Henrotte, Gayle A. 'Jesus Asleep in the Boat: A Thrice-Told Tale,' in John Miles Foley, ed. *De Gustibus: Essays for Alain Renoir* (New York: Garland, 1992).

Herbert, Kathleen. *Looking for the Lost Gods of England*. (Pinner: Anglo-Saxon Books, 1994).

Hillgarth, J.N., ed. *Christianity and Paganism, 350-750*. (Philadelphia: University of Pennsylvania Press, 1986)

Hofstra, Tette. 'Zu Veenbaas' Helianddichter-Hypothesen,' *Niederdeutsches Jahrbuch* 115 (1992), 177-182.

Holthausen, F. *Altsächsisches Elementarbuch*. (Heidelberg: Winter, 1921).

Holthausen, F. 'Zum Heliand v. 5788,' *Zeitschrift für die Geschichte der deutschen Sprache und Literatur* 46 (1922), 337.

Ilkow, Peter. *Die Nominalkomposita der altsächsischen Bibeldichtung*. W. Wissmann and H.-Fr. Rosenfeld, eds. (Göttingen: Vandenhoeck & Ruprecht, 1968).

Jedin, Hubert, hrsg. *Handbuch der Kirchengeschichte*. Bd. III/1. 3rd ed. (Freiburg: Herder, 1965.)

Jente, Richard. *Die mythologischen Ausdrücke im altenglischen Wortschatz*. (Heidelberg: Winter, 1921).

Jones, Gwyn. *Egil's Saga*. (Syracuse University Press, 1960)

Kartschoke, Dieter. *Geschichte der deutschen Literatur im frühen Mittelalter*. 2. Aufl.. (München: Deutscher Taschenbuchverlag, 1994).

Kellermann, Volkmar. 'Germanische Altertümer,' in Wolfgang Stammler, hrsg. *Deutsche Philologie im Aufriß*, 2. Aufl., Band III. (Berlin: Erich Schmidt Verlag, 1967).

Kienle, Mathilde von. 'Der Schicksalsbegriff im Altdeutschen,' *Wörter und Sachen* 15 (1933), 81-111.

Klaeber, Fr. *Beowulf and the Fight at Finnsburg*. (Boston: D.C. Heath, 1941).

Klaeber, Fr. 'Beowulfiana,' *Anglia* 49 (1925), 195-244.

Klein, Thomas. 'Zu Veenbaas: "Bernlef und der Heliand",' *Niederdeutsches Jahrbuch* 115 (1992), 174-177.

References

Kluge, Friedrich. *Etymologisches Wörterbuch der deutschen Sprache*, 16. Aufl. bearbeitet von Alfred Götze. (Berlin: de Gruyter, 1953).

Kluge, Friedrich. *Etymologisches Wörterbuch der deutschen Sprache*, 22. Aufl. bearbeitet von Elmar Seebold, ed. (Berlin: de Gruyter, 1989).

Kolb, Herbert. 'Vora demo muspille,' *Zeitschrift für deutsche Philologie* 83 (1964), 2-33.

Krogmann, Willy. 'Praefatio in librum antiquum lingua Saxonica conscriptum' in Jürgen Eichhoff and Irmengard Rauch, eds., *Der Heliand* (Wissenschaftliche Buchgesellschaft: Darmstadt, 1973).

Lauffer, O. "Die Pferdeknechte im Heliand und der volkstümliche Gebrauch der Nachtweide" in *Die Heimat des Heliand*. 1912.

Lehmann, Winfred P. 'The Alliteration of Old Saxon Poetry,' in Jürgen Eichhoff and Irmengard Rauch, eds. *Der Heliand*. (Wege der Forschung: Band CCCXXI), (Wissenschaftliche Buchgesellschaft: Darmstadt, 1973).

Lexer, Matthias. *Mittelhochdeutsches Handwörterbuch*. (Stuttgart: Hirzel, 1970).

Liberman, Anatoly. 'Heliand,' in Will Hasty and James Hardin, eds. *Dictionary of Literary Biography*, Volume 148. (Gale: New York, 1995).

Lochrie, Karma 'The Structure and Wisdom of "Judgment Day I",' *Neuphilologische Mitteilungen* 87 (1986), 201-210.

Lonke, Alwin. 1946. 'Römer, Franken, Sachsen zwischen Ems und Elbe,' *Gießener Beiträge zur deutschen Philologie* 88 (1946), 5-48.

Markey, Thomas L. 'Germanic Terms for Temple and Cult' in Evelyn Firchow, et. al, *Studies for Einar Haugen*. (The Hague: Moulton, 1972), 365-378.

Markey, Thomas L. *A North Sea Germanic Reader* (München: Fink, 1976).

Marnell, William H. 1978. *Light from the West: The Irish Mission and the Emergence of Modern Europe*. (New York: The Seabury Press).

Marstrander, Sverri. *De skjulte skipene*. (Oslo: Gyldendal Norsk Forlag, 1986).

Martin, John Stanley. *Ragnarok: An investigation into Old Norse Concepts of the Fate of the Gods*. (Assen: van Gorcum, 1972).

McLintock, David R. 'Heliand' in *Dictionary of the Middle Ages*, Volume XX, pp. 150-151. (New York: Charles Scribner's Sons, 1985).

Meyer, Herbert. *Das Handgemal*. (Weimar: Böhlau, 1934).

Miller, David Harry. 'Sacral kingship, biblical kingship, and the elevation of Pepin the Short' in Thomas F.X. Noble and John J. Contreni, eds. *Religion, Culture, and Society in the Early Middle Ages*. (Kalamazoo: Medieval Institute Publications, 1987), 131-154.

Murphy, G. Ronald, S.J. *The Saxon Savior*. (New York: Oxford University Press, 1989).

Murphy, G. Ronald, S.J. *The Heliand: The Saxon Gospel*. (New York: Oxford University Press, 1992).

Murphy, G. Ronald, S.J. 'The Light Worlds of the *Heliand*,' *Monatshefte* 89 (1997), 5-17.

Myers, Henry A. and Herwig Wolfram. *Medieval Kingship*. (Chicago: Nelson-Hall, 1982).

Neill, Stephen. 1964. *Christian Missions*. (The Pelican History of the Church, Volume Six).

Nordal, Sigurður. ed. *Vǫluspá*. Trans. R.S. Benedikz and John McKinnell (Durham: Durham and St. Andrews Medieval Texts, 1978).

Norman, Vesey. *The Medieval Soldier*. (London: Barker, 1971).

North, Richard. *Pagan Words and Christian Meanings*. (Amsterdam: Rodolpi, 1991)

References

Nya Testamentet. Svenska Bibelsällskapet. (Stockholm: Gummessons, 1981).

Oakeshott, R. Ewart. *The Archaeology of Weapons.* (New York: Praeger, 1960).

Oxenstierna, Eric Graf. *Die Vikinger.* (Stuttgart: Kohlhammer, 1966).

Pokorny, Julius. *Indogermanisches etymologisches Wörterbuch.* (Bern: Franke, 1959).

Polomé, Edgar C. *Essays on Germanic Religion.* (Journal of Indo-European Studies Monograph Number Six) (Washington: Institute for the Study of Man, 1989).

Priebsch, R. *The Heliand Manuscript Cotton Caligula A VII in the British Museum* (Oxford, 1925).

Prokosch, E. *A Comparative Germanic Grammar.* (Linguistic Society of America: 1938).

Rathofer, Johannes. *Der Heliand: Theologischer Sinn als tektonische Form* (Köln/Graz: Böhlau Verlag, 1962).

Riché, Pierre. *The Carolingians.* (Philadelphia: University of Pennsylvania Press, 1993).

Russell, James C. *The Germanization of Early Medieval Christianity.* (Oxford: University Press, 1994).

Schmidt-Wiegand, Ruth. *'handgemælde (Parzival 6,19)'* in Kurt Gärtner und Joachim Heinzle, hrsg. *Studien zu Wolfram von Eschenbach: Festschrift für Werner Schröder zum 75. Geburtstag.* (Tübingen: Niemeyer, 1989).

Scholz, Bernhard Walter, trans. *Carolingian Chronicles: Royal Frankish Annals; Nithard's Histories.* (Ann Arbor: University of Michigan Press, 1972).

Schramm, Gottfried. *Namenschatz und Dichtersprache.* (Göttingen: Vandenhoeck & Ruprecht, 1957).

Schützeichel, Rudolf. *Althochdeutsches Wörterbuch.* (Tübingen: Niemeyer, 1969).

Schwab, Ute. arbeo laosa: *Philologische Studien zum Hildebrandslied*. (Bern: Francke, 1972).

Schwab, Ute. 'In sluthere bebunden' in Heiko Uecker, ed. *Studien zum Altgermanischen* (Berlin: de Gruyter, 1994)

Sehrt, Edward H. *Vollständiges Wörterbuch zum Heliand und zur altsächischen Genesis*. 2., durchgesehene Auflage. (Göttingen: Vandenhoeck & Ruprecht, 1966).

Sievers, E., ed. *Heliand*. (Halle: Verlag der Buchhandlung des Waisenhauses, 1878).

Sievers, E. 'Über Heliand Ed. Behagel,' *Zeitschrift für deutsche Philologie* 16 (1884), 110-114.

Smith, William, ed. *A Dictionary of the Bible*. (Cincinnati: National Publishing Co, 1869).

Steward, J.W. *The Snakes of Europe*. (Newton Abbot: David & Charles, 1971).

Störmer, Wilhelm. *Früher Adel*. (Stuttgart: Hiersemann, 1973).

Ström, Folke. 'Den egna kraftens män,' *Göteborgs Högskolas Årsskrift* 54 (1948), 1-79.

Ström, Folke. *On the Sacral Origin of the Germanic Death Penalties*. (Stockholm: Wahlström & Widstrand, 1942).

Swisher, Michael. 'The Sea Miracles in the Heliand,' *Neophilologus* 75 (1991), 232-238.

Taeger, Burkhard. 'Das Straubinger 'Heliand'-Fragment: Philologische Untersuchungen,' *Zeitschrift zur Geschichte der deutschen Sprache und Literatur* 101 (1979), 181-228.

Taeger, Burkhard. 'Ein vergessener handschriftlicher Befund: Die Neumen im Münchener "Heliand"' *Zeitschrift für deutsches Altertum* 107 (1978), 184-193.

Taeger, Burkhard, ed. *Heliand und Genesis* (Altdeutsche Textbibliothek 4) (Tübingen: Niemeyer, 1984).

Todd, Malcolm. *The Early Germans*. (Oxford: Blackwell, 1992).

References

Veenbaas, Redbad. 'Bernlef und der Heliand,' *Niederdeutsches Jahrbuch* 115 (1992), 159-173.

Vilmar, A. F. C. (August Friedrich Christian). *Deutsches Altertum im Heliand als Einkleidung der Evangelischen Geschichte : Beiträge zur Erklärung des altsächsischen Heliand und zur innern Geschichte der Einführung des Christentums in Deutschland.* (Marburg <s.n.>, 1845)

Weringha, Juw fon. *Heliand und Diatesseron.* (Assen: Van Gorcum, 1965).

Wiedemann, Heinrich. 1949. *Karl der Grosse, Widukind und die Sachsenbekehrung.* (Münster/Westf. 1949:23).

Wolf, Alois. 'Beobachtungen zur ersten Fitte des Heliand,' *Niederdeutsches-Jahrbuch* 98-99 (1975-1976), 7-21.

Wolfram, Herwig, ed. *Ionae Vitae Columbani Liber Primus* in *Quellen zur Geschichte des 7. und 8. Jahrhunderts* Herbert Haupt, translator. (Darmstadt: Wissenschaftliche Buchgesellschaft, 1982).

Wolfram, Richard. *Die gekreuzten Pferdeköpfe als Giebelzeichen.* (Wien: Verlag A. Schendl, 1968).

Woolf, Rosemary. 'The ideal of men dying with their lord in the *Germania* and in *The Battle of Maldon*,' *Anglo-Saxon England* 5 (1976), 63-81.

Young, Jean I., trans. *The Prose Edda.* (Berkeley: University of California Press, 1973).

A Brief Outline of Old Saxon Grammar

A. The Sound Systems of Primitive Germanic and Old Saxon

1.0) *The Primitive Germanic (PGmc) sound system*

1.1) Vowels:

	SHORT		LONG		DIPTHONGS	
	front	*back*	*front*	*back*	*front*	*back*
high	/i/	/u/	/i:/	/u:/		
			/e:$_2$/	/o:/		/eu/
low	/e/	/a/	/e:$_1$/	/a:/	/ai/	/au/

PGmc */a:/ is derived solely from earlier short */a/ which was lengthened when */n/ was vocalized in the syllabic string */anX/. Some instances of PGmc */i:/ and */u:/ were derived from earlier */i/ and */u/ in the strings */inX/ and */unX/, respectively.[1]

1.2) Consonants:

	LABIAL	DENTAL	PALATAL	VELAR	GLOTTAL
stops					
unvoiced	/p/	/t/		/k/	
spirants					
unvoiced	/f/	/þ/, /s/			/X/
voiced	/ƀ/	/ð/, /z/		/γ/	
resonant	/w/	/r/	/j/		
lateral		/l/			
nasal	/m/	/n/			

---

[1] Note: An asterisk (*) indicates a non-attested but reconstructed form, while (----) indicates non-attested. A colon (:) indicates that a vowel is long. In Old Saxon a circumflex (^) is used for the same purpose. Slanting lines (/ /) around segments indicate phonemic (underlyingly systematic) status, while square brackets ([ ]) indicate phonetic status (as pronounced).

A Brief Outline of Old Saxon Grammar

PGmc */ƀ/, */ð/, and */γ/ (the voiced bilabial, dental, and velar spirants, respectively) were voiced spirants (fricatives) except after nasals, where they were realized as *[b], *[d], and *[g], respectively, in the strings *[mb], *[nd], and *[ŋg]. Early on, these phonemes were realized as stops initially, e.g. Early PGmc **/ƀeran-/ became */beran-/, etc. In Old Saxon voiced /γ/ was palato-velar and generally written as <g> in Old Saxon but sometimes as <j> or <i>.

2.0) *The Old Saxon sound system*

2.1) Vowels:

	SHORT		LONG		DIPHTONGS	
	front	*back*	*front*	*back*	*front*	*back*
high	/i/	/u/	/i:/	/u:/	/iu/	/io/
	/e/	/o/	/e:/	/o:/	/ei/	
low	/ę/	/a/	/ę:/	/ǫ:/		/au/

2.2) New vowels:

(a) Old Saxon / ę:/ and / ǫ:/ were presumably open vowels derived from PGmc */ai/ and */au/, respectively. Old Saxon /ei/ and /au/ were derived from PGmc */ai/ and */au/ when these occurred before homorganic glides (/j/ and /w/, respectively).

(b) PGmc */i/ and */u/ were subject to lowering (from high to mid) and became Old Saxon /ñ/ and /o/, respectively. PGmc */i/ and */u/ remained as such in Old Saxon if (i) followed by */m/ or */n/ plus consonant, e.g. in strings like */ind/; (ii) contacted by a labial; or (iii) if the next syllable began with */j/ or contained the high vowels */i/ or */u/.

(c) Raising of PGmc */e/ to Old Saxon /i/ occurred under the conditions described at (b i-iii) for the retention of PGmc */i/ and */u/.

Phonology

2.3) Consonants:

	LABIAL	DENTAL	PALATAL	VELAR	GLOTTAL
stops					
voiced	/b/	/d/		/g/	
unvoiced	/p/	/t/		/k/	
spirants					
voiced	/ƀ/	/ð/	/j/	/γ/	
unvoiced	/f/	/þ/, /s/			/X/
resonant	/w/	/r/			
lateral			/l/		
nasal	/m/	/n/			

PGmc */ð/ became /d/ initially in Old Saxon and /dd/ when geminated; */ƀ/ became /b/ initially and /bb/ when geminated; */γ/ remained initially or merged with /j/ in that position, while it became /gg/ when geminated. (Note that /γ/ — whatever its quality when initial — alliterates with /j/ in the *Hêliand*.) In final position PGmc */ƀ/ was devoiced to /f/, and */f/ was voiced between voiced sounds, appearing there as /ƀ/. Hence */ƀ/ and */f/ merged as /f/ in final position and as /ƀ/ in voiced medial surroundings. PGmc */þ/ became /ð/ in voiced medial surroundings. PGmc */z/ merged with /r/.

In the *Hêliand* voiced /ð/ was written as <ð> or, occasionally, as <đ> (as in Uuarđ in ln. 291), while its voiceless allophone [þ] was written initially in words as <th>. The voiced bilabial spirant was written as <ƀ>.

2.4) Linear rules of sound change from PGmc to OS include:

(a) Umlaut (the fronting of a back vowel in stressed position in anticipation of a high, front vowel in the following syllable, i.e. */j/, */i/, or */i:/) of */a/ appears regularly as /e/ in Old Saxon except before consonant clusters of /X/ (spelled <h> and perhaps pronounced like [h]) plus a consonant, or before /r/ plus /w/. Indication of umlaut with other vowels is sporadic and possibly due to the influence of Frisian.

(b) Gemination (the doubling of a single consonant in medial position) occurred in West Germanic when any consonant (except */r/) was followed by */j/. The */j/ surfaced in Old Saxon as /i/

or /e/. Thus PGmc */kwaðjan/ became OS *queddian / queddien / queddean*, 'greet'. The doubled consonant was shortened after a long vowel or a diphthong. Gemination also occurred before PGmc suffixes containing */l/, */n/, or */r/, e.g. */akraz/ > *akkar* 'field' (cf. Gothic *akrs*).

(c) Loss of nasals before fricatives: Old Saxon (along with Low German dialects generally, including Anglo-Frisian) underwent loss of a PGmc nasal before tautosyllabic */f/, */s/, or */þ/. A preceding short vowel was thereby lengthened (cf. German *fünf, Gans* vs. English 'five', 'goose'). Before */s/ and */þ/ a long /a:/ (from */an/) normally appeared as /ô/ in Old Saxon (cf. German *sanft, ander-* vs. English 'soft', 'other').

(d) Reduction of vowel length in unstressed syllables: In addition to the frequent loss of unstressed short vowels, unstressed polar vowels (*/i/, */u/, and */a/) tended to become centralized in Old Saxon; /i/ and /a/ frequently appear as /e/, while /u/ alternates with /o/.

(e) Simplification of terminal long consonants occurred in West Germanic. Examples in Old Saxon are *man* but *mannes, snel* but *snelle,* etc. (Compare English 'tap' but 'tapped' and 'tapping' or 'man' but 'manned' or 'manning' etc.

B. OLD SAXON REFLEXES OF GERMANIC VOWELS

3.0) *Short Vowels:*

*/a/ *fadar* 'father'; *gast* 'guest'; *salt* 'salt'. Umlaut: *sendian* 'send'; (but *mahtig* 'mighty' (cf. point 2.4 a). Loss of nasals: */anf/ - *sâft* 'soft'; */anþ/ - *ôðar* 'other' (cf. 2.4 c)

*/e/ *etan* 'eat'; *sehs* 'six'; *beran* 'bear, carry'; but *hilpu* 'I help' with raising : *helpan* 'help' (cf. 2.2 c), *bindan* 'bind, tie' (cf. 2.2 b.i).

*/i/ *skip* 'ship'; *uuika* 'week'; *quik* 'alive'. Lengthening: */inþ/ - *fîðan* 'find' (cf. 2.4 c).

*/u/ *jung* 'young'; *uuunda* 'wound'; *uuulf* 'wolf'; *fugal* 'bird'; *gumo* 'man'. Lowering: *opan* 'open'; *storm* 'storm'; *dohter* 'daugh-

ter'; *giboran* 'born' (cf. 2.2 b). Lengthening: */unX/ - *thûhta* 'seemed' (cf. 2.4 c).

3.1) Long Vowels

*/a:/ The only source of *â* in Old Saxon was from */anX/ (cf. 1.1): *thâhta* 'thought'; *brâhta* 'brought'; *fâhan* 'seize'.
*/e:$_1$/ *mâno* 'moon'; *dâd* 'deed'; *gâƀun* 'they gave'.
*/e:$_2$/ *hêr* 'here'; *mêda* 'reward'; *lêt* 'let'.
*/i:/ *tîr* 'fame'; *suuîn* 'swine'; *stîgan* 'climb'.
*/o:/ *stôd* 'stood'; *hôdian* 'guard'; *brôðar* 'brother'.
*/u:/ *hûs* 'house'; *bûan* 'dwell'; *trûon* 'trust'.

3.2) Diphthongs

*/au/ *bôm* 'tree'; *dôð* 'death'; *sôhta* 'sought'. Note: before */w/ *hauuuan* 'hew'; *thau* 'custom'.
*/ai/ *dêl* 'part'; *uuê* 'woe'; *êð* 'oath'. Note: before */j/ *tuueio* 'two' (genitive).
*/eu/ *dior* 'animal'; *liof* 'dear'; *fliogan* 'fly'; *liuhtan* 'gleam'; *bium* 'am'. Note: before */w/ when it followed by */a/ or */e/ or is final *treuuua* 'fidelity', *heu* 'hewed'.
Note: Old Saxon sometimes disambiguates otherwise "clashing" vowel concatenations by creating new diphthongs, as in the 3rd person plural subjunctive form *uuillean* < *wel-j+in, whose expected outcome would have been *uuillîn.

3.4) Consonants

*/w/ *uuulf* 'wolf'; *hîuuiski* 'family'; *niuuan* 'renew'. Vocalized to /o/ in *skado* 'shadow'; *garo* 'ready'. Lost in *thau* 'custom'.
*/j/ *giu* 'long ago'; *jâmar* 'sorrow'; *biddean* 'request'; *tuueio* 'two' (genitive)
*/r/ *rîki* 'realm'; *tharf* 'need', *erða* 'earth'; *hros* 'horse'; *ôðar* 'other.
*/l/ *lâri* 'empty'; *uuulf* 'wolf'; *salƀon* 'anoint'; *fugal* 'bird'.

A Brief Outline of Old Saxon Grammar

*/m/ *manag* 'many'; *simbla* 'always'; *bium* 'am'.

*/n/ *naht* 'night'; *bindan* 'bind'; *thunkian* 'seem'.

*/f/ *fregnan* 'ask, find out'; *tharf* 'need'; *thurƀan* 'need'; *uuulf* 'wolf'; *uuulƀos* 'wolves' (cf. 2.3 and English *wolf* : *wolves*).

*/þ/ *thunkian* 'seem'; *uuiðar* 'against'; *sôð* 'true, forsooth'.

*/s/ *skôni* 'beautiful'; *uuirs* 'worse'; *hûs* 'house'; *lesan* 'gather up'.

*/X/ *hûs* 'house'; *sah* 'saw'; *dohtar* 'daughter'; *sehs* 'six'; *hlahhian* 'laugh'.

*/ƀ/ *betara* 'better'; *geƀan* 'give'; *selƀo* 'self'; *hebbian* 'raise'; *lamb* 'lamb'.

*/z/ *nerian* 'rescue'; *mêr* 'more'; *curun* 'they chose'.

*/γ/ *geƀan* 'give'; *galgo* 'gallows'; *liggian* 'lie'; *magu* 'boy'; *lag* 'lay'; *iâr* 'year'.

*/p/ *plegan* 'play'; *diop* 'deep'; *dôpian* 'baptize'.

*/t/ *tîd* 'time', *lâtan* 'permit'; *settian* 'set'; *sat* 'sat'.

*/k/ *knio* 'knee'; *kiosan* 'choose'; *makon* 'make'; *ôk* 'also'.

*/ð/ *dragan* 'carry'; *brôðar* 'brother'; *fandon* 'tempt'; *tîð* 'time'; *uuiðerstande* 'resist'.

C. Strong Noun Declension

Abbreviations: N = nominative, G = genitive, D = dative, A = accusative, I = instrumental. Throughout the declensions, some Old English correspondences are provided for comparison but, since OE exhibits considerable morphological variation, reference should also be made to Old English grammars.

4.0) *Masculines*

4.1) *a*-stems

	sing	*OE*	*plur*	*OE*	*sing*	*plur*
N	dag 'day'	dæʒ	dagos, -as, -a	daʒas	hof 'court'	hoƀos, -as, -a
G	dages, -as	dæʒes	dago	daʒa	hoƀes, -as	hoƀo
D	dage, -a	dæʒe	dagon, -un	daʒum	hoƀe, -a	hoƀum, -un, -on
A	dag	dæʒ	dagos, -as, -a	daʒas	hof	hoƀos, -as, -a
I	dagu, -o				hoƀu, -o	

4.2) *ja*-stems

	singular	*OE*	*plural*	*OE*	*singular*	*plural*
N	hirdi, -e 'herder'	hyrde	hirdios, -eos	hyrdas	heri 'army'	herios, -eos, -ia
G	hirdies, -ias, -eas	hyrdes	hirdio, -eo	hyrda	heries, -ias, -eas	herio, -ea
D	hirdie, -ia, -ea	hyrde	hirdium, -iun, ion, -eon	hyrdum	herie, -ia, -ea	herium, -iun-ion, -eon
A	hirdi, -e	hyrde	hirdios, -eos, -a	hyrdas	heri, -e	herios, -eos, -ia
I	hirdiu				heriu	

A Brief Outline of Old Saxon Grammar

4.3) *wa*-stems

	singular	*OE*	*plural*	*OE*
N	sê, sêo, -u 'sea'	snāw 'snow'	-----	snāwas
G	sêuues, -as	snāwes	-----	snāwa
D	sêuue, -a	snāwe	-----	snāwum
A	sê, sêo, -u	snāw	-----	snāwas

4.4) *i*-stems

long stems[2]

	singular	*OE*	*plural*	*OE*
N	gast, 'guest'	ʒiest	gesti, -e	ʒiestas
G	gastes, -as	ʒiestes	gestio, -eo	ʒiesta
D	gaste, -a	ʒieste	gestiun, -ion, -eon	ʒiestum
A	gast	ʒiest	gesti, -e	ʒiestas

short stems[3]

	singular	*OE*	*plural*	*OE*
N	uuini, 'friend'	wine	uuini, -ios	wine, -as
G	uuinies, -ias	wines	uuinio	wina
D	uuini, -ie, -ia, -ea	wine	uuiniun, -ion	winum
A	uuini	wine	uuini, -ios	wine, -as

4.5) *u*-stems

	singular	*OE*	*plural*	*OE*
N	sunu, -o, 'son'	sunu	suni	suna
G	sunies, -eas	suna	suno, -io	suna
D	suno, -u, -e, -ie	suna	sunun, -iun	sunum
A	sunu, -o	sunu	suni	suna

---

[2] Long stems have two consonants following the first vowel (as /VC$_1$C$_1$/ or /VC$_1$C$_2$/), or they have a diphthong (/VV(C)/) or long vowel (/V:(C)/ with or without a following consonant.

[3] Short stems have one (or no) consonant after the first short vowel.

4.6) Root-stems

	singular	OE	plural	OE
N	man, 'man'	mann	man, men	menn
G	mannes, -as	mannes	manno, -a	manna
D	man, manne, -a	menn	mannum, -un, -on	mannum
A	man	mann	man, men	menn

4.7) *nd*-stems (masculine only, originally formed from present participles of verbs)

	singular	OE	plural	OE
N	friund, 'friend, kinsman'	frēond	friund, -os, -a	frīend
G	friundes, -as	frēondes	friundo	frēonda
D	friunde, -a	frīend, frēonde	friundum, -un, -on	frēondum
A	friund	frēond	friund, -os, -a	frīend

4.8) *r*-stems (names of relationship, such as *fader* 'father', *brôðar* 'brother')

	singular	OE	plural	OE
N	brôðar, -er, 'brother'	brōðor	brôðar, -er	brōðor
G	brôðar, -er	brōðor	-------	-------
D	brôðar, -er	brōðor	brôðarun, brôðrun, brôðron	brōðrum
A	brôðar, -er	brōðor	brôðar, -er	brōðor

A Brief Outline of Old Saxon Grammar

5.0) Neuters

5.1) a-stems

long stem

	sing	OE	plur	OE	sing	OE	plur	OE
					short stem			
N	uuord, 'word'	word	uuord	word	graf, 'grave'	fæt 'vat'	grabu	fatu
G	uuordes, -as	wordes	uuordo	worda	grabes, -as	fætes	grabo	fata
D	uuorde, -a	worde	uuordum -un, -on	wordum	grabe, -a	fæte	grabum -un,-on	fatum
A	uuord	word	uuord	word	graf	fæt	grabu	fatu
I	uuordu, -o				grabu, -o			

5.2) ja-stems

	singular	OE	plural	OE	singular	plural
N	erbi, 'inheritance'	ende 'end'	erbi	endas	flet(ti), 'room'	fletti
G	erbies, -ias, -eas	endes	erbio, -eo	enda	fletties, -eas	flettio, -eo
D	erbie, -ia, -ea	ende	erbium,-iun, -ion, -eon	endum	flettie	flettium, -iun, -ion, -eon
A	erbi	ende	erbi	endas	flet(ti)	fletti
I	erbiu, -io				flettiu, -io	

5.3) i-stems

	singular	plural
N	halsmeni, 'necklace'	halsmeni, -ios
G	halsmenies, -ias	halsmenio
D	halsmeni, -ie, -ia, -ea	halsmeniun, -ion
A	halsmeni	halsmeni, -ios
I	halsmeni, -iu	

5.4) *wa*-stems

	singular	OE	**plural**	OE
N	treo, -io 'tree'	trēo	knêo, 'knees'	cnēo(wu)
G	treuues, -as	trēowes	-----	cnēowa
D	treuue, -a	trēowe	-----	cneowum
A	treo, -io	trēo	knêo	cnēo(wu)

5.5) *u*-stems

	singular	**plural**
N	fehu, -o 'cattle, property'	-----
G	fehes, -as	-----
D	feho, -e	-----
A	fehu, -o	-----

6.0) *Feminines*

6.1) *ô*-stems (n.b: words in this declension often also have endings as in §7.3.)

	singular	OE	**plural**	OE
N	geƀa, 'gift'	ȝiefu	geƀa	ȝiefa, -e
G	geƀa, -u, -o	ȝiefe	geƀono	ȝiefa, -ena
D	geƀu, -a, -o	ȝiefe	geƀon, -um, -un	ȝiefum
A	geƀa, -e	ȝiefe	geƀa	ȝiefa, -e

6.2) *i*-stems

	long stem				short stem	
	singular	OE	**plural**	OE	**singular**	**plural**
N	fard 'journey'	fierd, 'army'	ferdi	fierde	stedi, 'stead'	stedi
G	ferdi, -e	fierde	ferdio	fierda	stedi, -e	stedio
D	ferdi, -e, -iu	fierde	ferdium, -iun	fierdum	stedi, -e; -iu	stediun
A	fard	fierd	ferdi	fierde	stedi	stedi

A Brief Outline of Old Saxon Grammar

6.3) *u*-stems

	singular	OE	**plural**	OE
N	hand, 'hand'	hond	hendi, handi	honda
G	----	honda	hando	honda
D	hand, -i	honda	handun, -on, -iun	hondum
A	hand	honda	hendi, handi	honda

6.4) Root-stems

	sing	OE	**plur**	OE	**sing.**	OE	**plur**	OE
N	burg, 'city'	hnutu, 'nut'	burgi	hnyte	naht 'night'	niht	naht	niht
G	burges	hnute	burgo -io, -eo	hnuta	nahtes	niht, -es	nahto	nihta
D	burg, -i	hnute	burgun, -ion, -eon	hnutum	naht, -a	niht	nahtun, -on	nihtum
A	burg	hnutu	burgi	hnyte	naht	niht	naht	niht

6.5) *r*-stems (names of relationship, such as *suuester* 'sister', *môdar* 'mother')

	singular	OE	**plural**	OE
N	suuester, -ar 'sister'	sweostor	suuester, -ar	sweostor
G	suuester, -ar	sweostor	------	sweostra
D	suuester, -ar	sweostor	suuestrun, suuestarun, -ron	sweostrum
A	suuester, -ar	sweostor	suuester, -ar	sweostor

6.6) Abstracts in -i

	singular	**plural**
N	helti, 'lameness'	helti
G	helti	helti, -io
D	helti	heltion
A	helti	helti

Morphology

D. WEAK NOUN DECLENSION

7.0) n-*stems*

7.1) Masculine

	singular	OE	*plural*	OE
N	gumo, -a, 'man'	ȝuma	gumon, -un, -an	ȝuman
G	gumen, -an, -on	ȝuman	gumono	ȝumena
D	gumen, -an, -on	ȝuman	gumon, -un	ȝumum
A	gumon, -an	ȝuman	gumon, -un, -an	ȝuman

7.2) Neuter

	singular	OE	*plural*	OE
N	herta, -e, 'heart'	ēaȝe, 'eye'	hertun, -on	ēaȝan
G	herten, -an, -on	ēaȝen	hertono	ēaȝ(e)na
D	herten, -an, -on	ēaȝen	hertun, -on	ēaȝum
A	herta, -e	ēaȝe	hertun, -on	ēaȝan

7.3) Feminine

	singular	OE	*plural*	OE
N	tunga, -e, 'tongue'	tunȝe	tungun, -on, -an	tunȝan
G	tungun, -on, -an	tunȝan	tungono	tunȝ(e)na
D	tungun, -on, -an	tunȝan	tungun, -on, -an	tunȝum
A	tungun, -on, -an	tunȝan	tungun, -on, -an	tunȝan

A Brief Outline of Old Saxon Grammar

E. Pronouns

(Old English equivalents are provided only where they are substantially different.)

8.0) Personal Pronouns

8.1) First Person

	singular	*OE*	*dual*	*OE*	*plural*	*OE*
N	ik, 'I'	iċ	uuit, 'we two'	wit	uui, uue, 'we'	we
G	mîn	mīn	unkero, -aro	uncer	ûser	ūre
D	mî, me	me	unk	unc	ûs	ūs
A	mik, mî, me	me	unk	unc	ûs	ūs

8.2) Second Person

	singular	*OE*	*dual*	*OE*	*plural*	*OE*
N	thû, thu, tu, 'thou'	þu	git, 'you two'	ʒit	gî, gi, ge, 'you'	ʒe
G	thîn	þīn	inkero, inka	inċer	iuuuar(o), -er(o)	ēower
D	thî, thi	þe	ink	inċ	eu, iu, giu	ēow
A	thî, thi, thik	þe	ink	inċ	gî, gi, ge	ēow

8.3) Third Person

	masculine				*feminine*			
	sing	*OE*	*plur*	*OE*	*sing*	*OE*	*plur*	*OE*
N	hê, hie 'he'	hē	sia, sea, sie	hīe	siu, 'she'	hēo	sia, sea, sie	hīe
G	is, es	his	iro, ira, era	hira	iru, ira	hire	iro, ira, iru, era	hira
D	imo, imu, im	him	im	him	iru, iro, ira	hire	im	him
A	ina, ine	hine	sia, sea, sie	hīe	sia, sie, sea	hīe	sia, sea, sie	hīe

Morphology

	sing	OE	**plur**	OE
	neuter			
N	it, et, 'it'	hit	siu, sia, sea, sie	hīe
G	is, es	his	iro, ira, era	hira
D	imo, imu, im	him	im	him
A	it, et	hit	siu, sia, sea, sie	hīe

8.4) Reflexive:

G/D/A forms of the Personal Pronouns are also used as reflexive pronouns, cf. *fâhit im* 'make for themselves'. See also §14.5.

9.0) *Demonstrative Pronouns*

	singular				*plural*	
	masculine	OE	**feminine**	OE	**masc/fem**	OE
N	the, thie, se 'that'	sē	thiu, thea, thia	sēo	thea, thia, thie, the, thâ	þā
G	the	þæs	thera, -o, -u	þǣre	thero, -a	þāra
D	themu, them	þǣm	theru, -o, -a	þǣre	them, then	þǣm
A	thena, thene, thana	þone	thea, thie, thiu	þā	thea, thia, thie, the	þā
I	thiu	þȳ				

	singular	OE	*neuter* *plural*	OE
N	that	þæt	thiu (or = masc/fem)	þā
G	thes, thas	þæs	thero, -a	þāra
D	themu, -o, them	þǣm	them, then	þǣm
A	that	þæt	thiu (or = masc/fem)	þā
I	thiu	þȳ		

A Brief Outline of Old Saxon Grammar

10.0) Compound Demonstrative Pronouns

	masculine singular	OE	plural	OE	feminine singular	OE	plural	OE
N	these, 'this'	þēs	these, -a	þās	thius	þēos	thesa, -e	þās
G	theses, -as	þisses	thesaro, -oro	þissa	thesara, -o, -oro	þisse	thesaro, -oro	þissa
D	thesumu, -amo	þissum	thesum -un, -on	þissum	thesaru, -o, -oro	þisse	thesum, -un	þissum
A	thesan, -en, -on	þisne	these, -a	þās	thesa, -e	þās	thesa, -e	þās
I	thius	þȳs						

	neuter singular	OE	plural	OE
N	thit	þis	thius	þās
G	theses, -as	þisses	thesaro, -oro	þissa
D	thesumu, -amo, -um, -un	þissum	thesum, -on	þissum
A	thit	þis	thius	þās
I	thius	þȳs		

11.0) Interrogative Pronouns

	masc/fem	OE	neuter	OE
N	huuê, huuie	hwā	huuat	hwæt
G	huues	hwæs	huues	hwæs
D	huuemu, huuem	hwǣm	huuemu, huuem	hwǣm
A	huuena, huuene	hwone	huuat	hwæt
I	------		huuî, huuiu, huueo, hû, huuô	hwī

12.0) *huueðar* and *huuilîk*

huueðar 'which of two' (OE hwæðer) stands as a pronoun or with a following genitive and is inflected as a strong adjective.

huuilîk 'which' (OE hwilċ) stands as a pronoun or a strong adjective and may have *sô/sulîk* 'so/such' as a correlative.

13.0) Indefinite Pronouns

ên 'a, one'
ênhuuilîk 'a certain (one)'
ênig 'any'
gihuuê 'each'
gihuuilîk 'every': *dago*
   gihuuilîkes 'every day'
huuat 'anything, something'
   manages huuat 'many kinds of'
iouuiht 'something'
man 'someone'
neuuethar 'neither'

nigên 'no, none'
nioman 'no one'
niouuiht 'nothing'
ôðar ... ôðar 'the one ... the other'
sô huuê sô 'each who'
sô huueðar sô 'whosoever'
sô huuilîk sô 'whosoever'
sum 'a certain one, some'
sum ... sum 'the one ... the other'
uuiht 'something'.

F. ADJECTIVE DECLENSIONS

14.0) Strong Declensions

14.1) *a*- and *ô*-stems

masculine

	singular	OE	plural	OE
N	hêlag 'holy'	gōd 'good'	hêlaga, -e	gōde
G	hêlagas, -es	gōdes	hêlagaro, -ero	gōdra
D	hêlagum, -om, -omu, -emo	gōdum	hêlagum, -un, -om, -on	gōdum
A	hêlagna, -an	gōdne	hêlaga, -e	gōde
I	hêlagu, -o	gōde		

feminine

	singular	OE	plural	OE
N	hêlag	gōd	hêlaga, -e	gōd
G	hêlagaro, -era	gōdre	hêlagaro, -ero	gōdra
D	hêlagaru, -eru	gōdre	hêlagum, -un, -omu, -emo	gōdrum
A	hêlaga, -e	gōde	hêlaga, -e	gōda

A Brief Outline of Old Saxon Grammar

	singular	OE	**neuter** plural	OE
N	hêlag	gōd	hêlag, hêlage	gōd
G	hêlages, -as	gōdes	hêlagaro, -ero	gōdra
D	hêlagu, -umu, -un, -um	gōdum	hêlagum, -un, -om, -on	gōdrum
A	hêlag	gōd	hêlag, hêlage	gōd
I	hêlagu, -o	gōde		

Monosyllabic words in the above class have *-an* or *-on* (like 'good': *gôdan* or *gôdon*) in the masculine accusative singular; in manuscript M the endings are commonly *-ana, -ane, -ene*.

14.2) *ja-* and *jô-*stems

These are inflected as in §14.1, except in the nominative singular masculine and feminine, and in the nominative singular and plural neuter, where they end in *-i*. The *-i* is often reduced to *-e*, particularly before a following *a* or *o*. Examples of this class are *skôni* 'beautiful'; *rîpi* 'ripe'; *nutti* 'useful'; *lâri* 'empty'; *hrêni* 'pure'; *derni* 'hidden'. The adjectives *spâhi* 'wise' and *skîr* 'pure, clean' often decline as *ja*-stems.

14.3) *wa-* and *wô-*stems

These too are inflected as 14.1, except where the *-e* or *-u* ending is followed by *w*, e.g. *garo* 'ready' G *garouues*; *glau* 'wise' N pl *glauuue*; or *blâo* 'blue' G *blâuues*.

14.4) *u-*stems

Very few historical *u*-stems still remained in Old Saxon. The form *filu, -o* 'many, much' was retained in the nominative and accusative singular, but *hard* 'hard', *quik* 'alive' are inflected as *a*-stems, *glau* 'wise' as a *wa*-stem, and *engi* 'narrow' as a *ja*-stem.

Morphology

14.5) Possessive adjectives:

These inflect as §14.1. They are *mîn* 'my, mine', *thîn* 'thy, thine', *sîn* 'his', *unka* 'both of our(s)', *inka* 'both of your(s)', *ûsa* 'our(s)', *euuua, iuuua* 'your(s)'.

15.0) *Weak Declension*

	singular						*plural*	
	masculine	OE	**feminine**	OE	**neuter**	OE	**masc/fem/neut**	OE
N	hêlago, -a 'holy'	gōda	hêlaga, -e	gōde	hêlaga, -e	gōde	hêlagun, -on, -an	gōdan
G	hêlagen, -an, -on	gōdan	hêlagun	gōdan	hêlagen, -an, -on	gōdan	hêlagono	gōdra, gōdena
D	hêlagen, -an, -on	gōdan	hêlagun, -on, -an	gōdan	hêlagen, -an, -on	gōdan	hêlagum, un, on	gōdum
A	hêlagon, -an	gōdan	hêlagun, -on, -an	gōdan	hêlaga, -e	gōde	hêlagun, -on, -an	gōdan

ja- and *wa*-stems are inflected in like manner.

G. COMPARISON OF ADJECTIVES

16.0) *Form*

The *comparative* form of the adjective is constructed by the addition of endings *-or-, -ir-, -ar-, -er-* e.g. positive *uuîd* 'far'; comparative *uuîdora* 'farther'. The *superlative* is formed by the addition of *-ost-* or *-ist-*, thus *uuîdost* 'farthest'.

16.1) Inflection

Any of these derived forms may be inflected. The *comparative* is inflected according to the weak adjective declension only. The *superlative* can show strong adjective declension in the nominative singular of all genders and in the accusative singular of the neuter. Otherwise the superlative shows weak inflection.

16.2) Suppletive Forms

In the following forms the positive derives from a different stem than the comparative and superlative:

	OE
gôd 'good' : *betera, -ara* 'better' : *best* 'best'	gōd : betera : bet(e)st
uƀil 'bad' : *uuirsa* 'worse': *uuirsist, uuirrist* 'worst'	yfel : wiersa : wierrest
mikil 'big': *mêra* 'more' : *mêst* 'most'	miċel : māra : mǣst
luttil 'little': *minnera, -ara* 'smaller', *minnist* 'smallest'	lȳtel : lǣssa : lǣst

Note: The comparative forms take weak adjective endings as per §15.0.

H. Adverbs

17.0) *Derived and non-Derived Adverbs*

Adverbs are frequently formed from adjectives by adding the suffixes *-o, -ungo, -lîko* or *-samo* to the stem, e.g. *derno* 'secretly'; *darnungo* 'secretly'; *gâhliko* 'quickly'; *friðusamo* 'peacefully'. Otherwise certain forms are adverbs by definition, e.g. *thô* 'then', *êr* 'previously', *atsamna* 'together', *bihuuî* 'why', *rûmor* 'farther away,' etc.

I. Numerals

18.0) *Cardinal Numbers*

18.1) The number 'one'

The number 'one', *ên* (Old English *ān*) is usually inflected as a strong adjective corresponding to the English 'a, an', but if it is preceded by an article, it is inflected weak and then has the meaning 'the one', 'alone', 'the only'.

Morphology

18.2) The number 'two'

		masculine	OE	feminine	OE	neuter	OE
N		tuuêne, tuuêna	twēȝen	tuuô, tuuâ	twā	tuuê	twā, tū
G		tuuêio	twēȝea	tuuêio	twēȝea	tuuêio	twēȝea
D		tuuêm, tuuên	twǣm	tuuêm, tuuên	twǣm	tuuêm, tuuên	twǣm
A		tuuêne, tuuêna	twēȝen	tuuô, tuuâ	twā	tuuê	twā, tū

18.3) The number 'three'

	masculine	OE	feminine	OE	neuter	OE
N	thria, threa, thrie	þrī	thria, threa, thrie	þrēo	thriu, thrû	þrēo
G	*thrio	þrēora	*thrio	þrēora	*thrio	þrēora
D	thrim	þrim	thrim	þrim	thrim	þrim
A	thria, threa, thrie	þrī	thria, threa, thrie	þrēo	thriu, thrû	þrēo

18.4) Higher Numbers

The numbers from 4 to 12 are:

	OE		OE
'4' *fiuuuar, fior, fiar*	fēower	'9' *nigun*	nigon
'5' *fīf*	fīf	'10' *tehan, tian, tein*	tīen
'6' *sehs*	siex	'11' *elevan*	endlefan
'7' *sibun*	seofon	'12' *tuuelif, tuuulif*	twelf
'8' *ahto*	eahta		

These may be inflected as strong adjectives following nouns or when used pronominally; all genders emply the endings: N -*i*, G -*io*, D -*iun*, A -*i*.

The numbers 13 to 19 add -*tein* to the simple number, for example '15' *fiftein*.

The denominations of ten from 20 to 60 add *-tig* to the simple number, as in '50' *fiftig*. These are old nouns and are followed by the genitive plural of what is being counted.

The numbers of ten from 70 through 99 are often formed by the prefix *ant-* or *at-* on a special form of the simple number, as in '80' *antahto(da)*.

The number 100 is *hund*. A compound number may appear as, for example, *fior endi antahtoda* 'four and eighty'.

19.0) Ordinal Numbers

	OE		OE
êrist, furist, formo 'first'	æresta, fyresta, forma	*sehsto* 'sixth'	siexta
		sibendo 'seventh'	seofoða
ôðar, andar 'second'	ôðer, æfterra	*ahtodo* 'eighth'	eahtoða
thridde 'third'	þridda	*niguða* 'ninth'	nigoða
fiorðe 'fourth'	fēowerða	*tehando* 'tenth'	tēoðā
fifto 'fifth'	fīfta	*ellifto* 'eleventh'	endlefta

20.0) Other Forms of Numbers

ênfald '(onefold), simple', *tuuêdi* 'half', *thrio* 'three times', *ôtherhalf* 'one and one half'; multiple 'times' may be written with *sîð*, as in *ôðar sîðu* 'twice'.

J. VERBAL TYPES

21.0) Strong Verbs

21.1) Class I

infinitive	past sg	past pl	past ppl	OE
skînan 'shine'	skên	skinun	giskinan	sċīnan sċăn sċinon sċinen
skrîban 'write'	skrêf	skribun	giskriban	scrīfan scrāf scrifon scrifen
giuuîtan 'go'	giuuêt	giuuitun	giuuitan	ȝewītan ȝewāt ȝewiton ȝewiten
snîðan 'cut'	snêð	snidun	gisnidan	snīðan snāð snidon sniden
farlîhan 'give'	-------	---------	farliuuan	

Morphology

21.1) Class I

infinitive	past sg	past pl	past ppl	OE
skînan 'shine'	skên	skinun	giskinan	sċīnan sċān sċinon sċinen
skrîban 'write'	skrêf	skribun	giskriban	scrīfan scrāf scrifon scrifen
giuuîtan 'go'	giuuêt	giuuitun	giuuitan	ȝewītan ȝewāt ȝewiton ȝewiten
snîðan 'cut'	snêð	snidun	gisnidan	snīðan snāð snidon sniden
farlîhan 'give'	-------	---------	farliuuan	

21.2) Class II

infinitive	past sg	past pl	past ppl	OE
biodan 'bid'	bôd	budun	gibodan	bēodan bēad budon boden
fliotan 'flow'	flôt	flutun	giflotan	flēotan flēat fluton floten
griotan 'weep'	grôt	grutun	gigrotan	ȝrēotan ȝrēat ȝruton ȝroten
kiosan 'choose'	kôs	kurun	gikoran	ċēosan ċēas curon coren
tiohan 'draw'	tôh	tugun	gitogan	tēon tēah tuȝon toȝen
N.B. bûgan 'bend'	bôg	bugun	gibogan	būȝan bēah buȝon boȝen

21.3) Class III

infinitive	past sg	past pl	past ppl	OE
(a)				
bindan 'bind'	band	bundun	gibundan	bindan band bundon bunden
drinkan 'drink'	drank	drunkun	gidrunkan	drincan dranc druncon druncen
(b)				
uuerpan 'throw'	uuarp	uuurpun	giuuorpan	weorpan wearp wurpon worpen
uueröan 'become'	uuarð	uuurdun	uuordan	weorðan wearð wurdon worden
helpan 'help'	halp	hulpun	giholpan	helpan healp hulpon holpen
brestan 'burst'	brast	------	--------	berstan bærst burston borsten
fregnan 'find out'	fragn	frugnun	--------	friȝnan fræȝn fruȝnon fruȝnen

21.4) Class IV

infinitive	past sg	past pl	past ppl	OE
beran 'bear, carry'	bar	bârun	giboran	beran bær bǣron boren
stelan 'steal'	stal	stâlun	gistolan	stelan stæl stǣlon stolen
kuman 'come'	quam	quâmun	(gi)kuman	cuman c(w)ōm c(w)ōmon cumen
brekan 'break'	brak	brâkun	gibrokan	brecan bræc brǣcon brocen
sprekan 'speak'	sprak	sprâkun	gisprokan	

21.5) Class V

infinitive	past sg	past pl	past ppl	OE
geban 'give'	gaf	gâbun	gigeban	ȝiefan ȝeaf ȝēafon ȝiefen
sehan 'see'	sah	sâuuun	gisehan	sēon seah sāwon sewen
uuesan 'be'	uuas	uuârun	-----	wesan wæs wāron ----
queðan 'say'	quað	quâdun	giquedan	cweðan cwæð cwǣdon cweden

A Brief Outline of Old Saxon Grammar

infinitive	past sg	past pl	past ppl	OE
jan-present				
liggian 'lie'	lag	lâgun	gilegan	licʒan læʒ læʒon leʒen
sittian 'sit'	sat	sâtun	gisetan	sittan sæt sæton seten
biddian 'ask for'	bad	bâdun	gibedan	biddan bed bædon beden

21.6) Class VI

infinitive	past sg	past pl	past ppl	OE
faran 'journey'	fôr	fôrun	gifaran	faran fōr fōron faren
slahan 'strike'	slôg	slôgun	gislagan	slēan slōʒ slōʒon slæʒen
jan-present				
hebbian 'raise'	hôf	hôƀun	gihaƀan	hebbian hōf hōfon hafen
n-present				
standan/stân 'stand'	stôd	stôdun	gistandan	standan stōd stōdon standen

21.7) Class VII

infinitive	past sg	past pl	past ppl	OE
(a)				
haldan 'hold'	held	heldun	gihaldan	healdan hēold hēoldon healden
gangan 'go'	geng	gengun	gigangan	gangan ʒēng ʒēongon gangen
fâhan 'catch'	feng	fengun	gifangan	fōn fēng fēngon fangen
(b)				
lâtan 'let'	lêt	lêtun	gilâtan	lǣtan lēt lēton lǣten
slâpan 'sleep'	slêp	slêpun	gislâpan	slǣpan slēp slēpon slǣpen
(c)				
hêtan 'be called, command'	hêt	hêtun	gihêtan	hātan hēt hēton hāten
(d)				
hrôpan 'cry out'	hriop	hriopun	gihrôpan	hrōpan hrēop hrēopon hrōpen
hlôpan 'run'	hliop	hliopun	gihlôpan	hlēapan hlēop hlēopon hlēapen
hauuuan 'hew'	heu	heuuun	gihauuuan	hēawan hēow hēowon hēawen
jan-present				
uuôpian 'weep'	uuiop	uuiopun	giuuôpan	wēpan wēop wēopon wōpen

22.0) *Weak Verbs*

22.1) Class I:

To this class belong certain verbs with a PGmc **jan*-suffix (-*ian*/*ean* in Old Saxon). The /j/ caused gemination (doubling) of the preceding consonant except for */r/ and */ð/. Under gemination */ƀ/ developed into /bb/. Umlaut of an */a/ to Old Saxon /e/ in the stem of the verb is normal. From the */j/ in the *jan-suffix /i/ is normally

Morphology

retained as a connecting vowel in the past tense and participle forms wherever the stem syllable was originally short; after a long stem the /i/ in this position disappeared before it could cause umlaut of the stem vowel */a/.

infinitive	past tense (3rd per sg ind)	past participle	OE
frummian 'accomplish'	frumida	gifrumid	fremman fremede ȝefremed
tellian 'tell'	talda	gitald	tellan tealde ȝeteald
fullian 'fill'	fullda	gifullid	fyllan fylde ȝefyld
kûðian 'make known'	kûðda	gikûðd	cýðan cýðde ȝecýðed
nerian 'rescue'	nerida	ginerid	nerian nerede ȝenered
kussian 'kiss'	kussta	gikusst	cyssan cyste ȝecyst
with no original connecting vowel			
sôkian 'seek'	sôhta	gisôht	sēcean sōhte ȝesōht
thenkian 'think'	thâhta	------	þencean þōhte ȝeþōht
thunkian 'seem'	thûhta	------	þyncean þūhte ȝeþūht
brengian 'bring'	brâhta	-brâht	brinȝan brōhte ȝebrōht
uuirkian 'work'	uuarhta	-uuarht	wyrcean worhte ȝeworht
buggian 'buy'	------	giboht	byċȝean bohte ȝeboht
bûan 'dwell'	bûida	------	būan būde ȝebūd

22.2) Class II: Here the adjunct to the stem is /o/.

infinitive	past tense (3rd per sg ind)	past participle	OE
makon 'make'	makoda	gimakod	macian macode ȝemacod
bedon 'pray'	bedoda	gibedod	
tholon 'suffer'	tholoda	githolod	þōlian þōlode ȝeþōlod

22.3) Class III

Four verbs may be listed for this group, the infinitive forms of which place them in Class I but whose past forms indicate late loss of a connecting vowel /e/ from */e:/

infinitive	past tense (3rd per sg ind)	past participle	OE
hebbian 'have'	habda	gihabd	habban hæfde ȝehæfd
seggian 'say'	sagda	gisagd	seċȝan sæȝde ȝesæȝd
libbian 'live'	libda	gilibd	libban lifde ȝelifd
huggian 'think'	hogda	gihogd	hyċȝan hogde ȝehogd

A Brief Outline of Old Saxon Grammar

23.0) Preterite-Present Verbs

Preterite-presents resemble, in their present tense forms, the past tenses of strong verbs (cf. § 21.1-6). Their past tense forms contain a dental preterite marker and, in some, an additional *s*. Subjunctive endings are as given in § 25. Corresponding Old English forms are given next to the Old Saxon. Because attestation is lacking, some infinitives and other forms are reconstructed and marked with an asterisk. For a thorough discussion, see Birkmann 1987.

		$1^{st}, 3^{rd}$ pres sg		2nd pres sg		3rd pres pl		$1^{st}, 3^{rd}$ past sg		3rd past pl
1)	*uuitan* 'know'	*uuêt*	wāt	*uuêst*	wāst	*uuitun*;	witan	*uuissa*	wisse	*uuissun*.
	êgan 'own, have'	--------	āh	------	āht	*êgun*	aȝon	*êhta*	āhte	*êhtun*[4]
2)	**dugan* 'be good for'	*dôg*	dēaȝ	------	----	*dugun*	dugon	**dohta*	dohte	-------
3)	**unnan* 'grant'	-----	ann	------	----	---------	unnon	*afonsta*	ūðe	-------
	**durran* 'dare'	*gidar*	dearr	------	dearst	**durrun*	durron	*gidorsta*	dorste	*gidorstu*
	thurban 'need'	*tharf*	þearf	*tharft*	þearft	*thurbun*	þurfon	*thorfta*	þorfte	-------
	kunnan 'be able to; know'	*kan*	cann	*kanst*	canst	*kunnun*	cunnon	*konsta*	cūðe	-------
4)	**skulan* 'ought to'	*skal*	sceal	*skalt*	scealt	*skulun*	sculon	*skolda*	scolde	*skoldun*
	**munan* 'believe'	*-man*[5]	man	*-manst*	manst	*munun*	munon	*-monsta*	munde	*-monstun*
5)	**mugan* 'be able to'	*mag*	mæȝ	*maht*	meaht	*mugun*	magon	*mahta*,	meahte,	-----
6)	*môtan* 'be permitted to'; 'be able to'; 'have to'	*môt*	mōt	*môst*	mōst	*môtun*	mōton	*mohta* *môsta*	mihte mōste	*môstun*

---

[4] It is not clear under which entry *êgan* belonged in this scheme.

[5] The forms *-man*, *-manst*, etc. are from the paradigm of *farmunan* 'scorn, deny'.

K. Verb Conjugations

24.0) Strong Verbs

infinitive: *kiosan* 'choose'; *sehan* 'see'; OE ćēosan; sēon

present

	indicative					subjunctive		
		OE		OE			OE	OE
Sg 1	kiusu, -o	ćēose	sihu, -o	sēo	kiose, -a	ćēose	sehe, -a	sēo
2	kiusis	ćŷst	sihis	syhst	kioses, -as	ćēose	sehes, -as	sēo
3	kiusid, -t	ćŷsð	sihid, -t	syhð	kiose, -a	ćēose	sehe, -a	sēo
Pl	kiosad, -t	ćēosað	sehad, -t	sēoð	kiosen, -an	ćēosen		sēon

imperative: 2nd sg. kios, kius; plural kiosad, *OE:* 2nd sg. ćēos; plural ćēosað
present participle: kiosandi; sehandi, *OE:* ćēosende; sēonde
gerund: kiosanne, kiosannes; sehanne, sehannes, *OE:* sēonne; ćēosenne

past

	indicative						subjunctive	
		OE			OE		OE	OE
Sg 1	kôs	ćēas	sah	seah	kuri	cure	sâuui, -e	sāwe
2	kuri	cure	sâuui	sāwe	kuris	cure	sâuuis	sāwe
3	kôs	ćēas	seh	seah	kuri	cure	sâuui, -e	sāwe
Pl	kurun, -on	curon	sâuuun, -on	sāwon	kurin	curen	sâuuin	sāwe

past participle: gikoran, gisehan; *OE:* ʒecoren, ʒesewen.

25.0) Weak Verbs

infinitive: fremman -ien, -ean 'carry out'; tholo(ia)n -ogean, tholian 'suffer, endure'; OE: sēċan, þolian

present

	indicative					subjunctive		
		OE		OE			OE	OE
Sg 1	fremmiu	fremme	tholon	þoliʒe	fremmea	fremme	tholo(ie), -ogea	þoliʒe
2	fremis	fremest	tholos	þolast	fremmeas	fremme	tholos	þoliʒe
3	fremid, -t	fremeð	tholod, -t	þolað	fremea	fremme	tholo(ie), -ogea	þoliʒe
Pl	fremiad, -ead, -t	fremmað	tholod, -oiad, -t	þoliað	fremmean, -ian, -ien	fremmen	tholo(ian)	þoliʒen

A Brief Outline of Old Saxon Grammar

imperative: 2nd sg fremi, tholo; plural fremmiad. *OE*: freme, fremmað
present participle: fremmiandi, -iendi, -eandi; tholo(gea)ndi, tholiandi. *OE*: fremmende, þoliʒende
gerund: fremmianne, fremmiannes; tholo(ia)nne, tholo(ia)nnes. *OE*: sēċenne, þoliʒenne

		past						
	indicative				*subjunctive*			
		OE		OE		OE		OE
Sg 1	fremida, -e	fremede	tholoda, -e	þolode	fremidi	fremede	tholodi	þolode
2	fremidas, -es	fremedes(t)	tholodes, -as	þolodest	fremidis	fremede	tholodis	þolode
3	fremida, -e	fremede	tholoda, -e	þolode	fremidi	fremede	tholodi	þolode
Pl	fremidun	fremedon	tholodun	þolodon	fremidin	fremeden	tholodin	þoloden

past participle: gifremid; githolod. *OE*: fremed, þolod

infinitive: hebbian 'hold, have'; seggian 'say'; *OE*: habban; seċʒan

		present						
	indicative				*subjunctive*			
		OE		OE		OE		OE
Sg 1	hebbiu; habbiu	hæbbe	seggiu, -o	seċʒe	hebbie, -ia; habbie	hæbbe	seggie	seċʒe
2	habes, -as	hæfst	sagis	sæʒst	hebbias	hæbbe	--------	seċʒe
3	habed, -ad	hæfþ	sagad	sæʒþ	hebbie, -ea	hæbbe	(bi)seggea	seċʒe
Pl	hebbiad; habbiad	hæbbaþ	seggiad	seċʒaþ	hebbean	hæbben	--------	seċʒen

imperative: 2nd sg habe, saga; plural hebbiad, seggiad. *OE*: hafa, seʒe; habbaþ, seċʒaþ
present participle: hebbiandi, seggiandi. *OE*: hæbbende; seċʒende
gerund: hebbianne, hebbiannes; (gi)seggianne, *seggiannes. *OE*: hæbbenne; seċʒenne

		past						
	indicative				*subjunctive*			
		OE		OE		OE		OE
Sg 1	habda, habda	hæfde	sagda	sæʒde	-----	hadde	-----	-----
2	habdes	hæfdest	sagdas	sæʒdest	-----	hadde	-----	-----
3	habda	hæfde	sagdas	sæʒde	habdi	hadde	sagdi	-----
Pl	habdun	hæfdon	sagdun	sæʒdon	habdin	hadden	sagdin	-----

26.0) Irregular Verbs

26.1) uuesan 'be'; dôn 'do'. *OE*: wesan, bēon; dōn

present

		indicative				subjunctive		
			OE		*OE*		*OE*		*OE*
Sg 1	bium, -n	eom, bēo	dôm, -n, duom	dō	sî	sī	sīe, bēo	dôe, dûa, dûe	dō
2	bist	eart, bist	dôs, duo	dēst	sîs	sīe, bēo	duoas	dō
3	is, ist	is, biþ	dôd, duod, duot	dēþ	sî	sīe, bēo	dôe, dûa, dûe	dō
Pl	sind(un)	sind(on),	dôt, duod, duat,	dōþ	sîn	sīen, bēon	dôan, dûon	dōn
	sindon, sint	bēoþ	dûan, duoian					

imperative: 2nd sg uuis, dô; 2nd pl uuesad, dôt, duad. *OE*: wæs, bēo; dō; wesaþ, bēoþ; dōþ.
present participle: uuesandi; ------; *OE*: wesende; dōende
gerund: uuesanne, uuesannes; duonne, duonnes; *OE*: wesenne; dōenne

past

		indicative				subjunctive		
			OE		*OE*		*OE*		*OE*
Sg 1	uuas	wæs	deda, -e	dyde	uuâri	wǣre	dâdi, dêdi	dyde
2	uuâri	wǣre	dâdi	dydest	uuâris	wǣre	dâdis, dêdis	dyde
3	uuas	wæs	deda, -e	dyde	uuâri	wǣre	dâdi, dêdi	dyde
Pl	uuârun	wǣron	dâdun, dêdun	dydon	uuârin	wǣren	dâdin, dêdin	dyden

past participle: ----; -duan. *OE*: -----, ʒebēon; ʒedōn

26.2) **uuillian** 'to will'

present

		indicative		subjunctive	
			OE		*OE*
Sg 1	uuilliu	wille	uuillie	wille
2	uuilis, uuilt, uuili	wilt	uuillies, -eas	wille
3	uuili, uuil	wile, wille	uuillie, -ea, uuellie	wille
Pl	uuilleat, -iad, -ead	willaþ	uuillean	willen

infinitive: uuillien, uuellian; *OE*: willan
present participle: uuilliandi; *OE*: willende
gerund: ------

A Brief Outline of Old Saxon Grammar

		past			
	indicative		subjunctive		
		OE		OE	
Sg 1	uuelda, -e; uualda; uuolda	wolde	uueldi; uuoldi	-----	
2	uueldeas, -es	woldest	--------	-----	
3	uuelda, -e; uualda; uuolda	wolde	uueldi; uuoldi	-----	
Pl	uueldun; uuoldun	woldon	uueldin	-----	

past participle: ----

Glossary

ALPHABETIZATION AND ORTHOGRAPHY:

In general, words will be listed in alphabetical order as they are found in the accompanying excerpts from the *Hêliand*. When verb forms are encountered which lack a corresponding attestation of the infinitive (the 'dictionary entry form'), that infinitive is listed in its canonical form. Forms which may be difficult for the less-experienced reader are cross-referenced to the dictionary entry form, e.g. the gloss of **huaraƀe** is listed as **huaraƀe : huarf**, which indicates that the primary reference is **huarf**.

a) If the same word is spelled both with **c** and **k**, e.g. **scarp** and **skarp**, the gloss will be given under the form with **k**. Entries of the type **scarp : skarp** refer the former to the latter.

b) Double **u** (**w**) is sometimes spelled **u** and sometimes **uu**. When single **u** is used, words containing the sound **w** can appear among words with **u** that has the value of **u**, e.g. the ordering **suêt, suht, suîð**.

c) Alternate forms with **e** for **a** or **i** are generally listed under **a** or **i**. Thus, for example, alternate forms with **ge-** for **gi-** are generally listed under **gi-**, although if a form with only **ge-** occurs in the readings, it is so listed.

Please note carefully: unstressed (unaccented) **a** can be spelled as **e**, **i** as **e**, and **u** as **o**. If only one variant appears in the readings, then it is listed as such. If, however, variants occur, they are not generally listed separately under different spellings. Beyond the statement at c), note variants like **hêlagna : hêlagne** (for **a : e**); **hêlian : hêlean : hêlien** (for both **i : e** and **a : e**), and **hêlagu : hêlago** (for **u : o**). Moreover, even the **o** from an underlying **u** can further weaken to **e**, as for example in the variant set **hêlagumu : hêlagomu : hêlagemu : hêlagemo : hêlagomo** and even **hêlagamo**. In bisyllabic adjective endings like **-umu** almost any combination is possible.

OTHER CONVENTIONS

1) A colon (:) indicates reference to the form listed behind it.

2) A paragraph mark (§) refers to a section in the accompanying BRIEF GRAMMAR OF OLD SAXON.

3) Not every participle used as an adjective is referred to its infinitive if that infinitive doesn't appear as such. For example, **giblandan** 'mixed' is listed, but its infinitive **blandan** 'mix', which doesn't occur here, is not listed.

4) Abbreviations: **adj** = adjective; **conj** = conjunction; **dem** = demonstrative; **indef** = indefinite; **interj** = interjection; **interrog** = interrogative; **per** = person; **pers name** = personal name; **pret-pres** = preterite-present; **num** = number; **ord** = ordinal; **poss** = possessive; **prep** = preposition; **pron** = pronoun; **A** = accusative; **D** = dative; **G** = genitive; **I** = instrumental; **N** = nominative; **sg** = singular; **pl** = plural; **str** = strong; **wk** = weak; **m** = masculine; **f** = feminine; **n** = neuter.

5) **Nouns** are identified as to gender and stem type, e.g. m-*wa*, as represented in the accompanying BRIEF GRAMMAR OF OLD SAXON. The stem type is left unmarked for *a*-stems. **Adjectives** are marked except for *a*- and *ô*-stems. **Verbs** are marked according to class, as represented in the accompanying BRIEF GRAMMAR OF OLD SAXON. The small-font type following the definition indicates further reference, e.g. **sêolîdandi** *ja*- and *jô*-stem adj - seafaring (men) str vb I, which indicates that this adjective is derived from a strong verb of class I.

6) With the assumption that those learning Old Saxon will start with the first sections, those are more closely glossed as to their individual forms than words in later sections.

Glossary

abad : *abiddian*
abâdin : *abiddian* str vb endings § 24
âband m - evening
aƀaro m *n*-stem - descendant
abiddian str vb V - request, ask for
abolgan adj - furious str vb III
aƀoro : *aƀaro*
Abraham pers name
ac conj - but
accar m - field
âðalandbâri n *ja*-stem - noble appearance
aðalboran adj - noble of birth str vb IV
aðalcnôsal m - noble family
aðalcuning m - king of noble family
aðalcunni n *ja*-stem - noble family
aðali n *ja*-stem - nobility
aðalordfrumo m *n*-stem - chief spear thruster (Cf. Commentary to §1)
Adam personal name
Adaman m A sg : *Adam*
adêldi : *adêlien*
adêlien wk vb I - render (judgement)
adôgen wk vb I - endure
adômian wk vb I - judge

âðom m - spirit
âdro adv - early
âðrum : *ôðar*
Aegypti - Egypt
af : *ef*
afgaf : *afgeƀen*
afgeƀe : *afgeƀen* str vb endings §24.0
afgeƀen str vb V - give up
afgrundi n *ja*-stem - abyss
afhaƀen : *afhebbien*
afhebbien str vb VI - raise; cause
afhôƀi : *afhebbien* §24.0
afhôƀun : *afhebbien* str vb VI
afôdian wk vb I - bear
afonsta : *afunnan*
afsebbian str vb VI - recognize
afsôf : *afsebbian*
afstâd : *afstanden*
afstanden str vb VI - remain
afsteppian str vb VI - step onto
afsuoƀun : *afsebbian*
aftar adv - later; after
aftar prep - according to; after; along; across
after : *aftar*
afunnan [+G] pret-pres vb - begrudge, envy
agâƀun : *ageƀen*
agangan str vb VII - disappear

295

ageƀan str vb V - give over, give up
ageƀe : *ageƀan* §24.0
ageƀen = *ageƀan*
agiƀid : *ageƀan* §2.2 b
aha f *ô*-stem - water
ahastrôm m - water stream
ahebbean str vb VI - raise, begin
ahlîdan str vb I - open up
ahlêd : *ahlîdan*
ahliopun : *ahlôpan*
ahlôpan str vb VII - run up
ahlûdian wk vb I - announce
ahsla f *ô*-stem - shoulder
âhtean [+G] wk vb I - hunt down
âhtean aldres - kill
âhtið : *âhtean*
âhtien : *âhtean*
ahto num - eight
ahton wk vb II - take care of, worry about
ahu : *aha* f *ô*-stem
akkar m - field
al : *all*
alah m - temple
alaiung adj - quite young
alârian wk vb I - empty
alâsun : *alesan*
alât : *alâtan*
alâtan [+G] str vb VII - release

alâte : *alâtan* §24.0
ald adj - old
aldar n - age
aldarlagu n - life
alderu : *ald* adj
aldiro : *ald* adj
aldre : *aldar*
aldron wk vb II - age, become old
aldru : *aldar*
aldun : *ald*
alêðian wk vb I - make oneself hated; spoil
alesan str vb V - gather up
aleskian wk vb I - extinguish
aleskie : *aleskian* §24.0
alettean wk vb I - withdraw
all adj - all
all adv - entirely, completely
alofat n - ale vessel
alomahtig adj - almighty
alôsdi : *alôsian*
alôseas : *alôsian* wk vb I, §25.0
alôsian wk vb I - redeem, remove
alôsid : *alôsian* §25.0
alothioda f *ô*-stem - humanity
alouualdo m *n*-stem - The All-Wielder, Creator
alung adj - eternal
ambahteo m *n*-stem - servant

Glossary

ambahtman m root-stem - servant
ambahtskepi n *i*-stem - service
an [+A/D] prep with various meanings
an giburdeon f *i*-stem - in birth
an halƀa : *half* - on (a) side
anbêt : *anbîtan*
anbiodan str vb II - summon
anbîtan str vb I - eat
anbôd : *anbiodan*
andbâri n *ja*-stem - appearance
ando m n-stem - anger
andôn §26.1 - open
Andreas pers name - Andrew
andrêdan (*andrâdan*) str vb VII - fear, dread
andrêdin : *andrêdan* §25.0
andrêdun : *andrêdan*
anduuard adj - present
anduuordi n *ja*-stem - answer
anduuordian wk vb I - answer
aneƀan [+A] prep - at the border of
angegen [+D/A] prep - towards
angegin adv - again; [+D] prep - toward
anginne n *ja*-stem - beginning
anginni : *anginne*
angul m - hook
Anna pers name
ansiuni n *ja*-stem - facial feature

ansprang : *antspringen*
anst f *i*-stem - favor, grace
ant prep - until
antahtoda num - eighty
antat : *antthat*
antbêt : *antbîtan*
antbindan str vb III - untie
antbîtan : *anbîtan*
antdrêd : *andrêdan*
antdrêdin : *andrêdin*
antfâhan str vb VII - receive
antfâhanne : *antfâhan* §24.0
antfâhen : *antfâhan*
antfallan str vb VII - fall off, shrivel
antfand : *antfindan*
antfel : *antfallan*
antfeng : *antfâhan*
antfengun : *antfâhan*
antfindan str vb III - find, perceive
antfôrian wk vb I - remove
antfunda : *antfindan*
antfundun : *antfindan*
anthaƀad : *anthebbien*
anthabde : *anthebbien*
anthebbien str vb VI - maintain; withstand
antheftid : *antheftien*
antheftien wk vb I - untie
anthêti *ja*- and *jô*-stem adj - devout

anthlîdan str vb I - open up
anthlidun : *anthlîdan*
anthrînan str vb I - touch
anthrên : *anthrînan*
antkennien wk vb I - recognize
antkiendun : *antkennien*
antklemmi : *antklemmian* §25
antklemmian wk vb I - force open
antlêddun : *antlêdean*
antlêdean wk vb I - bring
antlôc : *antlûcan*
antlocan : *antlûcan*
antloken : *antlûcan*
antlûcan str vb II - open up
antluki : *antlûcan* str vb endings §24.0
antsakan str vb VI - resist
antsiƀunta num - seventy
antspringen str vb III - jump up
antstandan str vb VI - endure
antsuok : *antsakan*
antsuôr m / n - answer
anttat : *antthat*
antthat conj - until
antuuarp : *antuuerpan*
antuuerpan str vb III - move
antuuindan str vb III - unwrap
antuundun : *antuuindan*
aquellian wk vb I - kill

araƀedi : *arƀedi*
aram : *arm*
arƀed f *i*-stem - effort; trouble
arƀedi n *ja*-stem - effort; trouble
arƀetsam adj - laborious
arƀidlîco adv - laboriously
arƀid : *arƀed*
Archelâus pers name - Archelaus
ard m *a*-stem - domicile
arês : *arîsan*
arîsan str vb I - arise
arm m - arm
arm adj - poor, humble
armlîc adj, §16.0 - wretched
armôdi n *ja*-stem - poverty
armon wk vb II - become poor, be poverty stric-ken
armscapan adj - miserable
ârundi n *ja*-stem - errand; message
asat : *asittian*
asittian str vb V - sit up
astandan str vb VI - arise; *te astandanne* § 25.0
astuodun : *a*standan
at [+D] prep with various meanings
at adv - at
athengean wk vb I - achieve
athenkean wk vb I - recall
atiohan str vb II - rear; draw

Glossary

atogan : *atiohan* adj
atôh : *atiohan*
atsamna adv - together
atsamne : *atsamna*
atuomian wk vb I - release
auuallan str vb VII - well up
auuardian wk vb I - devastate; harm
auuekkian wk vb I - arouse
auuellun : *auuallan*
auuerðan str vb III - perish
auuerdian : *auuardian*
auuinnan str vb III - acquire
auuirðid : *auuerðan*
auuîsien wk vb I - abstain
auuôstian wk vb I - lay waste

B

bac : undar bac
bað n - bath
bad : *biddian*
bâdun : *biddian*
bâg m - praise
bâggeƀo m *n*-stem - giver of rings, prince
bâguuini m *i*-stem - fellow recipient of rings given by a king
bald adj - brave
baldlîco adv - bravely
balg : *belgan*
balouues : *balu*

balu n *u*-stem - ruin; balefulness
baludâd f *i*-stem - evil deed
baluuuerc n - evil deed, evil event
baluuues : *balu*
bâm n - tree
ban m / n - order
bank f *i*-stem - bench, seat
bano m *n*-stem - murderer
bâra f *ô*-stem - bier
bâri : *beran*
barm m - lap
barn n - child
Barrabas pers name
Bartholomeus pers name - Bartholomew
baruuirðig adj - very worthy
bat adj - better
be : *bi*
bebrâcon : *bebrekan*
bebrekan str vb V - break
bêd : *bîdan*
beda f *ô*-stem - prayer; request
bedan : *bedon*
bêðe : *bêðie*
bedêlian. wk vb I - deprive
bêdian wk vb I - force; *Crist dôðes bêdian* - force the death of Christ
bêðie adj / conj - both

299

bêðiu : *bêðie*
bêðium : *bêðie*
bedon wk vb II - pray
bedriogan str vb II - betray
bedrôg : *bedriogan*
bedrôragad : *bidrôregan*
bedskepi n *i*-stem - marriage
bedu : *beda*
befal : *befelhan*
befelhan str vb III - commend; bury
befilhu : *befelhan*
befulhun : *befelhan*
beforan adv - in front
began : *biginnan*
behabd : *behebbian*
behangan adj - draped str vb VIIa
behebbian wk vb III - surround
behliden : *bihlidan*
behuî interrog pron / adv - why
behuiu : *behuî*
behuuelbean wk vb I - conceal
beiðero : *bêðie*
belgan str vb III - be angry
belôsien wk vb I - rob
belucun : *belûkan*
belûkan str vb II - lock
bemîðan str vb I - avoid
bên n - leg
benam : *biniman*
bendi f *i*-stem - bonds

beneglian wk vb I - nail
beniðiun = *beniuundiun* (?) (Cf. Commentary to §53)
beniuunda f *ô*-stem - baneful wound
benkeon : *bank*
benki : *bank*
benkia : *bank*
beo n *wa*-stem - harvest
beran str vb IV - bear, carry
bereg : *berg*
bereht : *berht*
berehtlîco : *berhtlîco*
berg m - mountain
berht adj - bright
berhtlîco adv - brightly
berôƀon wk vb II - rob
besinkon wk vb II - sink
best adj - best §16.2
besuîcan str vb I - betray
besunki : *besinkan* §24.0
besuuêc : *besuîcan*
betara suppletive adj - better §16.2
betaron : *betara* §15.0
bethiu adv - therefore
Bethleem place name - Bethlehem
Bethlemaburg f root-stem - Stronghold of Bethlehem
beuuarp : *biuuerpan*
beuunden : *biuuindan*

300

Glossary

beuuo : *beo*
bezt : *best*
bezton wk adj : *best*
bi [+D/I/A] prep with various meanings
biƀon wk vb II - quake
biclîƀen str vb I - cleave, stay fast
bicnêgan str vb VII - attain
bîdan str vb I - wait
biddian [+A/G] str vb V - ask [someone] for [something]
biddiende §25.0 - asking, begging
bidelƀan str vb III - bury
bidernien wk vb I - conceal
bidid : *biddian* § 25.0
bîdon wk vb II - wait
bidrôregan = *bidrôriad* (?) *a*- and *ô*-stem adj - bloodied
bidrôrian wk vb I - bloody
bidulƀun : *bidelƀan*
bidun : *bîdan*
bifâhan str vb VII - seize; encompass
bifâhe : *bifâhan* §24.0
bifalah : *bifelhan*
bifallan str vb VII - fall; seize
bifangan : *bifâhan*
bifel : *bifallan*
bifelahan : *befelhan*

bifelhan str vb III - command, commend
bifelhen : *befelhan*
bifellian wk vb I - cast
bifellun : *bifallan*
bifeng : *bifâhan*
bifengi : *bifâhan* §24.0
bifieng : *bifeng*
bifolhen : *bifelhan*
biforan prep / adv - in front (of); before
bifulhun : *bifelhan*
bigan : *biginnan*
bigeten str vb V - meet
biginna : *biginnan* § 24.0
biginnan str vb III - begin
bigraƀan str vb VI - bury
bigrôƀun : *bigraƀan*
bigruoƀon : *bigraƀan*
bigunni : *biginnan* § 24.0
bigunnun : *biginnan*
bihagon wk vb II - please
bihaldan str vb VII - hold; continue
biheld : *bihaldan*
bihelan str vb IV - conceal
bihêt m - threat
bihêtuuord n - threatening word
bihlîdan str vb I - surround
bihlidan : *bihlîdan*
biholan : *bihelan*

301

bihuî : *bihuuî*
bihuuî adv - why
bikonsti : *bikunnan*
bikunnan pret-pres vb - understand
bil n - sword
bilang adj - related
biliði n *ja*-stem - parable
biloken : *belûkan*
bilôsian wk vb I - rob, deprive
bilôsie : *bilôsian* §25.0
binâmin : *biniman*
binden str vb III - tie
biniman str vb IV - seize, deprive
binoman : *biniman*
bioƀan adv - above
biodan str vb II - offer, proffer
birid : *beran*
biscop m - bishop
biscriƀan str vb I - forego
biseggea : *biseggian* § 25.0
biseggian wk vb III - say
bisinkan str vb III - perish
bisittian str vb V - besiege
bismersprâka f *ô*-stem - lampooning
bist § 26.1 - art
bisuêc : *besuîcan*
bîtan str vb I - bite
bitengi *ja*- and *jô*-stem adj - allied

bithekkien wk vb I - cover
bitherƀi *ja*- and *jô*-stem adj - useful
bithîhan [+G] str vb I - accomplish
bithiu : *bethiu*
bithuingan str vb III - attack
biti m *ja*-stem - bite
bittar adj - bitter
bittro adv - bitterly
bium § 26.1 - am
biûtan conj - other than
biuuand : *biuuindan*
biuuarp: *biuuerpan*
biuuerpan str vb III - surround
biuuindan str vb III - wrap
biuundan : *biuuindan*
biuurpun : *biuuerpan*
blêk adj - pale
blîcan str vb I - shine
blîcandi : *blîcan* § 25.0
blicsmo m *n*-stem - lightning
bliði *ja*- and *jô*-stem adj - cheerful, optimistic
bliðlîc adj - cheerful
bliðon wk vb II - cheer up
bliðsea f *ô*-stem - cheer
bliðsean wk vb I - entertain, make happy; *te blið-seanne* § 25.0
blind adj - blind

blîtzea : *blîðsea*
blôð adj - timorous
blôd n - blood
blôdag adj - bloody
blôðora : *blôð* §16.0
blôian wk vb I - bloom
blômo m n-stem - flower
bôc : *bôk*
bôcna : *bôkan*
bôcno : *bôkan*
bôcstaƀo : *bôcstaf*
bôcstaf m - letter
bôd : *biodan*
bodal m - property
bodlo : *bodal*
boðme : *boðom*
bodo m n-stem - messenger
boðom m - bottom
bodskepi n *i*-stem - tidings, message
bôk f root-stem / n - book
bôkan n - sign
bôkne : *bôkan*
bôkspâh adj - learned
bôm m - tree
bômgardo m n-stem - orchard
bômin adj - wooden
bord n - shield
bôsma : *bôsom*
bôsom m - bosom
bôtian wk vb I - repair; heal; redress

bôttin : *bôtian* § 25.0
bôttun : *bôtian*
braht m - din
brâhte : *brengean*
brâhtin : *brengean* § 25.0
brast : *brestan*
brêd adj - broad, wide
brêdian wk vb I - disseminate
brêf m - document
bregdan str vb III - knit
brengean wk vb I - bring
breost : *briost*
breosthugi m *i*-stem - courage
brestan str vb III - burst; [+G] - lack
bringan str vb III - bring
brinnan str vb III - burn
brinnandi : *brinnan* §24.0
brinnu : *brinnan* §24.0
briost n [pl] - breast
briostgithâht f *i*-stem - courage
brôd n - bread
brôðar m *r*-stem - brother
brôder : *brôðar*
brûd f *i*-stem - wife, woman; *te brûdiu* - as a bride
brûdigumo m *n*-stem - husband
brugdun : *bregdan*
brunn(i)o m *n*-stem - source, well

Hêliand

bû n - dwelling
bûan wk vb I - dwell
buggean wk vb I - buy
bûland n - cultivated field
bundun : *binden*
buok : *bôk*
burg f root-stem - stronghold, town
burgliudi m *i*-stem - townspeople (Cf. Commentary to §3)
bûtan conj - except

C

cald adj - cold
can : *kunnan*
cara f *ô*-stem - sorrow, lamentation, grief
caron wk vb II - grieve
cliƀon wk vb II - grow, cling
clioƀan str vb II - split
cluƀun : *clioƀan*
cneo : *knio*
cnôsal n - clan
cnuosle : *cnôsal*
comanne : *kuman*
consta : *kunnan*
côpon wk vb II - purchase
côpstedi f *i*-stem - market site
corn n - grain
côs : *kiosan*
coston wk vb II - tempt
costondi §25.0, adj - temptor
craft m *i*-stem / f *i*-stem - might, power; crowd, mob
craftag adj - mighty
craftig : *craftag*
craftigost §16.0 - mightiest
craht : *craft*
cribbia f *ô*-stem / f *n*-stem - manger
Crist pers name - Christ
crûci n *ja*-stem - cross
crûd n - weed
cûð adj - known
cûðean wk vb I - make known
cuma : *cuman* §24.0
cuman str vb IV - come
cumbal n - sign
cumbl : *cumbal*
cûmian wk vb I - mourn
cume : *cuma*
cumi m *i*-stem pl - arrival, coming
cuning m - king
cuningsterro m *n*-stem - royal star
cuninguuîsa f *ô*-stem - in a manner suitable in the presence of a ruler
cunni n *ja*-stem - kin, clan
cunnun : *kunnan*
cuolon wk vb II - cool
cûsco adv - proper, decent

Glossary

cussian wk vb I - kiss
cust f *u*-stem - choice

D

dâd f *i*-stem - deed
dâdun : *dôn*
dag m - day
daguuerk n - day's work
dal n - valley, abyss
darno adv - secretly
darnungo adv - secretly, cunningly
Dauid pers name - David
deda : *dôn*
dedi : *dôn* §25.0
dedin : *dôn* §25.0
dedos : *dôn*
dêl m - part
dêlien wk vb I - part; divide, share
derƀi *ja*- and *jô*-stem adj - evil, coarse
dereƀi : *derƀi*
derni *ja*- and *jô*-stem adj - hidden, evil
dernian wk vb I - conceal
diap adj - deep
diapo adv - deeply
diopgithâht f *i*-stem - deep thought
disk m - table
diuƀal m - devil

diurða : *diuriða*
diuri *ja*- and *jô*-stem adj - precious
diuriða f *ô*-stem - glory, honor
diurian wk vb I - glorify, honor
diurie : *diurian* §25.0
diurlîc adj - precious; praiseworthy
diurlîco adv - preciously; illustriously
dô : *dôn* §26.1
dôan : *dôn* / *dôian*
dôđ : *dôð*
dôð m - death
dôd adj - dead
dôg : *dugan*
dohtar f *r*-stem - daughter
dôian wk vb I - die
dôie : *dôian* §25.0
dol adj - foolish
dôm : *dôn*
dôm m - judgment
dôn §26.1 - do
dôperi m *ja*-stem - baptist
dôpisli n *ja*-stem - baptism
dôpian wk vb I - baptize
dôpte : *dôpian*
dor n - gateway
dôs : *dôn*
dôt : *dôn*

Hêliand

dragan str vb VI - bring, take, present, carry
dranc : *drincan*
drêf : *drîban*
drîban str vb I - engage in, carry out; drive (out)
dribun : *drîban*
drincan str vb III - drink
driopan str vb II - drip
driosan str vb II - fall
drôbi *ja-* and *jô-*stem adj - depressed, saddened
drôbian wk vb I - become depressed
drôg : *dragan*
drôgin : *dragan* §24.0
drôgun : *dragan*
drohtin m - lord, leader
drôm m - dream; tumult, din
drômean wk vb I - dream; clamor
drôp : *driopan*
drôr m - blood from wounds
drôreg adj - bleeding
drugithing n - deceit
druhtfolc n - retinue
druhting m - member of a retinue
druhtskepi m *ja-*stem - retinue
druknian wk vb I - dry off
druncan : *drincan*
drunkun : *drincan*

druobost : *drôbi* §16.0
druog : *dragan*
duan : *dôn*
duat : *dôn*
dûba f *ô-*stem - dove
dugan pret-pres vb - suffice, be good enough
dugi : *dugan* §24.0
dugun : *dugan*
duncar adj - dark
dunide : *dunnian* § 2.4 b
dunnian wk vb I - make a din
duod : *dôn*
duom : *dôm, dôn*
duomdag m - day of judgment
duot : *dôn*
duru [Holthausen § 300] - door
duualm m - enchantment

E

Ebreo [G pl] - Hebrew
ecid n - vinegar
êcso m *n-*stem - owner
eð m - oath
eder m - fence
eðili adj - noble
eðiligiburd f *i-*stem - noble origin, descent
êdstaf m - 'oathstave' (Cf. Commentary to §18)
eðuuord n - words of oaths
ef conj - if

306

Glossary

efno adv - equally
eft adv - again; on the other hand; in return
eftha : *eftho*
eftho conj - or; *eftho ... eftho* conj - either ... or
êgan n - property
êgan adj - own
êgan pret-pres vb - own, have
eggia f *ô*-stem - edge, sword
êgi : *êgan* §24.0
êgin : *êgan* §24.0
egislîc adj - horrible
egiso m *n*-stem - horror, terror
êgun : *êgan*
Egypti place name - Egypt
êhta : *êgan*
êhti : *êgan* § 25.0
êhtun : *êgan*
ehuscalc m - stableboy
elcor adv - otherwise,
êld m / n - fire
eldi m *i*-stem - people
eldia f *ô*-stem - age
eldibarn n - children of men
Elias pers name - Elijah
elilendi *ja*- and *jô*-stem adj - foreign
elitheoda f *ô*-stem - foreign people; heathens
elithioda : *elitheoda*
elleandâd f *i*-stem - deed of strength

elleanrôf adj - famed for strength
elleanruoƀa : *elleanrôf*
en = *endi* conj - and
ên num - one, a certain
ênag adj - only
ênan m N pl wk adj - alone
êndago m *n*-stem - last day; day of one's death
endi m *ja*-stem - end, goal; beginning
endi conj - and
endion wk vb II - end
endon : *endion*
ênfald adj - sole; true, genuine
engi *ja*- and *jô*-stem adj - narrow
engil m - angel
engira : *engi* §16.0
ênhuuilic indef pron - anyone
ênig indef pron - any
êno wk adj - alone
ênôdi f *u*-stem (?) / n *ja*-stem - desert
enstio : *anst*
ênuald : *ênfald*
eo = *io*
êo m *wa*-stem - law; *ald êo* - Old Testament
eoridfolc n - cavalry
eouuiht indef pron - something
êr m *i*-stem - messenger
êr adv - prior; earlier

Hêliand

êr (than) conj - before
êra f ô-stem - esteem, respect; help; protection; honor
erbi n ja-stem - inheritance
erbiuuard m - heir, guardian of the inheritance
erða f ô-stem / f n-stem - earth
erðbûandi m ja-stem - earthly man
erðgraf n - earthen grave
erðgrabe : *erðgraf*
erðlîbigiscapu n - earthly fate
êri : *êr*
êrist adv / ord num - first
erl m - earl, man
Erodes pers name - Herod
Erodesan m A sg : *Erodes*
êron : *êra*
êron wk vb II - give a present
êrthungan adj - rich in honors
str vb III
ettha : *eftho*
ettho : *eftho*
eu : *iu*
êu : *êo*
Êua pers name - *Eve*
Êuan : *Êua*
êuangelium m - gospel
êuu : *êo*
euua poss adj - your
êuuandag m - eternity
euuar : *gî* 2nd per pron

êuua : *êo*
êuuan adj - eternal
euues : *euua*
êuuig adj - eternal
êuuin adj - eternal
Êva pers name - Eve

F

fadar m r-stem - father
faderôdil m - paternal inheritance; father's home
faði n ja-stem - walking; *an faðiun* - by foot
faðmos m - outstretched arms
fagar adj - fair, peaceful
fagonon wk vb II - rejoice
fagoro : *fagar* §16.0
fagorost : *fagar* §16.0
fâhan str vb VIIa - catch; [+G] take; [reflexive] make for oneself
fâhat : *fâhan*
fâhit : *fâhan*
faho wa- and wô-stem - little, few; *fahora sum* - a certain one of the few
fahs n - hair
fakla f n-stem - torch
fallan str vb VIIa - fall
fan [+D] prep - from
fand : *findan*
fandon wk vb II - pursue
fano m n-stem - cloth

Glossary

Fanuel pers name
far [+D/A] prep - in front of; for; because of
faran str vb VI - fare, go
farcôpon wk vb II - sell
farcuman adj - past str vb IV
fard f *i*-stem - going; trip
farduan adj - depraved, sinful
farfâhan str vb VII - catch, snare
farfeng : *farfâhan*
farfengin : *farfâhan* §24.0
farfion wk vb II - consume
fargâbi : *fargeban*
fargaf : *fargeben*
fargangan adj - past str vb VII
fargâtun : *fargetan*
fargeban str vb V - give
fargelden str vb III - pay
fargetan str vb V - forget
fargibid : *fargeban*
fargibu : *fargeban*
fargoldan : *fargeldan*
fargûmon wk vb II - neglect
farhardon wk vb II - harden
farhauuan str vb VIId - cut off
farhelan str vb IV - conceal
farhuerbian wk vb I - twist; dispoil
farhuggian wk vb I - despise, scorn

farlâtan str vb VIIb - leave, give up, avoid
farlêbian wk vb I - leave over, leave behind
farlêdean wk vb I - lead astray
farlêti : *farlâtan* §24.0
farlêtin : *farlâtan* §24.0
farlêtun : *farlâtan*
farlieti : *farlâtan* §24.0
farliosan str vb II - lose
farlîhan str vb I - give
farliuuan : *farlîhan*
farlôgnien [+G] wk vb I - deny
farlor m - ruin
farloren : *farliosan*
farlust f *i*-stem - ruin, death
farm m - onslaught, onrush, assault
farmerrian wk vb I - miss
farmunan pret-pres vb - scorn, deny
farmuonstun : *farmunan*
farnam : *farniman*
farniman str vb IV - destroy
farsehan str vb V - see
farsihit : *farsehan*
farspanan str vb VI - entice
farstandan str vb VI - understand; hinder
farstôdi : *farstandan* §24.0
farstuod: *farstandan*
fartald : *fartellian*

Hêliand

fartellian wk vb I - condemn
farterian wk vb I - destroy
fârungo adv - suddenly
farûtar [+A] prep - without
faruuardon wk vb II - govern
faruuarht : *farwirkian* adj - abandoned
faruuerkon wk vb II - sin against
faruuerpan str vb III - reject
faruuirkian wk vb I -sin against
faruuorpen : *faruuerpan*
fast adj - firm
fastnon wk vb II - fasten, bind; strengthen
fasto adv - firmly
fastunnia f ô-stem - fasting
fat n - vessel
feðarhamo m *n*-stem - feathershirt
fêgnes : *fêkan*
fêh adj - colorful
fehogiri f *i*-stem - greed
fehoscat n - goldpiece
fehta f *o*-stem - strife, fight
fehu n *u*-stem - cattle, livestock; property
fêkan n - cunning, malice
fêkni *ja*- and *jô*-stem adj - cunning
fel n - skin
feld n - field

feldin : *fellian*
felgian wk vb I - inflict, perpetrate
felis m - rock
fell : *fallan*
fellian wk vb I - throw off
fellie : *fellian* §25.0
fellun : *fallan*
fêmea f n-stem - woman
feng : *fâhan*
fer adj - distant, far
fer adv - far
fera : *ferah*
ferah n - life, spirit
ferahquâla f ô-stem - torture, death
feraht adj - devout, wise
fercal m / n - bolt
ferdi : *fard*
fergon wk vb II - request, demand
ferh : *ferah*
ferian wk vb I - ferry
ferid : *faran*
fern n - inferno, hell
fern adj - previous
ferr : *fer* adv
ferran adv - from afar
ferrist : *fer* adj
feteros n - fetters
fîbi : *fíf*

Glossary

fîðan : *findan* (Cf. Commentary to §6.)
fîf num - five
fîfto ord num - fifth
figa f n-stem - fig
fillian wk vb I - strike
filu adv - much, very
filuuuîs adj - very wise, experienced
findan str vb III - find
fingär m - finger
finistar n - darkness
finistri f i-stem [Holthausen § 293 A 2] - darkness
fîond m *nd*-stem - enemy
fîondscipi m i-stem - enmity
fior num - four
fiorðe ord num - fourth
fiori : *fior*
fiortig num - forty
firihos m [pl] - people
firina f ô-stem - sin
firindâd f i-stem - outrage, crime
firinquâla f ô-stem - torture
firinsprâka f ô-stem - slander, invective
firinun adv - very (much)
firinuuerk n - sin, crime
firinuuord n - slander, invective
firio : *firihos*
firiuuit n *ja*-stem - curiousity

firiuuitlîco adv - curiously
fisc m - fish
fiscari m *ja*-stem - fisher
fiscon wk vb II - fish
fisk : *fisc*
fiterios : *feteros*
fîund m *nd*-stem - enemy
fîundscepi m *ja*-stem - enmity
fiur n - fire
fiuuariun : *fiuuuar*
fiuuartig num - forty
fiuuuar num - four
flêsk n - flesh
flet n *ja*-stem - flat
flet(ti) : *flet*
flioten str vb II - flow
fliutid : *flioten*
flôd m / f *u*-stem - flood
flôt : *flioten*
fôdian wk vb I - bear, nourish
fôdie : *fôdian* §25.0
fôði : *fâði*
fol : *ful*
folc n - people, folk; group
folccuning m - king
folcskepi n i-stem - people
folctogo m *n*-stem - duke
folcuuer m - fellow countryman
folda f ô-stem / f *n*-stem - earth
folgan : *folgon*
folgodin : *folgan* §25.0

311

Hêliand

folgon wk vb II - follow
folk : *folc*
folmos m - hands
fon : *fan*
for : *far*
fôr : *faran*
fora : *far*
forabodo m *n*-stem - forerunner, herald
foran adv - in front of
forana adv - from in front
forasago m *n*-stem - oracle, prophet
forð adv - forth
forduolon : *forduuelan*
forðuuardes adv - forward; further
forðuueg m - the path leading away
forduuelan str vb IV - miss
foren : *foran*
forgaf : *fargeƀan*
forgang m - death
forgâti : *fargetan* §24.0
forgeƀan : *fargeƀan*
forgripan adj - damned str vb I
forht adj - in fear
forhta f *ô*-stem - fear
forhti : *forhtian* §25.0
forhtian wk vb I - fear
forhtlîk adj - fearsom, terrible
forhtlîcost : *forhtlîk* §16.0

forhugi : *farhuggian* §25.0
fôri : *faran* §24.0
fôrian wk vb I - carry
fôrin : *faran* §24.0
forlâtan : *farlâtan*
forlêdda : *farlêdean*
forlêt : *farlâtan*
forlêti : *farlâtan* §24.0
forlêtun : *farlâtan*
forliuuan : *farlîhan*
forlôgnide : *farlôgnien*
formo m wk adj - the first; *formon wordu* [I] - the word of the Leader; *an thene formon sîð* - the first time
formon wk vb II - help; protect
forn adv - formerly
fornam : *farneman*
forslîtan str vb I - tear, rend
forsliten : *forslîtan*
forstandan : *farstandan*
forstôd : *farstandan*
forsuuerian str vb VI - swear falsely
forsuerie : *forsuuerian* §24.0
forthuuerdes : *forðuuardes*
fôrun : *faran*
forûtar : *farûtar*
fôt m root-stem - foot
fôtscamel m - footstool
fragn : *fregnan*

Glossary

frâgoda : *frâgon*
frâgoian : *frâgon*
frâgon wk vb II - ask
frâho m *n*-stem - lord
frânisco adv - gloriously
frâo : *frâho*
frataha f *ô*-stem - jewelry
fratoho : *frataha*
fregnan str vb V - ask
fremiði *ja*- and *jô*-stem adj - foreign
fremidun : *fremmian*
fremis : *fremmian*
fremmian wk vb I - carry out
frêson [+G] wk vb II - tempt; waylay
frî n - woman
frîdhoƀe : *frîdhof* §2.3
frîdhof m - forecourt
friðu m *u*-stem - protection, security
friðubarn n - Child of Security; (Cf. Commentary to §10.)
friðusamo adv - peacefully
friðuuîh m - temple
friund m *nd*-stem - kinsman; friend
friundskepi m *i*-stem - friendship
frô : *frâho*
frôƀra f *ô*-stem - help, comfort
frôd adj - wise; old

frôen : *frâho*
frôfra : *frôƀra*
frôfre : *frôƀra*
frôhan : *frâho*
frôkno adv - boldly
frômôd adj - cheerful
frugnun : *fregnan*
fruht m *i*-stem - fruit
fruma f *ô*-stem - advantage, use
frumi : *frummian*
frumid : *frummian*
frumidon : *frummian*
frummead : *frummian*
frummian wk vb I - further; carry out
frumon : *fruma*
fruocno : *frôkno*
fruod : *frôd*
fugal m - bird
fugles : *fugal*
fuglos : *fugal*
fuglun : *fugal*
ful n - filling of the cup
ful adj - full
fulgangan str vb VIIa - obey, follow
fulgengun : *fulgangan*
fulle : *ful*
fullêsti m *ja*-stem - help, support
fullien wk vb I - fill, fulfill

fullisti : *fullêsti*
fullon wk vb II - fulfill
fundi : *findan* §24.0
fundun : *findan*
fuot : *fôt*
fur : *far*
furðor adv - farther; further
furður : *furðor*
furi [+D/A/I] prep - before; *furi thiu* - therefore
furi adv - previously
furisto m *n*-stem - the first, the highest
furndagos m - days gone by
fûs adj - eager, ready
fûsid adj - urged, forced wk vb I; *ôðar uuas fûsid an forðwegos* - the one was forced onto the path away

G

gâbi : *geban* §24.0
Gabriel pers name - Gabriel
gadoling : *gaduling*
gaduling m - close relative
gaf : *geban*
galgo m *n*-stem - gallows
Galilea f *ô*-stem - Galilee
Galilealand n - Galilee
galilêisk adj - Galilean
Galileo land = Galilealand

galla f *ô*-stem - gall
galm m - loud voice, yelling
gaman n - joy, celebration
gambra f *ô*-stem - tax, outlay
gang m - path, way; course
gangan str vb VIIa - go, walk
gard m - field; dwelling place
gardo m - garden
garo adv - fully
garu *wa*- and *wô*-stem - ready, prepared
garuuuian wk vb I - make ready, prepare
gast m *i*-stem - guest
gastiun : *gast*
gastseli m *i*-stem - guest hall
gat n - hole
ge 2nd per pron - you
ge conj = *giu*
geba f *ô*-stem - gift
geban m - ocean
geban str vb V - give
gebon wk vb II - give, present with
gebârean wk vb I - behave
gebâri : *giberan*
gebeodan : *gibiodan*
geberan str vb IV - bear
gebîdan str vb I - expect
gebiddien str vb V - invite
gebinden str vb III - bind, fetter

gebirgi n *ja*-stem - mountain
gebiudid : *gibiodan*
gebiudu : *gibiodan*
geblôid : *blôian* §25.0
gebod : *gibod*
gebôd : *gibiodan*
gebôknian wk vb I - show
geboran adj - born str vb IV
gebôtean : *gibôtian*
gebrac n - throng
gebrôðar m *r*-stem - brethern
gebundan : *gibindan*
geburd : *giburd*
gecoran adj - chosen str vb II
gecôs : *gikiosan*
gecûðian wk vb I - make known
gecurun : *gikiosan*
gedâd f *i*-stem - deed
gedranc : *gedrinkan*
gedregid : *gidragan*
gedrinkan str vb III - drink
gef : *geƀan*
gefastnod : *gifastnod*
gefôri : *gifôri*
gefragn : *gifregnan*
gefratohot *a*- and *o*-stem adj - decorated
gefrummian : *gifrummian*
gegariuui n *ja*-stem - adornment
gegariuui : *garuuuian* §25.0

gegariuuit : *garuuuian*
geginuuard adj - opposite, present, face-to-face
geginuuarð : *geginuuard*
gegnungo adv - clearly, in truth; directly
geha : *gehan* §24.0
gehaldan str vb VIIa - keep, hold
gehalon wk vb II - reach, achieve
gehan [+G] str vb V - affirm
gehêlean wk vb I - heal
gehêli : *gehêlean* §25.0
gehêt : *gihêtan*
gehêtun : *gihêtan*
gehôrien : *gihôrian*
gehue : *gihue*
gehues : *gihue*
gehuggean wk vb I - think up; bear in mind; consider
gehuilic indef pron - every, each
gehuilik : *gehuilic*
gehungrean wk vb I - hunger
gehuuem : *gihue*
gehuuilicas : *gehuilic*
gehuuilico : *gehuilic*
gêl adj - boisterous
gelâten adj - devoted str vb VIIb; *biûten te themu ênagun sunie al gelâten uuunnea endi uuillean* -

Hêliand

other than that all joy and energy [were] devoted to the one son.
devoted to the one son
geld n - reward; payment; sacrifice
geldan str vb III - reward; pay, repay
gêlhert adj - rowdy
gelîc : *gilîc*
gelîk : *gilîc*
gêlmôdig adj - unruly
gelôbian wk vb I - believe
gelôbo m *n*-stem - belief
gelouuo : *gelu*
gelp m - scorn
gelpquidi m *i*-stem - hubris, arrogance
gelu *wa*- and *wô*-stem - yellow
gemaco : gimaco
gemahlit : *gimahlian*
gemang : *gimang*
gemarcod : *gimarcon*
genâdig adj - merciful
genemnian wk vb I name
generid : *ginerian*
geng : *gangan*
gengin : *gangan* §24.0
gengun : *gangan*
geniudon wk vb II - enjoy
genôg : *ginôg*
genouuer adv - there

geoponot : *oponon*
gequeðan str vb V - tell
gêr m - spear
gêr n - year
gêrfiund m *nd*-stem - spear foe, enemy
gêrheti m *i*-stem - spear hate, mortal enmity
geriedi : *girâdan*
gerihtian wk vb I - reveal
gerîpod adj - ripened wk vb II
geriuuide : *garuuuian*
gern adj - eager
gerno adv - eagerly, willingly
geron wk vb II - desire
gêrtal n - year
gerûni n *ja*-stem - secret
gesagda : *giseggian*
gesah : *gisehan*
gesamnod : *gisamnon*
gescôp : *giskeppian*
gescriban : *giscrîban*
gesehan : *gisehan*
gesehas : *gisehan*
gesîði : *gisîði*
gesidli n *ja*-stem - dwelling place
gesîðos : *gisîð*
gesîðskepi m *i*-stem - retinue
gesittien : *gisittian*
gesiun n - face; appearance
geskêđ : *giskêđ*

geskerid : *giscerian*
gespôn : *gispanan*
gesprac : *gisprekan*
gesprak : *gisprekan*
gesprâkun : *gisprekan*
gesprecan : *gisprekan*
gêst m - spirit
gestanden : *gistandan*
gesteo : *gast*
gesti : *gast*
gestiun : *gast*
gêstlîc adj - spiritual, sacred
gestriuni n *ja*-stem - treasure
gestseli : *gastseli*
geswerian str vb VI - swear
gesuester f *r*-stem [Holthausen § 319] - sisters
gesuîkid : *gisuîkan*
gesund adj - healthy, uninjured
gesunfader m *r*-stem - son and father
gesuôr : *geswerian*
getald : *gitellien*
gethiged : *gethiggian*
gethiggian wk vb I - accept
gethîhan : *githîhan*
gethingod : *githingon*
gethologean : *githoloian*
gethring n - throng
gethuing n - distress
gethuuing : *gethuing*

getimbrod adj - built, timbered wk vb II
getiunean wk vb I - damage
geuuâdi : *giuuâdi*
geuuald : *giuuald*
geuuarht : *giuuirkian*
geuueld : *giuualdan*
geuuîhid : *giuuîhian*
geuuin n - strife; turbulence
geuuirkean : *giuuirkian*
geuuîsean : *giuuîsian*
geuuit n *ja*-stem - wisdom, understanding
geuuitscepi n *i*-stem - witness
geuunnan : *giuuinnan*
geuunst m - tribute; earnings, profit
geuureðien wk vb I - support
geuurht f *i*-stem - (evil) deed
gi : *g*iu
gi 2nd per pron - you
gia : *g*iu
giac = gi + ac conj - and
gialdrod : *aldron*
giâmar adj - sad
giâmarlîc adj - lamentable
giarmod : *armon*
gibâri n *ja*-stem - appearance, behavior
gibâri : *giberan* §24.0
gibârian wk vb I - behave

gibeddeo m *n*-stem - bed companion

gibenkeo m *n*-stem - bench companion

giberan str vb IV - bear (a child)

gibid : *geban*

gibiðig adj - given, bestowed upon

gibindan str vb III - bind, tie

gibiodan str vb II - command, order; be necessary

giblandan adj - mixed str vb VII

giblôðit adj - disheartened, intimidated

gibôd n - commandment

gibôd : *gibiodan*

gibodscip : *gibodskepi*

gibodskepi n *i*-stem - commandment, teaching

giboht : *buggean*

gibôknian wk vb I - show, indicate

gibolgan : *belgan*

giboran adj - born str vb IV

gibôtian wk vb I - heal, redeem

gibrâhti : *gibrengian* §25.0

gibrengian wk vb I - bring

gibrôcan adj - fastened, nailed

gibrôðar m r-stem - brothers

gibu : *geban*

gibunden : *gibindan*

gibuotian : *gibôtian*

giburd m *ja*-stem/ f *i*-stem [Holthausen § 299] - birth

gicoran : *gikiosan*

gicôs : *gikiosan*

gicoston wk vb II - enjoy thoroughly

gicûðian wk vb I - make known

gicûðdin : *gicûðian* §25.0

gidago adv - daily

gidar : *gidurran*

gideda : *gidôn*

gidêl n - part, share

gidêli n *ja*-stem - part, share

gidiurian wk vb I - glorify

gidôen : *gidôn*

gidôn § 26.1 - do, have done

gidôpean wk vb I - baptize

gidorsta : *gidurran*

gidorste : *gidurran*

gidorstun : *gidurran*

gidragan str vb VI - carry, bring; give birth

gidrog n - optical illusion

gidrôg : *gidragan*

gidroge : *gidragan* §24.0

gidrôgi : *gidragan* §24.0

gidrusnod adj - weakened wk vb II

giduan : *gidôn*

giduo : *gidôn*

Glossary

giduod : *gidôn*
gidurran pret-pres vb - dare
gie conj: *gie ... gie* - both ... and
gifâhan str vb VIIa - catch; fasten
gifaran : *faran*
gifaren str vb VI - travel
gifastnod adj - strengthened, fastened wk vb II
gifehod adj - endowed wk vb II
gifôdit adj - born wk vb I
gifôlien wk vb I - notice, observe
gifôri n *ja*-stem - advantage, use
giformon wk vb II - help
gifragn : *gifregnan*
gifrang : *gifregnan*
gifregnan str vb III - find out (about)
gifremidi : *gifremmian*
gifremmian wk vb I - accomplish
gifrôdod adj - wise; experienced; old wk vb II
gifrôdot : *gifrôdod*
gifrumid : *gifrummian*
gifrumida : *gifrummian*
gifrummian wk vb I - do, act, carry out
gifullid adj - fulfilled wk vb I
gifuogid adj - fitted together wk vb I

gifuolda : *gifôlien*
gifuolian : *gifôlien*
gigado m *n*-stem - match, equal
gigamalod adj - aged wk vb II
gigangan str vb VIIa - go
gigeng : *gigangan*
gigirnan wk vb I - succeed, achieve
gihauuuan str vb VIId - hew, strike
giheftian wk vb I - bind, fetter
gihêlian wk vb I - save; still [hunger]
gihelpan str vb III - help
giherdid : *herdian*
gihêrod adj - noble wk vb II
gihêt : *gihêtan*
gihêtan str vb VIIc - promise; order
giheu : *gihauuuan*
gihîuuian wk vb I - marry
gihnêg : *gihnîgan*
gihnêgian wk vb I - bow
gihnîgan str vb I - bow down
gihôrda : *gihôrien* §25.0
gihôrdun : *gihôrien* §25.0
gihôrien wk vb I - hear, listen to
gihôrig adj - obedient
gihrênon wk vb II - cleanse, purify
gihue indef pron - each
gihuem : *gihue*

Hêliand

gihuerebian wk vb I - roll aside
gihugde : *huggien*
gihuilic : *gehuilic*
gihuilikes : *gehuilic*
gihuue : *gihue*
gihuuem : *gihue*
gihuuilic : *gehuilic*
gihuuorban : *huuerban*
gikiosan str vb II - choose, select
gikoran : *gikiosan*
gikund n - good earth
gilag : *giliggian*
gilagu n [pl] - fate
gilêbod adj - lamed wk vb II
gilêstean wk vb I - do, carry out, accomplish
gilêsti n *ja*-stem - deed
gilêsto : gilêsti
gilîc adj - like, of the same kind
gilîcnissi n *ja*-stem / f *i-stem* - form, image
giliðen : *lîðan*
giliggian str vb V - lie
gilôbo : *gelôbo*
gilustian wk vb I - long for
gimaco m *n*-stem - match, equal
gimacon wk vb II - make, achieve
gimahalda : *gimahlian*

gimahlian wk vb I - speak
gimâlda : *gimahlian*
gimâlod adj - marked wk vb II
gimang n - crowd, group; *an gimang* - in crowds, thickly
gimanon wk vb II - remind; admonish
gimarcon wk vb II - determine; choose; appoint
gimârid : *mârian*
gimêd adj - foolish
gimôdi n *ja*-stem - reconciliation
ginâðig : *genâdig*
ginâhid adj - nigh, cf. nâhian
ginerian wk vb I - save, liberate
ginesan str vb V - be saved
ginist f *i*-stem - salvation
ginôg adj - enough, in abundance
gio : *io*
giôcan : *ôcan*
giopanod : *oponon*
giouuiht : *iouuiht*
girâdan str vb VIIb - provide; further
giriuuan : *garuuuian*
girôbi n *ja*-stem - clothing
girûni n *ja*-stem - secret, mystery
gisâhin : *gisehan* str vb endings §24.0

320

Glossary

gisâhun : *gisehan*
gisald : *gisellian*
gisamnon wk vb II - gather, collect
gisat : *gisittian*
gisâun : *gisehan*
gisâuuin : *gisehan* §24.0
giscapu n [pl] - fates
giscerian wk vb I - allot, apportion
giscînan str vb I - shine
giscôp : *giskeppian*
giscrîban str vb I - write
giscriban : *giscrîban*
giscuohi n *ja*-stem - shoes
giscuop : *giskeppian*
gisêgid : *sêgian*
giseggian wk vb III - tell, announce
gisehan str vb V - see; look at; observe
gisellian wk vb I - give, hand over
gisendid : *sendian*
gisêrian wk vb I - disable; injure
gisetta : *gisettian*
gisettian wk vb I - set, bring
gisettun : *gisettian*
giseuuan : *gisehan*
gisîð m - companion
gisîði n *ja*-stem - crowd; companions

gisihu : *gisehan*
gisittian str vb V - sit (down), settle
gisiuni n *ja*-stem - vision
giskêđ n *ja*-stem - information, decision; *witan/ kunnan giskêđ* [+G] - know about [something]
giskeppian str vb VI - create
gislekit : *slekkian*
gispanan str vb VI - urge on
gisprac : *gisprekan*
gisprak : *gisprekan*
gisprekan str vb IV - speak, tell, say
gisprikis : *gisprekan*
gistande : *gistandan* §24.0
gistandan str vb VI - stand firm; occur; be granted; redound
gistellit : *stellian*
gistôd : *gistandan*
gistriunid adj - adorned wk vb I
gistuod : *gistandan*
gisuêk : *giswîkan*
gisuercan str vb III - darken
gisuerkan : *gisuercan*
gisustruonion : *gisuuestar*
gisuuestar f *r*-stem - sisters
gisuuîkan str vb I - forsake; [+G] betray [a trust]
git 2nd per pron - you two

gital n - number
gitald : *gitellien*
gitellien wk vb I - count, reckon; say, tell
githâht f *i*-stem - thought; belief
githenkien wk vb I - think; prepare oneself
githigan : *githîhan*
githîhan str vb I - thrive, grow
githingodin : *githingon* § 25.0
githingon wk vb II - stipulate, determine (a price)
githionon wk vb II - serve; earn
githoloian wk vb I - suffer, endure
githrusmod adj - darkened, mirky wk vb II
githuld f *i*-stem - patience
githungan adj - excellent str vb III
gitiohan str vb II - pull up
gitôh : *gitiohan*
gitrûon wk vb II - believe, trust
gituîflean wk vb I - doubt
giu conj - and
giu : *io*
Giudio : *Iudeo*
giungaro m *n*-stem - disciple
giuuâdi n *ja*-stem - clothing
giuuahsan : *uuahsan*

giuuald f *i*-stem - power; dominion; realm
giuualdan str vb VIIa - have power over
giuuand n - turning point, end; rebuttal, doubt
giuuâpni n *ja*-stem - armor
giuuar adj - aware
giuuaragean wk vb I - punish
giuuaraht : *giuuirkian*
giuuard : *giuuerðan*
giuuardon [reflexive] wk vb II - take care of, watch over [oneself]
giuuarht : *giuuirkian*
giuuâron wk vb II - prove to be true
giuuêdie : *giuuâdi*
giuueld : *giuualdan*
giuueldun : *giuualdan*
giuuer n - insurrection
giuuerc n - act, effort
giuuercon wk vb II - do, accomplish
giuuerðan str vb III - occur, happen
giuuerk : *giuuerc*
giuuêt : *giuuîtan*
giuuîhian wk vb I - bless, hallow
giuuin n - battle, strife
giuuinnan str vb III - gain through struggle, achieve

giuuirkian wk vb I - do, make; bring about; achieve

giuuirkie : *giuuirkian* §25.0

giuuîsian wk vb I - show; teach; announce

giuuit n - wit, intelligence; understanding

giuuîtan str vb I - go, proceed [generally reflexive with *im*]

giuuitti : *giuuit*

giuuittig adj - wise

giuuitun : *giuuîtan*

giuulenkid adj - emboldened wk vb I

giuunnan : *giuuinnan*

giuuorðen : *giuuerðan*

giuurêt : *giuurîtan*

giuuritan : *giuurîtan*

giuurîtan str vb I - write

gladmôd adj - cheerful

gladmôdi *ja*- and *jô*-stem adj - cheerful

glau *wa*- and *wô*-stem - wise

glauu : *glau*

glîmo m *n*-stem - gleam

glîtan str vb I - glisten, shine

god m - God

gôd adj - good

godcund adj - divine

godcundi f *i*-abstract - divinity

gôdlic : *gôdlîc*

gôdlîc adj - good, goodly, magnificent

godouuebbi n *ja*-stem - precious cloth

godspell n - gospel

gôdsprâki *ja*- and *jô*-stem adj - well-spoken, eloquent

gôduuillig adj - devout, of good intention

gold n - gold

goldfat n - golden vessel

gôma f *ô*-stem - banquet

gômean wk vb I - watch out for, take care of; entertain

gomo : *gumo*

gornon wk vb II - mourn

gornundi : *gornon*

gornuuord n - lament

graƀe : *graf*

graƀu : *graf*

grâdag adj - greedy

graf n - grave

gram adj - hostile

gramhugdig adj - hostile, with hostile intent

gramo m *n*-stem - devil, evil spirit

grâtan str vb VIIb - weep

greot n - gravel, sand

griat : *grâtan*

griet : *greot*

grim adj - wrathful, grim, evil

Hêliand

grimman str vb III - rage
griolîco adv - horribly
grîpan str vb I - grasp, touch
gripun : *grîpan*
gristgrimmo m *n*-stem - grinding fury
grôni *ja*- and *jô*-stem adj - green
grôt adj - great
grôtean wk vb I - greet
grôtta : *grôtean*
grund m - bottom
gruotian : *grôtean*
guldin adj - golden
guldun : *geldan*
gumcunni n ja-stem - noble kin
gumo m n-stem - man
gumscepi n *i*-stem - crowd, people
guod : *gôd*
guodlîcost : *gôdlic* §16.0

H

habad : *hebbian*
habas : *hebbian*
habda : *hebbian*
habdi : *hebbian* §25.0
habdin : *hebbian* §25.0
habdon : *hebbian*
habdun : *hebbian*
habe : *hebbian* §25.0
habed : *habad*
habes : *habas*
habit : *habad*
haft adj - fettered
hafton wk vb II - fasten
hagustald m - young man
hâhan str vb VIIa - hang
hal : *helan*
hâlag : *hêlag*
halba : *half*
hald : *haldan*
haldan str vb VIIa - hold, keep, own
half adj - half
halla f *ô*-stem - hall
halon wk vb II - hale, fetch, bring
halsmeni n *i*-stem - necklace
halt adj - halt, lame
halt adv - more than; *halt ni* - even less
hamur m - hammer
hand f *u*-stem - hand
handcraft m *i*-stem / f *i*-stem - main strength, strength of hand
handgiuuerc n - work of one's hands, creation
handmagen n - main strength, strength of hand
handmahal n ja-stem - home district
hangon wk vb II - hang

324

Glossary

hangondi : *hangon* §25.0
hanocrâd f *i*-stem - cock's crow
hâr n - hair
hard adj - hard, severe; bold
hardlico adv - severely
hardmôdig adj - bold, brave
hardo adv - severely
harm m/n - misfortune, grief
harmquidi m *i*-stem - invective
harmscara f *ô*-stem - share of misfortune
harmuuerc n - grievous deed
hatandi m *ja*-stem - one who hates, enemy
hatola : *hatul*
haton wk vb II - hate, pursue
hatul adj - hostile
he 3rd per pron - he
heƀancuning m - heavenly king
heƀanrîki n *ja*-stem - heavenly realm
heƀanuuang m - heavenly meadow
hebbian wk vb III - have, possess, own
hebbian str vb VI - raise
hebbiu : *hebbian* wk vb III, §25.0
heƀen n - heaven

heƀentungal n - heavenly body, star
heƀenuuard m - guardian of heaven
hêdar adj - bright
hêdro adv - brightly
hêðron wk vb II - brighten, clear up
heftian wk vb I - fetter, bind
hêl adj - hale, whole, healthy
hel m/f *u*-stem [Holthausen § 285 Anm. 1] - hell
hêlag adj - holy; *hêlagaro stemnun* - with voices of the holy (ones); with a holy voice
hêlaglîc adj - holy
hêlaglîco adv - in a holy manner
helan str vb IV - conceal
hêlan : *hêlean*
hêland : *hêleand*
hêlandi m *ja*-stem - savior
held : *haldan*
heldin : *haldan* §24.0
heldun : *haldan*
hêlean wk vb I - heal, save, expiate
hêleand m *nd*-stem - savior
hêli : *hêlean* §25.0
Hêliand m *nd*-stem - Savior
helið m - man, person
heliðcunni n *ja*-stem - mankind

Hêliand

heliðhelm m - concealing helmet
helldor n - portal of Hell
hellia f ô-stem - hell
helligithuuing n - oppression of hell
helmberand m *nd*-stem - helmet bearer, warrior
helmgitrôsteo m *n*-stem - armed companion
hêlog : *hêlag*
help : *helpan* §24.0
helpa f ô-stem - help, salvation, redemption
helpan str vb III - help
hêm n - (ancestral) home
hêmsitteandi m *ja*-stem - ruler
hendi : *hand*
henginna f ô-stem - hanging
hêr adj - noble, sublime
hêr adv - here
herdian wk vb I - strengthen, harden
herdislo m *n*-stem - strength
heri m *i*-stem - host, troop, crowd
hêri = heri
hêri f *i*-stem - noble people, crowd
heriscipi : *heriskepi*
heriskepi n *i*-stem - host
heritogo m *n*-stem - ruler
herod adv - hither

hêrro m *n*-stem - lord
herta n *n*-stem - heart
hertcara f ô-stem - heartbreak
herton : *herta*
herubendi f *i*-stem - fetters, 'sword-bonds' (Cf. Commentary to §53)
herudrôrag adj - sword-bloody
herusêl n - death rope
heruthrum n - sword force, thrusting force
hêt n - heat
hêt adj - hot
hêt : *hêtan*
hêtan str vb VIIc - be called; order, command
hetelîc adj - hateful, malicious
heti m *i*-stem - hatred, enmity
hetigrim adj - filled with hatred, aggressive; hatefully grim
hêtin : *hêtan* §24.0
hêto adv - hot
hetteand m *nd*-stem - hater, enemy
hettendi : *hetteand*
hi : *he*
hie : *he*
hier : *hêr*
Hierichoburg place name - Stronghold at Jerico

Hierusalem place name - Jerusalem
Hiesu : *Iêsu*
hiet : *hêt*
hild f *i*-stem - battle courage
hildiscalc m - warrior
hilis : *helan*
hilp : *helpan*
himil m - heaven
himilfader m *r*-stem - heavenly father
himilisk adj - heavenly
himilporta f *ô*-stem - portal of heaven
himilrîki n *ja*-stem - realm of heaven
himiltungal n - heavenly body, star
hinan adv - from here; farther; further
hindag adv - today
hinfard f *i*-stem - death
hinginna : *henginna*
hiopo m *n*-stem - brier
hîr : *hêr*
hirdi m *ja*-stem - shepard, herder
hîuua f *n*-stem - spouse
hîuuisca = *hîuuiskea* : *hîuuiski*
hîuuiski n *ja*-stem - family, household
hladen str vb VI - put, load

hlahhian str vb VI - laugh
hlamon wk vb II - rush, rage
hlea f *ô*-stem - shelter, lee
hlear n - cheek
hlêo m *wa*-stem - shelter; grave
hleotan str vb II - take upon oneself
hlinon wk vb II - lean
hlôgun : *hlahhian*
hlôt m - lot
hlûd adj - loud
hlûdo adv - loudly
hlûdost : *hlûd* §16.0
hlust f *i*-stem - hearing, attention
hluttar adj - clear, clean
hluttro : *hluttar*
hluttro adv - uprightly
hnêg : *hnîgan*
hnîgan str vb I - bow down
hôƀda : *hôƀid*
hôƀdu : *hôƀid*
hoƀe : *hof*
hôƀid n - head
hôƀidband n - headband, crown
hôƀidstedi m *i*-stem - capitol, main city
hôƀiduunda f *n*-stem - head wound
hoƀos : *hof*

Hêliand

hof m - royal court; plaza; house and yard
hôfdes : *hôbid*
hofna f *ô*-stem - lamentation
hôfslaga f *ô*-stem - hoofbeat
hogda : *huggien*
hôh adj - high
hôhgisetu n - throne
hôho adv - high
hôhor : *hôho* §16.0
hôhost : *hôh* §16.0
hold adj - submissive, obedient; merciful, gracious
holm m - hill
holmclibu : *holmclif*
holmklibu : *holmclif*
holmclif n - cliff, steep hill
hônða f *ô*-stem - insult, affront, disgrace
hôp m - crowd
horð n - hord
hord : *horð*
hôrdin : *hôrien* §25.0
hôrien wk vb I - hear; listen; follow, obey
hornseli m *i*-stem - a building with horn-shaped gable decoration
horsc adj - clever
horu n *wa*-stem - filth
hosc m / n - scorn
hoscuuord n - word(s) of scorn

hrêncorni n *ja*-stem - pure (sifted) wheat
hrêni *ja*- and *jô*-stem adj - pure, clean
hrêo n *wa*-stem - corpse
hrêobeddi n *ja*-stem - shroud
hreopun : *hrôpan*
hreuuan str vb II - worry about, regret
hriop : *hrôpan*
hrisian wk vb I - tremble
hriuuig adj - dejected, worried, sad
hriuuiglîco adv - dejectedly
hrôm n - glory, fame
hrômag adj - happy
hrômie : *hrômien* §25.0
hrômien wk vb I - boast of
hrôpan str vb VIId - cry out
hrôrien wk vb I - move, stir
hros n - steed, horse
hruora f *ô*-stem - motion
huan conj - when; *huan êr* - when finally
huand : *huuand*
huar conj - where; how
huar adv - where; whither
huarabe : *huarf*
huarabondi : *huarbon* §25.0
huarbon wk vb II - turn, go; churn
huarf m - crowd

huarf : *huuerƀan*

huarod adv - whither, where to; somewhere

huat : *huuat*

hueðer : *huueðer*

hueðeron : *huueðer*

huemu : *huuê*

huene : *huuê*

huergin : *huuergin*

huerigin : *huergin*

huggien wk vb I - think (of); be mindful of; remember

hugi m - mind, thought, heart

hugid : *huggien*

hugiskefti f *i*-stem - disposition, way of thinking

huî : *huuî*

huîl : *huuîla*

huîla : *huuîla*

huilic : *huuilic*

huilik : *huuilic*

huît adj - white; brilliant

huldi f *i*-stem - grace, favor

hund m - hound, dog

hungar m - hunger

huô : *huuô*

huodian wk vb I - guard, watch

huof : *hebbian*

huoti *ja*- and *jô*-stem adj - threatening, angry

hurnidskip n - ship with a high prow

hûs n - house

hûsstedi f *i*-stem - housestead

huuand conj - for, because, when

huuanda : *huuand*

huuanna adv - at one time

huuat interrog / indef pron - what; what kind of

huuat expletive - truly

huuê interrog pron - who

huueðer §12.0 - which [of two]

huuem : *huuê*

huuerƀan str vb III - go, turn; direct

huuergin adv - somewhere, somewhat; anywhere

huuî interrog pron - why

huuîla f *ô*-stem - time; *managa huuîla* - for a long time; *uuegas endi waldes huuîlon* - constantly on roads and through forests

huuilic §12.0 - which; any, every

huuirƀid : *huuerƀan*

huuô interrog pron - how

huurƀun : *huuerƀan*

I

ia conj - and; *ia ... ia* - both ... and
iâ interj - yes
iac conj - and also
Iacob pers name - Jacob
Iacobus pers name - Jacob
iâmarmôd adj - distressed, sad
iâr n - year
ic : *ik*
idis f *i*-stem - woman
Iêsus pers name - Jesus
if : *ef*
ik 1st per pron - I
im 3rd per pron
imo 3rd per pron [frequently reflexive with verbs of motion in addition to its function as D sg of *hê* and *it*]
in adv - in, into
ina 3rd per pron
inan = *ina*
inca 2nd per pron - (both of) your(s)
incan 2nd per pron / poss pron
incun 2nd per pron / poss pron
inna (cf. *thar inna*)
innan adv - inside, within
innan prep - in, within
inuuiddi n *ja*-stem - evil, enmity
inuuidrâd m - evil counsel
io adv - ever, always
Iohannes pers name - John
Iordan : *Jordan*
Ioseph pers name - Joseph
iouuiht indef pron - something
ira 3rd per pron / poss pron - her(s)
irminman m root-stem - person
irminthieda f *ô*-stem - humanity
irminthiod f *i*-stem - humanity
iro 3rd per pron
iru 3rd per pron
is 3rd per pron
is §26.1 - is
Isaak pers name - Isaac
îsarn n - iron
Israhel place name - Israel
ist §26.1 - is
it 3rd per pron
iu 2nd per pron
iu : *io*
Iudas pers name - Judas
Iudeo m *n*-stem - Jew
iguðhêdi f *u*-stem - youth
iguði f *i*-stem - youth
iung adj - young
iungardôm m - service, discipleship

Glossary

iungoro m *n*-stem - disciple, servant
iungron : *iungoro*
iungrun : *iungoro*
iuuua 2nd per pron / poss pron
iuuuar 2nd per pron / poss pron
iuuuas 2nd per pron / poss pron
iuuuen 2nd per pron / poss pron
iuuuom 2nd per pron / poss pron
iuuuoru 2nd per pron / poss pron

J

Jordan - the river Jordan
jungoro : *iungoro*

K

kaflos m [pl] - jaw
Kaiphas pers name - Caiphas
kelik m - chalice
kên : *kînan*
kennian wk vb I - beget
kêsur m - caesar
kiasan : *kiosan*
kiosan str vb II - choose
kîð m - shoot
kînan str vb I - sprout
kind n - child
kindisc adj - childish
kindiski f *i*-stem - childhood
kindiung adj - juvenile
kinni n *ja*-stem - jaw
kiusid : *kiosan*

knio n *wa*-stem - knee
kniobeda f *ô*-stem - prayer while kneeling
korn n - grain
Krist pers name - Christ
kristin adj - christian
kûðdi : *kûðian* §25.0
kûðian wk vb I - make known
kûðe : *kûðian* §25.0
kûðlîco adv - openly, publicly
kuman str vb IV - come
kûmde : *cûmian*
kume : *kuman* §24.0
kumi m *i*-stem - arrival, *adventus*
kuning : *cuning*
kuningdôm m - rank, office of king
kuningstôl m - royal throne
kunnan pret-pres vb - be able to
kunni n *ja*-stem - kin; people
kunnun : *kunnan*
kus m - kiss
kussu : *kus*

L

lacan n - cloth; curtain
lag : *liggian*
lâgnian wk vb I - deny
laguliðandi m *ja*-stem - seafarer
lâgun : *liggian*

lagustrôm m - sea tide

lahan str vb VI - reprove, criticize, blame, rebuke, fault

lamb n - lamb

land n - land

landscaðo m *n*-stem - despoiler of the country, robber

landscepi n *i*-stem - realm, world

landuuîsa f *ô*-stem / f *n*-stem - custom of the realm

lang adj, adv - long

lango adv - long (time)

langsam adj - lasting, enduring

lâri *ja*- and *jô*-stem adj - empty

lastar n - guilt; sin; scorn

lat adj - slow, idle; late

lât : *lâtan* §24.0

lâta : *lâtan* §24.0

lâtan str vb VIIb - let, leave, allow; let down

latta : *lettian*

Lazarus pers name - Lazarus

lazt : *lat* §16.0 [< * lat+ist-]

lêbon wk vb II - remain

lêð n - evil

lêð adj - evil; hateful, hostile

lêdde : *lêdian*

lêddun : *lêdian*

lêdea : *lêdian* §25.0

lêdian wk vb I - lead, guide; bring

lêðlîc adj - ruinous, destructive

lêfhêd f *u*-stem - illness, weakness

legarbed n *ja*-stem - sickbed, sickness

legda : *leggian*

leggian wk vb I - lay

lêia f *ô*-stem / f *n*-stem - rock

leng : *lang*

lengron : *lang* §16.0, §2.4a

leoƀes : *liof*

leoƀost : *liof* §16.0

leoht : *lioht*

lêra f *ô*-stem / f *n*-stem - teaching, commandment

lêrean wk vb I - teach

lêriu : *lêrean* §25.0

lesan str vb V - gather

lêste : *lêstien*

lêstien wk vb I - carry out, fulfill; do

lêt : *lâtan*

lêtin : *lâtan* §24.0

lettian wk vb I - hinder

leutcunni n *ja*-stem - human race

Levias pers name - Levi

liaƀane : *liof*

liagan : *liogan*

liahto : *liohto*

lîƀa : *lôf*

Glossary

libbian wk vb I - live
libdi : *libbian*
libod : *libbian*
lŏbu : *lŏf*
lŏchamo : *lŏkhamo*
lŏcon wk vb II - please
liŏ m - limb, member
lŏŏ n - fruit wine
lŏŏan str vb I - pass, go, travel on
lŏŏi ja- and jǫ-stem adj -mild, generous, gracious
liŏubendi f *i*-stem - bonds, fetters
lieba : *liof*
lietun : *lâtan*
lîf n - life; body
lîflôs adj - lifeless
liggen : *liggian*
liggian str vb V - lie
ligid : *liggian*
lîhtlîc adj - light, weak
lîk n - body; corpse; flesh
lîkhamo m *n*-stem - body; corpse
likkon wk vb II - lick
lîkuunda f *ô*-stem - body-wound
lilli m *ja*-stem - lily
lîn n - linen
lînon wk vb II - learn
lioban : *liof* adj

liobes : *liof*
lioblîk : *lioflîc*
liobora : *liof* adj - dearer; more preferable; *liobora thing* - something more pleasant
liobost : *liof* adj, §16
liodan str vb II - grow
liof n *ja*-stem - love, goodness, delight
liof adj - dear, friendly
lioflîc adj - lovely, friendly, beautiful
liogan str vb II - lie
lioht n - light
lioht adj - light, clear, faithful
liohtean wk vb I - shine
liohtfat n - lamp
liohto adv - brightly, clearly, faithfully
liomo m *n*-stem - ray, beam; tongue of fire
list f *i*-stem - wisdom
listiun adv - wisely; cleverly, secretly
liudfolc n - people
liudi m *i*-stem - people
liudscaðo m *n*-stem - corrupter of people
liudscepi n *i*-stem - people
liudstamn m *i*-stem - people
liudstamna = *liudstemnio* G [pl]
liuduuerod n - people

Hêliand

liuhte : leohtean
liuhtien : leohtean
lo◊on wk vb II - praise
lôd : liodan
lof n - praise
lofsam adj - praiseworthy
lofuuord n - word of praise
logna f ô-stem / f n-stem - flame
lôn n - reward; punishment
lônon wk vb II - reward
lôs adj - free (of)
lôsien wk vb I - loosen; free, redeem
lôsuuord n - loose speech, evil word
Loth pers name - Lot
luƀig adj - devout
Lucas pers name - Luke
lud m - form, growth
luft m / f *i*-stem - air
lugina f ô-stem - lie
lungar adj - powerful
lust f *i*-stem - joy; desire
lustean wk vb I - desire
lût adj - small amount
luttic adj - little
luttil adj - little

M

macon wk vb II - make, do; put
mâđmundi *ja*- and *jô*-stem adj - mild-mannered
mag : *mugan*
mâg m - relative
magađ f root-stem [Gallée §340] - maiden
magad : *magađ*
magađhêd f *i*-stem - maidenhood
magu m *u*-stem - son
maguiung adj - youthful
mâguuini m *i*-stem - relative
mahal n - assembly; speech
mahlian wk vb I - speak
maht f *i*-stem - power, might
mahta : *mugan*
mahte : *mugan*
mahti : *mugan* §25.0
mahtig adj - powerful
mahtiglîc adj - mighty
mâki n *ja*-stem - sword
Malchus pers name
man m root-stem - man; servant
manag adj - many (a)
managa huîla : *huuîla*

managfald adj - manifold, great
mancunni n - mankind
mandrohtin m - lord, king
manega : *manag*
mangon wk vb II - merchandise
mann : *man*
mâno m *n*-stem - moon
manon wk vb II - exhort, order; drive
manslahta f *ô*-stem - manslaughter
mansterbo m *n*-stem - plague
manuuerot n - crowd
marca f *ô*-stem - boundary (land)
marcon wk vb II - mark, notice; determine
Marcus pers name - Mark
mârða : *mâriða*
mâri *ja*- and *jô*-stem adj - brilliant, notable, famous
Maria pers name - Mary
mârian wk vb I - announce, make known
mâriða f *ô*-stem - revelation, wonder
mârlîco adv - wonderously
Martha pers name - Martha
mat n - food
Matheus : *M*attheus

Mattheus pers name - Matthew
me 1st per pron
mêda f *ô*-stem, f *n*-stem - reward
mêdean wk vb I - pay
mêðom m - precious object, jewel
mêðomgebo m *n*-stem - benefactor
mêðomhord n - precious hord
megi : *magu*
megin n - power, might
megincraft m / f *i*-stem - main strength; crowd
meginfard f *i*-stem - show of strength, campaign
meginstrengi f *i*-stem - main strength, powerful force
meginsundia f *n*-stem - great sin
meginthioda f *i*-stem - great people; big crowd
meginthiof m - great thief
meldon wk vb II - turn in, betray
melm m - dust
mên n - sin, crime
mênda : *mênian*
mêndâd f *i*-stem - sinful deed, crime
mendian wk vb I - rejoice
mendiodun : *mendian*
mendislo m *n*-stem - joy
mêndun : *mênian*

mênêđ m - false oath, perjury
menegi : *menigi*
mengian wk vb I - mix
mêngithâht f *i*-stem - sinful, criminal thought
mênhuat adj - criminal
mênian wk vb I - mean; think; indicate; opine
menigi f *i*-stem - crowd
mennisco m *n*-stem - person
menniski f *i*-stem - human form
mênscađo m *n*-stem - criminal offender, malefactor
mênsculd f *i*-stem - sin
mênuuerk n - sinful deed
mêr adv - more; *ni ... than mêr* - no more, no longer; *thiu mêr* - the more
meregrîta f *n*-stem - pearl
meri f *i*-stem - ocean, sea
meristrôm m - sea current
merrian wk vb I - anger, disturb
mêst adj - most(ly); greatest
mêster m - lord, master
met : *mid*
metigêdea f *i*-stem - hunger, lack of nourishment
metod m - fate
metodigiscaft f *i*-stem - fate
metodogiscapu n - divine fortune

mi 1st per pron
mid prep - with; *mid manages huî* - with something of everything
mîđan str vb I - avoid; refrain from
middean : *middia*
middi *ja-* and *jô-*stem adj - mid
middia f *n*-stem - middle
middien : *middia*
middilgard m / f *i*-stem - earth
middilgarda f *ô-*stem / f *n*-stem - earth
middiun : *middi*
mîđe : *mîđan* §24.0
mik 1st per pron
mikil adj - great, big *mikilu betara* - better by a great deal
mildi *ja-* and *jô-*stem adj - generous, merciful
mîn 1st per pron / poss adj - my, mine
minnia f *ô-*stem - love
minnion wk vb I - love
minnist suppletive adj - least
mirki *ja-* and *jô-*stem adj - dark; diabolic
mislîk adj - different
mit : *mid*
môd m - spirit, heart, cast of mind

môdag adj - wrathful, malicious
môdar f r-stem - mother
môder : *môdar*
môdgithâht f i-stem - emotion, thought
môdkara f ô-stem - grief
môdkarag adj - grieving
môdsebo m n-stem - thought, mood, emotion
môdspâh adj - astute, shrewd
môdstark adj - contentious, bellicose
môdthraca f ô-stem - deprivation, heartache, woe
mohta : *mugan*
mohte : *mugan*
mohti : *mugan* §25.0
mohtun : *mugan*
moraganstunda f ô-stem - morning hour
morð n - murder, execution
morgan m - morning
morgno : *morgan*
mornon wk vb II - mourn
môs n - food
môst : *môtan*
môsta : *môtan*
môste : *môtan*
môsti : *môtan* §25.0
môstin : *môtan*
môstun : *môtan*
môt : *môtan*

môtan pret-pres vb - be able to; be permitted to
môti : *môtan* §25.0
môtin : *môtan* §25.0
môtis : *môtan* §25.0
môtun : *môtan*
Moyses pers name - Moses
mûð m - mouth
mûdspelli : *mûtspelli*
mugan §25.0 - be able to, be capable of
mugi : *mugan* §25.0
mugin : *mugan* §25.0
mugis : *mugan* §25.0
mugun : *mugan*
mund m - mouth
mundboro m n-stem - patron, mentor
mundburd f i-st - patron; protecion, aid
mundon wk vb II - aid, protect
munilîc adj - lovely
muod : *môd*
muodag : *môdag*
muoder : *môdar*
muodsebo : *môdsebo*
muosta : *môtan*
mûra f ô-stem - wall, palisade
mûtspelli n ja-stem - apocalypse

N

naco m *n*-stem - ship
nâðian wk vb I - dare, strive
nâðla f *n*-stem - needle
nâdra f *ô*-stem - adder
nagal m - nail
naglos : *nagal*
nâh adj - near
nâhian wk vb I - approach
nâhor : *nâh* §16.0
naht f root-stem - night
nam : *niman*
nâmin : *niman* §24.0
namom n-stem - name
narauuo adv - narrow(ly); tightly
narouuaro : *naru* §16.0
naru *wa*- and *wô*-stem adj - narrow
Nazarethburg place name - Stronghold at Nazareth
Nazarethburh : *Nazarethburg*
ne : *ni*
neba conj - other than that, except that
nebal m - fog, dimness
nebu : *neba*
nebulo : *nebal*
nec conj - nor
negên : *nigên*
negilid : *neglian*
neglian wk vb I - nail
neglitskip n - ship constructed using nails
nemnian wk vb I - name
nên interj - no
nênig adj - no (one)
neo : *nio*
neoman indef pron - no one
neotan : *niotan*
neouuiht indef pron - nothing
neri : *nerien* §25.0
neriand m *nd*-stem - savior
neriand adj - saving wk vb I
nerien wk vb I - save
neriendi : *nerien* §25.0
nêthuuanan = nê wêt huuanan - I know not from where
netti n *ja*-stem - net
neuan conj - except
ni adv - not
nia : *nio*
niate : *niotan* §24.0
nîð m - hatred, malice; treachery
nîd : *nîð*
niðana adv - from below
niðer adv - down
nîðhuat adj - urging confrontation
nîðhugdig adj - contemplating violence

nîðhugi m *ja*-stem - violent disposition
nîðscipi : *nîðskepi*
nîðskepi m *ja*-stem - hostility
nieuuiht : *neouuiht*
nigên indef pron - no, none
nigênon : *nigên*
nigiean : *nigên*
nigun num - nine
Nîlstrôm m - the river Nile
niman str vb IV - take, accept
niman an [+D] – take from; niman at [+D] – accept from
nio adv - never
niotan str vb II - enjoy
nis = ni is
niud m - need, desire
niudlîco adv - eagerly; carefully
niudsam adj - pleasant
niuson wk vb II - tempt
niuua : *niuuui*
niuuon : *niuuui*
niuuui *ja*- and *jô*-stem adj – new
nôd f *i*-stem - distress, hardship
nôdian wk vb I - force
Nôe pers name - Noah
noh adv - still, yet; up to now
norð adv - northwards
nu adv - now
nuon f *i*-stem - 3 p.m.

O

oƀana adv - from above
oƀanuuard adv - up above
oƀar prep - over
ôƀarfâhan str vb VIIa - cover over
oƀarfangan : *ôƀarfâhan*
oƀarhoƀdo m *n*-stem - ruler
oƀarmôdig adj - proud
ôƀean wk vb I - celebrate
ôc : *ôk*
ôcan str vb VII [Holthausen § 421] - impregnate
Octauiân pers name - Octavian
ôd n - wealth; happiness
ôdag adj - prosperous
ôdan adj - given
ôdmôdi n *ja*-stem - humility
ôðar adj- the second; the/an other; *ôðar huueðar* - one of the two; *ôðar ... ôðar* - the one ... the other; *ne ôðar huerigin* - nor any other anywhere
ôðarlîc adj - different; changed
ôðerhueðer indef pron - one of the two
ôði *ja*- and *jô*-stem adj - easy
ôðil m - inherited property, ancestral home
ôðo adv - easily
ôðra : *ôðar*
ôðrana : *ôðar*
ôðres : *ôðar*
ôðru : *ôðar*
ôðrun : *ôðar*
ôður : *ôðo* §17.0 - more easily
of : *ef*
ofsittian str vb V - possess
ofstôp : *afsteppian*
ofsuoƀun : *afsebbian*

Hêliand

oft adv - often
ôga n *n*-stem - eye
ôgian wk vb I - show
ôgun : *ôga*
ohtho : *eftho*
ôk adv - also
ôlat m - thanks
olbundeo m *n*-stem - camel
opan adj - open
opanlîco adv - openly
oponon wk vb II - open
ôra n *n*-stem - ear
orc m - jug
ord m - point
orlag n - war
orlaghuîle f *ô*-stem - fateful hour
ôrun : *ôra*
ôstan adv - from the east
ôstana = *ôstan*
ôstar adv - eastwards
ôstaruueg m - path in the east
ôstroni *ja*- and *jô*-stem adj - from the east

P

paradis n - paradise
pascha n - Passover, Passover meal
pêda f *ô*-stem - shirt, garb
Pêter pers name - Peter
Petrus pers name - Peter
Philippus pers name - Philip
Pilatus pers name - Pilate
plegan str vb V - be responsible for
Ponteo land place name - apocryphal association of Pilate probably with Pontus (Asia Minor)
porta f *n*-stem - portal

Q

quað : *queðan*
quaddiu = *queddiu*
quaddun : *queddian*
quâðun : *queðan*
qual : *quelan*
quâla f *ô*-stem - torment, torture
qualm n - death; murder
quam : *queman*
quâmi : *queman*
quâmin : *queman* §24.0
quâmun : *queman*
quân f *i*-stem - woman
quathie = quað + *he*
queðan str vb V - say, speak
quedda [= *quedida*] : *queddian*
queddian wk vb I - address; greet
queðe : *queðan* §24.0
quelan str vb IV - die
quelidin : *quellian* §25.0
quellian wk vb I - kill
quelm(i)an wk vb I - kill
queman str vb IV - come
quena f n-stem - woman
quic adj - alive
quîðean wk vb I - lament
quidi m *i*-stem - speech, words

R

râd n - teaching, counsel; help, support; gain, profit

râdan [+G] str vb VIIb - give counsel, advise; help

râdand m *nd*-stem - counselor

râdburd f *i*-stem - dominion

râdgeƀo m *n*-stem - counselor

radur m - vault of heaven, firmament

rakud m - temple

ran : *rinnan*

rasta f *ô*-stem/f *n*-stem - death; grave

reckean : *rekkien*

recon : *rekon*

reðia f *ô*-stem - account; *an reðiu standen* - be called to account

reðion wk vb II - speak

regangiscapu n [pl] - divine fates

reganogiscapu : *regangiscapu*

regin m - rain

reginscaðo m *n*-stem - malefactor

reht n - justice; law

reht adj - correct, just

reht sô adv - just as, as soon as

rehto adv - legally, correctly

rekkien wk vb I - tell

rekon wk vb II - prepare

reomo m *n*-stem - band, thong

rês : *rîsan*

resta : *rasta*

restien wk vb I - rest

rîci : *rîki*

riedun : *râdan*

rihtian wk vb I - erect; rule

rihtun : *rihtian*

rîkeost : *rîki* §16.0

rîki n *ja*-stem - realm, dominion

rîki *ja*- and *jô*-stem adj - powerful; rich

rîkiost : *rîki* §16.0

rink m - young man

rinnan str vb III - run, flow

rîsan str vb I - arise

roƀon wk vb II - rob

rôd adj - red

Rômanoliudi m *i*-stem - people of the Romans

rûm m - distance; *standan an rûm* - stand back

Rûma f *ô*-stem - Rome

rûmien wk vb I - prepare; cleanse

rûmo adv - far away

rûmor §17.0 - farther away

Rûmuburg f root-stem - Stronghold of Rome

rûna f *ô*-stem - secret counsel

ruoda f *n*-stem - rood, cross
ruof adj - infamous

S

saca f *ô*-stem - court case; accusation; guilt; crime; thing
sad adj - satiated
sâfto adv - easily
sâftur : *sâfto* §17.0
saga : *seggian* §25.0
sagda : *seggian*
sagdi : *seggian* §25.0
sagdun : *seggian*
sah : *sehan*
sâhi : *sehan* §24.0
sâhin : *sehan* §24.0
sâhun : *sehan*
sâian wk vb I - sow
salƀa f *ô*-stem - ointment, salve
salƀon wk vb II - annoint
sâlda f *ô*-stem - beatitude; bliss
sâlig adj - blessed; devout
sâliglîco adv - blessedly
salt n - salt
sama : *samo*
samad adv - together
saman : *samad*
samnoian wk vb I : *samnon*
samnon wk vb II - gather; assemble

samo adv - likewise; *sô samo* - as well; *sô samo sô* - just as
sâmquic adj - half dead
samuuurdi n *ja*-stem - unanimous agreement
sân adv - immediately
sâna : *sân*
sancte *ja*- and *jô*-stem adj - saint
sand m - sand; shore
sandi (= sendi) : *sendian* §25.0
sang m - song
sat : *sittian*
Satanas pers name - Satan
Satanasan : *Satan* [A sg]
sâton : *sittian*
satta : *settian*
sâtun : *sittian*
sâuuun : *sehan*
scaðo m *n*-stem - malefactor
scado m *wa*-stem - shadow
scadouuan wk vb I - shadow, shield
scaft m - shaft, spear
scal : *skulan*
scâla f *n*-stem - drinking bowl
scalc m - servant
scalden str vb VIIa - shove
scalt : *skulan*
scaltu : *skulan*
scama f *ô*-stem - shame
scap n - vessel

scapuuard m - wine steward
scard adj - cut, wounded
scarp adj - sharp
scat m - hord of coins; money; chattel
scauuoien wk vb I - see; view
scauuon wk vb II : *scauuoien*
scian m - overcast; cloud deck
scild m - shield
scîn : *skîn*
scôh m - shoe
scola f *ô*-stem - crowd
scolda : *skulan*
scoldi : *skulan*
scoldin : *skulan*
scoldis : *skulan*
scoldun : *skulan*
scolo m *n*-stem - debtor; *is lîbes scolo* - forfeit life
scônera : *scôni* §16.0
scôni *ja*- and *jô*-stem adj - beautiful, brilliant
scôniost : *scôni* §16.0
scrêd : *skrîdan*
scrîban str vb I - write
scribun : *scrîban*
scrîd : *skrîdan*
scriði : *skrîdan* §24.0
scuddian wk vb I - shake
sculd f *i*-stem - obligation
sculdig adj - obligated; guilty
sculun : *skulan*

sê : *sêo*
sea 3rd per pron
sebo m *n*-stem - spirit; emotion; disposition
seðal n - rest; seat
seðle : *seðal*
sedle : *seðal*
segel n - sail
segg m *i*-stem - man
seggennea : *seggian* §250
seggeo : *segg*
seggian wk vb III - say
sêgian wk vb I - sink, set
segnade : *segnon*
segnon wk vb II - bless
seh : *sehan* §24.0
sehan st vb V - see; look (at); notice
sehs num - six
sehsi N [pl] : *sehs*
sehsta ord num - sixth
selban : *self*
selbaro : *self*
selbes : *self*
selbo : *self*
selbun: *self*
seldîk adj - wondrous
selðon: *seliða*
self §15.0 - him/herself; same
seli m *i*-stem - *dwelling*
selihûs n - house
senda : *sendian*
sendi : *sendian* §25.0
sendian wk vb I - send

Hêliand

sêo m wa-stem - sea
seok adj - sick
seola f ô-stem / f n-stem - soul; life
sêolîđandi *ja-* and *jô-*stem adj - seafaring (men) str vb I
sêr n - grief, care
sêr adj - sad, distressed
sêragmôd adj - sad, distressed
sêreg adj - sad, distressed
sêro adv - very, sorely
sette : *settian*
settian wk vb I - set, put; compose
sêuua : *sêo*
sî : *wesan* §26.1
sia 3rd per pron
sibbia f ô-stem - family, relatives
sibun num - seven
sicur adj - without, free of
sîđ m - path, way; time; *an thana formon sîđ* - the first time; *ôđru sîđu* - another time
sîđ adv - later, afterwards
sîđa : *sîda*
sîda f ô-stem - side; loins
sido : *sidu*
sîđogean wk vb I : *sîđon*
sîđon wk vb II - travel, go
sîđor conj - after, since

sîđor adv - later, afterwards
sidu m *u*-stem - custom
sîđur : *sîđor*
sîđuuôrig adj - roadweary, wayworn
sie 3rd per pron
sîgan str vb I - sink; move ahead
sigidrohtin m - victorious lord
sigun : *sîgan*
silubar n - silver
simbla adv - always; nevertheless; in any case
simblon adv - always
sîmo m *n*-stem - rope
Sîmon pers name - Simon
sîn poss adj - his
sinc : *sink*
sincan str vb III - sink
sind : *wesan* §26.1
singan str vb III - sing
sinhîun : *sinhîuua*
sinhîuua n *n*-stem - spouse
sink n - treasure, hord
sinlîf n - eternal life
sinnahti n *ja*-stem - eternal night
sinscôni *ja-* and *jô-*stem adj - eternally beautiful
sint : *sind*
sînu = sih nû - see now §24.0

Glossary

sinuueldi n - endless forest
siole : *seola*
sîs : *wesan* §26.1
sitit : *sittian*
sittian str vb V - sit
siu 3rd per pron
siun f *i*-stem - vision; eye
skarp adj - sharp
skêðan str vb VIIc - cleave
skêđia f *ô*-stem - sheath
skên : *skînan*
skenkio m *n*-stem - cupbearer
skeppien str vb VI - scoop
skimo m *n*-stem - lustre, light
skîn m - shine, light
skîn adj - discernible; apparent, manifest
skînan str vb I - shine
skip n - ship
skîr : *skîri*
skîreas : *skîri*
skîri *ja*- and *jô*-stem adj - pure, sheer
skrêd : *skrîdan*
skreid : *skrîdan*
skrîdan str vb I - glide (past), pass
skulan pret-pres vb - ought to, should
slac adj - timorous
slahan str vb VI - strike; slay
slâpan str vb VIIb - sleep

slâpandi : *slâpan* §24.0
slekkian wk vb I - weaken, slake
slîði *ja*- and *jô*-stem adj - cruel, evil
slîðmôd adj - cruel, evil
slîðmuod : *slîðmôd*
slîðuurdi *ja*- and *jô*-stem adj - speaking with cruel words
sliumo = *sniumo*
slôg : *slahan*
slôgun : *slahan*
slôpi : *slôpian* §25.0
slôpian wk vb I - slip; loosen
sluogin : *slahan*
slutil m - key
smultro adv - gently
snel adj - bold
snelle : *snel*
snêo m *wa*-stem - snow
snêu : *snêo*
snîðan str vb I - cut
snîði : *snîðan* §24.0
sniumo adv - quickly; soon
so : *sô*
sô adv - so, thus, in such a way
sô conj - so; as; *al sô* - just as; *sô huan sô* - whenever; *sô huat sô* indef pron - whatever; *sô ... sô* - as ... as; *sô hue sô* indef pron - whoever; *sô hueðer sô* indef pron - whosoever; *sô*

huilîk sô indef pron - whosoever; *sô samo sô* - the same as; *sô* self - likewise

sôð n - truth

sôð adj - true; correct

sôðlîc adj - true

sôðlîco adv - truly

Sodoma place name - Sodom

Sodomoburg place name - Stronghold at Sodom

sôhta : *sôkien*

sôhtin : *sôkien* §25.0

sôhtun : *sôkien*

sôkien wk vb I - seek

Solomon pers name - Solomon

sômi *ja-* and *jô*-stem adj - proper

sorga f *ô*-stem - worry, apprehension; *lâtan* [+D] *sorga* - concern [oneself] with

sorgandi : *sorgon* §25.0

sorgon wk vb II - worry, be concerned

sorgondi : *sorgon* §25.0

spâhi *ja-* and *jô*-stem adj - wise, experienced

spâhlîco adv - wisely

spâhuuord n - eloquent word

spanan str vb VI - urge, drive

spel n - speech; word

spenit : *spanan*

sper m - spear

spildian wk vb I - kill

spîwan str vb I - (be)spit

sprac : *sprekan*

sprâca : *sprâka*

sprak : *sprekan*

sprâka f *ô*-stem / f *n*-stem - speech; conversation

sprâkun : *sprekan*

sprang : *springan*

sprecan : *sprekan*

sprekan str vb IV - speak

sprikis : *sprekan*

springan str vb III - spring

sprungun : *springan*

spunsia f *ô*-stem - sponge

spurnan wk vb I - stomp, tread on

stac : *stekan*

stâð : *stân*

stâd : *stân*

stað m - strand; bank

stamn m - stem, prow

stân : *standan*

standan str vb VI - stand

stank m - stench

stark adj - strong; powerful; hard

starkmôd adj - brave, dauntless

stêd : *stân*

stedi f *i*-stem - place

stekan str vb V - stick

Glossary

stellian wk vb I - place, set
stemna f *ô*-stem / f *n*-stem - voice
stemnia : *stemna*
stên m - stone
stendit : *standan*
stênfat n - earthenware jug
stênuueg m - paved road
stênuuerc n - stone construction
sterƀan str vb III - die
sterƀe : *sterƀan* §24.0
sterkian wk vb I - strengthen
sterro m *n*-stem - star
stês : *stân*
stîgan str vb I - climb
stigun : *stîgan*
stilli *ja*- and *jô*-stem adj - quiet
stillo adv - quietly;
stillon wk vb II - die down
stilrun : *stilli* §16.0
stôd : *standan*
stôdun : *standan*
stôl m - throne
stôpo m *n*-stem - footstep
strang adj - strong, powerful
strangost : *strang* §16.0
strâta f *n*-stem - road
strîd n *i*-stem - conflict, battle; eagerness
strîdda : *strîdian*

strîdhugi m *i*-stem - eagerness for battle
strîdian wk vb I - contest
strîdig adj - confrontational
strôm m - stream, flood
stuod : *standan*
stuodun : *standan*
sualt : *sueltan*
suang : *suingan*
suâr adj - heavy; serious
suarf : *suerƀan*
suart : *suuart*
suâs adj - own; dear
suâslîco adv - in a friendly manner
suâsost : *suâs* §16.0
sûƀri adj - clean
suefresta f *ô*-stem - bed
suek : *suîkan*
sueltan str vb III - die
suerƀan str vb III - wipe
suerd n - sword
suerdthegan m - warrior, 'sword thane'
suerea : *suerien* §24.0
suerien str vb VI - swear
suêt m - sweat; blood
suht f *i*-stem - disease
suîð : *suîði*
suîði *ja*- and *jô*-stem adj - powerful; right (side, hand)

347

suîðlîco adv - vehemently

suîðo : *suuîðo*

suigli *ja*- and *jô*-stem adj - bright, beaming

suîgon : *suuîgon*

suîkan [+G] str vb I - abandon, betray

suîkan umbi str vb I - be unfaithful towards

suiltit : *sueltan*

suîn n - swine

suingan str vb III - plunge

sulik adj - such

suluuian wk vb I - sully

sum indef pron - a certain; many (a); *fahora sum* - with a few people

sumbal n - banquet

sundar adv - alone; individually

sundea f *ô*-stem / f *n*-stem - sin

sundie : *sundea*

sundig adj - sinful

sundor : *sundar*

suni : *sunu*

sunna f *ô*-stem / f *n*-stem - sun

suno : *sunu*

sunu m *u*-stem - son

suoð : *sôð*

suôgan wk vb I - swoop

suotera : *suôti* §16.0

suôti *ja*- and *jô*-stem adj - sweet, agreeable

sus adv - so

suuart n - darkness

suuart adj - black, dark

suuefn m - sleep

suuerea : *suerien* §25.0

suuîðo adv - very; very much

suuîðor : *suuîðo* §17.0 - all the more

suuîgon wk vb II - remain silent

suuiri m *i*-stem - nephew

suulti : *sueltan*

T

talda : *tellian*

tand m - tooth

te prep - to, towards; at, and etc.; *te brêdiu* - as a bride; *te huî* interrog pron - for what? (purpose)

te infinitive marker; *te alôsienne* - to redeem

te adv - too; *te thio* : *te thiu*; *te thiu* - for this (purpose), until then; *ni is/uuas lang te thiu that* - it isn't/wasn't long until

tebrast : *tebrestan*

tebrestan str vb III - burst, rip

têcan : *têkan*

tedêlda : *tedêlian*

tedêlian wk vb I - separate

tefallen str vb VIIa - fall apart

Glossary

tefaran str vb VI - disperse; perish
tefôr : *tefaran*
teforan postpostion - before
tegegnes postposition - before, towards
teglîdan str vb I - perish
tehan num - ten
tehando m *n*-stem, §19.0 - tenth
tehinfald adj - tenfold
têkan n - sign
teklioƀan str vb II - cleave
teklôf : *teklioƀan*
telâtan str vb VIIb - disperse, scatter
telêt : *telâtan*
tellian wk vb I - tell, explain
teoh : *tiohan*
tesamne adv - together
teskrîdan str vb I - part
teslâad : *teslahan*
teslahan str vb VI - smash
tesuuingan str vb III - scatter
tesuungan : *tesuuingan*
teuuerpan str vb III - destroy; scatter
teuuirpit : *teuuerpan*
teuuorpan : *teuuerpan*
thâ : *the*
thagon wk vb II - be silent
thâhte : *thenkian*
thâhtun : *thenkian*

than adv - then
than conj - then; when; *than ... than* - then ... when; if ... then
thana : *than*
thanan adv - from there, thence; from the place where
thanc m - thanks, reward; grace, favor
thar adv - there; thereupon
tharƀon wk vb II - lack
tharf f *i*-stem - lack, need
tharft : *thurƀan*
tharo : *thero* dem pron - those
tharod adv - to there, thither
that dem pron - that
that conj - that
thau m *wa*-stem - custom
the general relative pronoun - which, who, that
the rel pron - that
thea : *the* dem pron
thegan m - thane, follower; man; servant
thegn : *thegan*
them : *the* dem pron
then : *the* dem pron
thena : *the* dem pron
thene : *the* dem pron
thenidun : *thennian*
thenkian wk vb I - think

thennian wk vb I - spread, stretch out
theoƀas : *thiof*
theoƀe : *thiof*
theodan : *thiodan*
theodo : *thiod*
theolîco adv - humbly
theonogean wk vb I : *theonon*
theonon : *thionon*
theotgod m - Almighty God
thera : *the*
thero : *the*
theru : *the*
thes : *the*
thesa compound dem pron - this; these
thesaro : *thesa*
thi 2nd per pron
thia : *the* dem pron
thiadan : *thiodan*
thiade : *thioda*
thicci *ja-* and *jô*-stem adj - dense
thie : *the*
thieda : *thioda*
thiedcuning : *thiodcuning*
thiggean wk vb I - receive; request
thigida : *thiggean*
thîhan str vb I - thrive, prosper; be of use
thik 2nd per pron
thimm adj - dark

thîn poss adj - thy, thine
thing n - court; place of assembly; court action, charge; matter; thing
thinghûs n - court house
thingon wk vb II - negotiate
thingstedi f *i*-stem - place of assembly, court
thiod f *i*-stem - people
thioda f *ô*-stem - people
thiodan m - king, ruler
thiodarƀedi n *ja*-stem - great misfortune
thiodcuning m - king of all the people
thiodgumo m *n*-stem - excellent man
thiodne : *thiodan*
thioduuelo m *n*-stem - great property, great weal; salvation
thiof m - thief
thionodi : *thionon* §25.0
thionoian : *thionon*
thionon wk vb II - serve, obey, follow
thionost n - service
thiorna f *n*-stem - maiden
thit compound dem pron - this
thiu dem pron *thiu bat* - the better; *thiu uureðra* - more wroth
thius compound dem pron - these
thiustri n *ja*-stem - darkness

thiustri *ja-* and *jô-*stem adj - dark
thiuu f *i-*stem - maid, servant
thô adv - then; *thô ... thô* - when ... then
thô conj - when; while
thoh adv - yet, still, nevertheless; *thoh ... thoh* - even though ... yet
tholoian wk vb I : *tholon*
tholon wk vb II - suffer, endure
Thomas pers name
thorfte : *thurƀan*
thorfti : *thurƀan* §25.0
thorn m [Holthausen § 304] - thorn
thorron wk vb II - perish
thram : *thrimman*
thrâuuerk n - misery, pain
thria num - three
thriddio : *thria*
thrimman str vb III - swell
thringan str vb III - crowd in; press, beset
thrîsti *ja-* and *jô-*stem adj - bold, confident
thrîstmôd adj - bold, confident
thrîstmuodi *ja-* and *jô-*stem adj - bold, confident
thrîtig num - thirty
thrîuuo adv - thrice

thrungi : *thringan* §24.0
thu 2nd per pron - thou
thuahan str vb VI - wash
thuahe : *thuahan* §24.0
thunkean wk vb I - seem
thuo : *thô*
thuôg : *thuahan*
thuoloian : *tholon*
Thuomas pers name - Thomas
thurƀan pret-pres vb - have cause to; need to
thurƀon : *thurƀan*
thurƀun : *thurƀan*
thurftig adj - needy, poor
thurh prep - through; by means of
thurhgangan str vb VIIa - go all the way (on)
thurhgengid : *thurhgangan*
thurhslôpien wk vb I - let slip through
thurstian wk vb I - thirst
thuru : *thurh*
thuruuuonon wk vb II - wait
thus adv - thus, thusly
ti : *te*
ti quellianne : *quellian* §25.0
tîd f *i-*stem - time; age
tid : *tîd*
tilêt : *telâtan*
tins m - tribute, tax
tiohan str vb II - pull; bring up

tiono m *n*-stem - crime, sin
tîr m - honor, fame
tîrlîco adv - in an honorable way
tiscrêd : *teskrîdan*
tô adv - to, towards (etc.)
tôgian wk vb I - show
tolna f *ô*-stem - tax duty
tômian wk vb I - set free
tômig adj - free from
torht adj - bright
torn n - anger, fury
tôuuardes adv - near
trâda f *ô*-stem - track
trahni m *i*-stem - tears
treo n *wa*-stem - tree, beam
treuhaft adj - faithful
treulogo m *n*-stem - one who breaks faith
treulôs adj - deceitful
treuua f *ô*-stem - good faith, loyalty
treuun : *treuua*
treuuon : *treuua*
trûodin : *trûon*
trûon wk vb II - trust, believe
tuâ num - two
tuê num - two
tueho m *n*-stem - doubt
tueio num - two
tuelibi : *tuuelibi*
tuêm : *tuuêm*

tuêna : *tuuêna*
tuêntig num - twenty
tuhin : *tiohan*
tugiðon [+G] wk vb II - grant
tuîfli *ja*- and *jô*-stem adj - inconstant, doubting
tuîflien : *tuuîflien*
tulgo adv - very; very much
tunga f *n*-stem - tongue
tungal n - constellation
tuo : *tô*
tuô num - two
tuomian : *tômian*
tuomie : *tômian* §25.0
tuuê num - two
tuuehon wk vb II - doubt, waver
tuuelibi num - twelve
tuuêm num - two
tuuêna num - two
tuuîflien wk vb I - doubt

U

ubil adj - evil, bad
ûðia f n-stem - wave
uestane adv - from the west
ûhta f *ô*-stem - early morning
umbi adv - around; about
umbi prep - around
umbi postposition - around
umbihuarf : *umbihuerban*

Glossary

umbihuerƀan str vb III - surround
un- negative prefix
unc 1st per pron
unca poss adj
uncro poss adj
uncun poss adj
undar adv - below; underneath
undar prep - under; among; *siu habda barn undar ira* - she was with child; *undar im* - among themselves; *undar tuisk* - among themselves
undar bac adv - backwards
undar thiu adv - meanwhile
undarfindan str vb III - inform; find out about
undarfundin : *undarfindan*
undarhuggean wk vb I - understand, realize
undartuisc prep - between
undaruuitan pret-pres vb - recognize
under : *undar*
underbadon wk vb II - frighten
undergripan : *undergrîpan*
undergrîpan str vb I - seize
undern m - morning
unefno adv - unevenly; not at the same time
ungeuuittig adj - foolish
ungiuuideri n *ja*-stem - storm

unhiuri *ja*- and *jô*-stem adj - eerie
unhuldi f *i*-stem - disrespect; enmity
unmet adv - immeasurably, very
unôδi *ja*- and *jô*-stem adj - difficult
unqueδandi n *ja*-stem - that which is unspeakable (Cf. *queδan* and §24.0.)
unreht n - injustice illegality; *an unreht* - unlawfully, wrongfully
unrîm n - a host
unscôni *ja*- and *jô*-stem adj - unsightly, unbecoming
unsculdig adj - innocent
unspuod f *i*-stem - delinquincy, misconduct
unsuôti *ja*- and *jô*-stem adj - odious
unthat : *antthat*
untreuua f *ô*-stem - faithlessness, disloyalty
untthat : *antthat*
unuuand adj - steadfast
unuuânlîc adj - lowly, insignificant
unuuîs adj - unwise, foolish
up adv - up; upward
upôd m - upper estate, heavenly property
upp : *up*

Hêliand

uppa adv - up (there)
uppan postposition - up; *an ... uppan* - up on
uppuueg : *upuueg*
upuueg m - upward path
urlagi n *ja*-stem - battle
ûs 1st per pron
ûsa poss adj
ûses : *ûsa*
ûsson : *ûsa*
ûst f *i*-stem - gust
ût adv - out
ut: *ût*
ûta adv - out, outside

UU

uuacon wk vb II - watch
uuâdian wk vb I - clothe
uuâg m - wave
uuâglîðand m *nd*-stem - wavefarer
uuah interj - woe
uuahsan str vb VI - grow, wax
uuahta f *ô*-stem / f *n*-stem - watch
uual m - wall, palisade
uuald m - woods, forest
uualdan [+G] str vb VIIa - wield, rule; preside
uualdand m *nd*-stem - ruler
uuallan str vb VIIa - well (up); flame up
uuallandi : *uuallan* §24.0
uuam n - evil, sin

uuamscaðo m *n*-stem - evil scather, malefactor
uuamscefti f *i*-stem - sinfulness
uuân m - hope, expectation
uuânam - adj - brilliant, gleaming
uuânamo adv - gleaming, brilliantly
uuancol adj - wavering, inconstant
uuânda : *uuânian*
uuândun : *uuânian*
uuang m - meadow
uuanga f *n*-stem - meadow, field; cheek
uuânian wk vb I - imagine; believe; hope for
uuânlîc adj - auspicious; hopeful
uuânlîco adv - beautifully
uuann : *uuinnan*
uuanon wk vb II - wane
uuanscefti f *i*-stem - misery
uuânum : *uuânam*
uuâpan n - weapon
uuâpanthreki [Sehrt, p. 640] - skill with weapons
uuâr f *ô*-stem/f *n*-stem - truth; *te uuârun* - in truth
uuâr adj - true, real
uuâr n - truth; *fan wâre* - from truth
uuarag : *uuarg*

Glossary

uuaragtreo n *wa*-stem - gallows, 'strangling tree'
uuarahta : *uuirkian*
uuarƀos : *uuarf*
uuarđ : *uuerðan*
uuarð : *uuerðan*
uuard m - guardian, protector
uuardon wk vb II - protect, care for; guard against
uuarf m - crowd
uuarg m - criminal, 'strangler; wolf'
uuarhte : *uuirkian*
uuâri : *uuesan* §26.1
uuârin : *uuesan* § 26.1
uuâron : *uuesan* str vb V - were
uuârlîc adj - true
uuârlîco adv - in truth, truly
uuarlîco : *uuârlîco*
uuarmien : *uuermien*
uuarolîco : *uuârlîco*
uuaron wk vb II - tend; take care of; watch; last
uuarp : *uuerpen*
uuârsago m *n*-stem - soothsayer, prophet
uuaruhtun : *uuirkian*
uuârun : *uuesan* §26.1
uuas : *uuesan* §26.1
uuastom m - growth; fruit; stature
uuatar n - water; river, lake

uue 1st per pron
uuê n - woe; suffering
uuêc : *uuêk*
uuedar n - weather
uuederuuîs adj - weatherwise
uueg m - way, road
uuêg m - wall
uuêgean wk vb I - torture
uuêgi n *ja*-stem - bowl, vessel
uuehslean wk vb I - change; exchange
uuehslon wk vb II = *uuehslean*
uuêk adj - weak, faint-hearted
uuekidun : *uuekkian*
uuekkian wk vb I - wake up [transitive]
uuel adv - well
uueldâd f *i*-stem - good deed
uuell : *uuallan*
uuelan : *uuelo*
uuelda : *uuillian*
uueldi : *uuillian*
uueldin : *uuillian*
uueldun : *uuillian*
uuell : *uuallan*
uuelliat : *uuillian*
uuelo m *n*-stem - weal, estate
uuendian wk vb I - turn; change
uuendie : *uuendian* §25.0
uuenkian wk vb I - deviate from, depart from

355

Hêliand

uueop : *uuôpian*

uuêpanberand m *nd*-stem - weaponbearer, warrior

uuer m - man

uuerc : *uuerk*

uuerd m - host; innkeeper

uuerð n - payment; reward

uuerð adj, §16.0 - worth; worthy

uuerða : *uuerðe*

uuerðan str vb III - become; happen; *uuerðan* + [past partic] - be + [part partic] (= passive construction)

uuerðe : *uuerðan* §24.0

uuerðlîco adv - in a worthy manner

uuerdskepi m *i*-stem - entertainment

uuerian wk vb I - prohibit; hinder; forbid

uuerk n - deed; action; work

uuerkean : *uuirkian*

uuermien wk vb I - warm

uuernian [+G] wk vb I - deny

uuerod n - people

uuerold f *i*-stem / m - world, earth; life(time)

uueroldaldar n - epoch

uueroldcuning m - powerful king

uueroldlust f *u*-stem [Holthausen § 306] - worldliness, worldly pleasure

uueroldlusta [nom.sg., cf. Sehrt, p. 665] = *uueroldlust*

uueroldrîki n *ja*-stem - worldly realm

uueroldsaca f *ô*-stem - worldly affairs

uueroldscat m - worldly chattel

uueroldstunda f *ô*-stem - one's time on earth

uuerpan str vb III - cast, throw

uuerran str vb III - confuse; press, attack

uueruld : *uuerold*

uuesan str v V - be §2.1

uuêst : *uuitan*

uuestan adv - from the west

uuestar adv - westward

uuestrani *ja*- and *jô*-stem adj - west

uuêt : *uuitan*

uui 1st per pron

uuîbe : *uuîf*

uuîbes : *uuîf*

uuîbo : *uuîf*

uuîbun : *uuîf*

uuîcan str vb I - give way, yield

uuið : *uuið*

uuið prep - with; against

356

Glossary

uuîd adj - wide, broad
uuiðar prep - against
uuiðarsaco m *n*-stem - opponent; enemy
uuiðaruuerpan str vb III - reject, spurn
uuîdbrêd adj - wide and broad
uuiđerstandan str vb VI - resist, enter action against
uuiđerstande : *uuiđerstandan* §24.0
uuiðeruuardes adv - backwards
uuiđeruuord adj - repulsive
uuîdo adv - widely
uuîdost : *uuîdo* §16.0
uuidouua f *n*-stem - widow
uuîf n - woman; wife
uuîg m - battle
uuîgand m *nd*-stem - warrior
uuiggeo : *uuiggi*
uuiggi n *ja*-stem - horse
uuîgsaca f *ô*-stem - battle
uuîh m - sanctuary
uuiht m / f *i*-stem [pl] [Gallée §323; Holthausen §298] - beings, spirits
uuiht n [Gallée §320 §323] - thing; anything
uuîk m *i*-stem - town, village
uuîki : *uuîcan* §24.0
uuil : *uuillian*

uuili : *uuillian*
uuillea : *uuillian*
uuilleo : *uuillian*
uuillian §26.2 - intend, want
uuillie : *uuillian*
uuilliendi : *uuillian*
uuillio m *n*-stem - will; intention; desire; *an is uuillion* - according to his will; *te uuillion* - for advantage (to), usefully; *uuillion* - eagerly; voluntarily
uuilspel n - welcome news
uuilt : *uuillion*
uuîn m / n - wine
uuînberi n *ja*-stem - grape
uuind m - wind
uuindan str vb III - wind; move; uundan gold - gold wound into an arm ring
uuîngardo m *n*-stem - vinyard
uuini m *i*-stem - comrade, friend
uuinitreuua f *ô*-stem - faithfulness to a comrade
uuinnan str vb III - struggle; acquire; endure
uuînseli m *i*-stem - wine hall
uuintar m - winter; year
uuintarcald adj - wintry cold

357

uuintergital n - number of years
uuiopun : *uuôpian*
uuiopin : *uuôpian* §24.0
uuirđi : *uuerđan* §24.0
uuirđid : *uuerđan*
uuirđig adj - worth; worthy
uuirđig : *uuirđig*
uuirkian wk vb I - work; carry out; do; prepare
uuirs adv - worse
uuîs adj - wise, knowledgeable
uuis adj - certain
uuîsa f *ô*-stem / f *n*-stem - manner; means, way
uuîsad : *uuîson*
uuîsare : *uuîs* §16.0
uuisbodo m *n*-stem - reliable messenger
uuiscumo m *n*-stem - one certain to come
uuîscuning m - wise king
uuîsde : *uuîsian*
uuîsdôm m - wisdom
uuîsian wk vb I - show; teach
uuîslîco adv - wisely
uuîslik adj - wise
uuîson [+ G] wk vb II - seek out, visit
uuissa : *uuitan*
uuisse : *uuitan*
uuissun : *uuitan*

uuissungo adv - certainly
uuit 1st per pron - we two
uuita interj - let us
uuitan pret-pres vb - know; understand
uuîtan str vb I - accuse
uuîti n *ja*-stem - punishment
uuitin : *uuitan* §25.0
uuîtnon wk vb II - injure; kill
uuitodes : *uuiton* §25.0
uuiton wk vb II - determine; intend; *thar siu iro nîđskepies uuitodes uuânit* - where it suspects an intended attack
uuitun : *uuitan*
uulank adj - bold; arrogant
uulbos : *uuulf*
uuliti m *i*-stem - brilliance; appearance; form; face
uulitig adj - shining; brilliant
uulitigost : *uulitig* §16.0
uulitiscôni f *i*-stem - brilliant beauty
uund adj - injured, wounded
uundan : *uuindan*; *uundan gold* - gold wound into an arm ring
uundar n - marvel
uundron adv - wondrously; extra-ordinarily
uundarlîc : *uunderlîc*

Glossary

uundartêcan n - miraculous sign
uunderlîc adj - wondrous
uunderlîco adv - miraculously
uunderquâla f ô-stem - appalling torture
uundraian wk vb I : *uundron*
uundron wk vb II - be amazed
uundrun : *uunder*
uundun : *uuindan*
uunnia f ô-stem - joy, delight
uunnun : *uuinnan*
uunon : *uuonon*
uunsam adj - delightful, blissful
uuôði ja- and jô-stem adj - sweet, pleasant
uuôdian wk vb I - rage, be furious
uuôdiendi : *uuôdian* §25.0
uuôðiera : *uuôði* §16.1
uuôi f i-stem - suffering; misfortune
uuôl m - disease; calamity
uuolcan n - cloud
uuolcnun : *uuolcan*
uuolda : *uuillian*
uuoldi : *uuillian* §26.2
uuonian wk vb I : *uuonon*
uuonon wk vb II - dwell; tarry; endure
uuonotsam adj - delightful, gratifying

uuôp m - lamentation
uuôpian str vb VIId - weep, lament
uuôpiandi : *uuôpian* §25.0
uuord n - word
uuordgimerki n ja-stem - letters of the alphabet
uuordhelpa f ô-stem - intercession
uuordspâh adj - eloquent
uuorold : *uuerold*
uuorolduuelo m n-stem - earthly possession
uuôsti ja- and jô-stem adj - desolate
uuôstunnia f ô-stem - wasteland
uuracsîð m - path into exile
uurð f i-stem - fate; ground
uurðegiskefti f i-stem - fates
uurdgiscapu n [pl] - fates
uurði : *uuerðan* §24.0
uurðun : *uuerðan*
uurecan str vb V - retaliate; pay back, punish
uurêð adj - anxious, concerned; angry
uurđean wk vb I - become angry
uureðian wk vb I - support
uurêðmôd adj - angry
uurekkio m n-stem - foreign warrior; expatriate

uurgil m - noose
uurisilîc adj - gigantic
uurîtan str vb I - write; carve, incise
uuritan : *uurîtan* §24.0
uurm m - snake
uurt f *i*-stem - root; herb, plant. flower
uuruogian wk vb I - accuse
uuulf m - wolf
uuunda f *n*-stem - wound
uuurhtio m *n*-stem - worker
uuurpun : *uuerpan*
uuurrun : *uuerran*
uuuruhteo : *uuurhtio*

Z

Zacharias pers name - Zacharias

www.ingramcontent.com/pod-product-compliance
Lightning Source LLC
Chambersburg PA
CBHW022008300426
44117CB00005B/82